STONES OF LAW, BRICKS OF SHAME
NARRATING IMPRISONMENT IN THE VICTORIAN AGE

EDITED BY JAN ALBER
AND FRANK LAUTERBACH

Stones of Law,
Bricks of Shame

Narrating Imprisonment
in the Victorian Age

UNIVERSITY OF TORONTO PRESS
Toronto Buffalo London

© University of Toronto Press Incorporated 2009
Toronto Buffalo London
www.utppublishing.com
Printed in Canada
ISBN 978-0-8020-9897-9 (cloth)

Printed on acid-free paper

Library and Archives Canada Cataloguing in Publication

Stones of law, bricks of shame: narrating imprisonment
in the Victorian age / edited by Jan Alber and Frank Lauterbach.

ISBN 978-0-8020-9897-9

1. English fiction – 19th century – History and criticism. 2. Imprisonment
in literature. 3. Imprisonment – Social aspects – Great Britain – History –
19th century. I. Alber, Jan, 1973– II. Lauterbach, Frank

PR878.P7S76 2009   823'.8093554   C2008-906779-7

University of Toronto Press acknowledges the financial assistance to its publishing program of the Canada Council for the Arts and the Ontario Arts Council.

University of Toronto Press acknowledges the financial support for its publishing activities of the Government of Canada through the Book Publishing Industry Development Program (BPIDP).

Contents

Acknowledgments

The publication of *Stones of Law, Bricks of Shame* would not have been possible without the help of numerous individuals. First of all, I would like to thank Frank Lauterbach, my co-editor, for his work on this collection. Second, I am indebted to Marie-Luise Egbert, Paul Goetsch, Adam Hansen, Jason Haslam, Greta Olson, David Paroissien, and Jeremy Tambling for their extremely helpful comments on an earlier version of the introduction. Third, I would like to thank Jeff Thoss for all his hard work on the collection's format, including the endnotes. Fourth, this collection owes its existence to the financial support that it has received. I would like to thank the DFG research project 'Recht, Norm, Kriminalisierung,' Napier University, Stanford University, Texas Tech University, and the Wissenschaftliche Gesellschaft e.V. in Freiburg for providing us with the funding that made the publication of *Stones of Law, Bricks of Shame* possible. I am also indebted to W.B. Carnochan, Monika Fludernik, Sean C. Grass, and Anne Schwan for their help in the process of securing the funding. Fifth, I would like to thank Jill McConkey, Barbara Porter, Richard Ratzlaff, Charles Stuart, the anonymous readers of the manuscript, and everyone else at the University of Toronto Press for all their hard work in connection with this collection. It is to Anja and Quirin Jetschke, though, that I owe the largest debt of gratitude. They have done the most to make this collection possible.

Jan Alber (Columbus, OH)

STONES OF LAW, BRICKS OF SHAME

Introduction

JAN ALBER AND FRANK LAUTERBACH

In nineteenth-century Britain, imprisonment was a matter with which few were unacquainted, either as the debtors' prison many knew from personal experience, or the penal institution whose reform was a rather obsessive concern of quite a few respectable gentlemen, or the place of confinement so present in many Victorian novels (and poems). A discourse on imprisonment dominated the public sphere for decades – a discourse that manifested itself in both a great number of tracts on prison conditions and some of the most important literary works of the time. While previous studies of the history of imprisonment have largely concentrated on the structure and effects of the prison, *Stones of Law, Bricks of Shame* shifts the focus to the functions that the very act of writing about prisons and their inmates had for and within the Victorian public at large.

The period of time under discussion in *Stones of Law, Bricks of Shame* is framed by two well-known phrases, from William Blake in 1790 and Oscar Wilde in 1897. In *The Marriage of Heaven and Hell*, Blake's diabolical speaker says that 'Prisons are built with stones of Law, Brothels with bricks of Religion.'[1] Many critics argue that Blake's 'Proverbs of Hell' inverts traditional dichotomies and condemns law and religion as 'mind-forg'd manacles' that restrain excessive emotions.[2] In other words, the repression of desires (through strict understandings of law and religion) may ultimately kill human happiness.[3] However, as Harold Bloom has shown, Blake does not merely celebrate excess and powerful actions. Rather, he invites us 'to move from a defiant celebration of heretofore repressed energies to a realization that the freed energies must accept a bounding outline.' From this perspective, prisons and brothels contain social elements that fail to accept this 'bounding line, a lessened but still existent world of confining mental forms,'[4] and instead indulge in the immediate gratification of impulse. Blake thus argues that prisons and brothels exist because certain individuals fail to control their heretofore repressed desires and drives and engage in forms of limitless excess. And since there will always be individuals who, for whatever reason, indulge in excess, prisons and brothels constitute a societal necessity for him.

A good century after Blake, Oscar Wilde, who engaged in what some considered to be 'excessive' behaviour and was imprisoned for acts of 'gross indecency,' shifts the perspective from the individual's responsibilities to the shameful horrors of life in a Victorian prison. The speaker of 'The Ballad of Reading Gaol' argues 'That every prison that men build / Is built with bricks of Shame.'[5] Richard Ellmann summarizes Wilde's poem as follows: 'The poem has a divided theme: the cruelty of the doomed murderer's crime, the insistence that such cruelty is pervasive, and the greater cruelty of his punishment by a guilty society.'[6] Wilde does not doubt that criminals exist. Yet he addresses the question of whether they have to undergo harsh punishments that ultimately deprive them of their status as human beings. More specifically, Wilde points out that the crimes committed by governors and prison officials should not be greater than the ones for which the inmates were sent to prison. 'The Ballad of Reading Gaol' thus highlights the fact that society's attempts to contain criminality and 'deviancy' may sometimes get out of hand and become rather excessive, too.

The two positions highlighted by Blake and Wilde mark the two poles between which nineteenth-century authors and the Victorian public oscillate with regard to the prison. On the one hand, they need the prison as an institution and a discursive emblem to contain excess and to uphold their 'untainted' identities by distancing their self-images from moral, social, sexual, and national Otherness. On the other hand, the Victorians gradually realize that they sometimes carry their desperate attempts to distance themselves from their cultural Others to excess, and thus begin to question themselves (sometimes in acts of self-congratulatory self-blame, but sometimes also in rather honest fashion). *Stones of Law, Bricks of Shame*, the title of this volume, highlights the Victorian public's construction of the prison as both a societal necessity and a shameful institution or idea. In this context, it is also worth noting that stones imply not only the tables of law but also what is 'natural,' while bricks are man-made and artificial.[7] The title of this collection thus also accentuates the Victorians' oscillation between the view that it was 'natural' or positive to use the prison to distance oneself clearly from cultural Otherness, and the growing awareness that identity constructions through radical exclusion from absolute difference were highly artificial and might be seen as having negative connotations.

The History of Victorian Prisons

A survey of the historical context illustrates that prisons played a dominant role in nineteenth-century British life. For example, before imprisonment for debt was ended in 1869, debtors' prisons (like Ludgate, the King's Bench, the Queen's Bench, the Fleet, and the Marshalsea) and jails, which also held debtors, were open to people from outside, and law-abiding citizens frequented them with the observational curiosity of zoo visitors. That is to say, at this point, imprisonment was still a public matter. Furthermore, the Victorians worried about the question of how to deal with the rising crime rates connected with the Industrial Revolution and the ongoing process of urbanization. For instance, in 1820 some 13,700 people had been convicted for serious offences, and this number increased to 27,200 by 1840.[8] Also, the loss of the Australian convict depositories – Botany Bay and Van Diemen's Land – in mid-century forced the government to find other solutions to crime.[9] Thus, the police system was reformed and over ninety 'new' reformatory prisons or penitentiaries were constructed or added to between 1842, when Pentonville Prison was established, and 1877, when the prisons were nationalized.

The development of the 'new' reformative penitentiary – based on solitary confinement, religion, and hard labour – was influenced by the works of early penologists, among which Cesare Beccaria's *An Essay on Crimes and Punishment* (1764), Jonas Hanway's *Solitude in Imprisonment* (1776), and John Howard's *State of the Prisons in England and Wales* (1777) were the most important.[10] Hanway and Howard in particular were explicit about the material goals that would distinguish the prisons of the past from the penitentiary of the future; they were convinced that the 'new' prison would lead to the moral reformation and rehabilitation of the inmate. Both Hanway and Howard believed that the demoralization of criminals could be controlled if the inmates were separated and exposed to solitude. For example, Howard describes the 'therapeutic' value of solitary confinement as follows: 'I wish to have so many small rooms or cabins that each criminal may sleep alone … Solitude and silence are favourable to reflection; and may possibly lead them to repentance.'[11]

The Penitentiary Houses Act of 1779 introduced many of the features that Hanway and Howard had proposed: solitude, religious instruction, and strict labour. However, it still took more than thirty years until the first 'new' prison, the General Penitentiary at Millbank, London, was opened in 1816. After the loss of the American convict colonies in 1776, the government extended its holdings of disused warships (the so-called hulks) that had been used to confine convicts awaiting transportation to the penal colonies. Henry Mayhew and John Binny describe this process as follows: 'The idea of converting old ships into prisons arose when, on the breaking out of the American War of Independence, the transportation of our convicts to our transatlantic posses-sions became an impossibility.'[12] At the same time, they remark that the hulk system was condemned from its origin. 'Originally adopted as a makeshift under pressing circumstances, these old men-of-war have remained during nearly half a century the receptacles of the worst class of prisoners from all jails of the United Kingdom.'[13] Ultimately, the state of the ships proved to be so unsatisfactory that in 1779 the House of Commons set up a committee to look for other options for transporting the undesired convicts out of Britain. In 1786, the government decided on Botany Bay on the eastern coast of Australia; later on, Van Diemen's Land became the new convict depository. When the first 'new' prison or penitentiary opened at Millbank in 1816, thousands of convicts were still being transported to Australia each year. It is also worth noting that even though Millbank attempted to isolate prisoners from one another to prevent criminal 'contamination,' it did not actually become a reformative penitentiary. In part the problem arose from the huge numbers of prisoners, which clearly overwhelmed the arrangements.

When Pentonville was established in 1842, it operated as an experiment in the so-called Pennsylvania (or 'separate') system, in which the prisoners were housed in separate cells for the entire period of their confinement. The peno-logical practices at the time were defined by the competing, but in many ways similar, Pennsylvania and Auburn systems.[14] Under the Pennsylvania system, the prisoners 'worked, ate, and slept in solitary confinement and were allowed to see only selected visitors.'[15] Under the alternative Auburn (or 'silent') sys-tem, prisoners slept alone but came together to eat and work in the prison shops. However, when they 'met' one another, they were not allowed to talk or even exchange glances. Both systems emphasized a steady routine of hard labour and moral instruction in the context of a regime of silence intended to prevent criminal 'contamination.' Auburn and Pennsylvania were modelled on the example of religious orders and their practice of penitence and monastic isolation. Both types of prison were meant to produce a reformed citizen who had seen 'the error of his ways.' Ultimately, the Auburn system was adopted by most states in the United States, while most British prisons followed the Pennsylvania design.[16]

Other factors influenced the form and function of prisons. In the 1860s, two types of prisons existed in Britain, namely, convict prisons and local prisons. The convict prisons, which had grown out of problems with the transportation of convicts to overseas colonies, held offenders who had been sentenced to a minimum of three years. The local prisons (such as Newgate), on the other hand, held petty offenders sentenced for shorter periods as well as those awaiting trial.[17] Philip Priestley summarizes the confusing pattern of London prisons by the middle of the nineteenth century as follows:

> there were three 'convict' prisons, at Millbank, Pentonville and Brixton, run by the government's commissioners of prisons, as well as some hulks on the river at Woolwich. Middlesex magistrates had two prisons for convicted criminals, at Coldbath Fields and at Tothill Fields, and one remand prison, the House of Detention at Clerkenwell. The Surrey justices were in charge of Wandsworth for convicted men and women, and Horsemonger Lane for the unconvicted. Finally the Court of Aldermen of the City of London reserved Holloway for convicts and Newgate for prisoners awaiting trial.[18]

Under the 1877 Prisons Act, the local prisons were nationalized and amalgamated under central administration together with the convict prisons.[19] Subsequently, in 1878, administrative power was transferred from the local magistrates to the Prison Commission in Whitehall, working under the chairmanship of Sir Edmund Du Cane, who considered criminals to be 'a class of fools' with 'a natural proneness to evil.'[20] The infamous first head of the newly nationalized prison system appointed a crudely utilitarian prison committee; one example of its 'wisdom' was the decision that prisoners sentenced to hard labour should daily ascend 8,640 steps on the treadmill. It is also worth noting that since Du Cane was convinced of the unavoidable uselessness of prison work, the inmates were not allowed to do useful work that might have produced something.[21] Furthermore, the committee established a progressive dietary regime that was 'so meager in its early stages as to constitute deliberate starvation.'[22] Many prisoners were so desperate by hunger that they ate beetles, railway grease, candles, paper, grass, or earthworms.[23] In both local and convict prisons, the inmates were strictly separated and the pleasure of reading was restricted to the Bible or books of religious exhortation to cause the inmates to repent and reflect upon 'the errors of their ways.'

Narrating Victorian Imprisonment

This collection addresses the question of how these Victorian prisons are narrated in nineteenth-century texts. Moreover, *Stones of Law, Bricks of Shame* interrogates how the representations of imprisonment in Victorian narratives work within the discursive delimitations of cultural categories such as morality, gender, class, and nation. The essays in this collection deal with the question of how the delimitations associated with the prison are linked to wider cultural demarcations, and address the prison's ambivalent role in marking important facets of Victorian identity constructions.

In nineteenth-century Britain, the prison becomes emblematic of threats to the cultural identity and hegemony of Victorian gentlemen. Prisons typically serve an important function within discourses that reflect upon identities and hegemonies – in particular in times when anxieties over the identity of the cultural self prevail. Prisons tend to enter the public debate more forcefully when dominant social groups perceive their status to be challenged. This process can be observed in the Victorian age as social changes and the rapid development of the culturally diverse British Empire suddenly challenged the self-perception of the Victorian bourgeoisie.

The Victorian age was a period of rapid change and, as a result, of great social and moral confusion. The identity of Victorian gentlemen was challenged in a wide variety of ways. The disorders that accompanied the Reform Bill agitation in the early 1830s, the disturbing images of an organized working class (for example, in the agitation led by the Chartists in the 1840s), and the development of the modern women's movement posed significant threats 'from within.' Threats 'from without' included the incompetent management of the Crimean War (1854–6) as well as problems in the colonies such as the disasters related to the Indian Mutiny of 1857. Another example is the Irish Famine of 1845–51, followed by the Home Rule Movement, which rises to the fore with the founding of the Home Government Association in 1870 and Gladstone's conversion to Home Rule in 1885. All of these threats correlate with the confrontation between the Victorian bourgeoisie and some kind of moral, sexual, social, or national Other, and, as will be shown, nineteenth-century narratives associate the undesired aspects of such confrontations with the discursive emblem of the prison.

Existing analyses of Victorian and other prisons fall into four different categories. The first group of critics emphasizes the disciplining or repressive nature of penal institutions. For instance, Philip Priestley analyses Victorian prisons as oppressive institutions. In his preface to *Victorian Prison Lives* (1985) he states that it was his intention 'to blend hundreds of personal narratives of life in the nineteenth-century English prison into a single, collective account.'[24] Priestley's work is an invaluable compilation of inside views of nineteenth-century British prisons that effectively recreates the dismal and bleak atmosphere of these institutions – from the induction process to the prisoner's release – with much attention to detail. Similarly, Stephen Halliday's *Newgate* (2006) is a meticulous analysis of the history of Newgate Prison that highlights the repressive nature of this notorious prison hell. In *Prison Literature in America* (1989), Howard Bruce Franklin sees a slightly different form of oppression at work. He analyses imprisonment in the white society of the United States as a continuation of slavery, and argues that a state-sanctioned racism underlies the incarceration of most American prisoners.[25] Finally, Ioan Davies looks beyond the specific cases of imprisonment in Victorian Britain or the United States and instead deals with the long history of Western penal oppression as well as the writings produced from the prison. According to Davies, those who write in prison try 'to overcome violence, stare death in the face and provide the basis for human affirmation.'[26]

A second strand of literary criticism celebrates the potentially liberating effects of the prison on the inmate despite adverse circumstances. For example, Victor Brombert points out that in French literature, the prison is frequently conceived of 'as the protected and protective space, the locus of reverie and freedom.'[27] Similarly, Sigrid Weigel highlights that many German inmates see the prison as a space 'which promises autonomy and freedom within bondage' ('ein [...] Raum [...], der Autonomie und Freiheit verspricht').[28] Finally, W.B. Carnochan, Christa Karpenstein-Eßbach, and Martha Grace Duncan also accentuate the paradoxical dialectic between confinement and mental flight, or, more specifically, between physical incarceration on the one hand, and imaginative liberties on the other.[29] In contrast to the above-mentioned two schools of criticism, this collection deals not only with the effects of the Victorian prison but also with its broader cultural significance, that is, the refashioning of the penal experience in relation to notions of morality, gender, class, and nation.

A third group of critics investigates potential connections between structural attributes of prisons and narrative form, where 'form' relates either to metaphors or a narrative strategy such as 'omniscience.' In *Discipline and Punish* (1975), Michel Foucault ascribes primary importance to Jeremy Bentham's plans for a Panopticon with regard to the 'birth' of the prison and the development of disciplinary society at the beginning of the nineteenth century.[30] Bentham envisioned the Panopticon as a circular prison with a central tower, from which the inspectors could observe all cells located on the outer perimeter. In addition, strategically positioned venetian blinds on the watch-tower would prevent the prisoners from observing the guards, while allowing the officers an unobstructed view of the prisoners.[31] Following Michel Foucault's arguments about the centrality of the Panopticon, Mark Seltzer, John Bender, D.A. Miller, Audrey Jaffe, and Natalie McKnight argue that many nineteenth-century novels reproduce Bentham's Panopticon because the position of the 'omniscient' narrator in these novels is seen as being similar to the position of the prison officer in the watchtower of Bentham's architectural arrangement. For instance, Mark Seltzer argues that 'the most powerful tactic of supervision achieved by the traditional realist novel inheres in its dominant technique of narration – the style of "omniscient narration" that grants the narrative voice an unlimited authority over the novel's "world," a world thoroughly known and thoroughly mastered by the panoptic "eye" of the narration.'[32] Furthermore, D.A. Miller and John Bender maintain that tyranny surfaces in passages of free indirect discourse. According to Miller, free indirect discourse camouflages the abiding power of the 'master voice' and 'simultaneously subverts their [the characters'] authority and secures its own.' In other words, the master voice 'continually needs to confirm its authority.'[33] Bender is even more explicit about the putative link between structural attributes of the penitentiary and free indirect discourse. For him, 'the penitentiary habilitates, in its own technical practices, devices parallel to those of free indirect discourse. The mode of literary production and the social institution present collateral images of one another.'[34]

This collection rejects easy analogies between prison architecture and narrative form. To begin with, in contrast to the prison officer, the 'omniscient' narrator cannot threaten his characters, nor can they be physically compelled to obey his will. The alleged parallel between free indirect discourse and penal practices is odd since in actual prisons, prison officers can only gain 'external' knowledge about the inmates. As Dorrit Cohn has argued, guards cannot perceive the prisoners' minds, though they may of course 'adhere to the illusory belief that a show of obedience reflects psychic conformity.'[35] Also, the use of free indirect discourse in narrative fiction does not typically correlate with tyranny or authoritarianism; it usually signals 'a willingness to incorporate otherness rather than merely objectify or reify it.'[36]

Furthermore, this volume seeks to move away from the alleged importance of the Panopticon for historical reasons. As Sean C. Grass has shown, 'no [Victorian] prisoner ever spent a day in the Panopticon, nor probably in a prison much like it ... The exercise of power in the Victorian prison had very little to do with surveillance. Rather, it had to with locking the self in solitude, inscribing guilt upon it, forcing it to account for its own disordered identity and guilty desire, and seizing the power to subject that self-account to the inventive power of the authorial other.'[37] Indeed, someone convicted of a crime in Victorian Britain was more likely to be thrown into one of the squalid and dark debtors' prisons; held in overcrowded and filthy jails; forced to work on the dilapidated hulks; transported to the convict colonies at Botany Bay or Van Diemen's Land; or exposed to lengthy periods of solitary confinement in one of the country's 'new' penitentiaries. Debtors' prisons, jails, hulks, Australian colonies, and 'new' prisons that conformed to the 'separate' system – these are the prisons that are discussed in this volume, and it is worth noting that they have very little to do with Bentham's plans for a Panopticon, not least because surveillance played only a minor role in them.[38]

Foucault's *Discipline and Punish* certainly initiated an interest in both prisons and prison narratives. However, at the same time, Foucault limited the discussion to the roles of disciplinary mechanisms, surveillance, and the Panopticon. A proper Panopticon penitentiary 'was never erected in Britain'[39] because 'the English rejected Bentham's ideas.'[40] Grass concludes that under these circumstances, 'it is worth wondering whether recent scholarship focused upon surveillance has forged provocative links between the novel and the prison or only between the novel and Foucault.' He thus argues that 'first-person narration, more than surveillance, is the means by which the novel reflects the prison's power.' This occurred, according to him, because chaplains began to write down the prisoners' stories and ensured that these first-person accounts would say the 'right thing' about the value of the 'therapeutic' separation in prison. Grass describes the power of the Victorian prison as follows: 'Prison authorities all wished ... to hear convict self-accounts that began in depravity and ended in the glorious awakening engendered by separate discipline. After all, confessing the fullness of one's guilt was the essential first step in reform, and prison authorities devoutly wished for reform to happen.'[41]

W.B. Carnochan, Monika Fludernik, and Jan Alber address the form and function of prison metaphors. Carnochan deals with 'the larger, metaphorical pattern that includes all manner of restraint on human action.'[42] Fludernik[43] and Alber[44] discriminate between two types of prison metaphors, namely, metaphors of imprisonment that use the prison as tenor (PRISON IS X) and proper prison metaphors that use the prison as vehicle (X IS PRISON). Metaphors of imprisonment that describe the prison in terms of, say, a womb, a tomb, or a cage play an important role with regard to the rendering of the prison experience and usually occur in narratives that are set in prison. Prison metaphors, on the other hand, project the image of the prison onto domains outside a penal context in order to accentuate forms of restraint beyond the world of the prison, and can be found in all types of narratives.[45] This collection also discusses metaphorical extensions of the prison theme. However, at the same time, it transcends existing analyses by showing that Victorian narratives primarily use prison metaphors to associate a particular social group, value, or lifestyle with the prison.

Finally, a fourth strand of criticism deals with the cultural significance of the prison, and it is to this new and methodologically challenging domain that

Stones of Law, Bricks of Shame belongs. In *Fitting Sentences*, Jason Haslam deals with 'the way in which imprisoned authors detail the relationship of the prison to other social institutions, to the members of society, to various forms of the exercise of power, and to the people directly affected by it.'[46] Similarly, in their introduction to *Captivating Subjects*, Haslam and Julia M. Wright point out that their volume addresses the connections between captivity narratives and other cultural categories. More specifically, their 'contributors delve into the heart of contemporary debates surrounding identity, politics, history, and writing, shedding new light on the ways in which captivity has aided the formation of both the modern nation state and its concomitant subjectivities.'[47] For example, in his contribution to their collection, Frank Lauterbach shows that many Victorian prisoner autobiographies reproduce middle-class values by concentrating on the perspective of their gentlemanly author-narrators who corroborate the demonization of 'common' criminals but openly exempt themselves from this class.[48]

In similar fashion to *Captivating Subjects* (2005), this volume deals with the ways in which prisons are emblematized and woven into the textual fabric of Victorian novels and reform tracts. *Stones of Law, Bricks of Shame* demonstrates that through various associations and dissociations, the prison develops into a discursive emblem or trope that serves as an important focal point of the Victorian public discourse through which bourgeois gentlemen conceive of their cultural selves against moral, social, sexual, or national Otherness.

Corpus and Methodological Issues

In contrast to the discussions in Franklin, Davies, Haslam, and the collection by Haslam and Wright, all of which analyse first-person narratives by inmates or prison officials, this volume does not deal with first-hand writings *from* the prison. Rather, the essays collected here look at the ways in which the prison is narrated in writings that emerged from what Jürgen Habermas calls the bourgeois public sphere, that is, the 'world of a reasoning reading public.'[49] This collection looks at fictional narratives and reform tracts that were both written and read by representatives of the *pensée bourgeoise* of Victorian society. This focus on gentlemen and 'respectable' members of the middle class (as opposed to first-hand prison accounts) allows us to get a sense of how such writers use the prison as a discursive emblem to negotiate their own identities in relation to cultural Otherness.

The essays collected here cover a long period of rapid social, cultural, and literary change, from early Dickens before 1840 to fairly late Henry James in the 1890s (followed by an epilogue on the neo-Victorian Sarah Waters).

Stones of Law, Bricks of Shame places a major emphasis on Charles Dickens. Generally speaking, and in comparison with other nineteenth-century authors, it is in Dickens's oeuvre that the prison figures most prominently. According to A.O.J. Cockshut, 'the paramount importance of prisons in Dickens's imaginative life hardly needs to be demonstrated.'[50] His father, John Dickens, was imprisoned for debt in the Marshalsea debtors' prison in 1824 and the whole Dickens family had to join him there. This traumatic experience was exacerbated by the fact that the twelve-year-old Charles had to work in a blacking factory. The adult Dickens returned to the prison again and again in his texts: many of his novels and non-fictional writings deal with the subject at length. But even without any biographical knowledge, every attentive reader must be aware of the dominance of the prison in Dickens's work. Dickens plays such a central role in *Stones of Law, Bricks of Shame* because he presents us with an immense range of prison experience, and additionally deals with the intimate connections between the prison and the lives of the free and respectable.[51]

David Paroissien addresses the conflicting rhetorics of punishment in Dickens's writings from 'Criminal Courts' (1834) to *The Mystery of Edwin Drood* (1870), and shows that passages which depict criminals (and prisoners) as beasts and sympathetic commentary always go hand in hand. Jeremy Tambling, on the other hand, investigates the connections between the development of the 'new' penitentiary and a new image of criminality in Dickens's fiction as well as in Charles Reade's prison novel *It Is Never Too Late to Mend* (1856). Tambling demonstrates that while earlier images of the criminal present us with tough masculinity in action, newer images are more complex in sexual terms, and perhaps even homosexually charged. Adam Hansen shows that the prisons in Dickens's *Barnaby Rudge* (1841), *American Notes* (1842), and 'Pet Prisoners' (1850) critique the 'separate' system, which Dickens rejected, while simultaneously threatening the integrity of the 'silent' system, which Dickens officially propounded as an alternative. Anna Schur, on the other hand, accentuates Dickens's rejection of the officially endorsed 'separate' system and the notion of 'pattern penitence' in 'Pet Prisoners' (1850) and *David Copperfield* (1849–50). Finally, Sean C. Grass looks at the connections between the Victorian prison and Dickens's *Great Expectations* (1860–1). He argues that this mature novel effectively recreates the power of the Victorian prison in its portrayal of imprisonment, guilt, solitude, and first-person narration.

Stones of Law, Bricks of Shame combines this focus on Dickens with analyses of non-canonical texts by Charles Reade, Frederick William Robinson, and E.D.E.N. Southworth. Also, our contributors look at narratives about imprisonment in the former colonies of Ireland (Anthony Trollope, William Makepeace

Thackeray) and India (Philip Meadows Taylor). And finally, this volume contains readings of important prison reform tracts and novels by Henry James, as well as an epilogue on Sarah Waters. We have decided to include a neo-Victorian author and an American writer in a deliberate attempt to avoid unnecessarily constraining the theme discussed in this collection. Furthermore, the inclusion of a non-British narrative provides an outside perspective on the dynamics of the Victorian prison trope, while the discussion of a postmodern author tells us something about how we see the Victorian prison today. This mix of canonical and non-canonical texts allows us to show in great detail how the prison had entered the cultural subconscious of the Victorian age and was negotiated in the popular imagination of the nineteenth century.

Matthew Kaiser shows that the confessions by the incarcerated Indian Ameer Ali in Philip Meadows Taylor's *Confessions of a Thug* (1839) allow the imperial reformer to perform an act of self-congratulatory self-blame that ultimately reproduces imperialism. Furthermore, the prison setting and the Anglicization of the Indian inmate align the self-flagellating imperialism of Taylor's novel with the liberal efforts to reform the Victorian prison system that are discussed by Paroissien and Carnochan in this volume. Laura Berol shows that *The Irish Sketch Book, 1842* and *The Luck of Barry Lyndon* (1844) by William Makepeace Thackeray as well as *The Macdermots of Ballycloran* (1847) by Anthony Trollope use the prison to explore and critique the destructive effects of British colonialism, and perceive Britain as imprisoning the Irish. W.B. Carnochan looks at three reform tracts, namely, William Hepworth Dixon's *The London Prisons* (1850), George Laval Chesterton's *Revelations of Prison Life* (1856), and *The Criminal Prisons of London and Scenes of Prison Life* (1862) by Henry Mayhew and John Binny. He demonstrates that like Dickens's texts, they oscillate between the analytical and the emotional. However, in this case the emotions are slightly more egotistical; the reformers are interested in tolerable prison conditions, but they also get thrilled by the 'deviant' counter-world of the prison. Anne Schwan analyses Frederick William Robinson's portrayals of female convicts in *Female Life in Prison* (1862), *Memoirs of Jane Cameron: Female Convict* (1863), and *Prison Characters Drawn from Life with Suggestions for Prison Government* (1866). Robinson's narratives constitute attempts to reinstate the voices of female convicts and other lower-class women, but they also reproduce the dominant concepts of social inequality of the Victorian age. Jason Haslam looks at the ways in which E.D.E.N. Southworth's *The Hidden Hand or, Capitola the Madcap* (1888) critiques the culture of punishment of the United States in the mid-nineteenth century. In this novel, the prison gives rise to tales of horror as well as to debates about the ethics of punishment, and, as Haslam shows, the latter discourse may gradually change society. Greta Olson traces Henry James's exploration of imprisonment from Millbank prison in *The Princess Casamassima* (1886) to the captivity of a telegraphist's mind in *In the Cage* (1898). While the reflector figures realize their own economic limitations, readers become aware of the gaps in their knowledge about the texts. Both the protagonists and the readers enter a state of mental imprisonment, and, according to Olson, this phenomenon is an integral part of the paradigm shift from Victorian realism to literary modernism. Finally, Rosario Arias revisits the Victorian age in her discussion of Sarah Waters's neo-Victorian novel *Affinity* (1999). She deals with the prison and the home, the two major sites of female confinement in the nineteenth century, and additionally addresses attempts to escape them.

The essays collected here cover a wide range of current approaches and methodologies, all of which address the central role of prisons in Victorian narratives. More specifically, some of our contributors engage in close readings of nineteenth-century texts to reveal tensions, ambiguities, and contradictions in the attitudes towards prisons (Parossien, Kaiser, Hansen, Carnochan, and Schwan). Others approach Victorian prisons from the perspective of new historicism and address the reciprocal relationship between the historical reality of imprisonment and its fictional representation (Tambling, Grass, Haslam). Furthermore, some contributors use the Bakhtinian notions of objectified discourse or heteroglossia to illuminate particular features of Victorian prison representations (Schur and Schwan). Again other essays discuss the role of nineteenth-century imprisonment within the framework of postcolonial criticism (Kaiser and Berol), while some of our contributors address prisons in relation to issues of class and social inequality (Schwan, Haslam, and Olson). A final group of essays is informed by feminist or gender theory and looks at Victorian prisons in relation to gender roles (Tambling, Schwan, Haslam, Olson, and Arias).

Despite these different theoretical frameworks, all our contributors move beyond the traditional paradigms of studying imprisonment in literature and focus on the prison as a discursive emblem rather than an oppressive, disciplining, or potentially liberating institution. *Stones of Law, Bricks of Shame* constitutes a synoptic examination of the multifarious functions of narrating imprisonment for the cultural self-perception of Victorian society. This collection is an explicitly post-Foucauldian intervention in the scholarship on Victorian imprisonment. Our contributors critique and extend Foucault and his *Discipline and Punish* in three major ways.

Adam Hansen's contribution uses Peter Linebaugh's notion of 'excarceration,' which denotes ways of escaping society's disciplinary mechanisms

through connections between people and places that society attempts to separate.[52] Hansen challenges Foucault's notion of the all-embracing 'panoptical'
society by suggesting ways of opposing disciplinary institutions. Similarly,
by highlighting how rational debates in the public sphere may become the
cure to unjust forms of punishment, Jason Haslam moves beyond Foucault's
notion of the disciplinary society and the creation of 'docile' bodies. Furthermore, Rosario Arias's analysis of Sarah Waters's fiction is informed by an
article by Lauren M.E. Goodlad[53] that detects a discrepancy between the
alleged relevance of 'panopticism' in the nineteenth century and the decentralized, self-governing society of Victorian Britain. A second group of
essays highlights that surveillance played only a minor role in Victorian prisons. Sean C. Grass and Anna Schur point out that Foucault's analysis of the
centrality of the Panopticon has made it difficult to see any other links
between the prison and the novel than the central role of observation. In contrast to earlier Foucault-inspired critics, they investigate the connections
between the Victorian prison and first-person narration, and highlight the
power prison officials exercised over the inmates' self-accounts. A final
group of contributors analyse the prison in Victorian narratives against the
foil of different works by Foucault. For instance, Jeremy Tambling focuses
on Foucault's *The History of Sexuality* (1976) to explore the relations
between gender construction and imprisonment in Dickens and Reade. Similarly, Anne Schwan's essay is informed by a series of lectures by Foucault
that move beyond the 'panopticism' of *Discipline and Punish* and concern
the recovery of subjugated alternative forms of knowledge.[54]

Results: Synchronic vs Diachronic Perspectives

What are the results of the investigations in this volume? *Stones of Law, Bricks
of Shame* seeks to combine the merits of synchronic and diachronic perspectives. As Lawrence Krader argues, one may 'analyze a social phenomenon by
tracing its passage from one point in time to another, or how it came, at the
later point, to be; alternatively, we may focus on its relations in a particular
society at a given time.'[55] On the one hand, the contributions in this volume
reveal a particular set of relations between the prison and cultural categories
on the synchronic level; on the other hand, the chronological order of the contributions allows this collection to ponder developments of prison representations along the diachronic axis.

As far as the synchronic level is concerned, this collection shows that the
prison in Victorian narratives fulfils three important discursive functions.
First, the prison serves a *moral* function because its thematization urges both

authors and readers to reflect upon the ethical implications of excluding 'deviancy.' This question closely correlates with the way in which law-abiding citizens view themselves and construct their own identities. Albeit with slightly different foci, Paroissien, Hansen, and Carnochan discuss the prison as a matrix of conflicting moral views. And, once again, Dickens is a very prominent example of the general ambiguous attitude towards the prison. As Philip Collins has shown, his 'concern with crime was ... more persistent and more serious than most men's. Extraordinary in character as well as in literary skill, he had strong and conflicting feelings about criminals.'[56]

Second, the prison fulfils a *social* function in so far as it is used to reproduce but frequently also to renegotiate traditional gender roles, forms of social organization, or manifestations of national hegemony. Tambling, Schwan, and Arias look at the prison as a schema of gender roles. The prison may feminize men or masculinize women, and it may also be used as a metaphor to emphasize that many Victorians saw the family or the home as a site of oppression. Haslam and Olson analyse the prison as a marker of social organization, and investigate connections between the prison and society. The prison may reproduce society's hierarchies in so far as members of underprivileged classes are more likely to be imprisoned than others. Equally, the prison is often employed as a metaphor to accentuate forms of social confinement. Lastly, the prison may also lead to a discourse of resistance that alters society. Kaiser and Berol deal with the prison as an icon of national hegemony, and address ways in which the Victorians utilize the prison to discuss the imperial project. On the one hand, the British administration of the colonies may be figured as a form of imprisonment with the consequence that binary oppositions inscribed in the imperial project are subverted; on the other hand, the prison can also be used to reproduce and stabilize the imprisoning aspects of colonialism.

Third, the prison fulfils a *narrative* function in so far as it invents and shapes the identities of its inmates. Schur and Grass discuss the prison as a frame of narrative structure. That is to say, they illustrate how Victorian prisons pushed their inmates to offer coherent accounts of their (disordered, fragmented, and multidimensional) identities as a sign of their willingness to reform. As has already been said, Victorian prisoners were often visited by chaplains who forced them to tell stories about the 'beneficial' influence of the prison on their character development. The chaplains then frequently altered the inmates' self-accounts by making them say what the officials wanted to hear.

Stones of Law, Bricks of Shame forcefully demonstrates that the prison was a vital discursive icon in the construction of Victorian identities. Its importance was to discover, display, organize, interpret, comment on, even generate and negotiate the moral, sexual, social, and national structure of Victorian Britain. Interestingly, the narratives discussed here not only use the prison as an emblem to reproduce 'respectable' middle-class attitudes towards morality, gender, class, and nation. Rather, the prison is frequently employed as an emblem to deconstruct society's hierarchies and binary oppositions. Since the prison by its very nature establishes lines of demarcation between entities, it is a particularly apt and multifunctional prism for processes of identity construction. The contributions collected here demonstrate that both the prison and the outside world are narrated as belonging (or not belonging) to a specific person or group that stands for a certain moral value, life style, or social, sexual, or national identity.

One may use Horst Turk's terminology to describe the ambivalent ways in which Victorian narratives use the prison to textualize difference. Turk uses the term 'alienity' (*Alienität*) for identity constructions that mark the Other off as belonging to a distinct and 'alien' systemic frame, while he uses the term 'alterity' (*Alterität*) to denote processes of identity construction in which the 'self' is associated with the 'Other,' so that the two become aspects of the same perceptual frame.[57] As the title of our volume suggests, Victorian narratives permanently oscillate between these two ways of constructing Otherness. More specifically, scenes in which the Victorians dissociate themselves from the prison and simultaneously confirm cultural hegemonies go hand in hand with segments in which they associate themselves with the prison and deconstruct societal hierarchies.

As far as the diachronic level is concerned, one can observe a gradual movement into the mind of the prisoner. As we move from early Dickens to late James, we telescope inwards, towards the mental states of inmates. In other words, we travel from narrative 'omniscience' and first-person narratives that were controlled by agents of the prison to first-person and reflector-mode narratives that focus on the actual prisoner and his or her plight. Examples and anticipations of this 'new' and narrower mode of narrating the prisoner are *Confessions of a Thug*, *Great Expectations*, and *The Princess Casamassima*. Moreover, this trend is continued in the twentieth century. As Carnochan has shown, 'recent prison fictions ... renounce narrative omniscience and, by looking outward from the confinement of a cell, intensify the conditions of narrative self-reflexivity.'[58] Prison novels of the twentieth century are either first-person narratives that focus on the thoughts, feelings, and motivations of an imprisoned narrator or they are reflector-mode narratives that deal with the internal processes of an imprisoned character.[59]

It is perhaps no coincidence that as the internal perspective of inmates is pushed into the centre of interest in fictional literature, the authority of the

Victorian prison was gradually being undermined. Writers of fiction, prison reformers, and the Victorian public became more and more interested in prisoner interiority and the question of how the treatment in prison actually affects the inmates. At the end of the nineteenth century, public unease at Du Cane's authoritarian and brutal regime led to the appointment of a Departmental Committee of Enquiry, which reinvented the idea of rehabilitation, allowed witnesses to have their say, and published its findings in the Gladstone Report of 1895. This report recommended more reformative and 'hopeful' measures in British prisons. For example, certain offenders (such as women, children, alcoholics, and first offenders) were accorded more humane treatment. Also, prisoners were allowed to do 'useful work,' the 'separate' system was abolished, and psychologists were introduced into the prisons. Du Cane was then finally replaced as Chairman of the Prison Commission by Sir Evelyn Ruggles-Brise, who redefined the purpose of imprisonment as being for the humanization of the individual. Sir Robert Anderson, the first Secretary of the Prison Commission after 1877, writes about Du Cane's achievements in retrospect: 'Under his rule very great improvements were effected in prisons and prison administration; and if criminals were mere animals, nothing more need be desired in either sphere. But criminals are human beings, and they ought to be treated as such.'[60]

Finally, Sarah Waters's postmodern reconsideration of the Victorian past allows us to qualify such teleological developments towards the better. Waters's return to the nineteenth century certainly correlates with her knowledge about the continuing oppression of women and the deplorable state of British prisons in the twentieth century. Waters does not create a false continuity between the past and the present. Rather, she uses history responsibly by reading it for traces of the 'uninterrupted narrative' not so much of class struggle, as Fredric Jameson would like to have it, but of female oppression and shocking prison conditions. Also, she brings this 'repressed and buried reality'[61] to the surface of the text. Indeed, as Séan McConville has shown, twentieth-century imprisonment in Britain was marked by a tenacious Victorian inheritance. British prisons were 'caught between inadequate funding and increased demands' and 'declined to levels of sordidness that would have appalled and shamed Victorian administrators, politicians and public alike ... If this century has seen English prison administrators grapple with their Victorian inheritance, their decisions have been erratic, uncertain, and marked by periods of administrative inertia and philosophical coma.'[62] Furthermore, between 1946 and 1986 the British prison population increased from fifteen thousand to forty-five thousand, and this rise made the situation even worse because it created serious problems of order and overcrowding.[63] Arias's epilogue thus reminds us that we have to be very cautious with regard to the conceptualization of history in terms of progress or a continuous change for the better. The history of British prisons is not just a history of gradual improvements or positive alterations; it frequently also correlates with a return to old forms of barbarism.

NOTES

1 William Blake, *The Marriage of Heaven and Hell* (1790; London and New York: Oxford University Press, 1975), xviii.

2 John Villalobos, 'William Blake's "Proverbs of Hell" and the Tradition of Wisdom Literature,' *Studies in Philology* 87, no. 2 (1990): 257.

3 Diana Hume George, 'Blake and Freud,' in *William Blake's The Marriage of Heaven and Hell*, ed. Harold Bloom (New York: Chelsea, 1987), 80.

4 Harold Bloom, introduction to *William Blake's The Marriage of Heaven and Hell*, 3.

5 Oscar Wilde, 'The Ballad of Reading Gaol' (1897), in *The Complete Works of Oscar Wilde, vol. I, Poems and Poems in Prose*, ed. Bobby Fong and Karl Beckson (Oxford: Oxford University Press, 2000), 213, l. 550.

6 Richard Ellmann, *Oscar Wilde* (New York: Knopf, 1988), 532.

7 We would like to thank Jeremy Tambling for this observation.

8 Randall McGowen, 'The Well-Ordered Prison: England, 1780–1865,' in *The Oxford History of the Prison: The Practice of Punishment in Western Society*, ed. Norval Morris and David J. Rothman (New York: Oxford University Press, 1995), 99.

9 John Hirst, 'The Australian Experience: The Convict Colony,' in Morris and Rothman, *The Oxford History of the Prison*, 292–3.

10 Cesare Beccaria, *An Essay on Crimes and Punishments* (1767; Boston: International Pocket Library, 1992); Jonas Hanway, *Solitude in Imprisonment* (London: British Library, 1776); John Howard, *The State of the Prisons in England and Wales* (1777; London: Dent, 1929).

11 Howard, *The State of the Prisons*, 22.

12 Henry Mayhew and John Binny, *The Criminal Prisons of London and Scenes of Prison Life* (London: Griffin, Bohn, and Company, 1862), 198.

13 Ibid., 201.

14 Ibid., 100–5.

15 David J. Rothman, 'Perfecting the Prison. United States, 1789–1865,' in Morris and Rothman, *The Oxford History of the Prison*, 117.

16 Ibid., 119, and Randall McGowen, 'The Well-Ordered Prison,' 100. For a discussion of Dickens's views on these two prison systems, see the contributions by

David Paroissien, Adam Hansen, and Anna Schur in this volume. For the American perspective, see Jason Haslam's essay.

17 Stephen Halliday, *Newgate: London's Prototype of Hell* (Gloucestershire, UK: Sutton, 2006), 158.

18 Philip Priestley, *Victorian Prison Lives: English Prison Biography 1830–1914* (London: Methuen, 1985), 7. For more on the complex pattern of Victorian prisons, see Jeremy Tambling's contribution in this volume.

19 Priestley, *Victorian Prison Lives*, 108.

20 Edmund F. Du Cane, *The Punishment and Prevention of Crime* (London: Macmillan, 1885), 3.

21 Edmund F. Du Cane, 'The Unavoidable Uselessness of Prison Labour,' *The Nineteenth Century* 40, July-December (1896): 632–42.

22 Séan McConville, 'The Victorian Prison: England, 1865–1965,' in Morris and Rothman, *The Oxford History of the Prison*, 147.

23 Priestley, *Victorian Prison Lives*, 161–2.

24 Ibid., xiii.

25 Howard Bruce Franklin, *Prison Literature in America: The Victim as Criminal and Artist*, expanded ed. (New York: Oxford University Press, 1989), xiii–xv.

26 Ioan Davies, *Writers in Prison* (Oxford: Blackwell, 1990), 18. Other studies that focus on the representation of the prison experience are Monika Fludernik, 'Carceral Topography: Spatiality and Liminality in the Literary Prison,' *Textual Practice* 13, no. 1 (1999): 43–77; Jan Alber, 'Das Gefängnis im Hollywoodfilm: Strafvollzug zwischen Fiktion und Realität,' *Zeitschrift für Strafvollzug und Straffälligenhilfe* 52, no. 1 (2003): 31–40; and Jan Alber, 'Bodies behind Bars: The Disciplining of the Prisoner's Body in British and American Prison Movies,' in *In the Grip of the Law: Prisons, Trials and the Space Between*, ed. Monika Fludernik and Greta Olson (Frankfurt: Lang, 2004), 241–69.

27 Victor Brombert, *The Romantic Prison: The French Tradition* (1975; Princeton: Princeton University Press, 1978), 3.

28 Sigrid Weigel, *'Und selbst im Kerker frei...!': Schreiben im Gefängnis: Zur Theorie und Gattungsgeschichte der Gefängnisliteratur (1750–1933)* (Marburg: Guttandin and Hoppe, 1982), 98.

29 W.B. Carnochan, *Confinement and Flight: An Essay on English Literature of the Eighteenth Century* (Berkeley and Los Angeles: University of California Press, 1977); Christa Karpenstein-Eßbach, *Einschluß und Imagination: Über den literarischen Umgang mit Gefangenen* (Tübingen: Edition Diskord, 1985); Martha Grace Duncan, *Romantic Outlaws, Beloved Prisons: The Unconscious Meanings of Crime and Punishment* (New York: New York University Press, 1996). Although *Writers in Prison* focuses on the central role of violence, Davies also sees the prison as 'a centre of intellectual activity' and prison culture as 'a culture that is set apart

from everyday culture, establishing a creative, experiential scheme in dealing with its own everyday world.' Ioan Davies, *Writers in Prison*, 3, 11.

30 Michel Foucault, *Discipline and Punish: The Birth of the Prison*, trans. by Alan Sheridan (1975; New York: Vintage Books, 1979), 205.

31 Jeremy Bentham, *The Panopticon Writings*, ed. with an introduction by Miran Božovič (London: Verso, 1995).

32 Mark Seltzer, *Henry James and the Art of Power* (Ithaca, NY: Cornell University Press, 1984), 54.

33 D.A. Miller, *The Novel and the Police* (Berkeley and Los Angeles: University of California Press, 1988), 25.

34 John Bender, *Imagining the Penitentiary: Fiction and the Architecture of Mind in Eighteenth-Century England* (Chicago: University of Chicago Press, 1987), 203. For further links between 'omniscient' narration and the Panopticon, see Audrey Jaffe, *Vanishing Points: Dickens, Narrative, and the Subject of Omniscience* (Berkeley and Los Angeles: University of California Press, 1991), 6–13; and Natalie McKnight, *Idiots, Madmen, and Other Prisoners in Dickens* (New York: St Martin's Press, 1993), 111.

35 Dorrit Cohn, 'Optics and Power in the Novel,' *New Literary History* 26 (1995): 15. The contributions by David Paroissien and Anna Schur in this collection both illustrate how the view that a show of obedience reflects psychic conformity is critiqued in Dickens's 'Pet Prisoners' and *David Copperfield*.

36 Monika Fludernik, *Towards a 'Natural' Narratology* (London: Routledge, 1996), 368.

37 Sean C. Grass, *The Self in the Cell: Narrating the Victorian Prisoner* (New York: Routledge, 2003), 6, 219.

38 For further evidence, see U.R.Q. Henriques, 'The Rise and Decline of the Separate System of Prison Discipline,' *Past and Present* 54 (1972): 61–93; Robert Alan Cooper, 'Jeremy Bentham, Elizabeth Fry and English Prison Reform,' *Journal of the History of Ideas* 42 (1981): 675–90; and the essays by Jeremy Tambling and Sean C. Grass in this volume.

39 Norman Johnston, *The Human Cage: A Brief History of Prison Architecture* (New York: Walker, 1973), 20.

40 Frank E. Hagan, 'Panopticon,' in *Encyclopedia of American Prisons*, ed. Marilyn D. McShane and Frank R. Williams III (London: Garland, 1996), 341.

41 Grass, *The Self in the Cell*, 7, 220, 35.

42 W.B. Carnochan, 'The Literature of Confinement,' in Morris and Rothman, *The Oxford History of the Prison*, 427. In *Confinement and Flight*, he points out that one might even argue 'that reality follows rather than precedes metaphor, that the history of real prisons recapitulates the history of the philosophical prisons that haunted the eighteenth-century imagination.' Carnochan, *Confinement and Flight*, 4.

43 Monika Fludernik, 'Prison Metaphors – The Carceral Imagery?' in Fludernik and
    Olson, *In the Grip of the Law*, 145–67; Monika Fludernik, 'Metaphorics and Met-
    onymics of Carcerality: Reflections on Imprisonment as Source and Target Domain
    in Literary Texts,' *English Studies* 86, no. 3 (2005): 226–44; and Monika Fludernik,
    'Metaphoric (Im)prison(ment) and the Constitution of a Carceral Imaginary,'
    Anglia 123 (2005): 1–24.

44 Jan Alber, *Narrating the Prison: Role and Representation in Charles Dickens' Nov-
    els, Twentieth-Century Fiction, and Film* (Youngstown, NY: Cambria Press, 2007);
    Jan Alber, 'Cinematic Carcerality: Prison Metaphors in Film,' *The Journal of Popu-
    lar Culture* (forthcoming).

45 Both Fludernik and Alber also deal with the question of how certain features of
    society or societal ranks are reproduced in prison. Monika Fludernik, 'The Prison
    as World – The World as Prison: Theoretical and Historical Aspects of Two Recur-
    rent Topoi,' *Symbolism* 3 (2003): 145–89; Alber, *Narrating the Prison*, 49–55, 194–
    223; Jan Alber, 'Darkness, Light, and Various Shades of Gray: The Prison and the
    Outside World in Charles Dickens' *A Tale of Two Cities*,' *Dickens Studies Annual*
    (forthcoming).

46 Jason Haslam, *Fitting Sentences: Identity in Nineteenth- and Twentieth-Century
    Prison Narratives* (Toronto: University of Toronto Press, 2005), 10.

47 Jason Haslam and Julia M. Wright, introduction to *Captivating Subjects: Writing
    Confinement, Citizenship, and Nationhood in the Nineteenth Century*, ed. Jason
    Haslam and Julia Wright (Toronto: University of Toronto Press, 2005), 4.

48 Frank Lauterbach, '"From the Slums to the Slums": The Delimitation of Social
    Identity in Late Victorian Prison Narratives,' in Haslam and Wright, *Captivating
    Subjects*, 113–43. For a more extensive discussion of his theoretial premises see
    Frank Lauterbach, 'Textual Errands into The Carceral Wilderness: Prison Autobiog-
    raphies and the Construction of Cultural Hegemonies,' in Fludernik and Olson, *In
    the Grip of the Law*, 127–43. Moreover, many prison narratives of the twentieth cen-
    tury focus on one newcomer who is wrongfully imprisoned and then suffers under a
    brutal system. And while the fate of this character is represented as being unjust, the
    attitude towards the mass of ordinary prisoners is complicit with the view that 'real'
    criminals have to be imprisoned. Also, these delimitations are connected with other
    cultural delineations. The newcomer is typically a member of the white and hetero-
    sexual middle class, while the 'real' criminals are frequently black or coded as
    homosexuals. Alber, *Narrating the Prison*, 3–4, 118–19, 131–2, 179–80, 233–5.

49 The original phrase is: 'Welt [d]es räsonierenden Lesepublikums.' Jürgen
    Habermas, *Strukturwandel der Öffentlichkeit: Untersuchungen zu einer Kategorie
    der bürgerlichen Gesellschaft*, new ed. (Frankfurt: Suhrkamp, 1990), 183.

50 A.O.J. Cockshut, 'Prison Experiences in Dickens's Novels [1962],' in *Readings on
    Charles Dickens*, ed. Clarice Swisher (San Diego, CA: Greenhaven Press, 1998), 40.

51 Important studies on the representation of prisons and criminals in Dickens are Lionel Trilling, *The Opposing Self* (London: Secker and Warburg, 1955); Philip Collins, *Dickens and Crime* (London and New York: Macmillan and St Martin's Press, 1962); Jeremy Tambling, 'Prison-Bound: Dickens and Foucault [1986],' in *Great Expectations. Charles Dickens*, ed. Roger D. Sell (Houndmills, UK: Macmillan, 1994), 123–42; Jeremy Tambling, *Dickens, Violence and the Modern State: Dreams of the Scaffold.* (Houndmills, UK: Macmillan, 1995); Jeremy Tambling, *Lost in the American City: Dickens, James, and Kafka* (New York: Palgrave, 2001). For a comprehensive analysis of Dickens's oeuvre, see David Paroissien, ed., *A Companion to Dickens* (Oxford: Blackwell, 2007).

52 Peter Linebaugh, *The London Hanged: Crime and Civil Society in the Eighteenth Century* (London: Penguin, 1991), 3.

53 Lauren M.E. Goodlad, 'Beyond the Panopticon: Victorian Britain and the Critical Imagination,' *PMLA* 11, no. 3 (2003): 539–56.

54 Michel Foucault, *'Society Must Be Defended': Lectures at the Collège de France, 1975–76*, ed. Mauro Bertani and Alessandro Fontana, trans. David Macey (London: Lane, 2003).

55 Lawrence Krader, 'Beyond Structuralism: The Dialectics of the Diachronic and Synchronic Methods in the Human Sciences,' in *The Unconscious in Culture: The Structuralism of Lévi-Strauss in Perspective*, ed. Ino Rossi (New York: Dutton, 1974), 336.

56 Collins, *Dickens and Crime*, 1.

57 Horst Turk, 'Alienität und Alterität als Schlüsselbegriffe einer Kultursemantik,' *Jahrbuch für internationale Germanistik* 22, no. 1 (1990): 10–12.

58 Carnochan, 'The Literature of Confinement,' 442.

59 For a list of examples, see Alber, *Narrating the Prison*, 242.

60 Sir Robert Anderson, *The Lighter Side of My Office Life* (London: Hodder and Stoughton), 83.

61 Fredric Jameson, *The Political Unconscious* (Ithaca, NY: Cornell University Press, 1981), 20.

62 McConville, 'The Victorian Prison,' 155.

63 For an analysis of the current state of British prisons, see David Ramsbotham, *Prison Gate: The Shocking State of Britain's Prisons and the Need for Visionary Change* (London: Free Press, 2003).

1 Victims or Vermin? Contradictions in Dickens's Penal Philosophy

DAVID PAROISSIEN

Charles Dickens wrote extensively about imprisonment and wrongdoing. Murder, misdeeds, and jails feature in all fourteen of his novels. Bloodshed lies at the heart of his unfinished fifteenth, which would have concluded in the condemned cell had Dickens lived to complete it. Travel to the United States with him in 1842 and follow a tourist trail that missed no opportunity to visit state and federal penitentiaries. A year abroad in Italy two years later documents similar interests. Dickens met men fighting for Italy's independence and inspected prisons in France, Switzerland, and Italy. Even a public beheading in Rome made its way into his holiday agenda. The brilliant essays he contributed to *Household Words* and *All the Year Round* offer more of the same. Twelve volumes of personal correspondence close the case. One cannot read Dickens without running into those who break the law, whether they steal and rob in order to stay alive, burgle out of greed, or poison or bludgeon someone to death as the expression of long-held resentment or passion momentarily inflamed by anger or sexual jealousy. The whole range of criminal behaviour seems to fall under his scrutiny as he provides some of the most searching studies of the criminal intellect on record.

Critics seek various explanations for this phenomenon. Some turn to Dickens's life and evaluate the impact of hard experiences in boyhood, compounded by the humiliation Dickens suffered when his father was arrested and incarcerated for debt in 1824. The fiction that followed, it has been argued, springs from an attempt to digest those early shocks and hardships. 'For the man of spirit whose childhood has been crushed by the cruelty of organized society,' wrote Edmund Wilson in 1939, 'one of two attitudes is natural: that of the criminal or that of the rebel.'[1] Dickens in his fiction played both.

Others look to the formative years Dickens spent as a shorthand reporter, first in Parliament and then as a journalist employed by various London newspapers.

The first experience introduced him to reformist penal discourse of the 1830s and the second to court practices as they prevailed in the same decade. Who stood in the dock charged with what offence? Were those at the bar 'ill-looking' young fellows charged with 'acts of the grossest brutality,' like the thug ordered to stand before his victim in 'The Hospital Patient' (*Sketches by Boz*, 1836)? Or were the perpetrators of crimes victims themselves, youthful subjects of a harsh legal system that refused even to recognize the concept of juvenile offenders until 1847? Did 'summary justice' constitute justice or merely strengthen preju-dicial assumptions about guilt in order to sweep problems out of sight, prefera-bly to Britain's penal settlements in Australia?

Alternative explanations for Dickens's continuing interest in crime are sought by considering rhetorical strategies he employed as a novelist. 'I wants to make your flesh creep,' says the Fat Boy in *The Pickwick Papers* (1836–7).[2] Might stories about thieves and thief-takers and men awaiting death in the condemned cell serve this end? Much of *Oliver Twist* (1837–9) turns on such material. But by relying on conventions literary reviewers associated with the 'Newgate novel,' Dickens ran into opposition. The genre was as controversial in the 1830s as it was popular. To write about the lives of real criminals, whose notorious deeds had been recorded in a popular collection of criminal bio-graphies published in 1773 as *The Newgate Calendar; or, The Malefactors' Bloody Register*, was thought to condone and even advocate criminal behav-iour. Why gorge the novel-reading public with 'blood and foul Newgate gar-bage,' asked William Makepeace Thackeray in 1839. If people really want to read about 'cut-throats, burglars, [and] women of bad life,' go to the real source: the cheap newspapers and popular ballads sold in one of London's slums. Thackeray, a reviewer for *Fraser's Magazine*, and critic of Dickens's apparent glamorization of low-life criminals, confessed he could hug rogues in private. 'In public, it is, however, quite wrong to avow such likings, and to be seen in such company.'[3]

Moving people to tears proved a less inflammatory strategy. Dickens knew from experience that he could attract readers that way. By such means he could enlarge his readership without drawing charges of polluting the culture. Accordingly, he could turn his practical knowledge to account and reveal what he had learnt as a reporter about the nightly conditions prevailing in London's public 'station-houses,' as police courts were originally known. Throughout the Metropolis, the narrator of *Oliver Twist* confides, 'enough fantastic tricks' are played daily on those charged with offences 'to make the angels blind with weeping.'[4] This situation had arisen on account of changes in trial procedure introduced in the 1750s. In an attempt to combat rising crime rates before the introduction of the Metropolitan Police in 1829, London magistrates had been invested with 'a summary and arbitrary power.' Under this dispensation, court officials substituted for trial by jury trial by magistrates. As a result, impatient and unscrupulous stipendiary magistrates made a mockery of British liberties. This 'ain't the shop for justice,' complains the Artful Dodger, when he is taken into custody and charged with stealing. Dickens uses the occasion of the Dodger's arrest late in *Oliver Twist* to parody the kind of comic interchanges that often occurred between magistrates and young offenders, much to the amusement of the spectators.[5] Earlier in the same novel, he had sounded a more serious note. Men and women 'are every night,' observed the narrator, 'confined on the most trivial *charges* – the word is worth noting – in dungeons, compared with which, those in Newgate, occupied by the most atrocious felons ... are palaces.'[6]

Once in court, those charged with summary offences were hardly any better off. Possible offences included minor larceny such as stealing handkerchiefs as well as vagrancy, drunkenness, and prostitution. Most unfortunate were those brought before the notorious Allan Stewart Laing (1788–1862). Pilloried as Mr Fang in the same novel, this real London magistrate earned an unenviable reputation. His stock-in-trade included bullying witnesses, making stupid comments, treating the young with severity, and handing out harsh sentences. Many young boys, like Dickens's own fictional Artful Dodger, were shipped off 'abroad' for stealing 'a common twopenny-halfpenny sneezebox!'[7] Transporting adolescents for misdemeanours was common practice in England and resulted in boys of fourteen or younger receiving sentences of seven or fourteen years or even life when convicted for stealing a penny tart or a small loaf of bread, according to one well-informed observer.[8]

Explanations for Dickens's sustained interest in crime, we might therefore conclude, require a generous perspective. Dickens remains hard to pin down. His attitudes towards crime and those charged with breaking the law admit no single embracing label. Consider him 'hard' on some issues and elsewhere contradictory evidence emerges. Passages that depict criminals as beasts prone to acts of violence sit side by side with informed, sympathetic commentary. Antisocial behaviour is not without complexity. Nor is it a subject unfit for serious fiction. The narrator who confidently likens Fagin in chapter 19 to an obscene reptile crawling forth at night into London's ordure-packed streets 'in search of some rich offal for a meal' can also move well beyond these uncomfortable limitations. Later, during Fagin's trial scene, in chapter 52, Dickens enters the mind of this alien species in order to render his consciousness with a sympathetic omniscience that pushes the Newgate matter of *Oliver Twist* well beyond its moral and formal limits. Similarly, the brutal housebreaker Bill Sikes, on the run after beating Nancy to a bloody death, evinces a vulnerability rarely displayed by the novel's criminals. In short, Dickens's works fore-ground contradictory responses to crime. While embracing some popular prej-udices, he can deftly explode others, destabilizing popular cultural modes that brought instant literary success. Seeking both to entertain and to educate on matters of penal discourse, Dickens reveals a complexity and ambiguity that merits respect.

I have chosen three snapshots of Dickens's penal philosophy in action to make this point. And while all three are presented in chronological order, each attempts to move beyond the limits of oppositional thinking and of endorsing the conclusion that in middle age Dickens renounced the radicalism of his youth. Dualities, I contend, characterize his thinking about crime. They are present from the start and abound throughout his works irrespective of their date of composition. True, changed and deepened perceptions occur as Dickens extends his novelistic range in the course of mastering his craft. Yet even when most committed to creating affective responses among his readers, he can suddenly switch textual modes and stigmatize criminals as a breed apart, animals stripped of their common humanity.

Dickens and Newgate

Dickens's visit to Newgate Gaol in November 1835 confirmed his impression that the city of London's principal detention centre would yield rich copy. The name itself was enough to strike terror in the heart of many. A local prison since the twelfth century, the old building had been strengthened, extended, rebuilt in 1770, attacked and destroyed a decade later during the anti-Catholic riots led by Lord George Gordon, and then rebuilt in 1783. Massive blocks of granite, iron-barred windows, a display of fetters above the entrance, and a collection of ropes used by the hangman signalled the building's intimidating function. 'We shall never forget the mingled feelings of awe and respect with which we used to gaze on the exterior of Newgate in our schoolboy days,' comments the narrator of an early sketch published in 1834.[9] And if public architecture spoke so threateningly, what stories might be culled by visiting those hidden behind such an impenetrable exterior? A year later, Dickens toured the jail as a visitor, requiring only two hours of intense and silent obser-vation to find out. His excursion, he reported later, yielded 'lots of anec-dotes.'[10]

Dickens was equally confident about how to use the material he had gath-ered. Not for him the dreary recitation of statistics, measurements, tables, and quantitative details characteristic of the reformist discourse of Parliamentary Reports committed to fact-gathering. 'We took no notes, made no memoranda, measured none of the [prisoners'] yards, ascertained the exact number of inches in no particular room,' he told readers in the account he subsequently published in February 1836.[11] Rather, 'we saw the prison, and saw the prisoners; and what we did see, and what we thought, we will tell at once in our own way.'[12] True to his promise, Dickens lost little time in getting to the point. The one subject that riveted his attention was the condemned cells, those stone dungeons stripped to their essentials. Each contained a bench, a rug, a Bible, and a prayer book. Wan light struggled in from small high windows during the day. A candleholder fixed into the wall supplied a feeble artificial light during the hours of darkness. What thoughts go through the mind of a man spending his last night on earth in such circumstances? What torments visit his brain? What images pursue him as his final hours glide away, the time marked by the deep tolling of the bell of St Paul's Cathedral nearby?

Dickens's invitation to readers to respond subjectively clearly signals his rhetorical purpose. 'A Visit to Newgate' remains a brilliant piece of affective commentary, a classic exercise in sympathy, as readers respond to small, particularized details designed to move their imaginations and bring them into emotional intimacy with the psychological state of a man sentenced to die. What crime did he commit? Whom did he kill? Did his victim suffer excruciating pain? Was she or he bludgeoned to death? All such questions are brushed aside as we enter the imagination of the felon and share his agony, a man staring at death when the clock strikes eight in the morning. He hears the bell strike one on his last day alive; 'it has roused him. Seven hours left! He paces the narrow limits of his cell with rapid strides, cold drops of terror starting on his forehead.'[13] Seven hours! Two more quarters strike, then three, then four. 'Six hours left. Tell him not of repentance! Six hours' repentance for eight times six years of guilt and sin! He buries his face in his hands, and throws himself on the bench.'[14] Punishment and repentance under these circumstances fade into abstraction. Instead readers face the consequences of judicial murder, of a system that puts its victims to death with ritualistic precision.

But might not the perpetrator deserve his deserts, sceptics will ask? Suppose he had acted like a wild beast consumed with 'Blind Jackass-like passion,' taken a rolling pin and beaten a woman to death. Can students of human nature who have observed crimes of the most intolerable kind believe that such an individual, left to the chance of murdering again, would not act in the same manner? Given the 'pitiless compound of stupid conceit and deliberate cruelty' that fills such breasts, can society permit the existence of blind passion like this 'in its midst'? Dickens put these questions to a friend some thirty-six years later. 'I desire, as much as any man can, that [capital punishment] should not be,' he explained in August 1868, offering arguments in favour of a penalty he had once vociferously opposed. 'But I am reduced to the admission that I do not know what is to be done with the doers of such deeds of violence short of sending them out of this world.'[15]

The combination of an expressed distaste for judicial murder and despair at finding an appropriate response for 'wild beasts' characterizes Dickens's writing throughout his career. Within months of publishing 'A Visit to Newgate,' he had embarked on *Oliver Twist*, a full-length novel whose criminal subject matter brought him face-to-face with these issues. On the one hand, the novel's most complicated (and sympathetic) character, Nancy, expresses concern for prisoners in Newgate awaiting execution. As Nancy and Sikes cross a large open space in the vicinity of the prison, Nancy counts off the strokes of a nearby bell. The chimes come from St Sepulchre's, whose bell traditionally tolled on the morning of executions.

> 'Eight o'clock, Bill,' said Nancy, when the bell ceased.
> 'What's the good of telling me that; I can hear, can't I?' replied Sikes.
> 'I wonder whether *they* can hear it,' said Nancy ... 'Oh, Bill, such fine young chaps as them!'
> 'Yes; that's all you women think of,' answered Sikes. 'Fine young chaps! Well, they're as good as dead, so it don't much matter.'[16]

Later in the same novel the perspective shifts. In a scene unmediated by Nancy's compassion, we view a knot of decidedly unpleasant individuals. The details appear to have been taken from personal observation and can be corroborated by factual accounts provided by knowledgeable observers. Chapter 26 opens with an insider's view of the patrons of one of London's 'flash houses.' At such places, public houses of a low and disreputable sort, thieves, fences, gamblers, and prostitutes gathered. Typically a landlord reigned supreme. The establishment provided food, drink, and entertainment; the landlord kept a watchful eye over the whole, arranging robberies, connecting experienced thieves with fences, and dishing out stolen profits. Entertainment in the form of obscene songs, dancing, and sexual debauchery predominated. Describing those gathered at the fictional Three Cripples, the narrator comments as follows:

> It was curious to observe some faces which stood out ... There was the chairman himself, (the landlord of the house,) a coarse, rough, heavy-built fellow, who, while the songs were proceeding, rolled his eyes hither and thither, and, seeming to give himself up to joviality, had an eye for everything that was done, and an ear for everything that was said – and sharp ones, too. Near him, were the singers:

receiving, with professional indifference, the compliments of the company: and applying themselves, in turn, to a dozen proffered glasses of spirits and water, tendered by their more boisterous admirers; whose countenances, expressive of almost every vice in almost every grade, irresistibly attracted the attention, by their very repulsiveness. Cunning, ferocity, and drunkenness in all its stages, were there, in their strongest aspects; and women: some with the last lingering tinge of their early freshness, almost fading as you looked: others with every mark and stamp of their sex utterly beaten out, and presenting but one loathsome blank of profligacy and crime: some mere girls, others but young women, and none past the prime of life: formed the darkest and saddest portion of this dreary picture.[17]

What opportunity for reform or rehabilitation exists among those so irretrievably damned? The narrator's judgmental language conveys a sense that all here are lost, damned, the personification of the seven deadly sins, people for whom redemption seems impossible. Their alterity defined in these terms, criminals so loathsomely profligate in their ways, elicits horror and scant sympathy.

Elsewhere in the novel we meet equally unredeemable types, individuals like Fagin and Sikes, figured in metaphors that immediately criminalize them in such a way as to remove them from empathetic consideration. Sikes, for example, simply exudes brutality. As the novel's expert cracksman, he embodies the physicality we expect of one who uses force when faced with locks and stout doors. Accordingly, his potential (and capacity) for violence mark him both visually and linguistically as a monster. Quick to seize a poker or a large clasp knife when he meets with resistance from a man, woman, or dog, Sikes more nearly resembles the ugly and pugnacious cur that constantly skulks at his feet. When called to heel in 'the very harshest key of a very harsh voice,' Bull's-eye keeps his distance, growling fiercely 'like a wild beast.' Ferocious imprecations fail to move him, until the housebreaker assails 'the animal most furiously' as the snapping, growling, and barking dog and the thrusting, swearing, and blaspheming man fuse into a single identity. In his fury Sikes proves an apt adversary for the reptilian Fagin, who attempts to intervene. '"I wish you had been the dog, Fagin, half a minute ago."' In answer to Fagin's forced smile and query, Why? Sikes responds: '"Cause the government, as cares for the lives of such men as you, as haven't half the pluck of curs, lets a man kill a dog how he likes," shutting up the knife with a very expressive look; "that's why."'[18]

Let the patrons of the Three Cripples assemble in London's streets and supply them with an ostensible cause. It could be one as remote from their interests as that championed by the mentally unsound Lord George Gordon in *Barnaby Rudge* (1841). This actual historical figure served as the rallying point for the Protestant Association, a group formed to resist any measure of Catholic Emancipation and the Catholic Relief Act of 1778. Drawn to a march against Parliament organized by the association in 1780, criminals flocked to the demonstrations and took control. They rampaged through London, attacked private homes, and destroyed public property. A cause, any cause, Dickens feared, all too easily might serve as a catalyst and unleash a vortex of collective violence. The fictional criminals who join Lord Gordon are depicted in unmistakably brutish and destructive terms. Hugh, for example, mistakenly enlists under the impression that the protesters' cry of 'No Popery!' was really 'No Property!'[19] But he cares little for his error so long as the cause allows him to express his violent nature. Called a 'centaur' by his father, Hugh is threatening and dangerous, the illegitimate offspring of an effete and calculating hypocrite.[20] And yet at the same time, he is not without allure. The original illustrations by H.K. Browne reinforce this point. One shows a powerful dark-skinned man seated in repose, his shirt open at the chest and with long, wild hair straggling around a handsome face.

Suggestions of a contradictory attitude in the portrayal of Hugh – he is likened to 'a handsome satyr' by the narrator on one occasion – hint at further complications. For all Dickens's middle-class denunciation of violence and depiction of the mob as 'the very scum and refuse of London,' the respectable Victorian in him yields to a frisson of inner excitement when he describes the rebels in action. 'I have let all the prisoners out of Newgate, burnt down Lord Mansfield's, and played the very devil. Another number will finish the fires,' he wrote to John Forster on 18 September 1841. 'I feel quite smoky when I am at work.'[21] Self-dramatization of this sort was one of Dickens's specialties. But the relish shown here is surely consistent with an imaginative sympathy responsible for conflicting attitudes. Consider the treatment of the brutal Sikes, into whose mind we enter when we see him hunted and haunted by guilt after murdering Nancy. That same imaginative compassion turns Fagin the Devil into Fagin the man. When *Oliver Twist* concludes Fagin has become a crushed human being: a man with 'blood-shot eyes,' his head wounded by missiles thrown by the crowd, hands raw from beating futilely against the heavy door of the cell, his thoughts recalling in a few disjointed fragments words he could hardly hear when they were delivered in court by the judge wearing his black cap: 'To be hanged by the neck, till he was dead – that was the end. To be hanged by the neck till he was dead.'[22] In the novel's penultimate verdict on the whole system, the narrator comments: 'Those dreadful walls of Newgate, which have hidden so much misery and such unspeakable anguish, not only from the eyes, but, too often and too long, from the thoughts, of men, never held so dread a spectacle as that.'[23]

Misery and anguish also lay outside the prison walls in plain view and for all to see. To expose their causes required far less work and perhaps rather different tactics, a literary strategy suited to realism leavened by romance. Accordingly, one aspect of *Oliver Twist* examines what Thomas Carlyle called two years later 'The-Condition-of-England Question.' 'A feeling very generally exists that the condition and disposition of the Working Classes is a rather ominous matter at present,' wrote Carlyle, in the opening words of 'Chartism' (1839).[24] That something ought to be said and that something ought to be done struck both Carlyle and Dickens as self-evident.

One specific condition offering material to the realist owed much to recent attempts to reform England's antiquated Poor Laws, legislation dating back to the sixteenth century, when Tudor governments began to nudge the state into taking increasing responsibility for the poor, the indigent, the sick, and the infirm. The crown and its ministers acted in response to a vacuum created by the dissolution of the monasteries, which, in an unwritten partnership with England's parishes, attempted to help those in need of assistance. Such voluntary policies as they existed flowed primarily from an old and Christian concept of charity, whereby one helped one's neighbours as an expression of love for one's fellows. The steady growth of England's population during the ensuing centuries, together with the effects of industrialization and urbanization, laid an unworkable burden on the old system a host of later reformers attempted to correct, starting in the mid-eighteenth century. After the Royal Commission of 1832–4, extensive fact-gathering, a full report, and prolonged debate, the newly constituted Whig government passed the New Poor Law Amendment Act of 1834. This important piece of legislation attempted radical changes. Among them, the act set up a new breed of local and national bureaucrats armed with tables, guides, and policies all designed to decrease the number of those eligible for support and weed out those who didn't deserve it. Even those who received harsh, minimalist treatment. Central policies attempted to mandate the amount of food paupers were served, keep inmates from breeding by separating married paupers, and reduce the amount of aid in the form of bread, money, and coals for those living outside of newly built workhouses, whose architecture bore a distinct resemblance to prisons. Children, not surprisingly, received an even worse deal. They were fed 'at discretion,' poorly schooled, if at all, and then put to work as soon as they were able. The whole system, as the novel's officious Beadle cynically explains, was based on a simple principle: 'give the paupers exactly what they don't want; and then they get tired of coming.'[25]

Little imagination was required to see possible disastrous consequences arising from such treatment. Riots and demonstrations throughout England brought home to many the act's flaws. Rather than ameliorate the lives of the poor, the new policies of denial tended to criminalize them. Add the effects of a harsh winter and by 1837 Dickens had copy enough at hand. In fact, he only had to take 'a glance at the New Poor Law Bill' to awaken readers to conditions prevailing throughout the country. Particularly compelling, and central to the story Dickens chose to tell, was the plight of the young.

The novel's original title, *Oliver Twist; or the Parish Boy's Progress*, conveys a movement suggestive of one of William Hogarth's ironic pictorial 'Progresses.' Mistreat children, starve them, beat them, ignore them, fail to educate and equip them for work, and you sow seeds whose crops will eventually turn bad. In self-preservation, children will run away. London will provide the lure; once there, they will fall into the hands of adult criminals. Within eight chapters, Oliver is happily received into Fagin's den, where he finds the food and warmth denied him by those appointed by the government to supply the means of support. Readers of course know that Oliver is not destined to be hanged, that the conventions of the eighteenth-century novel will supply long-lost relatives, wealth, and stability. Counter elements of romance and fairy tale make it clear that Oliver won't stray from the primrose path. But he can be – and is – tempted. Thus, despite the sentiment and promise of salvation built into the ending, Dickens's point remains a serious one. The bullying sneak thief Noah Claypole eventually follows Oliver, with his employer's till in hand and maid-of-all-work in tow. The couple seeks accommodation at the Three Cripples and Noah enlists in Fagin's gang, eager to engage in forms of petty theft that required low cunning and stealth rather than courage and skill. After proving adept at stealing money from children and pewter and tin pots of beer hung on railings for collection, Fagin recruits him for 'a piece of work' that requires 'great care and caution': 'dodging' a young woman.[26] Eventually, when the gang is broken up, Claypole turns 'respectable' and earns his living as a police informer. Deny the young an education, alienate them by ill treatment, and hold no high expectations for how they will turn out.

Dickens's Visit to the United States in 1842

Alternatives of course existed, and government-initiated steps could be taken to treat the poor decently, help the sick, and provide schooling and training for the young. As an observer familiar with the power of circumstances to corrupt those who lived amidst dirt and squalor, Dickens understood the importance of concerted action. Constructive social policies, implemented on a wide scale by the government, could combat crime and antisocial behaviour. This was a point he sought constantly to convey.

The time Dickens spent in Boston in 1842 furnished models for the sort of action of which he approved. Into two busy weeks he packed visits to several of Boston's institutions and the textile factories of nearby Lowell, renowned for their pastoral care of the young women who made up the workforce. 'The American poor, the American factories, the institutions of all kinds – I have a book already,' he wrote to John Forster on 4 February.[27] Boston and its institutions, Dickens quickly concluded, offered a persuasive example of 'How to Do It.' Most impressive, he thought, was the predominance of state support and assistance over private charity. A public charity, he told readers in *American Notes* (1842), the book that resulted from the trip, 'is immeasurably better than a Private Foundation, no matter how magnificently the latter may be endowed.'[28] Such policies prevailed at Boston's State Hospital for the Insane, the House of Industry (for 'old or otherwise helpless paupers'), the Boylston School for Neglected Boys, the House of Reformation for Juvenile Offenders, and the Massachusetts House of Correction. State support or state assistance, he pointed out, made them all 'emphatically the people's,' an attitude that had not proved popular 'in our own country.'[29]

A second key element in Boston's success lay in attitude. Orphans, paupers, and poor children were not written off as 'evil-disposed and wicked people.' Rather than 'flourish threats and harsh restraints,' enlightened administrators displayed their regard for their fellows by looking on the destitute and afflicted as 'improvable creatures.'[30] As evidence, Dickens cited the Boylston School for Neglected Boys and the House of Reformation for Juvenile Offenders. In the first, the boys, though not criminals in deed, would soon have earned that designation had they not been taken 'from the hungry streets' and fed and educated. In the second, the youths had already begun their descent into crime, sure candidates to deserve the label 'the Dangerous Members of Society.' Intervention, however, stayed their fall. The boys had been given gainful employment ('basket-making, and the manufacture of palm-leaf hats') and taught basic reading skills. The point, Dickens noted, was the 'design and object' of this institution. It set out 'to reclaim the youthful criminal by firm but kind and judicious treatment' to make his prison a place of purification and improvement, not of demoralization and corruption. Such a combination of 'humanity and social policy,' he concluded, requires 'no comment.'[31]

Other disciplinary matters did. Penal policies common in U.S. state and federal penitentiaries for adult prisoners proved a different matter altogether. Elsewhere in *American Notes*, we see clearly that Dickens's trip to the United States in 1842 did not turn him into a 'soft-hearted psalm singer.' Bill Sikes uses the phrase as a term of contempt for religiously motivated reformers. Many of these held a naïve belief in the ability of a carefully controlled environment to promote repentance, sorrow for past deeds, and the resolution to lead a better life. By reflecting on one's past actions, Quakers and Evangelical reformers argued, one could reach a new understanding through the process of self-reflection.

This idea reaches back into the mid-eighteenth century and had proved particularly powerful in the United States, where Quakers in Philadelphia had been among the first to address the horrific conditions to which prisoners were subject in privately run prisons of the kind so graphically described and exposed by John Howard in his *State of the Prisons in England and Wales* (1777). When the city's civic authorities authorized the rebuilding of Philadelphia's Walnut Street Jail in 1790, they were determined to introduce new features. Individual cells were built to house single prisoners instead of crowding men, women, and children promiscuously together. Convicts were fed at the expense of the institution and not expected to provide for their own welfare. They were also put to work, a practical means of keeping them usefully occupied and offsetting costs towards maintaining them.

Serving as a model for general imitation, the Walnut Street Jail inspired further attempts to mitigate the severity of criminal law as it had developed in Hanoverian England. Legislation in 1818 and 1821 authorized the construction of two new prisons in Philadelphia, one for the western and the other for the eastern division of the state. Dickens visited both. But it was the city's Eastern Penitentiary that caught his eye. Invited by local officials to inspect the facility upon his arrival in the city, he passed the whole day there. He went from cell to cell and conversed with the prisoners. 'Every facility was given to me and no constraint whatever imposed upon any man's free speech.'[32] What Dickens saw furnished material that kept his mind occupied for the rest of his life.

The harsh verdict he delivers in chapter 7 of *American Notes* took U.S. prison officers by surprise. They had every reason to feel confident when they bid Dickens welcome and gave him carte blanche to roam and interrogate at will. First, the penitentiary built in 1821 incorporated the latest in prison design. The Eastern Penitentiary made no pretence of its admonitory function. But it also sought through its architecture to make a subtler point. Seven wings radiated from a central hub, from which point officials empowered with an omniscient perspective kept their eyes on prisoners housed in rows in the wings. The design was that of British-born architect John Haviland, who successfully incorporated Jeremy Bentham's notion of a Panopticon, a perceptual prison in which the inmates could be kept under the watchful eyes of the guard at all times without their knowledge.

Isolation from fellow prisoners and all staff except the prison chaplain constituted the other design feature. Confined thus, those held would have ample time for reflection. Inmates would contemplate their fallen behaviour and thereby initiate their own reform. Driven by necessity into the self, they would come to see their past in all its depravity and so seek consolation from religion. William Crawford, a British government official sent to the United States in 1834 to report on the American system, put the case thus. In the silence of the cell, deprived of all companions, the convict is compelled 'to reflect and listen to the reproofs of conscience.' In this state, he will dwell on his past errors, cherish any better feelings he once had, and so in time see the affections 'reclaim the heart.' Crawford expressed full confidence in this process. 'The mind becomes open to the best impressions,' he predicted, 'and prepared for the reception of those truths and consolations which Christianity alone can impart.'[33]

At least, that was the theory. In practice, Dickens concluded that two things went disastrously wrong. Kind and humane though their intentions may be, he conceded, the benevolent gentlemen who deprived the inmates of all contact with others 'did not know what they were doing.' Such conditions, Dickens believed, exacted a terrible toll. Dickens knew because he could read what he saw written on the faces of those cut off from all but the prison officers. 'I hold this slow and daily tampering with the mysteries of the brain, to be immeasurably worse than any torture of the body.'[34] To confine men thus is to bury them alive, he warned.

The second consequence was no less disturbing. For the majority not destroyed by solitary confinement, a tough few managed to resist the educative process. Some even turned the tables on well-intentioned reformers. Dickens saw evidence of this in an English thief and a tall, strong black burglar. He spoke to both during his tour and concluded that each possessed survival mechanisms capable of subverting the system. The English thief, a 'villainous, low-browed, thin-lipped fellow,' seemed impervious to treatment and was ready, 'for the additional penalty,' to stab Dickens with his shoemaker's knife. The burglar in a nearby cell was an allied type. Though near to the end of his time, he remained bold and defiant. He continued to relish his unlawful exploits and entertained Dickens with 'a long account of his achievements.' More to the point, Dickens thought, it would require only 'the slightest encouragement' on his or on anyone else's part to get him to mingle with 'his professional recollections the most detestable cant' of the kind Dickens believed prison chaplains encouraged. 'I am very much mistaken if he could have surpassed the unmitigated hypocrisy with which he declared that he blessed the day on which he came into that prison, and that he would never commit another robbery as long as he lived.'[35]

This was not a new insight. Dickens could easily have been alerted to such complications by earlier observers. Take for example warnings contained in prison reports and evidentiary materials gathered by William August Miles in the 1830s. Miles, a sympathetic observer of young offenders, was nevertheless alert to the way hardened felons quickly learnt to exploit the efforts of religious reformers anxious to believe in the benefits of their own intervention. Prisoners, he argued, could easily deceive them. Miles had come to this realization while working on behalf of a Select Committee of Gaols, whose conclusions he delivered to the House of Lords on 29 June 1835: 'I have no hesitation in asserting that these visitors to the prisons do harm to society and to the offenders because the prisoners dupe them daily, and being duped they dupe the public by statements concerning the good they may imagine they have effected, when ... they have been doing a positive mischief, by inducing among prisoners a system of positive hypocrisy and deceit.'[36]

The reservations Dickens expressed about Philadelphia's 'Solitary Prison' evidently had a similar audience in mind. The presence in his library of a copy of Crawford's *Report on the Penitentiaries of the United States* (1834) provides no conclusive proof that he had read it. But it seems inescapable that Dickens knew that his verdict stood as a powerful indictment of mid-century Anglo-American penology. 'The system here, is rigid, strict, and hopeless solitary confinement. I believe it, in its effects, to be cruel and wrong,' he wrote in a comment that frames his whole indictment of the prison.[37] Consensus seems to have prevailed in England that the Americans had established a system to be emulated, that they led the way in penal reform. By 1834, seventeen of the twenty-four states comprising the Union had set up their own penal facilities. Each was under the immediate control of inspectors, most of whom were paid by the state and accountable to the state legislature or governor. A general concern with the health and well-being of inmates, together with one for strict prison discipline, characterized them. Ensuring adequate funding, creating positions for inspectors, and making administrators accountable represent advances in penal practice worthy of introduction in England. But those responsible for the solitary and silent regime, Dickens concluded, did not know what they were doing. Very few men, in fact, were capable of 'estimating the immense amount of torture and agony which this dreadful punishment, prolonged for years, inflicts upon the sufferers.' Subsequent novels treat the issues Dickens raised in persuasive detail. Few others, he might have added, understood how clever felons could feign the penitent behaviour urged on them by chaplains exhorting them to read the Bible.[38]

The Criminal Intellect: 'A horrible wonder apart'

Dickens's encounter with Philadelphia's 'Solitary Prison' fertilized his thinking about penal matters in opposing ways. The insights he derived apparently follow from his sympathetic identification with what it meant to lock a man away for years, denying him any contact with his wife, children, home, or friends. To look on no human countenance save that of the prison officers was to bury a man alive, 'to be dug out in the slow round of years.' And if 'the benevolent gentlemen' did not know what they were doing, Dickens did. Speaking in full disclosure of his own reservations, he explains how if he hesitated once about the wisdom of the practice, tried only in certain cases and then 'where the terms of imprisonment were short,' he was now ready 'solemnly' to repudiate it altogether.[39]

Seventeen years later, the consequences of burying a man alive supplied one of the central conceits of *A Tale of Two Cities* (1859). Dickens develops the idea in the story of the Dr Manette, the 'unfortunate physician' who suffers permanent damage to his mind after a long period of solitary confinement in the Bastille, served solely to protect a French aristocrat guilty of rape. The monotony of prison life and the doleful effects of isolation permanently disable him. Even rescued and released, he remains a victim of the regime. 'Hope has quite departed from my breast ... I am weary, weary, weary – worn down by misery,' he recounts later.[40]

Consistent with Dickens's ability to entertain simultaneously opposing ideas, the same novel hints at a different insight: the inscrutability of the human countenance. 'A wonderful fact to reflect upon,' comments the narrator, 'that every human creature is constituted to be that profound secret and mystery to every other.' Such is the level of indecipherability, the narrator muses during a night walk in the city of London, that in the houses of those asleep around him there lies one beating heart lying next to another whose breast harbours 'imaginings, a secret to the heart nearest to it!'[41]

An inability to read the human countenance had consequences for the managers of prisons and other disciplinary institutions. Failure to detect duplicity and hypocrisy proved a severe handicap to legal authorities and to the police. Combine that disadvantage with expectations of repentance supplied by prison chaplains and you have a prescription for further trouble. Dickens explores this concern in 'Pet Prisoners,' published in *Household Words* on 27 April 1850, and in the concluding scenes of *David Copperfield*, written seven months later. In the novel's final double number, David and Tommy Traddles visit a fictional version of England's Pentonville Jail, a vast and solid building constructed at great expense, the purpose of which was to reshape convicts' lives by means of strict isolation. In the words of the guide, David and Traddles witness 'the only true system of prison discipline; the only unchallengeable way of making sincere and lasting converts and penitents – which, you know, is by solitary confinement.' The two bright exhibits are none other than Uriah Heep, espied in his cell 'reading a Hymn Book,' and Litimer, the insinuating former valet of

Steerforth. Brought forth and questioned, each professes the most becoming humility. 'I see my follies now, sir,' Littimer assures the presiding magistrate, a statement whose incredibility can only be exceeded by Heep's that 'There's nothing but sin everywhere – except here.'[42]

Greater discursive space in 'Pet Prisoners' provides room for a further gloss on the implications of this scene. In addition to coining the useful phrase, 'pattern penitence,' to describe what happens when sharp prisoners pick up signals sent by clergymen anxious to encourage repentance, the essay also comments on the consequences of misguided solicitude. 'A strange absorbing selfishness – a spiritual egotism and vanity, real or assumed – is the first result.' This state of mind, Dickens continues, seems to characterize murderers, particularly when they are confined to the condemned cell. A further result seems to be the tendency to eclipse entirely 'the murdered person,' who disappears entirely 'from the stage of their thoughts.' Entering the felon's mind, the narrator effaces himself to allow the condemned to say 'I make no enquiry of the clergyman concerning the salvation of the murdered person's soul; *mine* is the matter; and I am almost happy that I came here, as to the gate of Paradise.'[43]

The combination of extreme selfishness and absence of empathy for the victim – actual or intended – characterizes for Dickens the sine qua non of the murderer. His comments here and elsewhere leave little doubt that he found such figures 'members of the vermin race,' a phrase whose language sets them apart in terms reminiscent of those chosen for Fagin. By mid-century, however, Dickens had come to understand the need for greater vigilance and a different vocabulary. Casting one's eyes around the interior of places like the Three Cripples would no longer serve to identify criminal types. Rather the detective gaze required caution when judging by appearances. Essays like 'Pet Prisoners' and 'A Detective Police Party' reinforce this insight and make a related point. They remind readers that even the professed students of crime can be misled by looks and confounded when they insist on attempting to reconcile 'the criminal intellect' with 'the average intellect of average men.'[44] To do so, is to imitate the error of Rosa Bud, 'the poor girl' in *The Mystery of Edwin Drood* (1870). When Rosa is confronted by Jasper's villainy, she can get no further than conclude that 'he *was* a terrible man, and must be fled from,' but she cannot understand him. The narrator explains that her failure to do so rests on her inability to see the mind of Jasper as 'a horrible wonder apart.'[45]

Elsewhere, I have argued that the prosecution of Dr William Palmer for murder in May 1856 offers an analogue for Jasper's behaviour in the novel.[46] The point of contention here is the extent to which the mantle of respectability can mask homicidal intentions and so prove baffling to the unwary. Palmer, for example, came before the public as a respectable surgeon; Jasper, the choirmaster, stood in comparable regard among the residents of the fictional town of Cloisterham. Palmer so resolutely maintained his calm gaze and air of tranquillity during twelve days of hostile testimony when charged with murder that reporters and spectators alike seem persuaded of his innocence. Likewise, thought Rosa, how could Jasper be responsible for the death of a nephew to whom he had so openly professed love? How could he have maintained his unceasing wish to find the person responsible for the murder? Since no one else suspected him of foul play, Rosa concludes that to do so is her error: 'Am I so wicked in my thoughts as to conceive a wickedness that others cannot imagine? she wonders.'[47]

Dickens, who attended Palmer's trial, entertained no doubt about the surgeon's guilt and wrote 'The Demeanour of Murderers' as 'a quiet protest' against the misinformed accounts of his bearing during the trial by members of the press. Newspaper depictions of Palmer as collected and self-possessed, Dickens warned, 'are harmful to the public at large' and are 'even in themselves, altogether blind and wrong.'[48] The case he makes echoes concerns that had agitated him as early as 1842, when he alerted readers to the fact that clever felons could easily dupe those who held them captive and then encouraged them to repent. While many had been confounded by the fact that Palmer never looked 'like a murderer' on account of his manner and poised behaviour, experts, like himself, Dickens argued, could discern 'marks' on the man's countenance – a countenance so seemingly at odds with guilt.

Dickens based his assumption of wrongdoing on two clues. First, Palmer's studied coolness signalled a capacity for cruelty and the ability to plan murders without alarming his victims. To dispatch as many as Palmer indicated the absence of 'any lingering traces of sensibility' in the man, who had betrayed his Hippocratic oath by making it his trade 'to be learned in poisons.' Further, Dickens reasoned, the state of mind required to plan and execute serial murder called for the ability to extinguish any concern for the victims. 'If I had any natural feeling for my face to express, do you imagine that those medicines of my prescribing and administering would ever have been taken from my hand?' 'Demons' like Palmer, Dickens concluded, conveyed an air of imperturbable composure because they lacked a capacity for pity or sentiment.[49]

The incomplete state of *The Mystery of Edwin Drood* prevents any final conclusion about Jasper's guilt, especially since we know nothing about his childhood and upbringing. But for all Dickens's willingness to explore the dark corners of the mind open to thoughts of jealousy and murder, the novel also offers an antidote to its many sombre colours. Rather than meet ill treatment with anger and injustice with further wrong, when provoked, one can, in New Testament terms, turn the other cheek. So counsels Canon Crisparkle, the manly proponent of forgiveness when faced with 'adverse circumstances.' 'You have the wisdom of Love,' observes Crisparkle to the twin of the aggrieved Neville Landless, who, like Helena, his sister, suffered beatings and ill treatment as a child. It 'was the highest wisdom ever known upon this earth, remember.'[50]

Conclusion

What significance can we assign to the presence of opposing ideas this essay has documented? Do we conclude that Dickens is an undisciplined thinker prone to constant self-contradiction? That his mind was muddled and indecisive? Or that, alive to complexity, he understood how matters of appropriate punishments for variously defined crimes admitted different responses? Read contextually, do his ideas record the fluxes of mid-Victorian thinking, of the need for the liberal treatment of young offenders and a stern form of discipline for the less malleable? Formalist critics have traditionally welcomed contradictions and pointed to their presence as indicative of a sought complexity. More recently, academic methodology has taken 'complexity' one step further. Encouraged by the application of linguistic theory, postmodernists have lauded decentring. To find evidence of self-reflexivity, a preoccupation with writing, a willingness of the text to question its own apparent affirmations, these and similar criteria constitute maturity. Taken further, readers conclude that texts can never serve as an unproblematic repository of human values.

Jeremy Tambling's remarks on *Great Expectations* illustrate such claims. 'Prison-Bound: Dickens and Foucault' (1986)[51] is cited as one of two essays to question 'traditional conceptions about the affirmations offered by *Great Expectations*' and push analysis in different directions.[52] Flush with the theories Michel Foucault set forth in *Discipline and Punish*, Tambling deepens our sense of the extent to which oppression in its multiple forms operates in society. From the forge to Satis House, to Jaggers's office and beyond, Pip encounters overt and covert manifestations of disciplinary powers. Most disturbingly and most pertinent to Tambling's thesis is Pip's continuing encounter with 'self-oppression,' a form of constriction, literal and linguistic, which challenge claims that Pip learns and so fulfils the reader's expectations of traditional *Bildungsroman* fiction. To seek knowledge, which Pip does, is only to find oneself imprisoned in various kinds of discourses, all of which dole out the same oppressive fate. For Tambling, the book charts only oppression and the production and reproduction of the same, an endless cycle from which escape seems impossible.

I prefer a milder and more cautiously optimistic conclusion: that the voice of the Pip who recounts his experiences at the end of the novel belongs to an older and wiser man rather than to the blinded and self-deluded figure Tambling sees. The story after all is told when Pip is about sixty years old.[53] Almost forty years earlier, he had learned to love Magwitch and to accept him, a damaged and violent man without question, but also one who had genuinely meant to be Pip's benefactor and who had acted towards him 'affectionately, gratefully, and generously ... with great constancy through a series of years.'[54] Such affection and loyalty count for something, as does the ability to recognize them as operative in one's life. The ability to love also mitigates roughness and the fact that this same man capable of gentleness could simultaneously inspire in the face of his old enemy an expression of 'white terror' Pip felt he could 'never forget.' Magwitch is no gentle man like Joe Gargery, who would settle his differences with a foe by sharing a pot of beer 'in a peaceable manner.' Rather, he would sacrifice his own chance of escape by lunging for Compeyson, cloaked and shrinking in the pursuing customs galley. And when the two go over the side, he tells Pip afterward that 'he did not pretend to say what he might or might not have done' when he laid hands on Compeyson. What happened in the water when the two went down, 'fiercely locked in each other's arms,' might be anybody's guess. Magwitch says that they struggled, that he disengaged himself, 'struck out,' and swam away. 'I never had any reason to doubt the exact truth of what he thus told me,' comments Pip.[55]

Exact truth in this instance might be something that Pip has to take on faith. Is he blind or self-deluded to do so? Or is his willingness to accept Magwitch at his word a sign of maturity? Is this not the position of the narrating older 'I,' who is capable of allowing opposing truths to emerge? On the one hand, he can fault refractory felons who, better fed than soldiers or paupers, set fire to their prison 'with the excusable object of improving the flavour of their soup.'[56] On the other, he can feel his former repugnance to 'the shackled creature' before him melt away to reveal 'a man who had meant' to be his benefactor. Most readers, too, applaud Pip when he resolves that henceforth his place was to be by Magwitch's side 'while he lived.' A brutal man, yes, but a 'wretched creature' who calls to mind sympathy rather than the horror we reserve for reptiles, vermin, and other loathsome creatures. That sympathy and concern jostle with horror and condemnation remains perhaps the only final truth about Dickens's penal philosophy.

NOTES

1 Edmund Wilson, 'Dickens: The Two Scrooges,' in *The Wound and The Bow: Seven Studies in Literature* (1939; London: Methuen, 1961), 13.

2 Charles Dickens, *The Pickwick Papers*, ed. James Kinsley, Clarendon Edition (Oxford: Clarendon Press, 1986), 119.

3 William Makepeace Thackeray, 'Horae Catnachianae,' *Fraser's Magazine* 19 (April 1839): 408.

4 Charles Dickens, *Oliver Twist*, ed. Kathleen Tillotson, Clarendon Edition (Oxford: Clarendon Press, 1966), 65.

5 Ibid., 300.

6 Ibid., 61.

7 Ibid., 295.

8 'The Schoolmaster's Experience in Newgate,' *Fraser's Magazine* 5 (June 1832): 525.

9 Charles Dickens, 'Criminal Courts,' in *Sketches by Boz, The Dent Uniform Edition of Dickens' Journalism*, 4 vols, ed. Michael Slater, vol. 1 (Columbus: Ohio State University Press, 1994–2000), 194.

10 Charles Dickens, *The Letters of Charles Dickens*, 12 vols, ed. Madeline House, Graham Storey, et al., Pilgrim Edition (Oxford: Clarendon Press, 1965–2002), 1:88.

11 Charles Dickens, 'A Visit to Newgate,' in Slater, *The Dent Uniform Edition of Dickens' Journalism*, 1:200.

12 Ibid.,1:200.

13 Ibid., 1:209.

14 Ibid.

15 Dickens, *Letters,* 12:177.

16 Dickens, *Oliver Twist*, 98–9.

17 Ibid., 164.

18 Ibid., 93.

19 Charles Dickens, *Barnaby Rudge* (Harmondsworth: Penguin, 1973), 359.

20 Cf. ibid., chapters 15, 23, 75.

21 Dickens, *Letters*, 2:385. For further forms of excarceration in Dickens's oeuvre, see Adam Hansen's article in this collection.

22 Dickens, *Oliver Twist*, 360.

23 Ibid., 361.

24 Thomas Carlyle, 'Chartism,' in *Thomas Carlyle: Selected Writings*, ed. Alan Shelston (Harmondsworth: Penguin, 1971), 151.

25 Dickens, *Oliver Twist*, 148.

26 Ibid., 307.

27 Dickens, *Letters*, 3:50.

28 Charles Dickens, *American Notes* (Harmondsworth, UK: Penguin, 1972), 78.

29 Ibid., 78.

30 Ibid., 97, 78.

31 Ibid., 99–100.

32 Dickens, *Letters*, 3:123.

33 William Crawford, *Report of William Crawford on the Penitentiaries of the United States* [British Parliamentary Papers: Crime and Punishment Prisons, 2] (Shannon: Irish University Press, 1986), 12.

34 Dickens, *American Notes*, 147.

35 Ibid., 151, 150.

36 'Select Committee on Gaols' 2, cited in David Paroissien, *The Companion to 'Oliver Twist'* (Edinburgh: Edinburgh University Press 1992), 152.

37 Dickens, *American Notes*, 146.

38 Ibid., 147–8.

39 Ibid., 147.

40 Charles Dickens, *A Tale of Two Cities* (Harmondsworth: Penguin, 1970), 348, 359.

41 Ibid., 44.

42 Charles Dickens, *David Copperfield*, Norton Critical Edition (New York: Norton, 1990), 712, 717–18.

43 Charles Dickens, 'Pet Prisoners' [*Household Words* 27 April 1850], in Slater, *The Dent Uniform Edition of Dickens' Journalism*, 2, 220. For another analysis of this type of 'pattern penitence' in *David Copperfield* and 'Pet Prisoners,' see Anna Schur's contribution to this collection.

44 Charles Dickens, *The Mystery of Edwin Drood* (London: Penguin, 2002), 220.

45 Ibid., 220.

46 Cf. David Paroissien, introduction to Charles Dickens, *The Mystery of Edwin Drood* (London: Penguin, 2002), xxvi–xxx.

47 Dickens, *Edwin Drood*, 220.

48 Dickens, *Letters*, 8:128.

49 Dickens, 'The Demeanour of Murderers' [*Household Words* 14 June 1856], in Slater, *The Dent Uniform Edition of Dickens' Journalism*, 3:380.

50 Dickens, *Edwin Drood*, 108.

51 Jeremy Tambling, 'Prison-Bound: Dickens and Foucault,' *Essays in Criticism* 36, no. 1 (1986): 11–31.

52 Janice Carlisle, 'A Critical History of *Great Expectations*,' in Charles Dickens, *Great Expectations*, ed. Janice Carlisle (Boston: St Martin's Press, 1996), 459.

53 This calculation of Pip's age is based on 'The Sequence of Events in Pip's Narrative.' See David Paroissien, *The Companion to 'Great Expectations'* (Robertsbridge, UK: Helm Information, 2000), 423–34 [Appendix One].

54 Dickens, *Great Expectations* (London: Penguin, 1996), 446.

55 Ibid., 446.

56 Ibid., 260.

2 New Prisons, New Criminals, New Masculinity: Dickens and Reade

JEREMY TAMBLING

I

> He looked at the gateway, then fixed his gaze upon something that stood just above – something which the dusk half concealed, and by so doing, made more impressive. It was the sculptured counterfeit of a human face, that of a man distraught with agony. The eyes stared wildly from their sockets, the hair struggled in maniac disorder, the forehead was wrung with torture, the cheeks sunken, the throat fearsomely wasted, and from the wide lips there seemed to be issuing a horrible cry. Above this hideous effigy was carved the legend: 'MIDDLESEX HOUSE OF CORRECTION.'[1]

> Violence, when not in the hands of the law, threatens it not with the ends that it may pursue, but by its mere existence outside the law. The same may be more drastically suggested if one reflects how often the figure of the 'great criminal,' however repellent his ends may have been, has aroused the secret admiration of the public.[2]

The opening of Gissing's *The Nether World*, set some ten years earlier than its publication date of 1889, is in Clerkenwell Close, in London's working-class Clerkenwell area. Gissing's fascination with the prison shows his debt to Dickens. The image of madness staring from the gateway, as if saying *lasciate ogni speranza, voi ch'entrate* to entrants to its netherworld, who are already, however, in the netherworld of London poverty, makes the prison motif dominant, productive of extremities of behaviour. The allegorical figure, a solitary face, the body cancelled out, is a reminder of the Michelangelesque statues of Melancholy and Raving Madness that rested above the gateway outside Bethlem Hospital (Bedlam) when it stood in Moorfields (1676–1815). These statues of naked males who, because they are mad, are unashamed of their nakedness, had been designed by Caius Gabriel Cibber (1630–1700).[3] The latter sculpture, depicted in chains, inspired Hogarth's portrayal of madness in the last scene of *The Rake's Progress*; it is as if madness outside the prison was answered by madness within, the perfect reconstruction of madness by Hogarth fitting its hegemonic representation. Dickens certainly knew these statues by Cibber, which were transported from Bedlam at Moorfields to the new site in Lambeth in 1815, and certainly his fascination with criminality makes him produce something equivalently minatory and teasing in the two death masks of hanged criminals above Mr Jaggers's desk in Little Britain, 'with the twitchy leer' that Wemmick so jauntily cleans up, remarking that one had murdered his master (perhaps Dickens is thinking here of Courvoisier, hanged in 1840 for the same, and pleading reading *Jack Sheppard* by way of excuse), and the other, 'with the genuine [hanged] look … as if one nostril was caught up with a horsehair and a little fish-hook,' had 'forged wills.'[4]

To explore the power of what I take to be Dickens's obsessional interest in criminal, which in this case leads him to give them an afterlife by visualizing them and presenting them to the reader with complete case histories, means thinking about something that probably transcends everything in the novelist's conscious discourse, or that of his contemporaries. To begin to explore that fascination, and to chart its development, which also includes fascination with the prison and the changes in prison discipline, is the concern of this paper. Certainly, Dickens's interest in these matters is way outside Henry Mayhew's meliorist and bourgeois-utilitarian viewpoint about criminals, when, writing about prisons, Mayhew says that 'our criminal tribes … may be regarded as that portion of our society who have not yet conformed to civilized habits,'[5] and identifies them with those who like a 'wandering and predatory' life, since 'though all have an instinctive aversion to labour, some find the drudgery of it more irksome than others.'[6] Dickens reveals what he thought of this view in the text of Magwitch's autobiography.[7]

The fictional prison in which the beginning of *The Nether World* is set corresponds to two prisons: the Clerkenwell Bridewell and the House of Detention. The former was an overflow of Bridewell, which, on the banks of the Fleet, had been a prison belonging to the City of London since 1553, so remaining till 1833, when it came under state control, before being closed in 1855. Bridewell was intended, according to Mayhew, for 'unruly London apprentices and sturdy beggars, and disorderly persons committed to jail for three months or less.'[8] The Bridewell at Clerkenwell, called the New Prison, opened in 1616. Later in that century it was rebuilt as a House of Detention, and an overflow prison for Newgate. One of its famous prisoners was Jack Sheppard (1702–24), who escaped from it, as he escaped twice from Newgate.[9] Enlarged in 1774, its prisoners were released during the attacks on it by the Gordon rioters in 1780, Dickens noting the detail at the end of *Barnaby Rudge*, in chapter 66, when he shows the mad heroism of the rioters, who would empty all London's prisons and set fire to Newgate.[10] In 1845, the prison at Clerkenwell was rebuilt on the lines of Pentonville, which had been built as a model, reforming prison. As such it is discussed by Mayhew.[11] It was closed in 1877, and demolished in 1890, a year after publication of *The Nether World*.

In this history of a Clerkenwell prison, which has as analogues first in Bridewell, then in Newgate and Pentonville, but which is seen by Gissing the novelist in essentialist or generic, non-historic terms, there is – because of Dickens's influence on Gissing – much to be thought on in relation to Dickens and prisons. The association in modern criticism of Dickens with the carceral comes in three phases. The first was Edmund Wilson's and Lionel Trilling's emphasis in 'Dickens: The Two Scrooges' (1941) and in the introduction to the Oxford *Little Dorrit* (1953), respectively, and it made Dickens a Romantic, constructing the prison as the symbol of modern society, with the free and spontaneous individual opposed to it. The second phase was the publication of Philip Collins's useful and influential *Dickens and Crime* (1962). This remains indispensable for anyone interested in prisons, the police, capital punishment, and the treatment of the criminal in Dickens. Though Collins consistently underrates Dickens in the name of his empirical research, and makes him the paradigm of the 'ordinary man,' whose own assessments of the prison are ruggedly empirical, his book's materials and evidence show the relevance of associating Dickens with both criminals and prisons. The third phase comes from readings drawing on Foucault, which, using *Discipline and Punish: The Birth of the Prison*, make the prison the paradigm for universal societal surveillance and for the production of docile bodies within a panoptical structure. More than anything, Foucault's argument justified the thesis that the prison was the symbol for society, as well as being the prototype for all institutions. Yet his argument leaves open questions about the possibility of resistance or reaction to this model, in which the subject is constructed through the compulsion to confess imposed by the prison regime.

Perhaps it is time to go beyond these three approaches. Foucault-inspired studies have engaged with madness, but given less attention to the production of the sexual in Dickens.[12] They have not responded so much to *The History of Sexuality*, with which Foucault continued; this paper will offer some comments on constructions of masculinity in relation to 'criminality.' Another approach, more empirical but no less valid, and also to be employed here, might reject the totalizing approach involved in discussing 'the prison,'[13] as though all prisons were panoptical, and will help to question the investment in prisons by mapping them, and asking which prisons are most allegorical for Dickens.

There is no doubt which prison was most written about. 'A Visit to Newgate' (February 1836) appears in *Sketches by Boz*, as the record of a visit made on 5 November 1835 with John Black, editor of the *Morning Chronicle*. Dickens followed the visit made to Newgate by the heroes of Pierce Egan's *Life in London* (1821) on the morning of an execution.[14] Mayhew's visit in 1857 should be compared with that of Dickens.[15] Newgate, rebuilt in 1782, to designs by George Dance the Younger, Clerk of the City Works, replaced the prison that was burned in the Gordon Riots of 1780, and until 1813 it held debtors as well as convicted criminals. Sexuality, and an evasion of the sexual, appears in the account of the visit to Newgate, which culminates in a description of three condemned men. The first has been identified as Robert Swan, age thirty-two, a soldier in the foot guards convicted of robbery with menaces, who had hope of a reprieve, which in fact happened. The other two were John Smith and John Pratt, convicted for homosexuality, or, in Collins, following Carlton, 'an unnatural offence.'[16] Both men were hanged on 27 November 1835. They had been committed for trial by Hesney Wedgwood, the magistrate at Union Hall in Southwark, and were the last two to be hanged for the 'offence' in England. Wedgwood said that they had been in a room in a lodging house, and 'the detection of these degraded creatures was entirely due to their poverty, [for] they were unable to pay for privacy, and the room was so poor that what was going on inside was easily visible from without.'[17] Though all three men were poor, there seems to be an implicit class difference: these homosexuals had not only infringed the law, but were in dire poverty (so the word 'degraded' has a double meaning). Hangings for sodomy, however this was defined, usually as 'indecent assault,' ended in practice in continental Europe in 1803, but in England continued till 1835, though the death penalty was only ended by the Offences Against the Person Act in 1861 (transportation, or ten-year terms in prison served instead). An attempt at legislation in 1841 had been unsuccessful. Some 46 people were hanged for the 'crime' between 1810 and 1835, 32 were reprieved, and 713 received the sentence of the pillory (discontinued after 1816) or were imprisoned. These figures need to be contextualized by the point that legislation in 1828 reduced the evidence required in trials of sodomy.[18]

Dickens's text notes the first man's stillness, but then, when he is seen again, he is walking up and down. Of the two other men, one is leaning against the fireplace, with his back to the visitors, while the other looks out of the window. The first homosexual is presented as melancholic, the second, with 'pale haggard face and disordered hair' a 'ghastly' appearance and with 'eyes wildly staring before him,' as maniacal, like Cibber's Bedlam representations, and both are 'as motionless as statues,'[19] as if already dead. These men have been made literary by the description; however, Dickens comments not at all on the offence, unless the sense of melancholia and madness represents his construction of it, putting the men beyond the self-control of Robert Swan, and within an eighteenth-century literary and artistic code for describing, imagining, and constructing men in despair. Dickens ends with an attempt at imagining a man's last night alive, the existence of which writing only regis- ters the impossibility of the attempt: a man who goes to his death takes his secrets of the prison house with him, and no novelist can follow his thoughts on his last night alive. Similarly, to write about one of the two homosexuals would have been to attempt to represent what could not be represented, but even in what he does with the man whose last night alive he imagines, the impossibility of writing the unknowable shows itself in the conventionality of the representation: the passage ends with the man recalling being with his wife 'before misery and ill treatment had altered her looks, and vice had changed his nature, and she is leaning upon his arm, and looking up into his face with tenderness and affection – and he does *not* strike her now, nor rudely shake her from him.'[20] The condemned man is a married Bill Sikes, a thuggish criminal whom Dickens had originally intended to die at Newgate, and the construction of masculinity in the Sketch moves from noting the dignified, even 'jaunty' soldier to the two figures of complete passivity, who are homosexual, to the man whose 'vice' shows itself in wife-beating as an index to his other crimes. The impossibility of representing adequately these figures does not, however, imply anything less than fascination with each of them, which is also, it seems, an interest in them as figures of masculinity.

Newgate reappears in 'The Jew's Last Night Alive,' chapter 52 of *Oliver Twist* (1837–9), after Dickens had visited it for a second time, on 27 June 1837, with Forster, Macready, and Halbot K. Browne. It is referred to again in chapter 4 of *Nicholas Nickleby*, where there is fascination with the prison as the symbol of London but as that about which nothing can be said, and with the prison as supremely the place of neither punishment, nor reform, but of execution, which shows up the impossibility of writing about it:

There, at the very core of London, in the heart of its business and animation, in the midst of a whirl of noise and motion: stemming as it were the giant currents of life that flow ceaselessly on from different quarters, and meet beneath its walls, stands Newgate; and in that crowded street on which it frowns so darkly – within a few feet of the squalid tottering houses – upon the very spot on which the vendors of soup and fish and damaged fruit are now plying their trades – scores of human beings, amidst a roar of sounds to which even the tumult of a great city is as nothing, four, six or eight strong men at a time, have been hurried violently and swiftly from the world, when the scene has been rendered frightful with excess of human life; when curious eyes have glared from casement, and house-top, and wall and pillar, and when, in the mass of white and upturned faces, the dying wretch, in his all-comprehensive look of agony, has met not one – not one – that bore the impress of pity or compassion.[21]

As Fagin in his last night reflects on how 'the drop went down' and 'they changed, from being strong and vigorous men, to dangling heaps of clothes,'[22] so 'strong' reappears to characterize the men who are killed, and with whom the passage identifies; they are the objects of pity while the onlooking crowd seems less than human.

The older Newgate had only been rebuilt after 1770, to a design by George Dance, and was not completed in 1780. It features as 'then a new building' in chapter 62 of *Barnaby Rudge* (1841), which had been planned as a novel as early as 1836, immediately after *Sketches by Boz*. Associated with the Old Bailey (as it is in *Sketches by Boz*), Newgate reappears in book 2, chapter 2 of *A Tale of Two Cities*, where it is implicitly paralleled by the Bastille. Here, it is the old Newgate of 1780, presented in a novel that echoes *Barnaby Rudge*: both novels open in 1775, and then move to 1780. Again associated with the Old Bailey, Newgate is also seen in *Great Expectations*, which begins with references to the hulks, a mode of imprisonment that began in 1776, when the American War of Independence ended transportation to America. Transportation to Australia began in 1787, and prisoners in the hulks often served a period of hard labour in the naval dockyards, such as at Woolwich, but the system was being run down from around 1840, as transportation began to come to an end, and the last hulks ship was burned at Woolwich in 1857.[23] *Great Expectations*, the last Dickens novel to feature a prison, describes prison methods that were, by the time of the novel's publication in 1860, firmly of the past, even though transportation did not end completely until 1867, a few months before the end of public hanging.[24] *Edwin Drood* it seems was planned to end with Jasper's last night alive in Maidstone prison, and here two points seem worth noting: first, how Jasper's obsessionalism – whether he is guilty or not of whatever crime Dickens meant him to commit – contrasts with Fagin's; second, that the prison is no longer in London, as though a connection between the city and the prison, implicit in *Nicholas Nickleby*, has been lost.

Before returning to Newgate, what can be said of the other London prisons Dickens refers to? Chapter 40 of *Pickwick Papers* uses the Fleet, the oldest prison – it was medieval – in the country; it appears again in *Barnaby Rudge* (chapter 67) as one of those fired in the Gordon Riots. *David Copperfield* has two prisons: the King's Bench and one that is, though not named, effectively Pentonville. The first is near the beginning of the novel (chapter 11), the other near the end (chapter 61), and they are separated, in the novel's diegesis, by some fifteen years. This mid-century novel represents two types of prison, old and new, working in nineteenth-century society: the debtor's prison, and the criminal prison. Pentonville, of which more later, derived from prisons described in *American Notes*. Dickens particularly discusses the Boston House of Correction for the State, which was run on the 'silent' system, where prisoners could see each other and work together but not talk. This is described and commented on in chapter 3, while in chapter 7 there is discussion of the prison model that also inspired both Millbank and Pentonville: the Eastern Penitentiary in Philadelphia, which practised the 'separate' system of incarceration, which involved the prisoner's total isolation. In *Bleak House*, Skimpole is nearly prison-bound for debt, and Mr George is put in prison – presumably Newgate – on suspicion of murder (chapter 52). One other novel makes the prison central: *Little Dorrit*, which begins in a prison in Marseilles, and features, complementing this in sound, the Marshalsea. A medieval prison, alongside others in Southwark, it had been newly built in 1811: John Dickens was confined there from February to May of 1824.[25]

Three other prisons indicate just how prevalent the penal institution was when Dickens began writing. Horsemonger prison in Southwark, on Newington Causeway,[26] built as a 'model prison' by George Gwilt between 1791 and 1799, was called Surrey Detentional Prison. Here Leigh Hunt was confined from 1813 to 1815, for insulting the Prince Regent. He describes the private room he was confined in within the prison infirmary in chapter 15 of his *Autobiography*. He describes watching the gallows being put up there, intended for, among others, 'one stout country girl, sitting in an absorbed manner, her eyes fixed on the fire. She was handsome, and had a little hectic spot in either cheek, the effect of some gnawing emotion.' The woman was to be hanged for murdering her baby. 'She heeded us not. There was no object before her but what produced the spot in her cheek. The gallows, on which she was executed, must have been brought out within her hearing; but perhaps she heard that as little.'[27] At this prison, which was closed in 1878 and demolished two years later, Dickens witnessed the hanging of the two Mannings in 1849.[28]

There were two Middlesex houses of correction: Coldbath Fields (men) and Tothill (boys and women). Houses of correction, which Mayhew says had been established as a concept in 1597, for those who would not work, or for vagrants,[29] served for those condemned to short terms of imprisonment, seven days to two years, and they contrasted with 'convict' prisons, for people to be transported, or for penal servitude (Millbank and Pentonville were the latter). Coldbath Fields was under the control of the Middlesex magistrates.[30] When Dickens visited it, he met its governor, Captain George Laval Chesterton, who had arrived in 1829, staying until 1854. In 1834 Coldbaths went over to the 'silent' system of punishment, which required a larger staff than the 'separate' system, as did other prisons with a punitive or reformatory discipline. It had few separate cells. Tothill Fields, in the area between Westminster Abbey and Millbank, whose desolate and desperately poor state Mayhew brings out, had been built as a bridewell in 1618, and it served Hogarth as a model in *The Rake's Progress*. Rebuilt in Francis Street, Westminster, in 1834, it was pulled down in 1885.[31] Dickens knew its governor, Lieutenant Augustus Frederick Tracey, RN. Like Coldbath, Tothill Fields worked the 'silent' system.

II

Today, prisons are not of the city, but are hidden outside it. Apart from Pentonville, not one of the London prisons discussed exists today; Dickens's fictional London is not ours, nor even that of his contemporaries. For one generalization may be made from thinking about Dickens's prisons, the point holding most for Newgate, but being valid for all. Each of Dickens's uses of Newgate refers to the period of the 'Newgate novel,' which was contemporary in writing with the time of Dickens's first visit there.[32] Like Bulwer's *Paul Clifford*, W.H. Ainsworth's two Newgate novels have highwaymen as heroes, Dick Turpin (thematized in a ballad in *Pickwick Papers*) for *Rookwood*,[33] and both are historical novels of the eighteenth century.[34] Ainsworth's *Jack Sheppard* in particular, a prose version of Hogarth's moral series *Industry and Idleness*, with the representative of idleness, Jack Sheppard, just as surely ending at Tyburn, may have created anxieties about identifying with the underclass, hence Thackeray's critique in *Catherine* (1839).[35] Yet Jack Sheppard is irrationally motivated by Jonathan Wild's influence, and Wild acts without motivation; hence the fears that were expressed over the criminality within the text.[36] In chapter 20 of *Oliver Twist*, the boy is forced by Fagin to read a book containing 'a history of the lives and trials of great criminals,' which, from the way it has been thumbed, seems to have been used by the thieves as a reference work. The most popular collection of tales was *The Newgate Calendar, or Malefactor's Bloody Register*, which first appeared in 1728 and reappeared in four volumes between 1824 and 1828. In chapter 43 of *Oliver Twist*, Charley Bates fears that the Artful Dodger will not make it into the Newgate Calendar, as his fate is to be transported to Australia. But *Oliver Twist* is firmly in Newgate-historical mode, and when Fagin tells Oliver on their first meeting that the Artful Dodger will be a 'great man,' he thinks back to Jonathan Wild, in Newgate in 1725, and of Fielding's version of him.[37] Dickens, in the 1850s and 1860s, never writes about his contemporary Newgate. By then it was in decline, closing in 1877 and destroyed in 1902.

The older Newgate created, at least in myth, strongly masculine 'great criminals' who risked execution. In discussing the work of Edward Gibbon Wakefield, author of *Facts Relating to the Punishment of Death in the Metropolis* (1831), which comments on how juveniles learned crime in Newgate, Heather Shore observes the 'precocious masculinity' in Dickens's description of juvenile thieves. She quotes Dickens: 'seated round the table were four or five boys: none older than the Dodger: smoking long clay pipes and drinking spirits with the air of middle-aged men.'[38] Oliver Twist is clearly different from these boy models. And the fascination with 'great criminals' we have already noted to have been Dickens's, and not Oliver Twist's. 'A Visit to Newgate' had noticed casts of the heads and faces of 'the two notorious murderers, Bishop and Williams,'[39] who were hanged at Newgate in 1831. This detail reappears in those death masks in *Great Expectations*, discussed already, allegorical dumb witnesses to Mr Jaggers's words and deeds, like Allegory to Mr Tulkinghorn, masks being, of course, forms of allegory.[40]

Where did this desire to see the criminal as 'great' come from? The beginning of an answer may be seen in considering the 1841 preface to the third edition of *Oliver Twist*, where it seems that Dickens drew Newgate from Hogarth and from Gay's *The Beggar's Opera*. The preface ends by mentioning Fielding, Defoe, Goldsmith, Smollett, Richardson, and Mackenzie, who all dealt with 'the very scum and refuse of the land.' Defoe's *Moll Flanders* (1722) and *Colonel Jack* (1722) both use Newgate, while Smollett, for whom violent masculinity is the norm, and whom Dickens followed so much in his fascination with the eighteenth century, knew London debtors' prisons, and made them part of the experience of each of his picaros. The pattern is observed by Dickens, as when Mr Pickwick is taken to the Fleet. In chapter 61 of *Roderick Random* (1748), Random is taken to the Marshalsea. Here he sees prisoners on the 'common side' of the prison, including a figure 'wrapt in a dirty rug, tied about his loins with two pieces of list, of different colours, knotted together; having a black bushy beard, and his head covered with a huge mass of brown periwig, which seemed to have been ravished from the head of some scarecrow.'[41] This is Melopoyn, a poet who narrates his misfortunes, leading Roderick Random into a state of melancholy that leads him to become a sloven. Simiarly, Peregrine Pickle is imprisoned in the Fleet (chapter 105).

The Marshalsea reappears in *Ferdinand Count Fathom* (1753), as do the Fleet and the King's Bench. *Sir Launcelot Greaves* (1762), which was written after Smollett had spent three months in the King's Bench prison – for libelling Admiral Knowles, who had commanded a West Indies expedition in 1740, where Smollett had been a surgeon's mate – 'descends into mansions of the damned' in chapters 20 and 21. The hero is

> conducted to the prison of the King's-bench ... [which] appears like a neat little regular town, surrounded by a very high wall, including an open piece of ground which may be termed a garden, where prisoners take the air, and amuse them- selves with a variety of diversions. Except the entrance, where the turnkeys keep watch and ward, there is nothing in the place that looks like a jail, or bears the least colour of restraint. The street is crowded with passengers ... At the farther end of the street, on the right hand, is a little paved court leading to a separate building, consisting of twelve large apartments, called state-rooms, well fur- nished, and fitted for the reception of the better sort of prisoners; and on the other side of the street, facing a separate division of ground, called the common side, is a range of prisons occupied by prisoners of the lowest order, who share the profits of a begging box, and are maintained by this practice, and some establishment and some established funds of charity. We ought also to observe, that the jail is provided with a neat chapel, in which a clergyman, in consideration of a certain salary, performs divine service every Sunday.[42]

The double standards for debtors – those who could pay, and those who were unable – informs the observation of the prison in *Pickwick Papers*.

Smollett's heroes pass through debtors' prison and survive, their masculin- ity unimpaired. But they are not criminals, and what they risk is different. In his history of the Fleet prison, Roger Lee Brown says that imprisonment for debt was synonymous with failure: both of the debtor, and the creditor to claim the debt. Such imprisonment backed up a system of credit on which the country's commercial life ran, but it made no distinction between the fraudu- lent debtor and the victim of circumstances.[43] Moses Pitt, in *The Cry of the Oppressed* (1691) on the iniquities of debtors' prisons, said that the debtor was in a worse state than the criminal, being 'kept a prisoner as long as it shall please God to lengthen out his life.'[44] The danger to the debtor, then, is of seeming to appear a failure, hence the significance of Roderick Random's Bedlam-like melancholia.

It has been said that 'in the eighteenth century, the gaols were perhaps the most medieval institutions in England.'[45] Punishment, as the aim of the prison, and with a view to reformation, is a nineteenth-century idea, stemming from late eighteenth-century moves towards prison reform. Collins's *Dickens and Crime* does not notice the difference between imprisonment for debt – a dying eighteenth-century practice – and imprisonment for a criminal offence – a growing nineteenth-century one – yet the distinction seems crucial. In the eighteenth century, over half the prisoners in the country were confined for debt; other prisoners were on their way to the gallows, or transportation, or were awaiting trial or sentencing; and most prisons were either for debtors or were 'detentional,' that is, they were for those who had been committed for trial by a magistrate, and were waiting their turn. At Newgate, primarily a detentional prison, most prisoners, well into the nineteenth century, stayed no more than three weeks, being on their way to trial or execution of sentence. Fagin is condemned on Friday, executed on Monday. Newgate, like the Fleet, the King's Bench, and the Marshalsea, also accommodated debtors. General Oglethorpe's prison *Enquiry* of 1729 examined the Fleet, King's Bench, and the Marshalsea, aiming at reducing the number of debtors, but the enquiry was forgotten, and at the end of the eighteenth century, in addition to these three prisons, and Newgate, there were several other debtors' prisons in 1800, all privately run.[46] A report on imprisonment for debt appeared in 1792, and further reports on prisons were published in 1814 and 1818, while the insolvent debtors' court, set up in 1813, marked the decline of the debtor's prison. *Pickwick Papers*, *David Copperfield*, and *Little Dorrit* deal with an institution that is almost an anachronism; the indignation about the Fleet expressed in *Pickwick Papers* reads strangely when it is considered that the Fleet and the Marshalsea both closed in 1842, and were demolished soon after.[47] The King's Bench, which was separated from the Marshalsea in the fifteenth century, and which stood in the Borough until it was rebuilt between 1755 and 1758 in St George's Fields, was another of those burned in the Gordon Riots (*Barnaby Rudge*, chapter 67). It was then rebuilt. Prisoners from the Fleet and the Marshalsea were decanted into it, but when imprisonment for debt was abolished in 1861, it became a military prison, until its demolition in 1880. Obsession with the debtors' prison shows the persistence of eighteenth-century modes of writing and illustrates how Dickens combined his fascination with prisons and criminality.

III

John Howard (1727–90) in *The State of the Prisons* (1777) had excited attention towards prison reform, including the classification of prisoners. His contemporary Jonas Hanway (1712–86), desiring to prevent jail fever, advocated solitary confinement. In 1779, under the leadership of Sir William Blackstone and William Eden, who was influenced by Beccaria and had produced

Principles of Penal Law in 1771, Parliament approved a Penitentiary Act, making Howard, along with Dr John Fothergill and George Whately, a supervisor for the construction of two national penitentiaries where prisoners would be kept separate. Nothing happened, except that Bentham, who had followed Howard and recommended solitary confinement and hard labour for criminals, submitted his plans in *The Panopticon or Inspection House* in 1791, changing his mind about solitary confinement, feeling that his system of inspection would make it unnecessary.

Between 1790 and 1820 the number of capital offences dwindled from two hundred to less than ten. The Holford Committee, under George Holford and including Wilberforce and Samuel Romilly, was remitted in 1810 to consider the possibility of a national penitentiary. The first national penitentiary, at Millbank, begun in 1816 and completed in 1821 at a cost of half a million pounds, incorporated some elements of Benthamism, but the Panopticon remained, in England, only a dream and a discourse about surveillance and punishment. Millbank also incorporated elements of the model prison that the magistrate George Onesiphorus Paul had instituted at Gloucester, hence it had separate cells. The Holford Committee concluded that the majority of prisoners could be reclaimed by penitentiary imprisonment, 'a system of imprisonment not confined to the safe custody of the prison, but extending to the reformation and improvement of the mind, and operating by seclusion, employment and religious instruction.'[48] Such prescriptions related not to debtors' prisons, but to making and reforming criminals. The Penitentiary Act of 1812, which instituted this, recommended that the prisoner would begin with solitude and hard labour, and then go on to work with a small group of other prisoners, retaining a small portion of the profits.[49] The Prisons Act of 1835, however, which brought prisons for criminals under the centralizing control of the Crown, reacted away from this by enforcing silence in prisons, or complete solitude, and hard labour, in which it followed the Philadelphia model.[50]

Dickens hardly marks the existence of Millbank, nor was its distinctiveness for nineteenth-century design recognized in *Dickens and Crime*, though Collins wrote on its successor, Pentonville, which emerged out of what was seen as Millbank's failure. Millbank became an ordinary prison in 1843, later appearing as the old-fashioned prison of James's *The Princess Casamassima*,[51] and it closed in 1890. But, in the spirit of the Prison Act of 1835, Lord John Russell, the Home Secretary, asked in 1839 for a new Model Prison to be built. It opened its doors, if that is what a prison does, in December 1842, with five hundred separate cells. Pentonville, according to Sir James Graham, Home Secretary, was intended for prisoners going to Van Diemen's Land after a reformatory period of eighteen months during which the inmates would learn a trade, though they were also to be punished with the crank, a hard-labour machine. In its first ten years, it seems to have induced high rates of insanity.[52] Pentonville, designed by Sir Joshua Jebb, Surveyor General of Prisons, used Haviland's Philadelphia model of 1829; indeed, while Dickens was looking at Philadelphia, Pentonville was under construction. Its radial wing design allowed for a single officer standing at the centre of the building to see each of the four wings in turn.[53] As older, eighteenth-century prison models faded out (the Fleet, the Marshalsea as debtors' prisons, Newgate as detentional, or as associated with executions), another, newer, more disciplinary model had arisen.

How far could Dickens, concentrating on older models, read this? *American Notes*, discussing Boston, but thinking too of Philadelphia, is uncertain about the implications for prisons of the newer regimes, which, in part, America was exporting to England. Dickens is caught between the different discourses of the prison. He says he found it hard in the 'house of correction' to persuade himself that he was really in a jail, 'a place of ignominious punishment and endurance. And to this hour I very much question whether the humane boast that it is not like one, has its root in the true wisdom or philosophy of the matter.' Saying that with his 'strong and deep interest' in prisons he does not wish to be misunderstood, he inclines 'as little to the sickly feeling which makes every canting lie or maudlin speech of a notorious criminal a subject of newspaper report and general sympathy, as I do to those good old customs of the good old times which made England, even so recently as in the reign of the Third George, in respect of her criminal code and her prison regulations, one of the most bloody-minded and barbarous countries on the earth.' He then expresses his contempt for the highwaymen and the prison turnkeys who 'had always been felons themselves and were, to the last, their bosom-friends and pot-companions.'[54] This is also the tone of the preface to *Oliver Twist* of 1841; wishing not to be identified with other Newgate novelists, but fascinated, like them, with the eighteenth century. As a tone, it continues in *David Copperfield*, with Copperfield's boyhood reading in eighteenth-century novels, saving the text of the eighteenth century, as it were, and it shows equally in Thackeray's comments in the preface to *Pendennis* on the novelist not being able, since the days of *Tom Jones*, to represent 'A MAN.' The context of Thackeray's comment is the impossibility of showing 'a real rascal.' 'You must make him so horrible that he would be too hideous to show.' So, too, for a hero, 'We must drape him, and give him a certain conventional simper. Society will not tolerate the natural in our art.'[55] Thackeray believes neither criminality nor masculinity may be represented. Nonetheless, this section of *American Notes* concludes that 'the subject of Prison Discipline is one of the highest importance to any community; and that in her sweeping reform and bright example ... America has shown great wisdom, great benevolence, and exalted policy. In contrasting her system with that which we have modelled upon it, I merely seek to show that with all its drawbacks, ours has some advantages of its own.'[56] The writer is caught between a literary, romanticized presentation of the eighteenth-century jail, unable to note the status of the poor debtors, who were at its heart, and the perception that the American prison does not look like a prison, and therefore fails to underline its disciplinary quality. Aligning his view as an outsider with that of the insider, he assumes that the prisoner is not adequately aware of being in prison, or of what that means.[57] This problem of how to read the model prison persists with the prisons in *David Copperfield*. Micawber's presentation in the King's Bench prison is eighteenth-century, Smollett-like, the dominant mode, despite the horror of the *mise en scène*, being comic. There is a jump to the middle of the nineteenth century in 'I Am Shown Two Interesting Penitents,' a chapter that followed hard on the writing of 'Pet Prisoners' in *Household Words* on 27 April 1850.[58] The satire against 'model prisoners' comes when Copperfield and Traddles are taken by the Middlesex magistrate Mr Creakle to see Uriah Heep and Littimer in their separate cells in Pentonville. It assumes a wholly deluded and disingenuous prison management and criminals who can play the system with as much freedom as the highwaymen of the previous century. Yet these examples of mid-Victorian prisoners are different. If they are 'great criminals,' it is not because they share the masculinity of either Jonathan Wild, or Tom Jones, or even Steerforth, the Byronic figure of *David Copperfield*, whose death by drowning six chapters earlier has differentiated him from both prisoners and made him superior. (To unpack this: Heep was Copperfield's unsuccessful rival for Agnes as Steerforth was the successful rival with Copperfield for Emily; Littimer was the attempted substitute for Steerforth with Emily, and his servant.)

Perhaps doubts about the adequacy of prison discipline accord with a gender anxiety; while the older prison attracted the 'great criminal,' the newer prison is for those who lack masculinity, or who are made to lack it. Those who rejected the idea of the prison as the place for reformation and as offering room for 'sympathy' objected to the idea of creating 'a new man,' because it was reshaping the British character. For William Frankland in 1811, the existing law suited the 'manly' traits of the nation: 'How comes it then that our laws are severe? It is because we love freedom and happiness; because we are jealous of previous restraint and control of our actions; because we wish to avoid the teasing vigilance of the perpetual superintendence of the law; because we would not purchase exemption from crime, by the loss of virtue ... Have severe laws broken down our spirit? Are we a mean, creeping, overawed people?'[59] But the words 'mean' and 'creeping' do describe the 'unmanly' Uriah Heep and Littimer. McGowen quotes J.S. Mill's essay 'Civilisation' (1836) on the disappearance of pain in modern society, and thinks that while the 'opulent classes' are becoming more 'amiable and humane,' this also entails a weakening. 'If the source of great virtues thus dries up, great vices are placed, no doubt, under considerable restraint.'[60] Great virtues spring out of the untrammelled conditions that permit pain; the 'great criminal' of Dickens is not wholly separable from either 'great virtues' or 'great vices,' which are, perhaps, in Mill's thinking, necessary to each other. Perhaps Dickens, in the wonderful comic drama that makes up the chapter – different comedy from that of Micawber in his prison – did not consciously register how much the Pentonville experiment manipulated those who were its sub-jects, and replaced a physical torturing with the constitution of the subject as criminal, through observation and forcing the prisoner to interiorize his deeds as motives and as characteristics of a personality – Foucault's theme. But per-haps he also intuits a weakening of manliness in the model prison, as a result of the forcing of the prisoner into self-inspection and self-analysis.

IV

In this light we may compare Dickens on the model prison with another novel discussing prison reform, by Charles Reade (1814–89), who, popular in his lifetime if not now, published seventeen novels and more than two dozen plays. *It Is Never Too Late to Mend: A Matter-of-Fact Romance* (1856), partly centred on the prison, is contemporary with *Little Dorrit*. Reade's two previous novels bore eponymous titles for their female protagonists: *Peg Woffington* (1851) and *Christie Johnstone* (1852). *It's Never Too Late to Mend* was inspired by *Uncle Tom's Cabin*, with its attack on slavery men-tioned in chapter 17; indeed, Reade attempts to do for prisoners what Stowe had done for slaves. Insofar as the novel is about the prison, Reade's interests are, from the title, reformatory, while the subtitle recalls Dickens's protest about the criminal aspects of *Oliver Twist* in the 1841 preface, and the Nancy episodes especially, that 'IT IS TRUE.' Reade's plot concerns George Fielding, a poor farmer who goes to Australia in order to secure the finances to wed his fiancée Susan Merton. His lodger is Thomas Robinson, whose crimes take him to an unnamed and unspecified prison, but for which Reade took the details from a scandal at Birmingham Borough Prison, the subject of a public enquiry. After Robinson is released from prison, he and Fielding go to Australia together, and after prospecting for gold, return to England, for Fielding to marry Susan Merton.

The scandal, which Reade read about in the *Times* in a series of articles beginning on 8 September 1853, came to light after a fifteen-year old convict, Edward Andrews, convicted for having stolen four pounds of beef (third offence), had hanged himself in prison on 28 April 1853. In Reade, this episode takes place in chapter 20, after much turning of the screw of punishment. At the time, the prison governor, who operated the 'separate' system, was Lieutenant William Austin, who had come to the post from Tothill Fields, and who was to be sentenced to six months' imprisonment for his practice of excessive punishment. The previous governor, Captain Alexander Maconochie, who was known to Dickens, and who before his return to England had been governor of Norfolk Island in the Pacific, had held that 'the proper object of prison discipline is to prepare men for discharge.'[61] Dickens drew on his ideas for awarding 'marks' for conduct when preparing his own 'prison' – Urania Cottage, for Angela Burdett-Coutts – in 1846,[62] and the same sentiments, as Wiener indicates, may be found in Mayhew, who opposed 'useless labour' in prison with what he calls a return 'to those natural laws which the Almighty has laid down for the regulation of human life, and making a man's food and enjoyments, whilst in prison, depend upon the amount of work he does, as is the case with the rest of the world *out* of prison.'[63] Maconochie appears in Reade's novel as Captain O'Connor, who is, in Reade's words, unaware 'that severe punishment of mind and body was the essential element of a jail.'[64] The prison chaplain was Ambrose Sherwin, who made a statement about the 'illegal and excessive punishments inflicted on the deceased and on other prisoners.' In the prison, the convicts had to turn the cranks at least ten thousand times per day, and whoever failed in this was put on a bread and water diet. In addition, there was the 'punishment jacket,' which was supposed to be used only for restraint. This is carried over into *It is Never Too Late to Mend*, using a character called Josephs who commits suicide, the chaplain becoming Mr Francis Eden, and the governor, Hawes.[65]

The prison is introduced in chapter 10, when Tom Robinson enters it to spend a year there before being transported for a period of ten years. The prison is, consequently, seen through his eyes and his experience.

> Tom Robinson had not been in jail these four years, and since his last visit, great changes had begun to take place in the internal economy of these skeleton palaces, and in the treatment of their prisoners. Prisons might be said to be in a transition state. In some, as in the county bridewell Robinson had just left, the old system prevailed in full force. The two systems vary in their aims. Under the old, jail was a finishing school of felony and petty larceny. Under the new, it is intended to be a penal hospital for diseased and contagious souls.[66]

Robinson is made to work the crank, and Reade emphasizes the power of surveillance: 'though no mortal oversaw the thief at his task, the eye of science was in that cell and watched every stroke and her inexorable finger marked it down ... On the face of the machine was a thing like a chronometer with numbers set all round, and a hand which ... always pointed to the exact number of turns the thief had made. The crank was an autometer, or self-measurer, and in that respect your superior and mine.'[67] Reade goes inside the model prison as Dickens does not. Robinson and the chaplain meet in chapter 15, and Reade, writing to his American publishers, called this part of the narrative 'the soul of it': 'the scenes in which a bad man is despaired of and tortured by fools, and afterward not despaired of by a wise and good man, but encouraged, softened, converted. These psychological scenes and the melodramatic scenes that follow, in which the thief's understanding is convinced as well as his heart, are the immortal part of the work.'[68] Yet, at the same time, Eden is 'his good angel,' as the end of chapter 23 puts it:[69] masculinity needs supplementing by something more sentimental, and Eden goes on, triumphantly, in chapters 24 to 26 to bring a successful case against Hawes.

Eden and Robinson together constitute 'a saint and a thief.'[70] The novel should have been named *Susan Merton*, but dropping the feminine referent in the title was only one way in which the book was seen by contemporary reviewers as a 'masculine' novel: one essay, at least, has been devoted to the masculine aspects of the text.[71] And it is if hysteria may be gendered as masculine, for the novel's tone, including its frequent capitalizations to enforce a point, is hysterical, especially when it comes to the succour and sympathy that Eden gives to Robinson. In chapter 42, Eden's system of government of the jail is seen, and how he makes prisoners write their lives for the use of the prison (encouraging confession). Chapter 43, set just before Robinson's transportation to Australia, where he will give true assistance to George Fielding, says of the autobiography that he has written that it is: 'a self-drawn portrait of a true Bohemian, and his mind from boyhood up to the date when it fell into my hands ... the reader has seen Robinson turned to a fiend by cruelty, and turned back to a man by humanity. On this followed many sacred, softening, improving lessons, and as he loved Mr Eden his heart was open to them.'[72] Reade, convinced by this vindication of the masculine hero, brought out separately the section of Robinson's life, which he had removed from *It's Never Too Late to Mend* as *The Autobiography of a Thief* (1858). Yet the portrayal of the 'Bohemian' Robinson shows how much further Reade has moved from eighteenth-century models of masculinity. The prisoner has no power of independence, even if desiring reform.

V

If great criminals told the truth – which, being great criminals, they do not – they would very rarely tell of their struggles against the crime. Their struggles are towards it. They buffet with opposing waves to gain the bloody shore, not to recede from it.[73]

Dickens's fascination with the 'great criminal,' which persists with his writing of the case of Bradley Headstone, a man who never sees the inside of a prison, has changed character from the time of Newgate and *Oliver Twist*. It was then masculinity in action, but it is now, in 1865, something more complicated in sexual terms, possibly homosexually charged in both Headstone and the later John Jasper, certainly obsessive, achieving crime against the odds, fighting to become bloody, contending against bourgeois society from a position just inside it. Murderousness becomes non-utilitarian madness in Headstone and Jasper, but madness now means something different from its signification in Cibber's statues: it now includes Jasper's drugged state.[74] If the criminal is no longer heroic – prison conditions, in both Reade's and Dickens's perceptions, render that impossible – he becomes, analeptically, more duplicitous, more inward. This paper can do no more than hint towards that newer sense of the 'great criminal,' leaving it for further study, which might develop previous work on Headstone and Jasper,[75] yet it should not be assumed too quickly that Headstone is a great criminal; he is too self-divided for that. He is more like a case of what Freud calls a 'criminal out of a sense of guilt.'[76] This type is a person who commits a crime to free himself of a pervasive sense of guilt, and who hopes that by so acting he will get relief from a guilt that has been implanted in him through his class consciousness, through his self-division within the educational system that, 'murdering the innocents,' to quote from Dickens's chapter title in *Hard Times*, is destructive of both the pupil and the teacher (and Headstone has been both), and through what looks like an attraction to Eugene Wrayburn, which is also repulsion.

To reintroduce the homoerotic here, to be able to consider Headstone, or Jasper, in the light of same-sex attraction, means moving a long way from the men convicted for homosexual offences seen in Newgate in *Sketches By Boz*. As a stage on that journey there is the figure of Steerforth, constructed as morally criminal and sexually ambiguous: he, in class terms, leads towards Wrayburn, not Headstone. But *David Copperfield* also contains Uriah Heep, who is also a figure of repulsion and attraction to the hero, and a parallel to Steerforth, and in class terms, like Headstone. And so, perhaps the other model prisoner, Littimer, may be read as sexually ambiguous; if so, the two men in Pentonville contrast strongly with the two men in Newgate. The point about Headstone, which is reflected in the words of the quotation that begins this section, is that he is treated outside the comic mode that characterizes Heep, or Littimer; the text sees him as a man marked by unconscious depths. He is passionate in his desire to be free of class and perhaps gender constraints, but he cannot be. Such figures as Rogue Riderhood and Charley Hexam, as well as Wrayburn himself, are for him shadowing, guilt-inducing, suggesting by their different forms of surveillance that the work of the prison in the nineteenth century is, quite apart from its literal existence, to structure people as always-already guilty, in need of confession, and if criminal, not so spontaneously, but as a reactive way of trying to break free that only entangles the self in further guilt.

Where the criminal becomes more self-conscious, and more modern, less like the obsessional case of Headstone or Jasper, is hinted at in Dickens's interest in and representation of William Palmer, who was hanged as a poisoner at Newgate in 1856. The case came four years after the period 1849–52, during which years Martin Wiener, though he does not discuss this case, notes a 'poison panic,' showing, too, how this was the only form of spousal murder for which more women than men were convicted, as if poisoning could therefore be perceived as more 'feminine' than masculine.[77] Dickens's article 'The Demeanour of Murderers' (1856), beginning by calling Palmer 'the greatest villain,' responds to those who noticed the calm demeanour of the man, which seemed to testify to his innocence. Dickens argues otherwise: there is nothing in the man but 'cruelty and insensibility ... the man is of a piece with his misdeeds; and it is not likely that he ever could have committed the crimes for which he is to suffer, if he had not this demeanour to present, in standing publicly to answer for them.'[78] It is a neat argument – the calmness proves the guilt – though arguing from an absence to a presence is likely to make guilt seem more and more prevalent, in all aspects of society. The approach produces in Dickens a detective mentality that looks for signs of restlessness and agitation in the man's hands in the trial (signs of obsessionalism), and which goes back at newspaper reports of other trials for murder that prove Palmer's case as common, creating a new archive of guilt, a new kind of Newgate Calendar.

Perhaps Dickens registers unconsciously that the changing conditions of the prison produce in their turn the man possessed of a more complete ability to keep his feelings as interior and as private as possible, despite a certain non-melodramatic psychopathology that is noticeable in his behaviour in the dock. He has not struck his wife down, he has poisoned her, along with his friend and his wife's brother, and he has done so with a calculation indicative of a new way of gendering masculinity. Whereas the movement within mid-century prison reform was towards closer control of the prisoner, sometimes in the disguised form of friendliness towards him, which makes Dickens say that the prison conditions are better than conditions for those outside, the novelist here argues another point. The prisoner has become more controlled, more machine-like, more hidden in his methods, just as being a 'Poisoner' – so different from being a highwayman – relies on new prison methods: secrecy, observation, and science. To finish with William Palmer and the fictional Bradley Headstone is to imply how much criminality proliferates for Dickens as the century progresses, and how distinctively new features it offers as the modern state comes more under the power of the police and the power of confessional tactics that call out other, and alternative, forms of desire and transgression.

NOTES

1 George Gissing, *The Nether World* (Oxford: Oxford University Press, 1992), 2.
2 Walter Benjamin, 'Critique of Violence,' in *One Way Street and Other Writings*, trans. Edmund Jephcott and Kingsley Shorter (London: Verso, 1979), 136.
3 Jonathan Andrews, et al., *The History of Bethlem* (London: Routledge, 1997), 153, 238–9.
4 Charles Dickens, *Great Expectations*, ed. Angus Calder (Harmondsworth, UK: Penguin, 1965), 223; Simon Joyce, *Capital Offenses: Geographies of Class and Crime in Victorian London* (Charlottesville: University of Virginia Press, 2003), 95–6.
5 Henry Mayhew and John Binny, *The Criminal Prisons of London and Scenes of Prison Life* (London: Griffin, Bohn, and Company, Stationers' Hall Court, 1862), 384.
6 Ibid., 285. For a detailed analysis of this text, see W.B. Carnochan's contribution in this volume.
7 Dickens, *Great Expectations*, chap. 42.
8 Mayhew and Binny, *The Criminal Prisons of London*, 81.
9 Keith Hollingsworth, *The Newgate Novel, 1830–1847: Bulwer, Ainsworth, Dickens, and Thackeray* (Detroit: Wayne State University Press, 1963), 131–47.
10 See also Adam Hansen's contribution to this volume.
11 Mayhew and Binny, *The Criminal Prisons of London*, 611–23.
12 Jeremy Tambling, '"Why should I call you mad?" Dickens and the Literature of Madness,' *Cahiers Victoriens et Edouardiens* 56 (2002): 59–77.
13 John Reed, *Dickens and Thackeray: Punishment and Forgiveness* (Athens: Ohio University Press, 1995), 45–61.
14 For *Life in London* in relation to Regency writing, see Deborah Epstein Nord, 'The City as Theater: From Georgian to Early Victorian London,' *Victorian Studies* 31 (1988): 159–88.

15 Mayhew and Binny, *The Criminal Prisons of London*, 588–611.
16 W.J. Carlton, 'The Third Man at Newgate,' *The Review of English Studies* 8 (1957): 406; Philip Collins, *Dickens and Crime* (London: Macmillan, 1962), 39.
17 Quoted in H.G. Cocks, *Nameless Offences: Homosexual Desire in the Nineteenth Century* (London: I.B. Tauris, 2003), 38.
18 For figures for hanging, see Graham Robb, *Strangers: Homosexual Love in the Nineteenth Century* (London: Picador, 2003), 22–5; Cocks, *Nameless Offences*, 23; and for the eighteenth-century and Regency context, Louis Crompton, *Byron and Greek Love* (London: Gay Men's Press, 1998), 12–62, and Matt Cook, *London and the Culture of Homosexuality, 1885–1914* (Cambridge: Cambridge University Press 2003), 7–14.
19 Charles Dickens, *Dickens's Journalism; Sketches by Boz and Other Early Papers,* ed. Michael Slater (London: Dent, 1994), 208.
20 Ibid., 210.
21 Charles Dickens, *Nicholas Nickleby*, ed. Mark Ford (Harmondsworth, UK: Penguin, 2003), 43.
22 Charles Dickens, *Oliver Twist,* ed. Stephen Gill (Oxford: Oxford University Press, 1999), 429.
23 Mayhew and Binny, *The Criminal Prisons of London*, 197–231.
24 Martin J. Wiener, *Reconstructing the Criminal: Culture, Law and Policy in England, 1830–1914* (Cambridge: Cambridge University Press, 1990), 100.
25 Trey Philpotts, *The Companion to Little Dorrit* (Mountfield, UK: Helm Information, 2003), 90–121.
26 See Mayhew and Binny, *The Criminal Prisons of London*, 623–34.
27 Leigh Hunt, *The Autobiography of Leigh Hunt*, ed., intro., and notes J.E. Morpurgo (London: Cresset Press, 1949), 248–9.
28 David D. Cooper, *The Lesson of the Scaffold: The Public Execution Controversy in Victorian England* (Athens: Ohio University Press, 1974), 9–11.
29 Mayhew and Binny, *The Criminal Prisons of London*, 274.
30 Coldbath Fields opened in 1794, and was accused, at the time of its opening, of being like the Bastille, equally containing innocent people. See Coleridge's and Southey's satire, *The Devil's Thoughts* (1799):
    As he went through Coldbath Fields he saw
    A solitary cell
    And the Devil was pleased, for it gave him a hint
    For improving his prisons in Hell.
    See *The Collected Works of Samuel Taylor Coleridge: Poetical Works*, vol. 1, pt. 1, ed. J.C.C. Mays (Princeton, NJ: Princeton University Press, 2001), 564. The prison closed in 1877, and was pulled down twelve years later.
31 Mayhew and Binny, *The Criminal Prisons of London*, 353–486.

32 Examples are Bulwer's *Pelham* (1828), *Paul Clifford* (1830), *Eugene Aram* (1832), *Ernest Maltravers* (1837), *Alice* (1838), *Night and Morning* (1841), *Lucretia* (1846), or W.H. Ainsworth's *Rookwood* (1834) and *Jack Sheppard* (1839).

33 Charles Dickens, *Pickwick Papers*, ed. Robert Pattern (Harmondsworth, UK: Penguin, 1972), 702.

34 Elliott Engel and Margaret F. King, *The Victorian Novel before Victoria: British Fiction during the Reign of William IV, 1830–1837* (London: Macmillan, 1984), 96–100.

35 John Harvey, *Victorian Novelists and Their Illustrators* (London: Sidgwick & Jackson, 1970), 44–51; Joyce, *Capital Offenses*, 59–100; Kathleen Tillotson, *Novels of the Eighteen-Forties* (Oxford: Oxford University Press, 1956), 75–7.

36 George J. Worth, 'Early Victorian Criticism of the Novel and Its Limitations: *Jack Sheppard*, A Test Case,' in *The Nineteenth-Century Writer and His Audience*, ed. Harold Orel and George J. Worth (Lawrence: University of Kansas Publications, 1969), 51–60.

37 Robert Tracy, '"The Old Story" and Inside Stories: Modish Fiction and Fictional Modes in *Oliver Twist*,' *Dickens Studies Annual* 18 (1988): 20.

38 Heather Shore, *Artful Dodgers: Youth and Crime in Early Nineteenth-Century London* (Woodbridge, Suffolk, UK/Rochester, NY: Royal Historical Society/ Boydell Press, 1999), 104; Dickens, *Oliver Twist*, 63.

39 Dickens, *Dickens's Journalism*, 200–1.

40 Other examples of interest in the criminal appear with James Blomfield Rush (1800–49), who shot the owner of Stanfield Hall on 28 November 1848 and was hanged for it at Norwich the following 21 April (Charles Dickens, *The Letters of Charles Dickens*, ed. Madeline House and Graham Storey [Oxford: Clarendon Press, 1965–2002], vol. 5, 473). This case produced four articles in *The Examiner* on prison and prison discipline: 'Prisons and Convict Discipline,' 10 March 1849, 'Rush's Conviction,' 7 April 1849, 'Capital Punishment,' 5 May 1849, and 'False Reliance,' 2 June 1849; mention of Rush in Dickens's second letter to the *Times* on capital punishment; and again in the article 'The Demeanour of Murderers' in *Household Words*, 14 June 1856 (see below, note 78), a piece which concentrates on the trial of William Palmer in 1856, hanged for poisoning, and reminding readers of John Thurtell, 'one of the murderers best remembered in England,' hanged in 1824, and also of Mr Manning (Charles Dickens, *'Gone Astray' and Other Papers from Household Words, 1851–59*, ed. Michael Slater [London: Dent, 1998], 377–83).

41 Tobias Smollett, *Roderick Random* (London: Everyman's Library, 1940), 369–70.

42 Tobias Smollett, *The Life and Adventures of Sir Launcelot Greaves*, ed. Peter Wagner (Harmondsworth, UK: Penguin Books, 1988), 205.

43 Roger Lee Brown, *A History of the Fleet Prison, London: The Anatomy Of The Fleet* (Lewiston, NY: Edwin Mellen Press, 1996), x.

44 Quoted in ibid., 29.

45 Ibid., viii.

46 Such as Poultry Compter, demolished in 1817, Giltspur Street Compter, almost adjacent to Newgate, and designed by George Dance the Younger, opened in 1791 and closed in 1854. It appears in *Nicholas Nickleby*, ch. 4. Another, Whitecross prison, opened in 1815 and closed in 1870.

47 Yet, in relation to *Little Dorrit*, it is worth noting that two prisoners transferred out of the Fleet had been there for over thirty years. Brown, *A History of the Fleet Prison*, 108.

48 Séan McConville, *A History of English Prison Administration* (London: Routledge and Kegan Paul, 1981), 131.

49 Robert Alan Cooper, 'Ideas and their Execution: English Prison Reform,' *Eighteenth Century Studies* 10 (1976): 73–93.

50 Robert Alan Cooper, 'Jeremy Bentham, Elizabeth Fry and English Prison Reform,' *Journal of the History of Ideas* 42 (1981): 675–90.

51 For an analysis of the prison in this novel see Greta Olson's contribution in this volume.

52 McConville, *A History of English Prison Administration*, 208.

53 See Terence Morris and Pauline Morris, *Pentonville: A Sociological Study of an English Prison*, assisted by Barbara Barker (London: Routledge, 1998).

54 Charles Dickens, *American Notes*, ed. F.S. Schwarzbach and Leonee Ormond (London: Everyman 1997), 64–5.

55 William Makepeace Thackeray, *Pendennis,* ed. John Sutherland (Oxford: Oxford University Press 1994), lvi.

56 Dickens, *American Notes*, 65.

57 Dickens as interested in prison discipline was not interested in the abolition of capital punishment, for instance, as the curt note sent to the Boston minister, the Reverend Charles Spear (14 April 1849, Dickens, *Letters*, 525), indicates. Spear had initiated the American Society for the Abolition of Capital Punishment in 1844, and Dickens's letter declines to contribute to his abolitionist journal *The Prisoner's Friend*.

58 Dickens, *David Copperfield*, ed. Jeremy Tambling (Harmondsworth, UK: Penguin, 2004), 849–61. See also Anna Schur's contribution in this volume.

59 Randall McGowen, 'A Powerful Sympathy: Terror, the Prison and Humanitarian Reform in Early Nineteenth Century Britain,' *Journal of British Studies* 25 (1986): 318.

60 Ibid., 332.

61 Collins, *Dickens and Crime*, 165. See also Wiener, *Reconstructing the Criminal*, 114–22.

62 Collins, *Dickens and Crime*, 94–116, 166–8.

63 Mayhew and Binny, *The Criminal Prisons of London*, 308.

64 Charles Reade, *It Is Never Too Late to Mend* (London: Collins, 1856), 100.

65 See Sheila M. Smith, 'Propaganda and Hard Facts in Charles Reade's Didactic Novels: A Study of *It Is Never Too Late to Mend* and *Hard Cash*,' *Renaissance and Modern Studies* 4 (1960): 165–89, and Sean C. Grass, *The Self in the Cell: Narrating the Victorian Prisoner* (London: Routledge, 2003), 81–101.

66 Reade, *It Is Never Too Late to Mend*, 99.

67 Ibid., 111.

68 Malcolm Elvin, *Charles Reade: A Biography* (London: Jonathan Cape, 1931), 112–13.

69 Reade, *It Is Never Too Late to Mend*, 275.

70 Ibid., 326.

71 Nicola Diane Thompson, *Reviewing Sex: Gender and the Reception of Victorian Novels* (New York: New York University Press, 1996), 25–45.

72 Reade, *It Is Never Too Late to Mend*, 388–9.

73 Charles Dickens, *Our Mutual Friend*, ed. Adrian Poole (Harmondsworth, UK: Penguin, 1997), 535.

74 Wiener discusses the new pleas of insanity brought in after the case of Daniel McNaughten, who killed Peel's secretary in 1843, which ruled that a man was not responsible for his crime only if, at the time of committing it, he was unable to know that it was illegal and wrong. Such convicted people who were sent to asylums were 'criminal lunatics.' Wiener, *Reconstructing the Criminal*, 86–91. See also Martin J. Wiener, *Men of Blood: Violence, Manliness and Criminal Justice in Victorian England* (Cambridge: Cambridge University Press, 2004), 279–88.

75 Jeremy Tambling, *Dickens, Violence and the Modern State: Dreams of the Scaffold* (London: Macmillan, 1995), 174–85, 202–15. I discuss Headstone further in my *Going Astray: Dickens and London* (London: Longman, 2008), 253–8.

76 Sigmund Freud, 'Art and Literature,' *The Penguin Freud*, vol. 14 (Harmondsworth, UK: Penguin, 1985), 317–19.

77 Wiener, *Men of Blood*, 129–30.

78 Charles Dickens, 'The Demeanour of Murderers,' in *Selected Journalism 1850–1870*, ed. David Pascoe (1856; Harmondsworth, UK: Penguin, 1997), 383. See above, note 40.

3 Facing a Mirror: Philip Meadows Taylor's *Confessions of a Thug* and the Politics of Imperial Self-Incrimination

MATTHEW KAISER

Critics generally agree that Philip Meadows Taylor's 1839 *Confessions of a Thug* – the most popular and ideologically influential Anglo-Indian novel of the nineteenth century – constitutes a paradigmatic expression of liberal imperialism, a meditation upon the cultural, political, and psychological tensions between a Western self and an Indian Other. The former assistant superintendent of police in the Nizam in the late 1820s and early 1830s, Taylor presents his novel, which is based on his experience interrogating captured Thugs, as the jailhouse confession of Ameer Ali, a notorious north Indian Thug, who gives a vivid account of his life and the 719 murders he committed. His litany of crime, his occasional professions of remorse, and his defiant statements of self-justification are assiduously recorded by an anonymous colonial law enforcement officer, whom Ameer Ali obligatorily addresses as 'Sahib,' and who is, for the most part, silent, interrupting his loquacious interlocutor every few chapters with a bureaucratic 'tsk, tsk,' before receding with scientific detachment to the margins of the text. The novel's vexed self-Other opposition has attracted in the last two decades an increasing amount of critical attention. Writing in 1988, Patrick Brantlinger, one of the first critics to take *Confessions of a Thug* seriously, reads the novel as a propagandistic rallying cry for British imperialism, as an act of political and moral self-justification, with Thuggee, or *thagi* – a criminal cult devoted to the ritualistic robbing and strangling, according to British officials, of as many as forty thousand Indians annually – functioning as a stand-in for India itself.[1] Writing in 1996, in the wake of Homi Bhabha's work on colonial mimicry, Parama Roy reads the novel instead as an inherently anxious and ambivalent text, unsettled by the racial and cultural Otherness against which it falteringly strives to define a stable and knowable Western subject.[2] In a sign that the novel is inching towards canonicity, towards interpretative inexhaustibility, Mary Poovey, writing in the post-9/11 environment of New York City, reads *Confessions of a Thug* as a devastating indictment by Taylor of Britain's imperial project, the novel tacitly encouraging its readers, Poovey argues, to identify with the Thug.[3] Poovey supplements her reading with a metacritical meditation upon the ease with which historicist interpretative strategies can fall prey to 'presentism,' to a critic's postcolonial sympathies, for instance. She demonstrates how one can convincingly historicize the text in such a way that it appears either decidedly anti-imperialist or decidedly pro-imperialist in its ambitions. Although she privileges the former reading over the latter, the fact that such radically irreconcilable interpretative outcomes are practicable, indeed, historically viable, should be a warning, she suggests, to us *all*.

What makes Taylor's novel so paradigmatic an expression of liberal imperialism, however, is not the irreconcilability of the divergent readings that it inspires, or its purported ideological undecidability, but the certainty, the confidence, with which it seamlessly reconciles the critique of imperialism with its valorization. *Confessions of a Thug* is a passionately anti-imperial text, as Poovey demonstrates, but it is also a passionately pro-imperial text, as Brantlinger contends. Imperialism becomes coterminous in the novel with its own critique. The novel's ideological two-facedness, then, its reconciliation of self-critique and self-justification, manifests itself not as ambivalence but as the self-congratulatory logic of liberal guilt, the ethic of self-incrimination that underlies and fuels the Victorian culture of liberal reform. With liberal guilt, one casts oneself as villain and hero of the same psychological-political narrative. Hence: *I will save you from myself.* Or, more specifically: *I will lift you from the poverty/oppression/injustice/bigotry that I have been complicit in perpetuating.* Take, for instance, the Christian socialist Romney Leigh in Elizabeth Barrett Browning's 1856 *Aurora Leigh.* The mid-Victorian epitome of self-aggrandizing liberal guilt, of a guilt that is more performative than paradigm-shifting, he proposes marriage to a working-class woman whom he does not love – in the words of cynical Lord Howe – '*By symbol,* to instruct us formally / To fill the ditches up 'twixt class and class.'[4] Taylor's self-flagellating imperialism, his veiled attacks on British rule in India, the numerous parallels that he draws between the British and the Thugs, function not to destabilize imperial ideology from within, to radicalize his readers, but to inoculate imperialism and his readers against that very radicalism, and to position himself as the enlightened spokesperson for a more just imperialism.

Critics tend to gloss over the novel's carceral setting, reading it, if they analyse it at all, as a metaphor for the imperial relationship between the British and their Indian subjects. This essay makes the case, however, that Taylor's employment of the confessional mode, specifically within the context of a prison, aligns his imperial novel formally and politically with contemporaneous liberal efforts to reform the Victorian prison system, to recast it as a site of confession, of reciprocal self-incrimination, in which prisoners contemplate their past crimes, and in which reform-minded prison administrators contemplate the sociological and structural conditions that produce those crimes – conditions which society and the prison system, it turns out, are complicit in perpetuating. The prisoner's confession becomes, as does Ameer Ali's in *Confessions of a Thug*, an opportunity for the prison reformer, or the imperial reformer in Taylor's case, to perform self-congratulatory self-blame, mirroring himself in the prisoner's face, taking guilty pleasure in the momentary resemblance. The fleeting sense of intimacy that is kindled rhetorically between prisoner and prison administrator – and by extension between the prisoner and society at large – masks the violence of the criminal justice system. Ethical self-reflection becomes a substitute for radical change, rather than its trigger. With its anti-imperial imperialism, *Confessions of a Thug* performs liberal guilt on a geopolitical scale, turns India into a kind of penitentiary.

At the novel's start, Ameer Ali sits in chains before the anonymous framing narrator, 'denouncing all [his] old confederates,' and giving a detailed account of his life, from childhood sorrows, through adolescent angst, to the glories of manhood.[5] Some readers have viewed Taylor's Thug as a transparent window onto Indian otherness, a window which renders visible, exposes, as Robert Williams puts it, the 'dark, inscrutable secret buried beneath the breast of India.'[6] Brantlinger, too, chooses to treat Ameer Ali as inherently 'transparent,' as a 'penetrated' surface, his 'hidden' and 'secret life' having been irradiated by the panoptic gaze of empire, and the '[a]uthoritarian silence' of the framing narrator having 'wrap[ped] a steel cage of implicit rationality around the Thug's irrational discourse.'[7] Rather than a window onto otherness, however, Taylor's Thug functions as a reflective surface on which the imperial subject confronts his own predatory designs on India. *Ameer* is *a mirror*: an apparatus of British self-recognition, a looking glass in which the scrutinized Other turns out to be none other than a distorted reflection of the Western self. In the unsettling figure of Ameer Ali, the Victorian reader faces a mirror. Taylor achieves this *trompe l'oeil* by cultivating in his reader, as Poovey demonstrates, identification with, indeed, sympathy for, his Thug protagonist. Taylor sustains this identification by anglicizing Ameer Ali, endowing him with an uncannily British temperament: a taste for domesticity and commerce; a disdain for native superstition and disorder; a tourist's fascination with the Indian landscape through which he travels; a subjugator's condescension towards the population on which he preys. Indeed, so gentlemanly is the Thug, so congenial, so familiar, that the framing narrator finds himself – to his surprise – touched by Ameer Ali's pathetic accounts of his suffering: the death of his beloved wife, his father's brutal execution at the hands of corrupt local officials, the loss of his daughter.

At first glance, Taylor's anglicized Thug seems to illustrate perfectly Bhabha's notion of colonial mimicry: the 'process by which the look of surveillance returns as the displacing gaze of the disciplined, where the observer becomes the observed and "partial" representation rearticulates the whole notion of *identity* and alienates it from essence.'[8] Ameer Ali takes fetishistic delight in mimicking the British, whom he admits he 'respected,' praising them for being 'good and brave soldiers.'[9] Before strangling one of his victims, a notorious Pindharee soldier whom the British, too, sought to bring to justice, Ameer Ali offers the man some English wine and a decidedly English 'Hip, hip, hip!'[10] From our postcolonial vantage, what is *most* striking about *Confessions of a Thug* is not that it employs strategies of mimicry (which it does) to critique British imperialism, to induce epistemological slippage between self and Other, to discombobulate and unsettle its Victorian readers. On the contrary, what is most striking (and sobering) about the novel is the disturbing ease with which Taylor's very deconstruction of imperial logic, of racial superiority, indeed, of identity, functions paradoxically to inspire a new and improved imperial ideology, in which imperialism becomes interoperable with its critique, and in which the imperial subject is *strengthened* by any attempt to decentre or disorient it. Though Taylor was often critical of the East India Company, especially its policy of non-interference, whereby territory was conquered and neglected rather than emancipated and civilized, he remained a dedicated and committed colonial official. Taylor was never a direct employee of the East India Company per se, working instead as an administrator in various semi-autonomous client states. In exposing the violence inherent in imperial ideology, in encouraging the reader's identification with the predacious yet eerily familiar Ameer Ali, who evokes in turn the picaresque Newgate hero, the sentimental Victorian patriarch, the savvy capitalist entrepreneur, Taylor triggers in his reader self-reflection, a more enlightened, self-critical imperialism, in which liberal guilt functions as a built-in moral corrective, and in which a guilty deconstruction of the self becomes a substitute for radical action. In the end, of course, Taylor's reformist model of self-incriminating imperial subjectivity is as insidious as the jingoistic cultural supremacy it modifies. British imperialism is recast homeopathically as both the disease from which India suffers and its only possible cure. In Taylor's imperial psychodrama, the white man saves India not – as in Gayatri

Spivak's classic formulation – from India itself but from *himself*, from his own unconscious thuggishness.[11] Like Ameer Ali, the imperial subject serves as villain and hero of the same confessional narrative, redeeming himself by incriminating himself.

The Politics of Self-Blame

Taylor's stated goal in writing *Confessions of a Thug* was to awaken his countrymen to an unseen enemy, to instigate a public outcry for the increased funding of counter-Thuggee operations. The most daunting obstacle to the eradication of Thuggee, however, was not the craftiness of the Thugs themselves, who proved relatively easy to neutralize with the requisite manpower and resources; rather, it was Britain's chronic indifference towards its Indian subjects and its reluctance to pay for their security. In his introductory remarks, Taylor laments the fact that '[t]hroughout the whole of India' 'only eighteen officers are employed as' 'agents for the suppression of Thuggee.' He goes on to 'hope ... that *oeconomical* considerations do not prevent the appointment of others.' [12] Taylor frames his novel not so much as a confrontation between a Briton and a Thug but as a pitched battle between two imperial logics: his own liberal-reformist view, on the one hand, that Britain has a moral duty to bring enlightened justice to India, and the pragmatic-conservative view, on the other, which held that, because Indians are morally inferior to Europeans and thus incapable of justice, they should be left to their own peculiar devices, so long as they yield a steady stream of tax revenue and commerce. In Taylor's eyes, Britain's *own* predatoriness, its history of viewing the subcontinent – as do his fictional Thugs – as its divine prize, impedes the successful suppression of Thuggee. The company's 'questionable policy of non-interference,' as Taylor terms it in an 1843 article, its moral neglect, enables Thuggee to proliferate, creating a causal connection between the imperialist and the Thug, between British cupidity and Indian lawlessness.[13] Taylor's campaign against Thuggee is inseparable from his crusade against the British colonial government's often irresponsible and exploitative treatment of its Indian subjects. Taylor conceived of himself, in the words of his contemporary, Henry Reeve, as 'a protector and a friend' of 'the natives' of India, as a moral corrective to Indian self-destructiveness and to British exploitation.[14] Reeve even suggests that Taylor's 1877 autobiography, *The Story of My Life*, be assigned reading for any 'young Englishman' who 'enter[s] upon the duties of an Indian career.'[15] '[W]ith this book in his pocket,' Reeve waxes hyperbolic, a young man will surely 'develop and improve his own character and attainments,' learn 'to promote the welfare of the people committed to his charge.' Reeve presents Taylor's life story, then, as a model of ethical imperialism, and his autobiography as a pedagogical instrument for tempering and countering the potentially unethical imperial impulses lurking within every Englishman.

Taylor is not the only student of Indian history to discern a disturbing causal connection between Thuggee and British imperialism. The dramatic increase in Thuggee activity in the late eighteenth century, in fact, has been blamed, by some twentieth-century historians, on the British themselves, on the demographic displacement and economic turmoil unleashed by their incursive and annexational policies, by Britain's insatiable hunger for the rights of taxation that went with the ownership of territory. As Kate Teltscher reminds us, the East India Company's 'cruel negligence' of its Indian subjects in 1769–70 led to a famine of unprecedented proportions, with a quarter of the population of Bengal starving to death, and vast numbers of the survivors turning vagrant.[16] Although Thugs had been operating for centuries, their number swelled during this British-induced catastrophe. Nineteenth-century critics of the East India Company, too, saw causal connections – both direct and indirect – between British imperialism and Thuggee. Captain William Sleeman, for instance, who, like Taylor, was a committed reformer (and the target of Taylor's professional jealousy), suggests in his 1839 report, *The Thugs or Phansigars of India*, that the increase in Thuggee activity after 1808 in the territories 'of the Nizam and of the Mahrattas' is due, at least in part, to a growing number of Thugs abandoning their traditional hunting grounds in 'the Company's territories' and in 'districts' that have since been 'ceded' to the British.[17] Likewise, in *Confessions of a Thug*, Taylor conceives of the British as the unconscious accomplices, the unwitting enablers, of Thug gangs. Before Ameer Ali departs on his maiden Thug expedition, his adoptive father and fellow Thug informs him that their impending success is due to the social and political chaos unleashed by Britain's martial enterprises in India: '[W]e have determined to take advantage of the confusion at present produced by the wars of Holkar and Sindea with the Feringhees [or British][;] we anticipate much work and a stirring season, and the men are impatient for employment, after a long period of inactivity.'[18] The Thug is the shadow cast by the British imperialist, the spectre at his heels.

Even more biting a critique of company heavy-handedness and misrule is Sleeman's assertion that the 'ruthless vigilance of the Thugs' is fuelled, in part, by the fate of the once 'numerous' 'inns or serais in India,' which have 'gone entirely to ruin' '[u]nder the extortion of the earlier English government in India' 'and the consequent impoverishment of the country.'[19] In the seventeenth century, Sleeman explains, 'Mohammedan princes' and 'native rulers'

built a vast network of 'beautiful,' 'splendid' inns, in order to ensure the safety
of their subjects, and to provide travellers with dependable shelter, where 'a
regular establishment of guards and servants was maintained.' The company's
virtual destruction of this paternalistic hospitality system – through extortion,
neglect, and mismanagement – 'renders,' Sleeman concludes, 'the operations
of the Thugs so practicable.'[20] Taylor and Sleeman are joined by other nineteenth-century experts on Thuggee in accusing the British themselves of either
indirectly or unthinkingly enabling the phenomenon, of turning a blind eye to
the unforeseen consequences of British imperialism. In his 1837 *Illustrations
of the History and Practices of the Thugs*, Edward Thornton links the proliferation of Thuggee in the late eighteenth and early nineteenth centuries to the
lackadaisical morality and bureaucratic lassitude of the conservative colonial
government, who 'regarded' the 'evil' of Thuggee 'in much the same light as
the fixed inconveniences of the climate, or the accidental inclemency of unfa-
vorable seasons.'[21] Thornton claims that this 'languid and desultory' pragmatic-conservative approach, which he considers profoundly immoral, was 'at
length succeeded by a better system' under the liberal-reformist administration of Governor-General Lord William Bentinck in the late 1820s.[22]
Bentinck's efforts to eradicate both *sati* and Thuggee, as well as to neutralize
the mercenary Pindharee armies that pillaged whole regions, 'indicat[e] an
advancing regard to the principles of public morality in the Government.'[23]

Taylor, too, draws a sharp contrast between the 'humanity and benevolence'
of Bentinck, a decidedly 'enlightened nobleman,' and the 'crooked and
unworthy' 'political conduct,' indeed, the 'vices,' of conservative colonial
officials.[24] In his autobiography, Taylor reserves special scorn for Governor-
General Lord Ellenborough, for whom 'anything but fighting' seemed
'beneath his notice,' as well as for Ellenborough's controversial Major-
General Sir Charles Napier, whose 'aggressive policy' towards the Sind in
1843 – deliberately engineering a war in order to destabilize and annex a
region – constitutes, in Taylor's mind, 'a dark blot on the record of Indian history.'[25] For interventionary reformers like Thornton, Sleeman, and Taylor, the
Thug serves as a powerful and sensational symbol not of the inherent immorality – as some twentieth-century critics suggest – of the Indian people, who
were, after all, the Thug's unwitting victims, but of the East India Company's,
and by extension the British government's, moral shortcomings: its failure to
protect its subjects, its inability to resist the temptation to exploit the vast population over which it proclaimed itself steward. Taylor agreed with Sleeman,
whose investigative efforts he admired, and whose fame he envied, that the
'members at the head of the [colonial] administration have always had a toler-
ably correct idea of the oppressive nature of the British rule in India, and of

the light in which it is held by the natives; but it has always been a primary object to prevent this knowledge from reaching the English public.'[26] With *Confessions of a Thug*, Taylor informs a vast middle-class readership, for the first time, of the existence and extent of Thuggee in British India, knowledge of which an uneasy and image-conscious colonial government prefers to conceal, lest it 'produce,' in Sleeman's words, 'a considerable sensation and excite inquiry' into its own complicity.[27] In betraying the secret of Thuggee, however, in exposing the company's dirty laundry, Taylor simultaneously exposes the thuggishness of the British colonial government: its moral neglect, its reckless expansionism, its role as Thuggee's catalyst rather than its antidote. As we shall see, Taylor's appreciation of the parallels between imperialist and Thug, his recognition of the interoperability of their predatory agendas, explains why he so aggressively anglicizes Ameer Ali, why he avoids overtly 'Othering' him, why he encourages his British reader both to identify with and to condemn his rapacious protagonist.

The extent to which Taylor's Victorian readers were cognizant of Ameer Ali's reflective function is of course difficult to verify. Poovey points out that early reviews of *Confessions of a Thug* 'hint … at' 'resemblances' between Ameer Ali and the British but stubbornly resist reading the text as an indictment of English rule.[28] This, however, is precisely the *aim* of Taylor's brand of self-incriminating imperialism. His Thug's ability to decentre imperial subjectivity rallies rather than dampens the imperial spirits of his readers. The genius of *Confessions of a Thug* lies in its ability to appropriate in the name of imperialism imperialism's deconstruction. Destabilizing the self-Other opposition at the heart of imperial ideology, then, inspires rather than undermines imperialism. At the level of popular culture, this phenomenon is evidenced in the speed and enthusiasm with which the word 'thug' was incorporated into English, thoroughly anglicized, both lexically and psychologically. Within two decades of the publication of *Confessions of a Thug*, the word 'thug' had come to mean roughly what it means today, 'common criminal' or 'hoodlum,' its initial connotations of racial otherness having been gradually displaced and overwritten by connotations of class otherness. The foreignness of 'thug,' then, was not erased in the mid-nineteenth century so much as domesticated, redirected at the otherworldliness of the British underclass: hence, George Sala's burlesque 'The Key of the Street,' which was featured in the September 1851 edition of *Household Words*, and which playfully enumerates the 'recent achievements in the strangling line' of 'Tom Thug and his gang.'[29] Taylor's novel created an insatiable appetite for Thugs in British and Western European popular culture. As Wendy Jacobson has documented, Eugène Sue's *The Wandering Jew* (1844–5), Wilkie Collins's

The Moonstone (1868), Edward Bulwer-Lytton's 'A Strange Story' (1861–2), and Charles Dickens's *The Mystery of Edwin Drood* (1870), as well as works by lesser writers, contain blatant and veiled references to Thugs, the existence of Thuggee having become, by the early 1840s, thanks in part to Taylor, a source of lasting 'excitement' and 'common knowledge.'[30] By transplanting the Thug into a British context, shattering Thuggee's geographical boundedness, Dickens, for instance, reinforces the notion, with the mysterious figure of John Jasper, that the Thug's magnetism derives from his familiarity as much as from his foreignness, from his uncanny proximity to the British reader as much as from the unbridgeable distance between them.

Ever since Britain commenced its colonial project in India, Hindi, Persian, and Gujarati words and phrases had been shipped to Britain for domestic consumption. Words such as 'veranda,' 'sherbet,' 'pundit' (from the Hindi for 'learned man'), and 'shampoo' (from the Hindi for 'massage') imparted to their British users an air of cosmopolitanism. Over time, however, these alien words ripened into full-fledged English words, as awareness of their lexical origins faded with use. In general, Indian words with inanimate objects as their referents, such as 'pajamas' (from the Hindi for 'pants') and 'tank' (from the Gujarati for 'artificial pond'), were assimilated into English more seamlessly than words that had as their referents categories of people or social arrangements, such as 'thug' or 'mogul,' which were idiomatically embedded in cultural-historical contexts without parallel in English. The nineteenth-century term 'railroad mogul,' for instance, retains an aura of Oriental despotism, conjures images of India's Mughal emperors. The derogatory English word 'nabob,' which results from clumsily anglicizing *nawab* (Hindi for 'governor'), emerged in the early 1770s as a means of dismissing '*arrivistes*,' to quote historian Lawrence James, 'who had come home from India with a fortune' and 'thrust themselves into fashionable society and politics.'[31] The word suggests that the nabob's acquisition of wealth was somehow unwholesome or un-British, that it had blossomed unnaturally, in jungly profusion, beneath a tropical sun. The word also betrays the public's growing anxiety about the 'Oriental' changes that the imperial experience had wrought on the British psyche, the despotic impulses that it had brought to the surface. In 'nabob,' 'mogul,' and 'thug,' in these *foreign* words, the British confronted reflections of their own violent urges.

Taylor's Anglicized Thug

In his introduction to the 1920 edition of Taylor's *The Story of My Life*, Henry Bruce, who met the author on a voyage to India in 1875, observes that Taylor 'dwells,' in his novels, 'upon the likenesses, not the unlikenesses, between his readers and his characters.'[32] This, despite the fact that Taylor's characters, who 'can never be white,' 'go about barefooted' and 'eat with their own fingers.' Through the fog of his racist condescension, Bruce nevertheless manages to put his finger on one of the salient features of Taylor's liberal-imperial representations of India: his strategy of anglicizing rather than 'othering' his native protagonists, underscoring his characters' familiarity, their function as sites of identification rather than contrast. It is no coincidence, therefore, that both Ameer Ali and the British imperialist view themselves as morally superior to India's largely Hindu population, or that both justify their exploitation of India on economic and religious grounds. Both the imperialist and the Thug survive, in fact, in a land where they are vastly outnumbered, by bribing local functionaries and dubious rajahs, whose friendship is seasonal, whose cooperation is always precarious. The Thugs and the British often find themselves in competition for partnership with the same native princes. Ameer Ali recounts with frustration how the Rajah of Jhalone scraps his 'confederacy' with the Thugs for a 'treaty' with 'the English Government.'[33] Both the British and the Thugs are forced to look constantly over their shoulders, in paranoid anticipation of the population turning against them. Both are masters, therefore, of dissimulation and inveiglement, of masking their true agendas with claims of friendship, with promises of security and profit.

Like the British colonist, the Thug is a foreigner in India. He faces inevitable language barriers. He gets entangled in embarrassing cultural misunderstandings. Confusions abound. Like the British, Ameer Ali relies upon native informants, collecting knowledge of local customs and notables in order to master his prey. Ameer Ali's displacement, his sense of being out of place, outside India's social fabric, is reinforced by the fact that he is adopted, raised by the leader of the Thug gang that murdered his wealthy parents when he was a child. Although he is gracious, courteous to the locals he encounters, he insists upon preserving his distance. Ameer Ali possesses all the qualities of an English gentleman: he has a 'polite demeanour,' a 'smooth tongue,' and an all-important sense of 'tact.'[34] Even the novel's framing narrator, the anonymous prison official who transcribes his confession, feels compelled to inform the reader, in a friendly aside, that Ameer Ali is not only physically attractive but that his noble good looks are decidedly European. We are made to understand that the Thug has a 'strikingly handsome' 'face,' a 'broad' 'forehead,' and a 'complexion' that 'is fair for a native.'[35] 'His manner,' the police officer adds, 'is graceful, bland, and polite, – it is indeed more than gentlemanlike.'[36] This portrait of Ameer Ali echoes Taylor's description six years earlier, in an 1833 article in *The New Monthly Magazine*, of the unexpectedly gentlemanly bearing of the Thugs whom he had interviewed in captivity. 'Solicitous about their dress,' about maintaining a 'respectable' and 'decent appearance,' the Thugs, Taylor writes, 'seem to be men of mild and unobtrusive manners, possessing a cheerfulness of disposition entirely opposed to the violent passions and ferocious demeanour that are usually associated with the idea of a professed murderer.'[37]

Ameer Ali experiences India, in fact, as an English tourist would, or as a Victorian travel writer. His narrative is replete with visits to landmarks and monuments. He plays up their exoticism, sharing fragments of their lurid or tragic history with his British interlocutor. Haunted by the ambiance of the locales through which he passes, by an otherworldly energy to which he achieves only fleeting and partial access, Ameer Ali describes the sunlight dancing upon Hyderabad's 'hundreds' of 'bright gilt spire[s]' and 'slender white minarets,'[38] as well as the 'gloomy' song of the 'bats and wild pigeons, whose cooing re-echo[es] within the lofty domes' of the royal tombs at which he 'loiter[s].'[39] When his gang of Thugs approaches the 'stupendous' and 'extraordinary' rock formations that lie outside Hyderabad, shrouded in '[w]reaths of mist,' Ameer Ali turns eagerly to his Hindu guide, Bhudrinath, for a traditional Hindu account of their purportedly divine origin.[40] An amateur Orientalist, Ameer Ali takes periodic breaks from thugging to visit Mughal ruins, where he ponders, like Shelley in 'Ozymandias,' their warning to arrogant outsiders. 'Piles upon piles of old ruined palaces,' he reflects, 'in many places built upon the walls themselves, and all nodding to their fall,' 'were a lesson to humble proud man – to teach him that he too must moulder in the dust.'[41] He appraises the various vistas and views that the ruins afford, as if he were sharing vacation photos, rather than recounting his crimes, with his interrogator: '[F]rom the terrace out of which the huge dome proudly reared itself the view of the city was superb,' he earnestly explains, 'but it was not equal to the one I have before described to you, for we saw none of the white buildings.'[42] In his autobiography, Taylor describes touring many of the same attractions, and does so with the same enthusiasm, the same aesthetic sensitivity.

A decidedly European eye shapes Ameer Ali's descriptions of the Indian population, his accounts of the 'thickly peopled' towns, with their Eastern crowds.[43] In a passage reminiscent of De Quincey's agoraphobic hallucinations in Confessions of an English Opium Eater, Ameer Ali recounts the 'sickening' sublimity of the festival of the Mohorum, which 'pour[s]' through the narrow street' beneath his second-story window: a deindividuating chaos, a 'sea of human heads,' 'whirling' bodies 'closely wedged together,' with their 'strange and uncouth antics,' 'painted' torsos, and 'fantastic dresses.'[44] From the vantage of his window, above the 'agitated' and 'deafening' 'multitude,' above the 'blaze of a thousand blue lights,' the Thug watches in horror as a 'mad-dened' elephant, scorched by a wayward torch, 'rush[es] into the crowd,' 'seize[s] an unfortunate wretch by the waist,' and 'dash[es] him against the ground.' Ameer Ali repeatedly contrasts his own bodily coherence with the herd mentality of the natives. As his gang push their way through the Mohorum crowd, their foreignness becomes manifest: they find themselves 'exposed' 'to the jeers and abuse of the multitude,' 'recognised' from their 'dress and language' 'as strangers.'[45] The deindividuating multitude, with its tendency to liquefy all distinctions, is literalized for Ameer Ali when he sur-veys a riverbank from atop a bridge, beholds 'the various and motley groups in the bed of the river': 'there were thousands assembled; the banks of the river and the bed were full, – so full, it seemed as if you might have walked upon the heads of the multitude.'[46]

Ameer Ali's foreignness is reinforced by his religion. He identifies, after all, not with India's predominantly Hindu population but with its Mughal invaders, the Muslim forerunners of East India Company bureaucrats. Ameer Ali's father even links the origin of Thuggee to the 'invasion by our forefathers of India.'[47] Sleeman, too, advances a similar theory of Thuggee's foreign origin: '[I]f, as I have been informed, Arabia and Persia be infested by Phansigars [or Thugs], little room is left to doubt that these murderers came along with the Moham-medan conquerors into India, and that they have followed the progress south-ward of the Mohammedan arms.'[48] Not surprisingly, Ameer Ali contrasts his own nobility with 'the present degeneracy,' with the 'mean and sordid' charac-ter, of 'the present miserable generation,' a 'degenerate race.'[49] He repeatedly laments the 'superstitious fear' plaguing not only the population at large but some of the less sophisticated members of his own gang.[50] He conceives of him-self as 'a scourge' on India's 'wickedness,' an enforcer of divine law, for 'the hand of Alla,' he muses, 'was upon all our doings.'[51] Ameer Ali delivers 'retrib-utive justice,' as he calls it, to a Pindharee soldier who brutally tortures an old man by meticulously wrapping the man's fingers and hands in oil-soaked cloth, before setting them on fire.[52] Like the British, in fact, who famously suppress the Pindharee armies during the Bentinck administration, Ameer Ali views Pindharees as a decidedly 'wicked set.'[53] Disgusted at the sight of native police officials torturing a bandit, who is forced to inhale 'burning-hot ashes' before 'both sinews of his legs' 'above the heels' are 'cut,' Ameer Ali and his comrade congratulate themselves upon their own relative humanity: '[I]t makes me sick; what a contrast this is to our work, where he who is to die scarcely knows that the handkerchief is about his neck before he is a dead man!'[54]

The line between Ameer Ali and the British all but disintegrates by novel's end, once the captured Thug turns informant and then undercover agent for the

British, leading a party of his captors to one of the secret 'lurking-places' of a notorious Thug.[55] Temporarily released from prison in order to lead his captors to the hideout, Ameer Ali, though shackled, is given a sword and six men with which to subdue the wanted man. In chains, with a weapon at his side, he is prisoner and police officer in one, an embodiment of the blurring line between British law and Thuggee. Likewise, the six soldiers, who have been carefully disguised as Thugs, guard Ameer Ali, prevent his escape, but also follow his orders. He aligns himself politically and psychologically with the counter-Thuggee enterprise, conflating himself grammatically with his British captors: if he 'ever escaped from *us*,' Ameer Ali assures his captors, 'I alone could tell where he was to be found.'[56]

Earlier in the novel, in a metafictional exchange between captive and captor, between Thug and framing narrator, Ameer Ali's mirror-like quality becomes manifest. Waiting for Ameer Ali to collect his thoughts, the narrator takes the opportunity to provide the reader with a detailed account of his prisoner's physical appearance, which, as we have already witnessed, is graceful and attractive. 'Reader, if you can embody these descriptions, you have Ameer Ali before you; and while you gaze on the picture in your imagination and look on the mild and expressive face you may have fancied, you, as I was, would be the last person to think that he was a professed murderer.'[57] Ameer Ali asks unexpectedly to hear the narrator's description. It is the only time during the interview that he has shown any interest in what his interrogator has written about him. His request granted, he compliments a momentarily disoriented and somewhat self-conscious narrator: 'It is a faithful picture, such as I behold myself when I look in a glass.'[58] For a fleeting moment – a moment, however, that reverberates throughout the text – Ameer Ali seizes hold of his own representation in the imperial metanarrative, turning his objectification at the hands of his captor into a vehicle for narcissistic reflection, a mirror in which his own physique and the narrator's descriptive powers are mutually flattered, affirmatively entangled, made to reflect each other. In a flash of self-recognition and guilty pleasure, the narrator sees in Ameer Ali's narcissism *himself* in the act of narrating, watches himself watching. Already hailed, the reader, too, is implicated in this hall of mirrors, for, in listening to the narrator's sketch, in scrutinizing Taylor's words, Ameer Ali becomes for an instant the text's audience, another one of its silent spectators.

The Carceral Context

By way of concluding, I would like to turn our attention to the materiality of Ameer Ali's confession. What made *Confessions of a Thug* so popular with nineteenth-century readers was its self-proclaimed realism, the aura of authenticity and urgency that accrued around its unknown author, who insisted somewhat disingenuously that he wrote the novel not to entertain, not to make money, but to alert the public to the reality of Thuggee. In the manner of a fictionalized 'leaked memo,' the novel recreates for its readers the sensation of perusing an official government document, and it replicates the formal and rhetorical conventions of two confessional genres that operated within the nineteenth-century British criminal justice system. First and foremost it is a deposition, the written record of a witness's out-of-court testimony. It will be used presumably to apprehend, prosecute, and convict other Thugs. In exchange for their cooperation, Thug informants or 'approvers,' as they were called, were often spared the death penalty. Second, it is a fictional example of the moral interrogations, the exercises in criminal self-analysis, that were adopted by an increasing number of British penitentiaries in the 1830s and 1840s to gauge the redemptive potential and moral self-awareness of hardened criminals.[59] Ameer Ali's narrative fluctuates stylistically between these two confessional genres. On the one hand, *Confessions of a Thug* is the blood-soaked deposition of a criminal, a litany of murder and braggadocio that takes the form of an adventure story. On the other hand, it is a conversion narrative, a *Bildungsroman* of sorts, in which a subject – almost in spite of himself – meditates upon the consequences of his life choices.

Taylor only fleetingly describes the material reality of the prison in which Ameer Ali is giving his confession. At the beginning of the text, for instance, the Thug asks for and is granted a drink of water. Swept up in the recitation of a childhood memory, Ameer Ali 'got up,' we are informed, 'and walked across the room, his irons clanking as he moved.'[60] As the novel progresses, however, Ameer Ali's irrepressible chattiness and the prison official's relative passivity have the effect of dematerializing the prison, drowning out its sights and sounds, including those irons, in the convivial and seemingly unmediated stream of discourse that flows for forty-nine chapters from Indian mouth to English ear. Perhaps because Taylor himself downplays the material reality of his novel's carceral setting, criticism on *Confessions of a Thug* tends to do so, too, either brushing past its meta-setting with a cursory nod of the head, or abstracting it even further, viewing Taylor's prison interrogation conceit as a metaphor for the panoptic logic of British imperialism. By reading the text not merely as an imperial novel but as a *prison* novel, by taking into account the historical particularity of confessional technologies in the context of British carceral reforms in the 1830s and 1840s, we can recapture the historical materiality of imprisonment in *Confessions of a Thug* – a materiality that operates, as I've said, at the level of *form* in the novel.

As Sean C. Grass has documented, in the wake of the Prisons Bill of 1839 – the year, not coincidentally, when Taylor's novel was published – new disciplinary technologies aimed at individualizing 'the reformative endeavor' were implemented throughout the British penal system. Prisoners were placed in isolation, encouraged to contemplate 'the origins of [their] criminality' and 'the commission of [their] crime[s].' Endless acts of self-narration would trigger (so the theory went) their 'moral reformation.'[61] If literate, they were asked to pen their own psychological-sociological self-studies. If illiterate, they recited their life stories to the prison chaplain or schoolmaster, who assiduously transcribed their words. The goal was to instil prisoners with an ethic of contemplation, an epistemology of the self, which would echo therapeutically in their heads, nurtured by the monastic silence of their cells. In the early and mid-1840s, the Reverend John Clay – a prison reformer and chaplain of Preston Gaol – collected hundreds of pages of these 'short narratives' of 'self-examination,' as he termed them, many of which were dictated to him, and which detail prisoners' 'lives, their delinquencies, their self-convictions, and their penitence.'[62] Needless to say, these innovations in incarceration did not extend to Britain's vast network of overseas colonial prisons and penal colonies. In India, captured Thugs met very different fates than the 'Anglo-Saxon' men from 'the labouring classes' with whom Clay worked. According to historian Clare Anderson, Thugs were either executed or 'transported' by the East India Company to the island of Mauritius, where they were 'employed within the expanding plantation economy,' in other words, where they served as slaves.[63]

That the reform-minded Taylor spares Ameer Ali this fate and instead subjects him to the regime of didactic self-contemplation that was foisted upon *British* convicts in *English* penitentiaries, has the *prima facie* effect not just of anglicizing the Thug but of suggesting, in the face of his stubborn incorrigibility, that even *he* is redeemable, that his criminality – and that criminality more generally – is the product of environment, of nurture rather than nature. Prison reform, indeed, the very logic of *reform*, is premised on the assumption that criminals are made not born, that improved material conditions, both in the prison and in society at large, will inevitably produce a better class of people. It is not that Taylor wants to reform Thugs. Nor does he want to implement in India Britain's penitentiary experiments. Rather, by imagining a scenario in which a Thug performs a carceral self-study, with its assumptions about the *social* origins of crime and the protean nature of man, Taylor launches a sweeping political attack against British mismanagement in India, shifting the debate from the Thug's moral character to the colonial conditions that cause Thuggee to proliferate in the first place. Though the purpose of the carceral self-study is therapeutic self-incrimination, ownership of one's crime, the triggering of guilt *within the prisoner*, these documents also provide prison reformers with a vicarious and equally therapeutic experience of guilt. Reformers read in the faces of prisoners the fruits of their own broken criminal-justice system, of a flawed and mismanaged society. The prisoner's self-study, then, constitutes a site of guilty reciprocity, cathartic self-blame, between prisoner and prison administrator. Prisoners became, in the eyes of reformers, *reflections* of the failings of Britain's penal system, symptoms of its structural deficiencies, and opportunities for its redemption.

In his prison reports from the 1840s, Clay captures perfectly the self-flagellating yet messianic logic of reform that Taylor invokes in an imperial context. Clay's reports are not meditations upon the moral failings of criminals so much as passionate denunciations of the broken prison system that his reforms attempt at the local level to fix. He views prisoners as victims of a dubious philosophy of incarceration, their criminality the product of its implementation. Many of them had been inmates in the older penal institutions, in which prisoners, instead of being confined separately, were forced to live together, forming societies and gangs – one vast 'finishing school of crime,' a house of 'vicious education.' 'It was once a truth so fully recognized as to be proverbial,' he writes, that *'a criminal came out of prison worse than when he came in.'*[64] It is a favourite formulation of reformers. It echoes through the corridors of their writings. It makes an appearance, for instance, in Charles Reade's classic prison reform novel, *It Is Never Too Late to Mend* (1856): 'Under the old [system], the jail was a finishing school for felony and petty larceny. Under the new, it is intended to be a penal hospital for diseased and contagious souls.'[65] Prison is the disease from which the criminal suffers; it is his only hope for a cure. Such is the logic of liberal guilt. I oppress you; I save you. It is the logic, too, of Philip Meadows Taylor's *Confessions of a Thug*, of his imperial *prison* novel. In an Indian man's confession, in *a mirror*, a white man catches guilty glimpses of himself, then pledges to India: 'I will rescue you from myself.' I am your disease; I am your cure. Taylor's self-incriminating liberal imperialism is more dangerous, in some ways, than the genocidal logic of white supremacy to which it presents itself as moral corrective, as ideological antidote. *That*, at least, we do not mistake for progress.

NOTES

1 See Patrick Brantlinger, *Rule of Darkness: British Literature and Imperialism, 1830–1914* (Ithaca, NY: Cornell University Press, 1988), 86–90. From the Hindi verb *thugna* (to deceive), 'Thuggee,' as the British termed it, was a secret religious

cult whose adherents stalked unwitting wayfarers before strangling them with a silk handkerchief or *roomal*. Though victims, who bodies were expertly buried and often never discovered, were nominally sacrificed to Kali, the Hindu goddess of destruction, who was also called Bhowanee or Devi, Thuggee nonetheless attracted a significant number of Muslim adherents, Muslim Thugs purportedly believing that Kali functioned as an instrument of Allah's will. Though criminal gangs certainly existed in late-eighteenth- and early-nineteenth-century India, some historians argue that Thuggee is more a colonial ideological construct than a historical reality, in much the same way that 'Islamic terrorism' functions today as an unparticularized catch-all, a convenient metaphor for any and all guerilla activity by Muslims against Western economic and military interests.

2 See Parama Roy, 'Discovering India, Imagining *Thuggee*,' *Yale Journal of Criticism* 9 (1996): 121–3. See also Shuchi Kapila, 'Educating Seeta: Philip Meadows Taylor's Romances of Empire,' *Victorian Studies* 41 (1998): 216, and Javed Majeed, 'Meadows Taylor's *Confessions of a Thug*: The Anglo-Indian Novel as a Genre in the Making,' in *Writing India 1757–1900*, ed. Bart Gilbert-Moore (Manchester: Manchester University Press, 1996), 86–110.

3 See Mary Poovey, 'Ambiguity and Historicism: Interpreting *Confessions of a Thug*,' *Narrative* 12 (2004): 4.

4 Elizabeth Barrett Browning, *Aurora Leigh*, ed. Kerry McSweeney (Oxford: Oxford University Press, 1993), 4.754–5; emphasis added.

5 Philip Meadows Taylor, *Confessions of a Thug* (1839), ed. and intro. Patrick Brantlinger (Oxford: Oxford University Press, 1998), 15.

6 Robert Grant Williams, 'Shadows of Imperialism: Canonical Typology in Taylor's *Confessions of a Thug*,' *Dalhousie Review* 72 (1992–3): 485.

7 Brantlinger, *Rule of Darkness*, 88–9.

8 Homi K. Bhabha, *The Location of Culture* (London: Routledge, 1994), 127.

9 Taylor, *Confessions of a Thug*, 442.

10 Ibid., 393.

11 See Gayatri Chakravorty Spivak, 'Can the Subaltern Speak?' in *Colonial Discourse and Post-Colonial Theory: A Reader*, ed. Patrick Williams and Laura Chrisman (New York: Columbia University Press, 1994), 93.

12 Taylor, *Confessions of a Thug*, 12.

13 Philip Meadows Taylor, 'The State of Thuggee in India,' *British and Foreign Review* 15 (1843): 279.

14 Henry Reeve, preface to *The Story of My Life* (1877), by Philip Meadows Taylor (London: Oxford University Press, 1920), xxxvii.

15 Ibid., xxxvi.

16 Kate Teltscher, *India Inscribed: European and British Writing on India, 1600–1800* (Delhi and Bombay: Oxford University Press, 1995), 127.

17 William Henry Sleeman, *The Thugs or Phansigars of India: Comprising a History of the Rise and Progress of that Extraordinary Fraternity of Assassins*, 2 vols. (Philadelphia: Carey and Hart, 1839), 1:38.
18 Taylor, *Confessions of a Thug*, 36.
19 Sleeman, *The Thugs*, 1:51.
20 Ibid., 1:52.
21 Edward Thornton, *Illustrations of the History and Practices of the Thugs* (London: William H. Allen, 1837), 328.
22 Ibid., 334.
23 Ibid., 467.
24 Taylor, 'State of Thuggee,' 285.
25 Philip Meadows Taylor, *The Story of My Life* (1877) (London: Oxford University Press, 1920), 199, 230, 232.
26 Sleeman, *The Thugs*, 1:57.
27 Ibid., 1:58.
28 Poovey, 'Ambiguity and Historicism,' 14.
29 George A. Sala, 'The Key of the Street,' *Household Words* 3 (September 1851): 571.
30 Wendy S. Jacobson, 'John Jasper and Thuggee,' *Modern Language Review* 72 (1977): 527.
31 Lawrence James, *Raj: The Making and Unmaking of British India* (New York: St Martin's/Griffin, 1997), 45.
32 Henry Bruce, introduction to Taylor, *The Story of My Life*, xviii.
33 Taylor, *Confessions of a Thug*, 492.
34 Ibid., 90.
35 Ibid., 265.
36 Ibid., 266.
37 Philip Meadows Taylor, 'On the Thugs,' *New Monthly Magazine* 38 (July 1833): 286.
38 Taylor, *Confessions of a Thug*, 164.
39 Ibid., 227.
40 Ibid., 160.
41 Ibid., 238.
42 Ibid., 227.
43 Ibid., 164.
44 Ibid., 177–9.
45 Ibid., 166.
46 Ibid., 182.
47 Ibid., 48.
48 Sleeman, *The Thugs*, 1:48.
49 Taylor, *Confessions of a Thug*, 239, 226–7.

50 Ibid., 413.
51 Ibid., 72–3.
52 Ibid., 375.
53 Ibid., 388.
54 Ibid., 150, 152.
55 Ibid., 544.
56 Ibid., 544; emphasis added.
57 Ibid., 266.
58 Ibid., 267.
59 See also the contributions by Sean C. Grass and Anna Schur in this collection.
60 Taylor, *Confessions of a Thug*, 20.
61 Sean C. Grass, *The Self in the Cell: Narrating the Victorian Prisoner* (New York: Routledge, 2003), 31.
62 Walter Lowe Clay, *The Prison Chaplain: A Memoir of the Rev. John Clay* (1861; Montclair, NJ: Patterson Smith, 1969), 274.
63 Clare Anderson, 'The Genealogy of the Modern Subject: Indian Convicts in Mauritius, 1814–1853,' in *Representing Convicts: New Perspectives on Convict Forced Labour Migration*, ed. Ian Duffield and James Bradley (London: Leicester University Press, 1997), 164.
64 Clay, *The Prison Chaplain*, 272; emphasis in original.
65 Charles Reade, *It Is Never Too Late to Mend* (1856; Whitefish, MT: Kessinger, 2004), 113. See also the second part of Jeremy Tambling's contribution to this volume.

4 'Now, now, the door was down': Dickens and Excarceration, 1841–2

ADAM HANSEN

> Let it be impressed upon our readers that the existing question is, not between this
> system and the old abuses of the old profligate Gaols (with which, thank Heaven,
> we have nothing to do), but between this system and the associated silent system.[1]

By the time Charles Dickens published these lines in April 1850, it may have
been true that he, like his country, had 'nothing to do' with the 'old profligate
Gaols.' Yet nine years before, Dickens had issued *Barnaby Rudge*, a novel animated by the destruction of the typically 'profligate' Newgate Prison in 1780.
Equally, along with many other commentators on penal policy, Dickens knew
that in the 1850s the 'old abuses' still existed despite reforms, alongside many
new abuses caused *by* reforms. Dickens's parentheses are therefore disingenuous: he seems to acknowledge and repress the awareness that while new prisons appeared to have spatial and moral integrity, they only partially solved a
long-standing problem; similarly, despite Dickens's attempt to make the
phases of penal practice discrete, he knew no such separation was possible.

The penal practice favoured by the British government from the mid-1830s
onwards was termed the 'separate' system. This system was intended to keep
prisoners in solitary confinement, while they studied the Bible or laboured.
The authoritarian Dickens reviled it, not because of any mental anguish
inmates suffered, but because it was insufficiently punitive. As he put it in 'Pet
Prisoners,' the 'separate' system encouraged and indulged alienated egotism,
'pattern penitence,' and 'assumed repentance.'[2] By individuating prisoners,
the system had deleterious consequences for their moral state and the possibility of their proper reformation:

> A strange absorbing selfishness – a spiritual egotism and vanity, real or assumed
> – is the first result. It is remarkable to observe, in the case of murderers who

become this kind of object of interest, when they are at last consigned to the condemned cell, how the rule is ... that the murdered person disappears from the
stage of their thoughts, except as a part of their own important story; and how
they occupy the whole scene. *I* did this, *I* feel that, *I* confide in the mercy of
Heaven being extended to *me*; ... I don't want the forgiveness of this foully murdered person's bereaved wife, husband, brother, sister, child, friend; I don't ask
for it, I don't care for it. I make no enquiry of the clergyman concerning the salvation of that murdered person's soul; *mine* is the matter.[3]

Yet Dickens also deplored this system because the isolation it deemed necessary for improvement was actually counterproductive. Solitary confinement
failed to inculcate in inmates any sense of the intersubjective sympathy or
affiliation (strongly suggesting familial relations) that Dickens considered
fundamental to reforming the deviant and uniting the social body. Ultimately,
the 'separate' or 'solitary' system denied the very bonds of community upon
which Dickens perceived moral life to be based. Dickens himself attempted to
cultivate such familial and emotive bonds when petitioning 'fallen women' to
consider submitting to the benevolence of Urania Cottage by imagining himself as one of them: 'I mean nothing but kindness to you, and I write as if you
were my sister.'[4]

Such instances indicate that to Dickens writing – narrative and creative
imagining – could recreate the bonds threatened by social dissolution and
moral degeneracy. While the nineteenth century's copious jeremiads indicated
that the world was breaking up, Dickens made an effort to comprehend and
respond to the problems of connection in the 'superstructure.'[5] Writing in his
Memoranda, Dickens was clearly intoxicated by the idea that, as medium and
as communication, he might synergize disparate peoples and places with
unprecedented immediacy: 'Open a story by bringing two strongly contrasted
places and strongly contrasted sets of people, into the connexion necessary for
the story, by means of an electric message. Describe the message – *be* the
message – flashing along through space – over the earth, and under the sea.'[6]

As Raymond Williams affirmed, Dickens relentlessly strove to contrive
this comprehensive connection in the social and symbolic architecture of his
fiction.[7] Developing such ideas, Allon White offered the reading of connection that is perhaps most useful for thinking about the kinds of connections
Dickens creates in his representations of prisons. White suggested that there
were (at least) two senses of 'connection' relevant to Dickens. One is 'the
order of narrative and chronological connection (coherence, continuity)'; the
other is 'the nineteenth-century form of the word, "connection," those private, intersubjective links between people bound by consanguinity, kinship,

and close friendships.' Ultimately, these two meanings 'coalesce,' 'so that narrative and logical connection are inextricably joined to intersubjective connection, of which "natural" family bonds are the highest type.'[8] White identifies this in *Bleak House* (1852–3). But such narrative imagining could also re-constitute the bonds threatened by the 'separate' system.

The destruction of Newgate in *Barnaby Rudge* might thus be seen to fantastically obliterate what was dysfunctional about the 'old' prisons. But this is a reductive reading. Destruction *is* brought about by chaotic forces that threaten the stability of society as a whole. Yet, perversely, as will become clear, the destruction of Newgate and the excarceration it involves actually exemplify the permeable, incontinent qualities of the 'old profligate' prisons, to restore the very social bonds that the *new* prisons threaten.

In both 1842 and 1850 Dickens offers an alternative to both 'profligate' and 'separate' prisons, with the quality of a compromise: the associated 'silent' system. In 'Pet Prisoners,' Dickens argues that this system is 'less objectionable' than the 'separate' system because it is 'severe,' 'much less expensive,' 'and not calculated to pamper the mind of the prisoner and swell his sense of his own importance.'[9] Yet the crucial element of association (without communication) allowed prisoners to consider how the consequences of their crimes affected others. Thus, in the associated 'silent' system a prisoner is 'preserved from contamination' while also 'still one of a society of men, and not an isolated being, filling his whole sphere of view with a diseased dilation of himself.'[10] This system, in other words, excised excrescent, unhealthy, distended immoral growths, thereby curing the individual as well as the social corpus. As Thomas Carlyle asserted in *Past and Present* (1843): 'Men cannot live isolated: we *are* all bound together, for mutual good or else for mutual misery, as living nerves in the same body.'[11]

By realizing moments of excarceration, Dickens's narratives create connections. These connections work against the discrimination and separations enforced by new modes of incarceration (as in the 'solitary' prison Dickens visited in Philadelphia). Yet Dickens realizes these connections with such power that they threaten the integrity of the type of incarceration he did advocate. Thus, what seems to be a critique of the 'separate' system actually also records Dickens's anxieties about the associated 'silent' system.[12] These anxieties are conceived precisely in terms of the narrative-familial connections Dickens did so much to cultivate in 1841–2, connections revived and made more pressing by his prison writing in the 1850s.

After outlining the notion of 'excarceration,' this paper combines historical detail with close textual analysis to explore how Dickens realizes excarceration in *Barnaby Rudge*, in *American Notes* (1842), and in 'Pet Prisoners'

(1850). This involves situating these realizations in the 'now' of a specific historical moment in English penal policy and Dickens's work, but also suggests that what Dickens says about any given 'now' resonates in other phases of his writing.

Excarceration and Dickens

With the publication of *Surveiller et punir: Naissance de la prison* (translated into English as *Discipline and Punish: The Birth of the Prison* in 1977), Michel Foucault offered a rereading of the history of 'the birth of the prison' that was as polemical as it was influential. For as historians, criminologists, sociologists, anthropologists, and cultural critics have realized, Foucault described more than the genesis of a particular institution. He analysed an interrelated range of material and ideological structures: 'Prison continues, on those who are entrusted to it, a work begun elsewhere, which the whole of society pursues on each individual through innumerable mechanisms of discipline.'[13] With their factories, schools, and penal institutions, Western societies operated on the basis of a 'carceral continuum': 'the power to punish is not essentially different from that of curing or educating.'[14] Disciplining institutions had the power to contain transgression; moreover, they had the capacity to create transgression that necessitated containment: 'The carceral network does not cast the unassimilable into a confused hell; there is no outside ... In this panoptic society of which incarceration is the omnipresent armature, the delinquent is not outside the law; he is, from the very outset, in the law, at the very heart of the law ... The delinquent is an institutional product.'[15] Foucault historicized his analyses by describing the development of this 'carceral continuum' as a process that began in the early modern period as a means to counter the 'momentary saturnalia' and 'centres of illegality' generated by events such as public execution, an 'uncertain festival in which violence was instantaneously reversible' and in which 'rules were inverted, authority mocked and criminals transformed into heroes.'[16] Penal and punitive processes were now involved in separating the condemned from the innocent and the licit from the illicit. Foucault traced this process as it took new forms in the eighteenth century: 'The "Enlightenment," which discovered the liberties, also invented the disciplines.'[17] As Foucault described it, discipline became ever more insidious, pervasive, and subtle, as society became putatively more civilized. Reform was actually a new means of control in a great confinement, whether embodied in Jeremy Bentham's *Panopticon; Or the Inspection House* (1787) or in progressive French movements in the early nineteenth century. By this period, the role of discipline in discriminating criminals from everyone else had assumed comprehensively material and ideological forms. In the prisons demanded by nineteenth-century European reformers, separation within prisons and between prisoners and all others, was paramount: 'The first principle was isolation. The isolation of the convict from the external world, from everything that motivated the offence, from the complicities that facilitated it. The isolation of the prisoners from one another.'[18]

Forceful as Foucault's analyses were, in *Discipline and Punish* and elsewhere, they have not gone uncontested, primarily because of the determinism inherent to the historical narrative he proposes, and in the power and prevalence of the confinements he identifies. Thus, one of Foucault's most cogent challenges came from the historian Peter Linebaugh in *The London Hanged: Crime and Civil Society in the Eighteenth Century* (1991). Looking specifically at the period from the early eighteenth century to the early nineteenth century, Linebaugh examines 'the growing propensity, skill and success of London working people in escaping from the newly created institutions that were designed to discipline people by closing them in.' Linebaugh goes on to offer his own definition of this 'counter-tendency' to Foucault's description of a great incarceration: 'excarceration.'[19] If confinement isolates and discriminates, excarceration causes or reveals connections between people and places that authorities and ideologies try to keep separate. It is transgressive, associative, confusing. The revolutionary implications and bases of excarceration were especially evident in the exploits of the prison-breaker Jack Sheppard in the early 1720s: 'Sheppard's escapes were compared to the revolutionary activities of the Levellers. Sheppard's partner went on to help found the Sons of Liberty, the revolutionary organization in New York.'[20]

Yet for Linebaugh, these revolutionary, excarceratory impulses that could not be confined were also apparent in the delivery of Newgate Prison during the Gordon Riots of 4–9 June 1780. The 'liberation' of 'hundreds of prisoners' then was an 'extension' of the impulse Sheppard embodied 'from an individual to a mass scale.'[21] Given that 'the overwhelming majority' of those liberated were imprisoned for 'crimes against property,' such as housebreaking, it is clear to Linebaugh that the riots and the assault on Newgate exemplified a whole social system based on the incontinence of material boundaries: 'The delivery of Newgate demonstrated some weaknesses in the practice of confinement. Many of those delivered had demonstrated weaknesses in the practice of locking things up.'[22]

But what has all this historiography and penal theory got to do with Dickens? On a general level, as many critics have shown, Dickens was preoccupied by prisons. Following his father's incarceration in the Marshalsea debtors' prison in 1824, this preoccupation was personal. Yet his preoccupation was also publicly and extensively evident in his fictional and non-fictional works, texts animated by what Philip Collins termed a 'novel-tradition of rogues and villains,' and texts that intervened in the nineteenth century's ongoing debates about penal policy.[23]

By focusing on the years 1841–2, this paper will examine a specific period in penal policy, and Dickens's responses to it. Pentonville Prison was built in 1840–2, as Dickens was publishing *Barnaby Rudge*, leaving England to visit the United States, and writing and publishing *American Notes*. Pentonville was intended as a place where men sentenced to transportation to Australia would serve probation. It was designed, then, to respond to the nineteenth century's ongoing and habitual crises of crime, prisons, and their populations; as Donald Thomas notes, in 1841, 25.6 per cent of all those committed to prison were reoffenders.[24] As Michael Ignatieff and Robin Evans have shown, and as reformers including Dickens complained, prior to the innovations of Pentonville, the 'old' prisons were afflicted by material permeability and moral dissolution.[25] Corruption was rife, with people and things passing in and out of supposedly continent penal institutions with outrageous ease. Pentonville therefore employed the 'separate' system, in which, according to the Surveyor-General of Prisons, 'each individual prisoner is confined in a cell, which becomes his workshop by day and his bed-room by night, so as to be effectually prevented from holding communication with, or even being seen sufficiently to be recognized by other prisoners.'[26]

However, such innovations were so desperately sought precisely because the incontinence that afflicted the 'old' prisons was still blatantly manifest in the first half of the nineteenth century, not least in the rebuilt Newgate, which was only modernized in 1858–60, and in operation until 1880. Thus, in 1836, one Henry Williams escaped from Newgate, despite looming granite walls, spiked railings, and guards.[27] Degeneracy prevailed there: an official inspection in 1835–6 found inmates 'giddy drunk.'[28] A report of 1836 lamented what happened to felons when incarcerated: 'Instead of seclusion, his time is passed in the midst of a body of criminals of every class and degree, in riot, debauchery, and gaming, vaunting his own adventures, or listening to those of others; communicating his own skill and aptitude in crime, or acquiring the lessons of greater adepts. He has access to newspapers ... He is allowed intercourse with prostitutes ... Having thus passed his time, he returns a greater adept in crime.'[29] From this overview of a specific period in English penological history, it is clear that as Dickens engaged in the protracted genesis of *Barnaby Rudge*, excarceration still existed though it was being countered by ever more intensive mechanisms of incarceration. In the novel, Dickens reflects on this historically specific dynamic, by envisioning the events of another historical

period: the Gordon Riots, complete with prison-breaking and multiple violations of spatial boundaries. With *Barnaby Rudge*, Dickens realizes certain
problems of and anxieties about prisons, problems and anxieties that were pertinent both to his own personal history and that of his historical context. Moreover, he does this most spectacularly in a text that purports to be a historical
novel. Crucially, then, the way he writes about prisons in this period at once
sustains and dissolves the differences between historical moments and spatial
locations. Indeed, just as the bounds of the prisons he describes in that novel
are transgressed and broken, so his reflections on prisons, like Henry Williams,
cannot necessarily be contained to one moment or location. A passage from
another of Dickens's novels (published in 1838–9) fittingly emphasizes this
mobility: 'There, at the very core of London, in the heart of its business and
animation, in the midst of a whirl of noise and motion: stemming as it were
the giant currents of life that flow ceaselessly on from different quarters, and
meet beneath its walls, stands Newgate.'[30] In this description, from *Nicholas
Nickleby*, Newgate Prison is shown standing stock-still and seemingly impervious to the world outside. As incarceration incarnate, it is a deathly stoppage, a
blockage, the end of flow, of vitality, of circulation. Yet as excarceration
embodied, the prison is also 'in the heart' and 'at the core' of the city: it com-
pels circulation, exchange, and connection.

In *The Novel and the Police*, D.A. Miller has argued that, with Dickens, 'the
English novel for the first time features a massive thematization of social discipline.'[31] This casts Dickens as a kind of representative of the confining energies Foucault identified. While we may choose to qualify such an assertion, it
is unarguable that discipline of one sort or another is codified in Dickens's
works.[32] Indeed, in many ways his writings on prisons in 1841–2 offer explicit
and latent formulations of this discipline. However, while these writings incar-
cerate, and show how politically and morally necessary such incarceration can
be, they also excarcerate. As the passage from *Nicholas Nickleby* indicates,
Dickens's prisons are at once powerful and permeable, and he realizes them in
ways that separate and connect those confined in them with those outside,
including himself.

Barnaby Rudge: Excarceration Here and Now

Philip Collins notes that *Barnaby Rudge* should have been Dickens's 'first
published novel, not his fifth.'[33] As early as May 1836 Dickens accepted £200
from John Macrone for a work to be called 'Gabriel Vardon, the locksmith of
London.'[34] Yet the renamed work was not released until 1841, under a different publisher. If the publication history and Dickens's conflict with Richard

Bentley are convoluted, so was Dickens's conception of the story. He worked on it fitfully, mulling over and rejecting ideas while writing and publishing *Oliver Twist* (1837–9), *Nicholas Nickleby*, and *The Old Curiosity Shop* (1840–1). Hence, while some critics have usefully explored the implications of conceiving *Barnaby Rudge* as a 'historical novel' (notably John Bowen and Patrick Brantlinger),[35] it has been equally profitably recontextualized in relation to the social-critical agendas of Dickens's works of the 'Angry Thirties.'

Thus, whether the politics of *Barnaby Rudge* are conservative or radical, that the novel is political is manifest. When Dickens wrote to Charles Ollier on 3 June 1841, regarding the representation of Lord Gordon in the novel, he employed a nicely negative construction that encapsulates the ambivalence he inscribed: 'As to the riot, I am going to see if I can't make a better one than he did.'[36] A reading that does not seek to terminate such ambivalence, but to sustain it, might consider how this ambivalence is borne out in Dickens's representations of prisons in the novel.

Perhaps *because* of this cultivated riotousness, *Barnaby Rudge* insistently reminds readers of the differences between the period described in the narrative and the period in which the narrative is described. The novel's opening paragraph remarks that 'sixty-six years ago' a 'vast number' of people 'could neither read nor write.'[37] That readers in the early to mid-1800s could understand the text at all, in a widely available and popular format such as *Master Humphrey's Clock*, affirms the difference with the late 1700s. London was different too: large parts of what is 'now' the city had 'no existence.' More houses had gardens in these as yet undeveloped areas. As such, there was 'an air of freshness breathing up and down, which in these days would be sought in vain.'[38] If the capital was less noisome in parts during the day, it was more obscure in others at night, and therefore presented 'to the eye something so very different in character from the reality which is witnessed in these times.' Indeed, 'it would be difficult for the beholder to recognise his most familiar walks in the altered aspect of little more than half a century ago.' Many 'courts and lanes' are 'left in total darkness.' Even the 'lightest thoroughfares' invariably lead 'at every turn' to 'some obscure and dangerous spot whither a thief might fly for shelter.'[39] Characters are conscious of temporal disjunction too, as this exchange between Dennis and Lord Gordon's secretary suggests: '"And in times to come," pursued the hangman, "if our grandsons should think of their grandfathers times, and find these things altered, they'll say 'Those were days indeed, and we've been going down hill ever since.' – Won't they Muster Gashford?"'[40] Given that the feckless apprentice Simon Tappertit also desires and promises an 'altered state of society,' it is evident that such changes are not necessarily for the better.[41] Some differences are good; some are bad; some are credible, others are depicted wryly.

By conceiving this temporal and topographic difference in terms of illegibility and impenetrability, the novel might then be considered a 'dark history' akin to that suspected by the locksmith Gabriel Varden when he encounters a figure we learn is Barnaby Rudge's murderous father.[42] Yet Dickens found history's darkness and distance tantalizing. Comparably, the novel's 'omniscient' narration might be seen to regulate the deviant forces the account unleashes, but it is only partially successful in doing so, not least because it admits the necessity of regulation. As Peter Garrett notes in *The Victorian Multiplot Novel*: 'the moments which epitomize this need for a distanced, inclusive point of view present scenes of threatening yet fascinating violence: the need for distance is psychological as well as epistemological.'[43] The possibility of losing control, and denuding the integrity of an identity that might guarantee such control, shadows the connecting gaze of the 'omniscient' narrator. Hence Dickens's description of his narratorial position, in a letter to John Landseer (5 November 1841): 'No looker-on from a window at the struggle in the street, beheld an Individual, or anything but a great mass of magistrates, rioters, and soldiery, all mixed up together. Being always in one or other of these positions, my object has been to convey an idea of multitudes, violence, and fury; and even to lose my own dramatis personae in the throng, or only see them dimly, through the fire and smoke.'[44] Thus, just as order and disorder are simultaneously realized by the narrative, so by constantly remarking on the distance between the past and present the narrative seems to simultaneously make that past both less and more legible. *Barnaby Rudge* recognizes but also mitigates darkness, confusion, and difference.

When, then, is the 'now' of this 'dark history'? Thinking about this issue is important, because it frames the way Dickens deals with prisons in the book, and illuminates the quote in the title of this paper: 'Now, now, the door was down.'[45] The passive voice of this phrase obscures agency and involvement – including Dickens's – yet the agency is evident. The repeated 'now' intensifies the action, conveying a sense of the unstoppable rhythmic energy and immediacy of the attack. Yet the repetition also evokes a sense of sequence and connection, a patterning and echo compounded by the assonance with 'down.' One 'now' is happening, has gone, and is replaced by another 'now.' The phrase impresses upon readers that the transgression it describes is specific and localized, but also that it relates to other violations and excarcerations in other places and times. There is as much temporal continuity – *simultaneity* – as there is fragmentary instantaneity.

Does the novel simply offer a critique of or attack on the prison system in the late 1700s, or does it condemn abuses in the 1840s? The violent excarcerations Dickens performs in *Barnaby Rudge* relate to his ongoing and pervasive anxieties about incarceration, political and personal, not just his disdain for the brutalities and injustices of England's past. By cultivating what is only ever a partial sense of temporal discontinuity, Dickens can do things to prisons *of* the 1840s that a novel obviously *set in* the 1840s might not allow.

Barnaby Rudge's Prisons

At times, the novel frames prisons as unambiguously bad places: 'Who would not rather see a poor idiot happy in the sunlight, than a wise man pining in a darkened jail!'[46] Prisons are bad because, like Newgate in *Nicholas Nickleby*, they are deathly, morbid, stultifying places. Hence the description of Emma Haredale's room at the Warren, 'the liveliest room in the building': 'The chamber was sombre like the rest for the matter of that, but the presence of youth and beauty would make a prison cheerful (saving alas! that confinement withers them).'[47] Yet the novel offers more complex and ambivalent representations of prisons. Such ambivalence is registered in this description of Gabriel Varden's locksmith's workshop: 'There was nothing surly or severe in the whole scene. It seemed impossible that any one of the innumerable keys should fit a churlish strong-box or a prison-door. Cellars of beer and wine, rooms where there were fires, books, gossip, and cheering laughter – these were their proper sphere of action. Places of distrust, and cruelty and restraint, they would have left quadruple-locked for ever.'[48] As Steven Connor has suggested, *Barnaby Rudge* acknowledges the ambiguous power of keys.[49] But this passage suggests that such ambiguity extends to the locations that keys lock or open. It is sensible to ensure prison doors stay shut: they keep distrust and cruelty away from decent places like the Maypole. But prison doors cause restraint that is itself distrustful and cruel. To Connor, the 'interesting uncertainty' of this passage 'reflects Dickens' own political uncertainty regarding the question of restraint and liberty.'[50] Equally, restraint is never complete or terminal. As Connor notes, *Barnaby Rudge* realizes 'the dissolution of space and its construction.'[51]

Befitting the novel's Gothic tenor, in *Barnaby Rudge* the intangible and the material coalesce, and much that seems substantial dematerializes. In a 'high wind,' Varden sees London literally disintegrating: 'falling tiles and slates ... masses of bricks and mortar or fragments of stone-coping rattling upon the pavement near at hand, and splitting into fragments.'[52] When Joe Willett departs England from Chatham, the capital he leaves behind him is soon 'a mere dark mist – a giant phantom in the air.'[53] A comparable insubstantiality appears to affect restraints, within and without prisons. As Barnaby's father remarks to the blind man with whom he is confined: 'Fancy! Are you real?

Am I? Are these iron fetters, riveted on me by the smith's hammer, or are they fancies I can shatter at a blow?'[54] Capitalizing on this insubstantiality, *Barnaby Rudge* accordingly stages many spatial violations: of Parliament; of the doors, windows, and 'inviolable drawers' of John Willett's Maypole inn; of the Warren; of seventy-two 'private houses' in London, including the residence of the magistrate Sir John Fielding; and of many, many prisons, 'among them the Borough Clink in Tooley-street, the King's Bench, the Fleet, and the New Bridewell.'[55] This fulfils Hugh's promise to destroy, not just Newgate, but 'every jail in London.'[56]

In the novel, prisons are therefore also problematic (and fascinating) because they are dysfunctional, and dysfunctional in the way that the 'old' prisons deplored by reformers were. If such prisons lacked physical and moral integrity, in *Barnaby Rudge* they facilitate criminality, stimulate revolutionary transgression and chaotic confusion, and dissolve the spatial boundaries they are meant to preserve. Thus though the 'vast throng' following Lord Gordon contains some 'honest zealots,' it is 'composed for the most part of the very scum and refuse of London, whose growth was fostered by bad criminal laws, bad prison regulations, and the worst conceivable police.' Duly, in Parliament, this throng stops carriages, wrenches off wheels, and shivers glass 'to atoms': 'Lords, commoners, and reverend Bishops, with little distinction of person or party, were kicked and pinched and hustled.'[57]

Yet if the novel displays precisely what most horrified reformers about the 'old' prisons, and who or what such prisons were supposed to contain, it is, for all that, a display, conscious and cultivated: Dickens stages excarceration and the confusing connections it allows even as he manifests the terrors of such confusions and connections. Thus when Barnaby, Hugh, and Dennis are incarcerated in their individual condemned cells near the novel's close, Dickens creates connections between them. If the world outside prisons is affected by the connective transgressions they foster, so too are internal states. Certainly, prisoners bear the strain of these confusions: '"Better be mad than sane, here," said Hugh. "Go mad."'[58] For the condemned of *Barnaby Rudge*, confined in isolation, going mad is not a matter of choice:

The wandering and uncontrollable train of thought, suggesting sudden recollections of things distant and long forgotten and remote from each other – the vague restless craving for something undefined, which nothing could satisfy – the swift flight of the minutes, fusing themselves into hours, as if by enchantment – the rapid coming of the solemn night – the shadow of death always upon them, and yet so dim and faint, that objects the meanest and most trivial started from the gloom beyond, and forced themselves upon the view – the impossibility of holding the mind, even if they had been so disposed, to penitence and preparation, or of keeping it to any point while all that hideous fascination tempted it away – these things were common to them all, and varied only in their outward tokens.[59]

This passage presents a mimetic fragmentation and concatenation. Incarceration both concentrates and dissipates the mind. Focal points and perspectives shift. Yet in this fragmentation, concatenation, and shifting, Dickens powerfully encodes his perception of what prisons might and should do. Ethically, this psychological and spatial fragmentation is counterproductive – fear individuates and distracts inmates and consequently prevents them from thinking wholly about repentance. Nonetheless, while the prisoners are powerless, suffering, lonely, and alone, comforted and tormented by memory, the narrative voice does what the prison and the prisoners cannot. It realizes familiarity, continuity, and commonality, the connections between past and present and victim and crime and each other that the condemned apprehend only dimly.

Confounding the separations caused by incarceration, and confirming the relations between states inside and outside prison, this commingling approximates Barnaby's waking dream visions, Varden's 'dog sleep' (tempered by Maypole ale), and also the quality of the narrative and history itself, when 'events so crowd upon each other in convulsed and distracted times.'[60] As the narrator observes: 'A man may be very sober – or at least firmly set upon his legs on that neutral ground which lies between the confines of perfect sobriety and slight tipsiness – and yet feel a strong tendency to mingle up present circumstances with others which have no manner of connexion with them; to confound all consideration of persons, things, times, and places; and to jumble his disjointed thoughts together in a kind of mental kaleidoscope, producing combinations as unexpected as they are transitory.'[61] The connections effected by Dickens's excarceratory impulses are thus potent and profound. As Linebaugh indicates, and as a comparison between *Barnaby Rudge* and its context suggests, the destruction of Newgate was a politicized act, whether in 1780 or in 1841. But in the novel, the energy and cohesion necessary for this act are articulated in terms of familial or quasi-familial connections realized by narrative, precisely those types of connection Allon White identified. The ranks of those attacking Newgate incorporate 'a great number of people who were relatives or friends of felons in the jail.' Those imprisoned include 'not only the most desperate and utterly abandoned villains in London' but also 'some who were comparatively innocent.' Several women in the mob are 'bent upon the rescue of a child or brother.' They stand shoulder to shoulder with 'the two sons of a man who lay under sentence of death.' Boys seek to liberate 'fellow pickpockets'; more 'miserable women' want to release 'some other fallen creature as miserable as themselves.' Violation paradoxically restores right relations. It manifests a 'general sympathy – God knows,' which 'moves' the 'dense crowd,' psychologically and literally.[62] These forces of consanguineous and communal sympathy combine with still greater power: even Barnaby and his father are (momentarily) reunited, 'passed from hand to hand' by the 'dense crowd,' and saved from the 'burning pile,' like all other inmates, with 'wonderful rapidity.'[63] Clearly, it is not just the speed of the liberation that is incredible, sensational, or awe inspiring. The reconnections between fathers and sons and within a mass of people that liberation makes possible are also 'wonderful,' if maddened and maddening. Of course, Barnaby's father does not repent despite having opportunity to do so. He therefore remains incarcerated and unnamed until his execution, as alienated inside prison as he was in his outcast state. It is appropriate that his recalcitrance also isolates him from his family: 'in the savage terror of his condition he had hardened, rather than relented, to his wife and child.'[64] But while Barnaby's father does not repent, notably even he once looked a prison as a 'refuge.'[65]

Connor notes that *Barnaby Rudge* 'is energised by the *frisson* of representing familiar places torn apart by conflict.'[66] One might modify this acute observation to suggest that conflicts tear families apart (especially fathers and sons), and that familial bonds lead to destruction. But excarceration reconstitutes such bonds to exemplify the novel's key themes, and one of Dickens's key concerns, before, during, and after the 1840s.

For *Barnaby Rudge*, of course, insists upon the permanence and significance of consanguineous bonds, despite, indeed, *because* of the efforts of some to resist anyone rejoining the 'scattered links' of social, narrative, and familial chains.[67] Sir John Chester, for example, protects himself against the 'jail-fevers' of Newgate with camphor circles, and insulates himself against those he considers beneath (or behind) him, thereby enforcing what he terms 'natural class distinctions.'[68] Yet Chester's efforts are ineffectual, not least because his own desires have caused familial relations that transgress such distinctions.[69]

By recovering such bonds, and by showing how they are imperilled by incarceration and reaffirmed by excarceration, *Barnaby Rudge* does more than exemplify one of Dickens's perennial concerns. It also engages fiercely with contemporaneous penological discourses: 'Around the end of the Napoleonic Wars, a language of discipline free from familial or animal-taming connotations began to make its appearance. The word 'cell' replaced the word 'apartment,' with its association to the household dwelling. Discipline replaced economy. Prison populations, not families, were referred to in official parlance.'[70] *Barnaby Rudge* is an incarcerator's critique of the 'old,' degenerate, dissolute permeable prisons, and an authoritarian's condemnation of 'those shameful tumults' that 'reflect disgrace upon the time in which they occurred,' as Dickens put it in his preface to the Cheap Edition of 1849.[71] But it is also an excarcerator's assault on the social, familial, and psychological disintegrations and losses caused and represented by some of the reforms brought about under the new 'separate' system: these 'tumults' may be shameful, but they 'teach a good lesson.'[72] Dickens would continue this assault, and both learn and offer more lessons, in America.

Philadelphia's Solitary Prison, 8 March 1842

If *Barnaby Rudge* (fitfully) employs the insulation of temporal distance to attack prisons old and new, so Dickens used geographical distance when discussing prisons in *American Notes*. For the latter text, like the former, related strongly to domestic concerns. The first building Dickens describes in chapter 7 of the first volume of *American Notes* (1842), 'Philadelphia, and its Solitary Prison,' is not a prison. But given its appearance and Dickens's ambivalence about it, it might as well be. Under the 'sombre influence of the night,' precisely because this building is 'constructed of white marble,' it is at once 'handsome' and offers a 'mournful ghost-like aspect, dreary to behold.' Even in the morning, when Dickens anticipates 'groups of people' passing in and out, the door to this building is 'still tight shut': 'the same cold cheerless air prevailed.' Only then does Dickens realize and reveal what this building is: 'the Tomb of many fortunes, the Great Catacomb of investment; the memorable United States Bank.' The sepulchral bank manifests the same kind of 'stoppage' and 'ruinous consequences' as a prison: lives and livelihoods are lost in it.[73]

Sure enough, Philadelphia's prison, like countless others in Dickens's work, is a deathly, tormented place. Every cell is a 'stone coffin.'[74] Each prisoner wears a 'black hood,' a 'dark shroud' that serves as a 'curtain dropped between him and the living world': 'He is a man buried alive.'[75] A German prisoner arranges his room with his bed in the centre; it looks 'by the bye like a grave.'[76] Dickens is clearly haunted by what he observes. Thus, just as he does in the Gothic nightmare world of *Barnaby Rudge*, Dickens imagines each prisoner to be haunted by 'the terrors' of the 'hateful corner' of their cell: 'Now, it is every night the lurking-place of a ghost: a shadow – a silent something, horrible to see, but whether bird, or beast, or muffled human shape, he cannot tell.'[77] Repulsive as these scenes of haunting are, Dickens is compelled to communicate with the horrors they throw up, for interpretation is predicated on such communication: 'Ideas, like ghosts ... must be spoken to a little before they will explain themselves.'[78] Thus, again in a similar way to *Barnaby Rudge*, Dickens gives body and thought and voice to the prisoners. Indeed, he imagines himself as a prisoner to whom 'the scene' of 'captivity' is 'disclosed … in all its dismal monotony.'[79] Dickens is only able to enter into the situations and psychology of others because he has the commensurate ability (and privilege) to penetrate into, pass out of, and move through the prison, describing what he observes. Accompanied by 'two gentlemen officially connected to the management,' Dickens spends the day 'in going from cell to cell': 'Nothing was concealed or hidden from my view.'[80] This is a fantasy of omniscience realized, exemplifying a disciplinary, incarceratory gaze. Yet such mobility brings about interconnection between prisoners and between observer and subject. These interconnections have an excarceratory power whereby the narrative voice works against the demarcations established by the prison and the society it serves. Indeed, Dickens goes so far as to satirize the racial discrimination that governs the provision of 'refuge' for young offenders in the city: 'Noble aristocracy in crime!'[81]

Unsurprisingly, given all this ghostly ghastliness, Dickens unequivocally condemns the Philadelphia Solitary System as 'rigid, strict, and hopeless'; its effects are 'cruel and wrong.'[82] As seen above, the solitary system is wrong because while it is 'meant for reformation,' inmates all too easily parrot 'detestable cant' with 'unmitigated hypocrisy.'[83] Incarceration is not doing its job. But, most importantly for Dickens in *American Notes*, this lack of reformative power is exacerbated by the way in which prison inhibits the very communicative connection he desires. In fact, it makes people illegible: 'I hold this slow and daily tampering with the mysteries of the brain, to be immeasurably worse than any torture of the body: and because its ghastly signs and tokens are not so palpable to the eye and sense of touch as scars upon the flesh; because its wounds are not upon the surface, and it extorts few cries that human ears can hear; therefore I the more denounce it, as a secret punishment which slumbering humanity is not roused up to stay.'[84] The 'solitary' system silences sympathy, diminishes connection, and exacerbates an individuation that curtails the moral responsibility demanded of its inmates and, significantly, those incarcerating them. The omniscient fantasy is baffled, whether incarceratory or excarceratory, authoritarian or transgressive: Dickens admits he is 'guessing' by trying to read what is 'written upon' the 'faces' of prisoners.[85] Yet this only provokes his curiosity and prompts him to try to read and represent them even more: 'Semantic stoppage engrossed Dickens. The metaphor of circulation which had catalysed his imagining of social process made unintelligibility (or mystery) an object of compelling horror. The worst and most exciting evil was that which kept people apart by obscuring what they said to one another.'[86] The brilliance and irony of Dickens's writing on Philadelphia's Eastern Penitentiary is that it evinces how this 'solitary' prison is not in the least bit solitary. Everyone is implicated in its workings. Disciplinary demarcation affects the whole environment, within and without the prison, and not just the bank. This is a city where repression, guilt, and condemnation hang so heavy that Dickens feels himself changing 'beneath its quakerly influence.' The streets are 'distractingly regular.' Even water is 'dammed,' held back, restrained, and perhaps murkily foul.[87]

Dickens's closing and characteristically 'curious' story of the man who voluntarily incarcerates himself to cure his 'irresistible propensity to get drunk' seems then to exemplify the pervasiveness of a Foucauldian 'carceral continuum.' Driven by guilt, self-hate, and social disapprobation, what he endures in prison only consolidates what he suffered outside. Yet this unfortunate has not internalized carceral discipline so completely: when he encounters the freedom of a 'dusty road ... all shining in the light,' glimpsed through an open 'outer gate,' 'he no sooner raised his head' than he fled 'with the involuntary instinct of a prisoner.'[88] Dickens realizes a crowning irony here. The man has been so thoroughly assimilated into prison life that he has also absorbed a prisoner's desire for freedom. The 'solitary' system incites the will to liberation, not to remain rotting within. Even a man who initially wanted to be there would escape when given the chance.

Evidently, as part of his critique of modern prisons, Dickens cannot resist recording excarceration, even when all hope of such resistance to restraint seems lost and carceral powers seem omnipresent. Yet Dickens does something in this non-fictional analysis of a prison that he does not explicitly do in *Barnaby Rudge*. He advocates his alternative: 'All the instances of reformation that were mentioned to me, were of a kind that might have been – and I have no doubt whatever, in my own mind, would have been – equally well brought about by the Silent System.'[89] As has been seen, this alternative was attractive to Dickens. Moving beyond the confines of 1841–2, as means of a conclusion, we might consider why it could equally have been repulsive to him.

Conclusion: Excarcerating Memory

On 27 April 1850 Dickens published 'Pet Prisoners,' his leading article for *Household Words*. The article was the latest instalment of interventions in penal policy debate, yet for all its currency, it also served as a means of answering those who had criticized his account of the Philadelphia Eastern Penitentiary. In a footnote, Dickens provides an itinerary of events for the day on which he visited the prison eight years before: 'In returning thanks for his health being drunk, at the dinner within the walls, he said that what he had seen that day was running in his mind; that he could not help reflecting on it; and that it was an awful punishment.'[90] 'It' bears a lot of semantic weight in this note. The confused, loaded pronoun suggests a pertinent question: what was an awful punishment, prison *then*, or the reflection on and memory of prison *now*? For Dickens was 'reflecting on' prisons at this time, with characteristic obsession. In addition to reconsidering his work on American penitentiaries, he may have been inspired by Carlyle's attacks on 'Model Prisons' in *Latter-Day Pamphlets* (1850). He may also have been animated by rereading the Newgate jail-break in the Cheap Edition of *Barnaby Rudge*, republished with a new preface in 1849. Finally, he may have been thinking of his father, John Dickens, who, after a long illness, eventually died on 31 March 1851. John Dickens was buried on 5 April 1851. On 3 April, as Ackroyd records, Dickens 'came to the somewhat surprising decision that he wanted to spend the night at a police stationhouse in order to write an article on the subject': 'It has been suggested that beneath this extraordinary wish there was a buried sense of guilt about his father's death, prompting the desire to be somehow near the police and near the cells. But is there perhaps not something equally extraordinary here? Is he not going back in sad reprise to the days of the Marshalsea Prison, when he and his father had been so intimately connected? When he and his family had been so closely bound together by prison doors?'[91] This compound of writing, family connections, incarceration and excarceration (in and from graves and jails), 'now' and 'then,' is a well-rehearsed aggregation, in this paper and elsewhere. But this compound is important, finally, in 1850, because it haunts, deconstructs, and compromises Dickens's attempts to formulate an incarceratory ideal. His own vision of prison suffers from excarceration; his critique of Model Prisons and the 'separate' or 'solitary' systems also discloses his concerns about the associated 'silent' system he propounds as an alternative:

We now come to enquire into the condition of mind produced by the seclusion ... That it is a consummation much to be desired, that a respectable man, lapsing into crime, should expiate his offence without incurring the liability of being afterwards recognised by hardened offenders who were his fellow-prisoners, we most readily admit. But, that this object, howsoever desirable and benevolent, is in itself sufficient to outweigh such objections as we have set forth, we cannot for a moment concede. Nor have we any sufficient guarantee that even this solitary point is gained. Under how many apparently inseparable difficulties, men immured in solitary cells, will by some means obtain a knowledge of other men immured in other solitary cells, most of us know from

all the accounts and anecdotes we have read of secret prisons and secret prisoners from our school-time onwards. That there is a fascination in the desire to
know something of the hidden presence beyond the blank wall of the cell ... is
in that constitution of human nature which impels mankind to communication
with one another, and makes solitude a false condition against which nature
strives. That such communication within the Model Prison, is not only probable, but indisputably proved to be possible by its actual discovery, we have no
hesitation in stating as a fact ... Undiscovered communication, under this system, we assume to be frequent.[92]

The 'condition of mind' of this passage is tortured, by memory, by emotion,
by ambiguity. The syntax shows this. Deploying adversative conjunctions and
negative constructions that connect yet also compartmentalize his prose,
Dickens sets up a series of argumentative, moral, and spatial separations –
'solitary' points – only to jeopardize their separation. Dickens fantasizes about
the possibility that an inherently decent 'respectable man' (like his father),
who has simply suffered a moment's lapse, might be able to 'expiate his
offence,' attain atonement, and ultimately leave prison and his past behind,
reformed with discretion and privacy, distinct from habitual criminals. But this
is *only* a fantasy, and he knows it. The prison invalidates reform, abuses discretion and makes change and the isolation change needs impossible. The
decent cannot be demarcated from the degenerate, not least because the nefar-
ious will learn and reveal the secrets of the fallen, in a network of tittle-tattle,
coded languages, circulated whisperings. Though doors and walls do not obviously 'come down,' as they do in *Barnaby Rudge*, the echoes of other places
and past voices, textual and actual, mingle and resound in the 'now.' Exemplifying the very narrative and social connections that Dickens did so much to
realize, fascination, curiosity, and the spatial and expressive logic of connec-
tivity combine, to keep ghosts and memories alive, vocal, present. As Dickens
notes in *Barnaby Rudge*: 'Whether people, by dint of sitting together in the
same place and the same relative positions, and doing exactly the same things
for a great many years, acquire a sixth sense, or some unknown power of
influencing each other which serves them in its stead, is a question for
philosophy to settle.'[93] Early in the passage from 'Pet Prisoners' cited above,
Dickens offers another Shakespearean allusion that suggests that there are
more things in heaven and earth than are dreamt of by philosophy, or settled
by reflection: 'it is a consummation much to be desired.' In fact, reflection
unsettles. John Forster related that 'the last words' said to Dickens by his
father before he was 'finally carried' to the Marshalsea Prison 'were to the
effect that the sun was set upon him forever.'[94] Last words, final journeys, the

end of days: insolvency, and the shameful imprisonment that results, are at once darkness and death, a seemingly interminable inky blackness, the doom of hope, of aspiration, of opportunity. The potential of all this and more is evoked by the context of the allusion Dickens revives in his article.

For in his soliloquy in act 3, obsessed by a ghostly father, Hamlet simultaneously offers fighting words, dirty talk, and almost surrenders to suicide, or merely to sleep. What compromises the consolations and consummations of conflict, desire, and death is the recognition that none offer completion, fulfilment, or termination. What seems securely done in, locked away, or dead and buried survives to haunt us and is thus beyond our ken and control. As Hamlet says, and as Barnaby Rudge might have mused, in dying, as in sleeping, no one knows 'what dreams may come.' Fittingly, Forster records Dickens speculating: '*What if ghosts be one of the terrors of the jails?*'[95]

The 'separate' system fails because it cannot shut people up or shut them away. Yet the associated 'silent' system is compromised for similar reasons. Both systems provoke and invoke uncanny excarceration, communication, and remembrance; both systems simultaneously inspire and punish transgressions, moral and spatial and narrative. In such places separations and silences are not possible. Little wonder that Dickens desperately deploys enclosing parentheses to formulate the fundamental dictate of the associated system: '(rigid silence we consider indispensable).'[96]

Additionally, just as he destroys Newgate in *Barnaby Rudge* in the name of family, so Dickens subtly disclosed the inconsistencies of the associated 'silent' system in comparable ways, albeit with less violence. Such a system malfunctioned because intersubjective, consanguineous sympathy would – *should* – connect people. As Dickens asserts in *Barnaby Rudge*: 'who that has a heart, ever fails to recognize the silent presence of another!'[97]

For Dickens, carceral institutions reformed their inmates, whether fallen women, bankrupts, or thieves, by making them consider the consequences of their deviant actions. In doing so, such institutions reminded inmates of their connection to others, not their continued alienation from them. Yet when Dickens realized these connections in the excarcerations of his fiction and his non-fiction, imagining inmates, giving voice to and sometimes liberating the imprisoned, he remembered and reconfigured his own vexed relations to prison. The 'now' of writing was shadowed by histories and memories, personal, cultural, textual.

In 1841–2 and beyond, Dickens envisioned prisons in ways that recreated the connections only ever partially prohibited, jeopardized, or silenced by incarceration. The power of the connections he had realized attracted and repulsed him in equal measure.

NOTES

1 Charles Dickens, 'Pet Prisoners,' in *The Dent Uniform Edition of Dickens' Journalism*, ed. Michael Slater (London: J.M. Dent, 1996), 2:225.

2 Ibid., 223. See also Anna Schur's and David Paroissien's contributions in this collection.

3 Ibid., 220.

4 Charles Dickens, 'An Appeal,' in *The Dent Uniform Edition of Dickens' Journalism*, ed. Michael Slater (London: J.M. Dent, 1996), 3:503.

5 Charles Dickens, *Dombey and Son*, ed. Peter Fairclough (1848; Harmondsworth, UK: Penguin, 1970), 151.

6 Charles Dickens, *Charles Dickens' Book of Memoranda*, transcribed and annotated by Fred Kaplan (New York: New York Public Library/Astor, Lenox and Tilden Foundations, 1981), entry 89.

7 Raymond Williams, 'Social Criticism in Dickens: Some Problems of Method and Approach,' *Critical Quarterly* 6, no. 3 (1964): 214–27.

8 Allon White, *Carnival, Hysteria, and Writing: Collected Essays and Autobiography* (Oxford: Clarendon Press, 1993), 92, 89.

9 Dickens, 'Pet Prisoners,' 216.

10 Ibid., 226.

11 Thomas Carlyle, *Past and Present* (1843), ed. Richard D. Altick (New York: New York University Press, 1965), 282.

12 See Sean C. Grass, 'Narrating the Cell: Dickens on the American Prison,' *Journal of English and Germanic Philology* 99, no. 1 (2000): 50–70.

13 Michel Foucault, *Discipline and Punish: The Birth of the Prison* (1975), trans. Alan Sheridan (New York: Vintage Books, 1979), 302–3.

14 Ibid., 303.

15 Ibid., 301.

16 Ibid., 60–5.

17 Ibid., 222.

18 Ibid., 236.

19 Peter Linebaugh, *The London Hanged: Crime and Civil Society in the Eighteenth Century* (London: Penguin Press, 1991), 3.

20 Ibid.

21 Ibid., 334.

22 Ibid., 336, 365.

23 Philip Collins, *Dickens and Crime* (London: Macmillan, 1962), 30.

24 Donald Thomas, *The Victorian Underworld* (London: John Murray, 1998), 265.

25 Michael Ignatieff, *A Just Measure of Pain: The Penitentiary in the Industrial Revolution, 1750–1850* (New York: Pantheon Books, 1978); Robin Evans,

The Fabrication of Virtue: English Prison Architecture, 1750–1840 (Cambridge: Cambridge University Press, 1982).

26 Henry Mayhew and John Binny, *The Criminal Prisons of London and Scenes of Prison Life* (London: Griffin, Bohn, and Company, 1862), 102, quoted in Thomas, *Victorian Underworld*, 262.

27 Thomas, *Victorian Underworld*, 253–6.

28 Ibid., 258.

29 Quoted in ibid., 260.

30 Charles Dickens, *Nicholas Nickleby* (1839), ed. Mark Ford (Harmondsworth, UK: Penguin, 1999), 43.

31 D.A. Miller, *The Novel and the Police* (Berkeley and Los Angeles: University of California Press, 1988), ix.

32 See Jasmine Yong Hall, 'What's Troubling about Esther?: Narrating, Policing, and Resisting Arrest in *Bleak House*,' *Dickens Studies Annual* 22 (1993): 171–94.

33 Collins, *Dickens and Crime*, 44.

34 Peter Ackroyd, *Dickens* (London: Sinclair-Stevenson, 1990), 196.

35 John Bowen, *Other Dickens: Pickwick to Chuzzlewit* (Oxford: Oxford University Press, 2000); Patrick Brantlinger, 'Did Dickens have a Philosophy of History? The Case of *Barnaby Rudge*,' *Dickens Studies Annual* 30 (2001): 59–74.

36 Charles Dickens, *The Pilgrim Edition of the Letters of Charles Dickens*, ed. Madeline House and Graham Storey (Oxford: Clarendon Press, 1969), 2:296.

37 Charles Dickens, *Barnaby Rudge*, ed. John Bowen (1841–2; Harmondsworth, UK: Penguin, 2003), 5.

38 Ibid., 38.

39 Ibid., 137.

40 Ibid., 312.

41 Ibid., 425.

42 Ibid., 60.

43 Peter K. Garrett, *The Victorian Multiplot Novel: Studies in Dialogic Form* (New Haven, CT: Yale University Press, 1980), 36; see Audrey Jaffe, *Vanishing Points: Dickens, Narrative and the Subject of Omniscience* (Berkeley and Los Angeles: University of California Press, 1991), 6–12.

44 Dickens, *Letters*, 2:418.

45 Dickens, *Barnaby Rudge*, 539.

46 Ibid., 208.

47 Ibid., 169.

48 Ibid., 338.

49 Steven Connor, 'Space, Place and the Body of Riot in Barnaby Rudge,' in *Charles Dickens*, ed. Steven Connor (London: Longman, 1996), 211–29.

50 Ibid., 219.

51 Ibid., 227.
52 Dickens, *Barnaby Rudge*, 49.
53 Ibid., 266.
54 Ibid., 514.
55 Ibid., 407–8, 450–1, 459–62, 605, 552–4, 558–9.
56 Ibid., 504.
57 Ibid., 407.
58 Ibid., 635.
59 Ibid., 636.
60 Ibid., 504.
61 Ibid., 32–3.
62 Ibid., 522.
63 Ibid., 540.
64 Ibid., 632.
65 Ibid., 155.
66 Connor, 'Space, Place and the Body,' 211.
67 Dickens, *Barnaby Rudge*, 631.
68 Ibid., 624, 221.
69 Ibid., 628.
70 Ignatieff, *A Just Measure of Pain*, 190.
71 Charles Dickens, preface to *Barnaby Rudge* (London: Cheap Edition, 1849), 700.
72 Ibid., 700.
73 Charles Dickens, *American Notes for General Circulation*, ed. Patricia Ingham (1842; Harmondsworth, UK: Penguin, 2000), 109–10.
74 Ibid., 118.
75 Ibid., 113.
76 Ibid., 114.
77 Ibid., 119–20.
78 Dickens, *Dombey and Son*, 243.
79 Dickens, *American Notes*, 118.
80 Ibid., 112.
81 Ibid., 116.
82 Ibid., 111.
83 Ibid., 115.
84 Ibid., 111–12. See also David Paroissien's contribution in this collection.
85 Ibid., 111.
86 David Trotter, *Circulation: Defoe, Dickens and the Economies of the Novel* (Basingstoke: UK Macmillan, 1988), 109; see also Grass, 'Narrating the Cell,' 69.
87 Dickens, *American Notes*, 110.
88 Ibid., 123–4.

89 Ibid., 122.
90 Dickens, 'Pet Prisoners,' 221.
91 Ackroyd, *Dickens*, 656.
92 Dickens, 'Pet Prisoners,' 219–20.
93 Dickens, *Barnaby Rudge*, 273.
94 John Forster, *The Life of Charles Dickens* (1874; London: J.M. Dent & Sons, 1927), 1:16.
95 Ibid., 1:231–2.
96 Dickens, 'Pet Prisoners,' 216.
97 Dickens, *Barnaby Rudge*, 169.

5 Irish Prisoners and the Indictment of British Rule in the Writings of William Makepeace Thackeray and Anthony Trollope

LAURA BEROL

In chapters 31–2 of *Pendennis*, Pen and his friend Warrington visit an Irish prisoner, the journalist Captain Charles Shandon, who has just completed the prospectus for a new journal. According to Shandon, the *Pall Mall Gazette* will be written by and for 'the gentlemen of England'; in it, 'the old laws and liberties of England' will be defended by the descendants of those who signed 'the deed which secured our liberties at Runnymede.'[1] Shandon is constructing a false pedigree for his journal, the principal contributor to which will be Shandon himself, not an English gentleman, but an Irishman familiar with the inside of a debtor's prison. When Shandon mentions Runnymede (an allusion to the Magna Carta), his publisher asks, 'What's that?' and Warrington facetiously replies, 'It's the Habeas Corpus, Mr Bungay.'[2] Warrington's remark highlights a further layer of irony in the prospectus for the *Pall Mall Gazette*. Not only is its Irish author prevented by the laws of England from enjoying liberty, since he is confined to Fleet Prison, but he belongs to a country where the liberties known in England – and particularly the right to a writ of habeas corpus – are frequently abridged. This passage of Thackeray's novel thus makes imprisonment appear to be a particularly Irish condition.

   This essay will consider two other works by Thackeray (*The Irish Sketch Book, 1842* and *The Luck of Barry Lyndon*) and one by Trollope (*The Macdermots of Ballycloran*) that examine scenes of imprisonment as a means of exploring the relations between Ireland and England. All three texts were published during the 1840s, a decade that saw the peak of the Home Rule movement followed by the Great Irish Famine – two notable crises in English-Irish relations.[3] The containment of Ireland's problems, through the legal imprisonment of individuals or by other means, was a major priority in British policy at this time. Although Thackeray and Trollope may appear to endorse such policies through their portrayals of Irish criminals, I will demonstrate that these authors subtly reveal the destructive effects of Britain's treatment of Ireland, suggesting that efforts at containment produce violence rather than restraining it.

The 1801 Act of Union between Great Britain and Ireland ostensibly made the Irish into equal subjects of the United Kingdom along with the English. However, throughout the term of the Union, social unrest in Ireland often served as a justification for repressive measures, including the repeated suspension of habeas corpus.[4] Since political disaffection was so widespread, witnesses willing to testify against lawbreakers could be hard to find, and thus the cause of law and order appeared to benefit from giving the government the power to imprison suspected criminals without trial.[5] Yet harsh legislation also contributed to the problem by arousing the hostility of the Irish people to English rule.

In England during the 1830s and '40s, public opinion commonly attributed the large numbers imprisoned in Ireland to the intractable spirit of the Irish, who were seen to be as yet too primitive to share fully in English liberties. The historian R.F. Foster quotes Sir Robert Peel, who served as Tory prime minister (1834–5 and 1841–6), referring to 'the Irishman's natural predilection for outrage and a lawless life which I believe nothing can control.'[6] The Whig political economist Nassau W. Senior explained Ireland's social unrest in similar terms: 'The insecurity of persons and of property in Ireland arises from the tendency to violence and resistance to law, which is the most prominent, as well as the most mischievous part of the Irish character. It is the quality which most distinguishes Ireland from Great Britain.'[7] Such statements, coming from both sides of the political aisle, reveal what Homi Bhabha has posited as a powerful motive in colonial discourse: the colonizers' 'desire for "authorization"' from the colonized.[8] In the same vein, Abdul R. JanMohamed has argued that 'the ideological function of ... colonialist literature is to articulate and justify the moral authority of the colonizer.'[9] Perspectives like those articulated by Peel and Senior, which positioned the Irish as inherently criminal, served to justify British rule in Ireland, and particularly to defend policies that were too repressive to be tolerated in England.

The policies advocated by both Peel and Senior reveal their belief that the Irish and the English could not be governed in the same way. In the words of Senior, 'To extend similar laws and institutions to countries not merely widely different but strongly contrasted, is to act in violation of all sound legislation and wise government.'[10] Peel attempted to pass a bill in 1846 that would have given Irish landlords coercive powers to stop agrarian outrages (although his party, divided over the contentious repeal of the Corn Laws earlier that year, refused him the support he needed for the bill's passage).[11] In the same year, Senior made a similar argument from the opposing political camp, asserting that Irish landlords needed the increased support of the law in evicting tenants.[12] In the eyes of many English observers, a primary responsibility of the British government in Ireland was to impose stricter control on the unruly lower classes. Thus, the Earl of Clarendon defended his efficiency as Lord Lieutenant of Ireland by claiming that more than one hundred people had been imprisoned during the suspension of habeas corpus in 1848.[13]

While such penal severity won the government popularity among the English and the landowning Protestant Ascendancy in Ireland, it turned many Irish Catholics against British rule. Those who opposed the Union between Great Britain and Ireland often viewed imprisonment as heroic martyrdom. As William Makepeace Thackeray notes in his *Irish Sketch Book, 1842*, Kilmainham Jail became a site of pilgrimage early in the nineteenth century due to widespread reverence for Robert Emmet, who was hanged there in 1803 for his attempted rebellion against British rule.[14] Similarly, Daniel O'Connell's incarceration in October of 1843 confirmed the popularity that he had acquired throughout a dramatic summer of monster meetings advocating the repeal of the Union, according to his biographer Oliver MacDonagh.[15] MacDonagh reports the adulation O'Connell received both on his way to prison and at his release,[16] and Anthony Trollope's early novel, *The Kellys and the O'Kellys,* dramatizes the enthusiastic support that the Liberator experienced during his trial.[17] Being convicted of a crime against the state could even be treated as a badge of honour; for instance, when John Mitchell was convicted and transported for treason in 1848, his successor as the editor of the *United Irishman* defiantly renamed the paper the *Irish Felon,* with apparent pride at his predecessor's status.[18]

Thus, the spectrum of opinions regarding British rule in Ireland in the 1840s was quite wide. Between the two extremes of justifying oppression and idealizing criminality, Thackeray's and Trollope's writings most resemble popular English discourse. *The Irish Sketch Book, Barry Lyndon,* and *The Macdermots of Ballycloran* all portray acts of lawlessness committed by Irish characters as destructive rather than praiseworthy. While these texts do not glorify the behaviour that leads to imprisonment, however, neither do they represent it as an unambiguous indicator of Irish depravity. Instead, they obliquely suggest English culpability through brief narrative gestures calculated to raise questions about what motivates the Irish. Neither novelist openly accuses his own nation of causing Ireland's ills. The power of their texts resides not in argument, but in suggestion. Behind each instance of imprisonment that they describe, these authors offer glimpses of systemic oppression that may fuel individual outbursts of criminality. Thus, unlike colonialist literature with its justifications of the colonizers' moral authority,

Thackeray's and Trollope's writings cast doubt on the moral authority of the British administration of Ireland.

Each author focuses on a different aspect of English-Irish relations: Thackeray blurs the boundaries between the Protestant Ascendancy and the Catholic majority to create a simple opposition between English and Irish, whereas Trollope explores in more complexity the tensions created by the existence of an anglicized elite ruling in place of the English over the Irish common people. In either case, however, they hint at the failure of the socio-political system established in Ireland under English domination. As D.A. Miller has shown in *The Novel and the Police*, Victorian novels generally take their setting in 'an everyday middle-class world ... that for the most part the law does not cover or supervise' because there exists 'another, informal, and extralegal principle of organization and control' that keeps lawlessness at bay.[19] In the Ireland portrayed by Thackeray and Trollope, however, such a principle of organization and control is lacking. The entire nation resides within the 'world of delinquency' that occupies only a limited space within the English novels Miller addresses.[20] Police supervision is applied to all aspects of Irish life in the texts this essay considers, and it fails to establish order in any of them. The scenes of imprisonment in Thackeray's and Trollope's Irish works, rather than containing criminality, propagate it.

I

The Irish Sketch Book, 1842, Thackeray's first full-length work about Ireland, is a partially fictionalized travel narrative. From the text's first appearance to the present, readers have disagreed profoundly on the perspective towards Ireland to be found in this book. The opinions presented in the *Sketch Book* do not come directly from Thackeray himself but are mediated through the persona of his narrator, Mr Michael Angelo Titmarsh, who voices a wide range of views without suggesting how they all may be reconciled. Some readers have accepted Titmarsh's harsh words regarding the Irish as expressions of Thackeray's own bigoted perspective, while others have asserted that Thackeray deliberately ironizes Titmarsh and that the *Sketch Book* lays bare the process by which derogatory stereotypes are constructed.[21] For every critical interpretation that has been advanced, however, a certain residue of the text resists its explanatory power.

One example of the *Sketch Book*'s irreconcilable ambiguity appears in its treatment of the Irish legal system. Titmarsh's account of the assizes in Waterford praises 'the extreme leniency, acuteness, and sensibility of the judge presiding' and describes how one of the prisoners 'was found guilty with perfect justice.'[22] Although Titmarsh here expresses confidence in the functioning of Ireland's courts, he later argues regarding a different group of prisoners, 'It is not revenge so much which these poor fellows take, as a brutal justice of their own.'[23] The claim that those who break the law are enacting 'their own' justice is double-edged, suggesting both that the lawbreakers have an idiosyncratic version of justice and that the legal system is failing to provide a form of justice that they can recognize. The criticism of the government implied in Titmarsh's argument is muted, but it is present, as the context of the statement makes clear.

The prisoners Titmarsh is discussing in this case are sawyers who were put out of work by the opening of a sawmill and who tried to protect their jobs by throwing vitriol (sulphuric acid) in the faces of the mill owners. Although Ireland was known more for agrarian outrages than for Luddism of this kind, Titmarsh treats the sawyers as representatives of all the lower-class Irish who are trying to protect their livelihood through extralegal violence. In describing the crowds who surround the courthouse to show solidarity with the vitriol throwers, Titmarsh uses language that combines sympathy and dismay:

> Look yonder at those two hundred ragged fellow-subjects of yours: they are kind, good, pious, brutal, starving. If the priest tells them, there is scarcely any penance they will not perform; there is scarcely any pitch of misery which they have not been known to endure, nor any degree of generosity of which they are not capable: but if a man comes among these people, and can afford to take land over their heads, or if he invents a machine which can work more economically than their labour, they will shoot the man down without mercy, murder him, or put him to horrible tortures, and glory almost in what they do. There stand the men; they are only separated from us by a few paces; they are as fond of their mothers and children as we are; their gratitude for small kindnesses shown to them is extraordinary; they are Christians as we are; but interfere with their interests, and they will murder you without pity.[24]

What fascinates Titmarsh about the Irish workers is that they are simultaneously like and unlike the English readers he imagines for his book. His rhetoric impels his readers to find likeness where they would expect only dissimilarity. In place of 'the Irishman's natural predilection for outrage and a lawless life,' to use Peel's phrase,[25] Thackeray's readers discover that the behaviour of the Irish is shaped by circumstances much as their own actions would be. Thus, the Irish workers become the uncanny doubles of the English readers, since, as Freud has explained, 'the uncanny is that class of the frightening which leads back to what is known of old and long familiar.'[26] Titmarsh asserts both the physical proximity of the Irish ('only separated from us by a few paces') and a corresponding moral similarity ('they are Christians as we are'). According to Titmarsh, the Irish 'are as fond of their mothers and children as we are'; since they live under conditions of misery and starvation, their violence against those who threaten the livelihood of their family is comprehensible. Yet the closeness, the comprehension, the sympathy Titmarsh encourages are not likely to make English readers comfortable, since the Irish cannot simply be assimilated into Englishness. The resemblance between the two groups is marked by difference; for instance, they may all be Christians, but they are not all Protestants, as Titmarsh highlights with his mention of penance. Titmarsh even suggests that the difference can be deadly, as he glides seamlessly from a scenario in which the Irish workers 'murder *him*,' a nameless opponent, to one in which 'they will murder *you* without pity.'[27] English readers may discover that they themselves are threats to Irish life and objects of Irish vengeance. Whereas many in England were content to explain Irish crime in terms of moral failings, this passage from the *Sketch Book* evokes the social factors driving the poor to desperate acts. In light of the sentence following this passage, which characterizes the vitriol throwing as 'a brutal justice of their own,' readers might begin to question how the English, working through the British government, should work to establish a more equitable economic system in Ireland.

Not all of Thackeray's readers recognized the implied critique of the administration of Ireland that I have identified here. In fact, John Wilson Croker cited the precise paragraph quoted above in his 1849 article 'Tours in Ireland' as evidence that Ireland's social upheavals resulted solely from the depravity of the Irish people and bore no relation to English policy.[28] Croker's simplistic reading, which constitutes little more than a character assassination of the whole Irish people, ignores not only the nuances of the quoted passage but also the surrounding text. Thackeray's narrator hints in the very next paragraph that the violence of the law mirrors and propagates the violence of crime: 'Now, will it seem a paradox to say, in regard to them and their murderous system, that the way to put an end to the latter is to *kill them no more!* Let the priest be able to go amongst them and say, The law holds a man's life so sacred that it will on *no account* take it away. No man, nor body of men has a right to meddle with human life: not the Commons of England any more than the Commons of Tipperary.'[29] Titmarsh's argument works on the assumption that the governed model their behaviour to some degree after the actions of their government. Thus, if the legal system kills as a means to justice, the lower classes will feel entitled to enact their own justice through killing. Titmarsh asserts the equivalency of homicide and execution even more strongly in an earlier passage, stating that he 'revolt[s] against murder, whether performed by a ruffian's knife or a hangman's rope.'[30] In his view, responding to crime with the death penalty aggravates rather than ameliorates the social ills that provoke lawlessness. Thus, the *Irish Sketch Book* makes an important contribution to the English discourse surrounding Irish crime by directing attention away from personal guilt to broader causes. True, it does not offer a systematic critique of British rule in Ireland; many of its passages, indeed, defend British policies and mock Irish complaints.[31] The critical force of the *Sketch Book,* as of all three texts I consider in this essay, appears through isolated moments of the text that raise disturbing questions for those readers who pause to consider them.

II

Thackeray's novel from 1844, *The Luck of Barry Lyndon,* similarly offers clues that institutional violence may lead to personal violence. The prisons that serve as the loci of violence in this text are, to a certain degree, metaphorical. They lack the particular social, legal, and architectural apparatus usually associated with the prison: the police, the trial, the cell. Yet these metaphorical prisons are grounded in other social institutions: the military, marriage, and British rule over Ireland. In this way, 'imprisonment' in *Barry Lyndon* includes multiple forms of societally endorsed oppressive restraint. The narrator (Redmond Barry, later Barry Lyndon) explicitly uses the language of imprisonment to describe both his experience in the Prussian army and his treatment of his wife, Lady Lyndon. Barry tells the reader that, during the Seven Years War, he was captured by Prussian recruiters and incarcerated in 'the town-prison of Fulda' before being sent to battle.[32] Whereas the Prussians make the town into a prison for Barry, Barry himself makes his home into a prison for his wife. As is characteristic of Barry, he condemns himself with his efforts at self-justification when he explains, 'I was bound to be on my guard that she should not give me the slip. Had she left me I was ruined the next day … Every man imprisons his wife to a certain degree; the world would be in a pretty condition if women were allowed to quit home and return to it whenever they had a mind.'[33] Deborah A. Thomas has astutely noted in *Thackeray and Slavery* that Barry's treatment of his wife re-enacts the brutality that Barry suffered earlier as a soldier in the Prussian Army.[34] Later in this essay, I will trace Barry's attitude towards his English wife back even further to his experiences of disempowerment as an Irishman in the British Empire. Thus, this novel, like the *Irish Sketch Book,* suggests how pathogenic social structures can create destructive individuals. Furthermore, the novel goes beyond the

Sketch Book to indicate that the individuals shaped by institutionalized oppression go on to reproduce oppressive institutions.

When Barry justifies his cruelty towards Lady Lyndon on the grounds that 'every man imprisons his wife to a certain degree,' the ironic text simultaneously indicts Barry (whose behaviour is certainly worse than the norm he invokes) and contemporary English marriage law, which allowed husbands oppressive power over their wives. Thus, Michael M. Clarke is right to argue that the novel attacks 'the sanctioning of women's subjection by social, legal, and even religious elements of Barry Lyndon's culture.'[35] Yet I find that the text not only critiques Barry's marriage but also uses that marriage as a figure for the relations between England and Ireland. Just as the novel challenges the misogynist assumptions that Barry holds,[36] it also challenges the common mid-nineteenth-century English view that the Irish alone had created their nation's problems.

Presenting a heterosexual couple as a metaphor for Ireland and England was a standard literary device at the time Thackeray composed *Barry Lyndon*. A century earlier, Jonathan Swift had published 'The Story of the Injured Lady' (1746), representing Ireland as a woman exploited by her lover. In the early nineteenth century, novels such as Sidney Owenson's *The Wild Irish Girl* (1806) and Maria Edgeworth's *The Absentee* (1812) used courtship as a way of examining the interactions between the two countries.[37] During the 1840s, writers of non-fiction regularly used the language of marriage to explain English policy towards Ireland. Thus, in 1846 the radical MP and essayist G. Poulett Scrope referred to Ireland as 'the partner of Britain's fortune, whether for weal or woe,'[38] echoing the traditional phrase 'for better, for worse,' which appears in both the Anglican and the Roman Catholic wedding vows. In 1848 Charles Trevelyan's monograph *The Irish Crisis* anticipated a future of mutual prosperity for Great Britain and Ireland as 'the true consummation of their union.'[39] In light of this trend, Thackeray's readers would be quick to see the marriage of the Irish Redmond Barry to the English Countess of Lyndon as a depiction of national relations in miniature.

Furthermore, Barry's genealogy and his personal conduct mark him as a representative figure of Ireland as a whole. His family history allies him with both of the groups struggling for dominance in Irish society, the Protestant Ascendancy and the Catholic majority. Barry's uncle, the so-called Chevalier de Ballybarry, still espouses the family's historic Catholic faith, while Barry's father converted to the Church of Ireland in order to seize his elder brother's property under the penal code that kept Catholics from inheriting land.[40] On his own account, Barry commits outrages that reflect the threats that the English feared from both the aristocracy and the common people of Ireland. Even before he imprisons his wife, Barry takes captive another young woman, Amelia Kiljoy, who is Lady Lyndon's ward. His assault on Miss Kiljoy borrows the tactics of agrarian secret societies. As Barry explains, 'there was a sort of rough-and-ready law in Ireland in those days which was of great convenience to persons desirous of expeditious justice.'[41] When he kidnaps Miss Kiljoy and forces her to marry his cousin, Barry sends word to Lady Lyndon that the deed has been accomplished by the fictitious bandit leader Captain Thunder. His goal is to convince Lady Lyndon that it is impossible for her to resist the will of her Irish suitor, since men of his nation will stop at nothing to obtain what they desire. The fear of insatiable lower-class Irish rapacity that Barry arouses haunted the English imagination during the 1840s, especially after the onset of the Great Famine in 1845. The Tory John Wilson Croker asserted in 1849 that '[t]he Irish patriots, as they call themselves' had received 'ten millions of alms' from England as 'only a paltry, ungracious, and forced restitution of a long series of robberies,' thereby asserting their right to a much larger degree of English support.[42] It is significant to note that the anxiety Croker expresses regarding Irish demands was shared well outside conservative circles. Both J.S. Mill and Nassau Senior (an economic adviser to successive Whig ministries) warned the government not to promise relief to the Irish poor, whom they imagined as a 'devouring monster' that could bring about 'the ruin of all that makes England worth living in.'[43]

Whereas Barry's treatment of Miss Kiljoy associates him with lower-class lawlessness, his marriage to Lady Lyndon constitutes a more aristocratic form of plundering, in which he denudes an English estate for the purpose of enriching an Irish one. Even as Barry describes his first entry onto the grounds of Hackton Castle, Lady Lyndon's Devonshire residence, the property linguistically melts away under his rapacity: 'There were many hundreds of stout people at the great lodge, which, with the park-wall, bounds one side of Hackton Green, and from which, for three miles, goes, or rather went, an avenue of noble elms up to the towers of the old castle. I wished they had been oak when I cut the trees down in '79, for they would have fetched three times the money; and I know nothing more culpable than the carelessness of ancestors in planting their grounds with timber of small value, when they might just as easily raise oak.'[44] With a change of verb tense, Barry obliterates the 'avenue of noble elms' before the reader can even perceive them. Similarly, he asserts the value of the Lyndon family diamonds by announcing the enormous sum for which he pawned them.[45] As a result, Lady Lyndon's estate appears already impoverished by Barry's greed at the moment he takes possession. He explains that he uses the money to buy 'the ancient lands of Ballybarry and Barryogue' in Ireland, the historic possessions of his family.[46] Although Barry can imagine 'nothing more culpable' than planting elms instead of oaks, his audience is certain to recognize a greater crime in his destruction of the estate's beautiful trees.

Barry's spoliation of English property for the sake of Irish property epitomizes the parasitism that English politicians claimed to detect in the Irish upper classes as a whole. In 1833 G. Poulett Scrope warned that 'we, simple fools, in Britain are paying enormous taxes for the maintenance of an army in Ireland, – to enable the Irish landowners to extort exorbitant rents from their starving tenantry.'[47] In Scrope's view, the Ascendancy was relying on Britain's resources to maintain their power and wealth instead of making the effort to establish a sustainable social order. Scrope, a Radical, tended to lay the responsibility for Irish ills exclusively on Ireland's aristocracy, but Charles Trevelyan, the Whig assistant secretary to the Treasury during the Irish Famine, found much to blame in both the lower and the upper classes. In 1848 Trevelyan argued that Britain's refusal of aid during the Famine had shattered this trend, but he asserted that, up to that point, Ireland had been characterized by 'the habitual dependence of the upper classes upon the Government.' According to Trevelyan, the experience of battling the Famine had taught the Irish to resolve, 'We will no longer be dependent on the precarious assistance received from other lands.'[48] Few in England, however, shared his confidence that Ireland had learned self-reliance. To the end of the 1840s and beyond, Britain's policymakers feared that any concession to Irish demands would, like Lady Lyndon's capitulation to Barry's suit, simply open the floodgates to Irish cupidity. Thackeray's novel confirmed popular English fears of what the Irish would do if they ever gained the upper hand.

So far, the details of Barry's career that I have discussed offer little reason to criticize the British administration of Ireland. From what I have said to this point, one may conclude that Barry is no better than Sir Kit Stopgap, the most despicable of the Irish landlords portrayed in Maria Edgeworth's *Castle Rackrent,* who marries 'the grandest heiress in England' and then locks her in her room for seven years because she refuses to turn her jewels over to him.[49] Barry is indeed a literary descendant of Sir Kit, but Thackeray's novel differs from Edgeworth's in the attention it pays to the experiences that shape the character of the abusive husband. The unremitting oppression Barry suffers provides a partial explanation, although not a justification, for his cruelty. In *Thackery and Slavery,* Deborah A. Thomas attributes the formation of Barry's character to his time of de facto imprisonment in the Prussian Army.[50] I contend, however, that Barry's brutality is already fully developed before he is captured by the Prussians. What initially distorts Barry's character is not physical confinement but the social and psychological constraint he experiences as an Irish subject under British rule. His later cruelty towards his wife may borrow Prussian methods, but it is fuelled by a more long-standing motive in Barry's life. Barry's abuse of Lady Lyndon is just one episode in his lifelong effort to get the better of the English in a world that has always assigned him a subaltern position.

From childhood, Barry is schooled in the mimicry of an English identity. His parents lose all their money as hangers-on in fashionable London society, and at his father's death, his mother returns to Ireland to establish a reputation as 'the *English* widow,' winning for her son the nickname of 'English Redmond.'[51] As Barry grows, his mother urges him, 'Support your name with your blood,' and his efforts to protect his family's honour bring him into battle with every boy around.[52] All these feats, however, count for nothing when Barry falls in love with his cousin Nora, who sneers 'that it was mighty well of Redmond to talk and boast of beating ushers, and farmers' boys, but to fight an Englishman was a very different matter.'[53] Even when Barry proves his superior courage against Nora's pusillanimous English suitor, the Englishman's financial power ultimately triumphs. Nora's brothers stage a duel and lead Barry to believe that he has killed Captain Quin, with the result that Barry flees to Dublin to avoid arrest, leaving Nora to marry the captain and secure his fifteen hundred pounds a year for her family. In his eagerness to be accepted as an Englishman, Barry falls into the hands of Dublin con artists, who pretend to believe his account of himself as long as he has money to spend. Once his funds run dry, Barry sees no alternative but to enlist.

In the British Army, Barry finds that the officers have 'a contempt for Irishmen' and becomes convinced that his nationality precludes him from advancement.[54] The life he must lead rewards nothing but aggression. In response to the view that military service is ennobling, Barry writes, 'Such knaves and ruffians do men in war become! It is well for gentlemen to talk of the age of chivalry; but remember the starving brutes whom they lead – men nursed in poverty, entirely ignorant, made to take pride in deeds of blood – men who can have no amusement but in drunkenness, debauch, and plunder.'[55] This description would be questionable if Barry presented it as an excuse for his actions, but, on the contrary, he glories in his degradation, proclaiming, 'though only a young lad of seventeen, I was the master of them all in daring wickedness.'[56]

The novel pictures Barry as proud, violent, and unprincipled by nature and chronicles how the British administration of Ireland nurtures his destructive traits. The pretensions of England's elite drive the foolish struggles of those on the margins, like Barry, who are desperate to be admitted into their charmed society. The British government depends on penniless, unscrupulous men like him to fight its battles. Thackeray's depiction of Barry Lyndon is by no means flattering to the Irish, but it insists that his cruelty results from societal and not merely personal failings. According to this novel, the English have no grounds for complaining, as John Wilson Croker does, that 'all of civilization, arts, comfort, wealth, that Ireland enjoys, she owes exclusively to England – all her absurdities, errors, misery, she owes to herself.'[57] Thackeray reveals that Barry's violence results from a social system that encourages such behaviour. Whereas many contemporary readers would have been content to view Barry's imprisonment of Lady Lyndon simply as evidence of Irish brutality, Thackeray's text indicates that the English have helped to produce the savagery under which she suffers.

III

Like Thackeray, whom he admired, Trollope wrote about Irish characters early in his literary career, before composing his more famous English novels. As Trollope reveals in his autobiography, his success as a member of the British civil service was established in Ireland, where he worked as a surveyor for the post office between 1841 and 1859.[58] Trollope's work involved extensive travel throughout Ireland, and his autobiography asserts regarding the Irish, 'I had the means of studying their character.'[59] Trollope's faith in his own insight was so great that when he proposed to an editor to write 'a handbook for Ireland,' he claimed 'that [he] knew the country better than most other people, perhaps better than any other person.'[60] Although the handbook was never completed, Trollope returned to Irish topics repeatedly throughout his literary career. His tendency in explicit political argument was to defend British policy in Ireland, as he did in a series of letters to the *Examiner*, published in 1849 and 1850, which discussed Britain's response to the Irish Famine.[61] Yet Trollope's fiction is less univocal, betraying an agonized personal effort to come to terms with the upheavals of Ireland's national life.[62] In this essay, I will be focusing on Trollope's first novel, *The Macdermots of Ballycloran* (1847), which chronicles the ruin of a struggling Irish Catholic family. Thady Macdermot kills his sister's seducer and is wrongfully convicted of murder by members of the Protestant Ascendancy. His imprisonment, trial, and execution show how justice can go awry under the British administration of Ireland.

   As a Catholic landowner, Macdermot occupies an ambiguous social position, alienated from the rest of his class by his religion, genealogy, and social ties. His fellow landlords distrust him for his cultural similarity to the lower classes, and, in fact, on one occasion Macdermot agrees to join an agrarian secret society in attacking their oppressors, including the revenue officer Ussher, whose relationship with Macdermot's sister Feemy is provoking gossip. Macdermot repudiates any involvement in the society the very next day, but his brief flirtation with lawlessness turns out to be fatal. After Ussher dies, the jury of Anglo-Irish landlords that weigh Macdermot's case will not believe his defence: that Ussher appeared to be abducting Feemy, and that Macdermot struck him to protect her. Instead, they find Macdermot guilty of premeditated murder. As Macdermot in his cell awaits hanging, knowing that 'through the stern will of certain powerful men' he will become 'a hideous, foul, and dislocated corse [sic],' he is a figure of Ireland's Catholic population, crushed under the harsh rule of the Protestant Ascendancy.[63]

Thus, Trollope's first novel does not directly address British policies, since those primarily responsible for Macdermot's tragedy are not English but Anglo-Irish, descendents of the English who settled in Ireland and appropriated Irish property during the sixteenth and seventeenth centuries. Failing to recognize this distinction, Coral Lansbury has identified 'English law' as the obvious culprit in the novel.[64] Although Lansbury is right to trace the ills in Trollope's text to the administration of law in Ireland, she is wrong to assume that that law is clearly English. Trollope's contemporaries, by contrast, would be likely to interpret Macdermot's wrongful conviction as an example of Anglo-Irish misgovernment, for, as I have mentioned above, English popular opinion was as likely to blame Ireland's elite for their country's problems as it was to blame the poor. Thus, *The Macdermots* assesses responsibility for Irish conditions in a more complicated way than Lansbury acknowledges. The novel explores the standard accusations levelled against both the native Irish and the Anglo-Irish, and only indirectly does it suggest how those in England may have helped create Ireland's distress.

At the time when *The Macdermots* was written, many in England accused Ireland's Catholic majority of impoverishing their nation with their addiction to indolent freedom. In 1848 Charles Trevelyan published *The Irish Crisis*, heralding the Great Famine as the ultimate enforcer of the work ethic. He claimed that, as long as the Irish farmer depended on the potato for food, he needed to spend only five and a half weeks a year cultivating that crop. '[D]uring the rest of the year,' Trevelyan wrote, 'he [was] at leisure to follow his own inclinations ... and poverty, discontent, and idleness, acting on his excitable nature, produced that state of popular feeling which furnishes the material for every description of illegal association and misdirected political agitation.'[65] In Trevelyan's eyes, the famine had been salutary because it had made food more difficult to cultivate. Trollope's own letters to the *Examiner* from 1849–50 echo Trevelyan's claims and also accuse the large tenants and landlords of adopting luxurious habits when they should have been working. Trollope attributes these trends to the national character, explaining, 'The prospect of a comparatively idle life is, I regret to say, seductive to an Irishman.'[66]

The early portions of *The Macdermots* appear to confirm this stereotype. The narrator explains that Macdermot's current hardships are due to his ancestors' ambitions to be 'estated gentlemen.' His grandfather 'planned, ordered, and agreed for a house, such as he thought the descendent of a Connaught Prince might inhabit without disgrace,' but 'it was ill-built, half finished, and paid for by long bills.'[67] As a result, Macdermot's life is a continual struggle to extract rents from his tenants in order to pay the interest on the mortgage, while he lives in fear of foreclosure. Macdermot is 'not so indomitably idle' as his forebears, the narrator reveals, 'but as he [knows] not what to do, he only [becomes] more gloomy and tyrannical.'[68] A family history of extravagance has trapped Macdermot in helpless bondage to debt.

Macdermot's behaviour after killing Ussher, however, shows that he is not satisfied with inaction, and, in fact, that he prefers activity, even with danger, over an inert safety. Initially, upon discovering that Ussher is dead, Macdermot flees into the mountains to seek refuge with the Ribbonmen, members of an agrarian secret society. Yet his travels to escape the police lead him to a confinement worse than prison. Macdermot spends two days in the cabin of an old man, Andy McEvoy, who embodies the epitome of native Irish indolence, sitting motionless and silent on his bed all day until his daughter brings him food. At first, 'Thady envie[s] his quiescence,' but eventually 'he [gets] almost alarmed at this old man,' wondering, 'why [does] he sit there so quiet, doing nothing – saying nothing – looking at nothing – and apparently thinking of nothing?'[69] When Macdermot attempts conversation, he finds that McEvoy 'neither interest[s] himself about his house, his food, his landlord, nor his family.' It is only when McEvoy's daughter arrives with some bacon that 'the man's apathy and tranquillity [vanish], and the voracity with which he devour[s] the unaccustomed dainty show[s] that ... the vulture in his stomach torture[s] him.'[70] McEvoy's existence is reduced to the barest minimum, with the consumption of food as his only interest and occupation. Far from embracing such idleness, Macdermot revolts from the torpor of a life in hiding and determines to turn himself over to the police. Having made that decision, 'he [is] much easier in his mind' because 'he ha[s] at any rate once more something to do.'[71] The activity of the legal process is attractive to Macdermot simply because it involves work towards an end, even though he foresees that that end will be 'the horrid touch of that dread man with the fatal rope.'[72] The narrator proclaims that, 'even ... in gaol and committed to take his trial for life,' Macdermot feels 'infinitely less wretched than he [did] whilst sitting in Andy McEvoy's cabin, wondering at the torpidity of its owner.'[73] Although

Trollope's letters to the *Examiner* represent laziness as a primary determinant of Irish behaviour, Macdermot's experiences suggest that some in Ireland, at least, may desire to improve their condition but find no productive outlet for their energies.

Those in England who defended the native Irish against charges of innate indolence argued that their sense of hopelessness proceeded from the exploitation that they suffered at the hands of the Ascendancy. J.S. Mill, for instance, argued in his articles for the *Morning Chronicle* in 1846 that the impossibly high rents in Ireland destroy 'all motive either to industry or to prudence.' Mill wrote, 'To what end should the tenant, who is hopelessly in arrear to his landlord, exert himself to raise a larger produce? There would only be the more for the landlord to take from him.'[74] *The Macdermots* offers evidence to uphold this point of view in the character of the Anglo-Irish landlord Jonas Brown, whose estate is 'all set at a rack rent' and who is 'careful to see that he [gets] the full twelve hours' work from the unfortunate men whom he hire[s] at five pence a day.'[75] Trollope links the mistreatment of the poor with the central tragedy of the novel by presenting Brown as a leading propagator of the case against Macdermot. Brown declares that 'unless that young man were hanged, there would be an end to anything like law in the country,' viewing Macdermot's killing of Ussher as an instance of 'the landlords themselves turn[ing] ribbonmen, and [teaching] the tenants all manner of iniquity.'[76] At the trial, the jurors believe the false report that Macdermot was a Ribbonman and convict him on that basis. Their paranoia is driven by real threats from others among the native Irish. The officer who takes over Ussher's position is intimidated out of performing his duties, and the lawyer who takes charge of Ballycloran after Macdermot's imprisonment is attacked and maimed. Knowing the hostility they have aroused among the native Irish, the Ascendancy executes Macdermot in the fear that he is encouraging revolt.

Thus, the text indicates that no sector of Irish society functions as it should. The poorer classes may be idle and violent, but those who rule over them are greedy and unjust. The entire social system apparently requires an external authority to intervene for the sake of order. And it is only when readers recognize this need that they can perceive the novel's implicit criticism of British policy – for, according to colonial ideology, the British government should have been able to play the role of the unbiased mediator. The multiple Coercion Acts that Parliament imposed on Ireland certainly increased the methods of law enforcement, as Trollope's narrator highlights when he remarks, 'Everyone knows that Ireland, for her sins, maintains two distinct, regularly organised bodies of police.'[77] By the end of the novel, however, readers are left wondering what good such measures have accomplished.

The only visible instance of English involvement in the novel is a minor and yet revealing reference to an absentee landlord, Lord Birmingham. After describing the abject conditions in which his tenants live, the narrator asks, 'Is the landlord then so hard a man? so regardless of those who depend on him in all their wants and miseries?' In answer to his own question, the narrator lists the numerous charities to which the landlord subscribes. He concludes:

> In short, is not everyone aware that Lord Birmingham has spent a long and bril-
> liant life in acts of public and private philanthropy? 'Tis true he lives in England,
> was rarely in his life in Ireland, never in Mohill. Could he be blamed for this?
> Could he live in two countries at once? or would the world have been benefited
> had he left the Parliament and the Cabinet, to whitewash Irish cabins, and assist in
> the distribution of meal?
>   This would be his own excuse, and does it not seem a valid one? Yet shall no
> one be blamed for the misery which belonged to him; for the squalid sources of
> the wealth with which Poles were fed, and literary paupers clothed?[78]

This passage criticizes absentee landlords for their heartlessness towards their tenants, but the narrator's analysis goes deeper than that. As he points out, 'everyone [is] aware' that Lord Birmingham is a great philanthropist. English society validates his behaviour, praising his generosity and his public service in government without enquiring into the origins of his wealth. England needs public leaders, and Lord Birmingham could not do his part in 'Parliament and the Cabinet' if he had to oversee his Irish estate. He acts with a clear conscience because everyone around him affirms his choices. Thus, instead of condemning the landlord alone, Trollope's narrator also indicts the system of British rule that enables absentee landlords to collect rent from near-destitute tenants without suffering from outraged public opinion. While *The Macdermots* overtly cri-tiques the paranoia of the Ascendancy, it also suggests more subtly that English practices add to the sense of desperation that drives Anglo-Irish injustice. The Anglo-Irish who cannot leave Ireland like Lord Birmingham are left to face the hostility that his behaviour creates. In a way, they are just as trapped as the poor, and therefore they respond with excessive force to put down threats such as they believe Macdermot represents.

To be sure, neither Trollope nor Thackeray portrays the Irish as helpless victims of English oppression. On the contrary, they reveal grave flaws in their Irish characters. The narrator of *The Irish Sketch Book* expresses horror at the 'murderous system' of the vitriol throwers.[79] Barry Lyndon ingeniously condemns himself more fully than his worst enemies could with his naive account of his own experiences. Thady Macdermot puts himself at risk with his muddled behaviour, repeatedly seeking the Ribbonmen for help and then repudiating them – and when he eventually suffers for his poor choices, his persecutors are Anglo-Irish, not English. Even Captain Shandon from *Pendennis* is fully responsible for his own imprisonment, as Warrington argues convincingly in response to Pen's protest over the Irishman's supposed mistreatment.[80] What makes Thackeray's and Trollope's writings extraordinary is that they simultaneously highlight the failures in England's treatment of the Irish. While acknowledging the evils current in Irish society, these authors show how harsh measures of law enforcement help to produce and extend those ills. Thackeray and Trollope suggest that Ireland needs not the suspension of habeas corpus and more prisoners in the jails, but greater justice: economic, political, and social.

NOTES

1 William Makepeace Thackeray, *The History of Pendennis: His Fortunes and Misfortunes, His Friends and His Greatest Enemy*, ed. John Sutherland (1848–50; Oxford: Oxford University Press, 1994), 408–9.
2 Ibid., 409.
3 The distressed condition of Ireland was a topic that few English novelists chose to address in their fiction during the nineteenth century. A steady flow of Anglo-Irish novels appeared throughout the century for the entertainment of English audiences: the nationalist romances of Maria Edgeworth and Sydney Owenson, Lady Morgan; the swashbuckling tales of William Hamilton Maxwell and Charles Lever; the Gothic horror of Charles Maturin and J. Sheridan Le Fanu; the naturalism of George Moore. English fiction on Irish topics, however, was generally limited to such obscure productions as Harriet Martineau's 1833 *Ireland: A Tale,* one of twenty-five works in her doctrinaire series *Illustrations of Political Economy.* Yet the writings of Thackeray and Trollope are notable exceptions. During the 1840s, both authors published significant texts that focus primarily on Irish scenes and people: Thackeray's travel narrative *The Irish Sketch Book, 1842*; his novel *The Luck of Barry Lyndon*; and Trollope's first two novels, *The Macdermots of Ballycloran* and *The Kellys and the O'Kellys.* In addition, Thackeray's greatest novels, *Vanity Fair* and *Pendennis,* both date from that decade and include important Irish characters. Irish topics continued to appear in Trollope's novels throughout his career (see endnote 62).
4 Virginia Crossman, *Politics, Law and Order in Nineteenth-Century Ireland* (New York: St Martin's, 1996), 28–9, 63, 86.
5 Crossman, *Politics, Law and Order,* 9–10, 88; R.F. Foster, *Modern Ireland, 1600–1972* (London: Penguin, 1989), 292–4; G. Poulett Scrope, *How Is Ireland to Be*

Governed?: A Question Addressed to the New Administration of Lord Melbourne in 1834, with a Postscript, in Which the Same Question Is Addressed to the Administration of Sir Robert Peel in 1846 (London: James Ridgway, 1846), 14, 16, 17; William Makepeace Thackeray, *The Irish Sketch Book of 1842*, in *The Paris Sketch Book of Mr. M. A. Titmarsh; The Irish Sketch Book; and Notes of a Journey from Cornhill to Grand Cairo* (1843; New York: John B. Alden, 1885), 294.

6 Foster, *Modern Ireland*, 294.

7 Nassau W. Senior, 'Ireland,' *Edinburgh Review* 79 (1844): 198.

8 Homi Bhabha, *The Location of Culture* (London: Routledge, 1994), 100.

9 Abdul R. JanMohamed, 'The Economy of Manichean Allegory: The Function of Racial Difference in Colonialist Literature,' *Critical Inquiry* 12, no. 1 (1985): 84. See also Matthew Kaiser's contribution in this volume.

10 Nassau W. Senior, 'Proposals for Extending the Irish Poor-Law,' *Edinburgh Review* 84 (1846): 267.

11 Crossman, *Politics, Law and Order*, 78; Peter Gray, *Famine, Land and Politics: British Government and Irish Society, 1843–1850* (Dublin: Irish Academic, 1999), 138–40.

12 Senior, 'Proposals,' 278–9.

13 Crossman, *Politics, Law and Order*, 86–7.

14 Thackeray, *The Irish Sketch Book*, 20.

15 Oliver MacDonagh, *The Emancipist: Daniel O'Connell, 1830–47* (New York: St Martin's, 1989), 241.

16 Ibid., 246–7, 251–2.

17 Anthony Trollope, *The Kellys and the O'Kellys: or Landlords and Tenants*, ed. W.J. McCormack (1848; Oxford: Oxford University Press, 1982).

18 John Martin, 'To All Whom It May Concern,' *Irish Felon, Successor to the United Irishman*, 24 June 1848, 8.

19 D.A. Miller, *The Novel and the Police* (Berkeley and Los Angeles: University of California Press, 1988), 3.

20 Ibid., 5.

21 Those readers who have accepted Titmarsh's words in the *Sketch Book* as transparent expressions of Thackeray's personal views include Gordon N. Ray, in his biography *Thackeray: The Uses of Adversity, 1811–1846* (New York: McGraw-Hill, 1955), 315; John Sutherland, in his essay 'Thackeray as Victorian Racialist,' *Essays in Criticism* 20 (1970): 442; Richard Michael Klish, in his PhD dissertation 'Thackeray's Travel Writings' (PhD diss., University of Michigan, 1974), 118; and Phyllis Weinroth Bernt, in her PhD dissertation 'William Makepeace Thackeray and the Irish: A Study in Victorian Prejudice' (PhD diss., University of Nebraska, 1979), 111. These critics are in accord with many early reviewers of the *Sketch Book*, including John Wilson Croker ('Tours in Ireland,' *Quarterly Review* 85

[1849]: 507–9) and the anonymous reviewer for the *Dublin Review* in 1843 (153, 168), who attribute quotations from the text directly to Thackeray himself. More recent critics have attempted to find irony in Thackeray's characterization of Titmarsh; for instance, Günther Klotz, in his essay 'Thackeray's Ireland: Image and Attitude in *The Irish Sketch Book* and *Barry Lyndon*,' in *National Images and Stereotypes*, vol. 3 of *Literary Interrelations: Ireland, England, and the World*, ed. Wolfgang Zach and Heinz Kosok (Tübingen: Narr, 1987), 96–8; and Kenneth L. Brewer, in his article 'Colonial Discourse and William Makepeace Thackeray's *Irish Sketch Book*,' *Papers on Language and Literature* 29 (1993): 265. These later readers follow in the footsteps of the anonymous reviewer of the *Sketch Book* for London's prominent Catholic newspaper the *Tablet* in 1843, who also tried to read Titmarsh's more bigoted statements ironically, and they face the problem that this reviewer articulates: although many of the narrator's statements seem outrageous, the author and the narrator are not clearly distanced from each other in the *Sketch Book,* as they are in earlier works by Thackeray. See *Tablet*, 13 May 1843, 291.

22 Thackeray, *The Irish Sketch Book*, 326.

23 Ibid., 361.

24 Ibid.

25 Foster, *Modern Ireland*, 294.

26 Sigmund Freud, 'The "Uncanny"' (1919), in *The Standard Edition of the Complete Psychological Works of Sigmund Freud*, vol. 17, ed. and trans. James Strachey et al. (London: Hogarth and the Institute of Psycho-Analysis, 1955), 220.

27 Emphasis added.

28 Croker, 'Tours in Ireland,' 508.

29 Thackeray, *The Irish Sketch Book*, 361.

30 Ibid., 296.

31 See, for example, pp. 351–2, of the *Irish Sketch Book,* in which Titmarsh asserts that the Irish blame England for the problems caused by Irish 'indolence,' 'impru-dence,' and 'vanity'; p. 362, in which Titmarsh argues against some Irishmen who claim that the English exploit Irish agricultural labourers; and p. 486, in which Titmarsh states that 'The people [of Ireland] are not politically worse treated than their neighbors in England,' and demands, 'Is it not too monstrous to howl about English tyranny and suffering Ireland?'

32 William Makepeace Thackeray, *The Luck of Barry Lyndon; A Romance of the Last Century*, ed. Edgar F. Harden (1844; Ann Arbor: University of Michigan Press, 1999), 70.

33 Ibid.

34 Deborah A. Thomas, *Thackeray and Slavery* (Athens: Ohio University Press, 1993), 32–8.

35 Michael M. Clarke, *Thackeray and Women* (DeKalb: Northern Illinois University Press, 1995), 60.

36 Ibid., 66.
37 See Jonathan Swift, 'The Story of the Injured Lady. Written by Herself' (1746), in *The Prose Works of Jonathan Swift, D D.*, vol. 7, *Historical and Political Tracts – Irish*, ed. Temple Scott (London: Bell, 1925), 93–103; Sydney Owenson, *The Wild Irish Girl*, ed. Kathryn Kirkpatrick (1806; Oxford: Oxford University Press, 1999); and Maria Edgeworth, *The Absentee*, ed. W.J. McCormack and Kim Walker (1812; Oxford: Oxford University Press, 1988).
38 Scrope, *How Is Ireland to Be Governed?*, 66.
39 Charles Trevelyan, *The Irish Crisis* (London: Longman, Brown, Green and Longmans, 1848), 201.
40 Thackeray, *Luck*, 3.
41 Ibid., 148.
42 Croker, 'Tours in Ireland,' 497.
43 John Stuart Mill, *Newspaper Writings, January 1835 – June 1847*, in *Collected Works of John Stuart Mill*, vol. 24, ed. Ann P. Robson and John M. Robson (Toronto: University of Toronto Press, 1986), 1070; Nassau W. Senior, 'Relief of Irish Distress,' *Edinburgh Review* 89 (1849): 268.
44 Thackeray, *Luck*, 173–4.
45 Ibid., 174.
46 Ibid., 177.
47 G. Poulett Scrope, *Plan of a Poor-Law for Ireland, with a Review of the Arguments for and against It* (London: James Ridgway, 1833), 63.
48 Trevelyan, *The Irish Crisis*, 188, 190.
49 Maria Edgeworth, *Castle Rackrent* (1800), ed. George Watson (Oxford: Oxford University Press, 1999), 23, 28–9.
50 Thomas, *Thackeray and Slavery*, 32–9.
51 Thackeray, *Luck*, 5–6.
52 Ibid., 11.
53 Ibid., 18.
54 Ibid., 53.
55 Ibid., 52.
56 Ibid., 53.
57 Croker, 'Tours in Ireland,' 497.
58 Anthony Trollope, *An Autobiography*, ed. Michael Sadleir and Frederick Page (1883; Oxford: Oxford University Press, 1999), 63.
59 Ibid., 65.
60 Ibid., 87.
61 Anthony Trollope, 'Trollope's Letters to the Examiner,' ed. Helen Garlinghouse King, *Princeton University Library Chronicle* 26, no. 2 (1965): 71–101.
62 Trollope's second novel, *The Kellys and the O'Kellys* (1848), offers a much more hopeful (if less convincing) view of Ireland than does *The Macdermots:* Catholic

tenants join with the Anglo-Irish elite to rid their country of evil, embodied in the character of the rapacious middleman Barry Lynch (whose name, perhaps not for-tuitously, echoes that of Thackeray's anti-hero Barry Lyndon). After the 1840s, Trollope's next major work about Ireland was *Castle Richmond,* published in 1860 but set during the Irish Famine with the explicit goal of demonstrating that 'the measures of the government [in response to the Famine] were prompt, wise, and beneficent.' Anthony Trollope, *Castle Richmond,* ed. Mary Hamer (1860; Oxford: Oxford University Press, 1992), 69. An Irish character next played a significant role in Trollope's fiction with the appearance of Phineas Finn, the Irish MP, as the epon-ymous protagonist of two novels in the Palliser series (*Phineas Finn* [1869] and *Phineas Redux* [1874]). Although the fraught relations between Ireland and England are not foregrounded in those novels, they surface violently in *An Eye for an Eye* (1879), which climaxes with an enraged mother (English, but Catholic and residing in Ireland) murdering the English Protestant seducer of her daughter. Trollope's last, unfinished novel, *The Landleaguers* (1883), portrays an Ireland in which murder is an everyday occurrence and terror defeats the rule of law.

63 Anthony Trollope, *The Macdermots of Ballycloran* (1847; London: Folio Society, 1991), 442.
64 Coral Lansbury, *The Reasonable Man: Trollope's Legal Fiction* (Princeton, NJ: Princeton University Press, 1981), 124.
65 Trevelyan, *The Irish Crisis,* 5–6.
66 Trollope, 'Trollope's Letters to the *Examiner,*' 78.
67 Trollope, *Macdermots,* 5.
68 Ibid., 6.
69 Ibid., 270.
70 Ibid., 273.
71 Ibid., 277.
72 Ibid., 271.
73 Ibid., 284.
74 Mill, *Newspaper Writings,* 891. Mill's defence of the lower-class Irish in this passage may appear to contradict the earlier quotation warning the British government not to provide relief to the Irish lower classes. In fact, the two statements are part of a single unified argument propounded by Mill regarding Ireland's economic problems. Since he believed that the exploitative landlord-tenant relations common throughout Ireland encouraged destructive habits among the Irish peasantry, he advocated reforming that inequitable system of land tenure rather than propping it up with charitable relief to the lower-class victims of that system. Mill's plan to create a class of peasant propri-etors on reclaimed waste lands in Ireland is detailed in approximately fifty leading articles that Mill published in the *Morning Chronicle* from the autumn of 1846 through the spring of 1847. See Mill, *Newspaper Writings,* 879–1078.

75 Trollope, *Macdermots*, 215, 217.
76 Ibid., 293–4.
77 Ibid., 16.
78 Ibid., 82–3.
79 Thackeray, *The Irish Sketch Book*, 361.
80 Thackeray, *The History of Pendennis*, 414–17.

6 The Poetics of 'Pattern Penitence': 'Pet Prisoners' and Plagiarized Selves

ANNA SCHUR

In 'Pet Prisoners,' the leading article that appeared in *Household Words* on 27 April 1850, Dickens resumed his polemic with the advocates and the practitioners of the so-called separate system of prison discipline, a polemic he began in *American Notes* with a poignant description of his visit to the Philadelphia Eastern Penitentiary in March 1842. In the article, Dickens rehearsed the arguments that were to reappear seven months later in chapter 61 of the final, November, instalment of *David Copperfield* (1849–50). This chapter, in which David, on a prison tour, is shown two 'interesting penitents' who turn out to be Uriah Heep and Mr Littimer, constitutes the most well-known of his inroads against the phenomena of the model prison and the 'model prisoner.'

As Philip Collins explains in his classic study *Dickens and Crime*, Dickens's vigorous rejection of the officially endorsed 'separate' system, a disciplinary regime based on complete isolation in individual cells for extended periods of time, was central to his position in the mid-century penological debate.[1] He favoured instead its rival: the associated 'silent' system, which required isolation only at night, while during the day prisoners worked together in common quarters but in strict silence enforced by prison guards.

Following Carlyle, who in *Latter-Day Pamphlets* (1850) railed against what he perceived as the pampering of prisoners in new model prisons, Dickens, too, believed that the inmate ought not to enjoy any material advantage over the honest poor struggling to survive outside prison walls. '[One] of the first essentials and requirements of a well-regulated Prison,' Dickens wrote in 'In and Out of Jail,' a *Household Words* article from 1853, 'is, that its inmates should be worse off in every imaginable respect than the bulk of honest paupers and honest labouring men.' The condition of criminals, Dickens continued, should 'in no particular, present a favourable comparison with the pauper's or the labourer's. Let it do so under any system, and I call that system, however plausible in theory, a manifestly false and absurd one in its practical application,' he claimed with an air of objectivity.[2]

Of the two competing systems, however, it was clearly the 'separate' that, in his estimation, was by far guiltier in presenting the criminal with undeserved and manifestly unfair advantages before the labouring poor.[3] This is in part why he pledged his allegiance to the 'silent' system, which, to his mind, displayed a more correct understanding of its own mission. Convinced that the primary function of a prison sentence was punitive, Dickens was naturally drawn to the advocates of the 'silent' system who shared this opinion. Repeatedly, he spoke in favour of a degrading and useless labour at the treadmill or the crank carried out under the 'silent' system and against the practice of having prisoners work at trades (or teaching them new ones) implemented by its rival. And repeatedly, he held up for ridicule the separatists' misguided doctrine that regarded the main goal of a prison sentence not as deterrence through the fear of painful and demeaning punishment but as spiritual reclamation through introspection, reflection, and religious instruction. It was this aspect of the separatist theory, which in practice led to an epidemic of fraudulent professions of spiritual awakening (most famously manufactured by Littimer and Uriah Heep), that further fuelled Dickens's distaste for the 'separate' system.

In a rough outline, this is a familiar account of Dickens's position within the penological debate of the 1840s and the 1850s, frequently reiterated in critical discussions of his views on punishment and crime management.[4] This paper attempts to provide further insight into Dickens's views on the penal policies of his time by focusing on the specifics of his objections to the champions of the 'separate' system. It argues that Dickens's discussions in 'Pet Prisoners' and *David Copperfield* foreground the reformers' assumptions about the centrality of language to the reformative process and point to the separatists' implicit understanding of moral reform as an aptitude to articulate appropriate content in an acceptable narrative form. In critiquing both the form and the content of 'patterned penitence,' the two texts expose the system's inability to distinguish between discourse and lived experience, and they shed light on some rarely discussed aspects of Dickens's position on (criminal) subjectivity, as well as the possibility and the nature of moral reform in the individual criminal.

Prison Sentence as a 'Narrative' Quarantine

That the association of inmates led to further moral contamination was an obligatory truism of all writers on prison questions. Regardless of their persuasion in other matters of prison discipline, reformers agreed that regulation of prisoners' association, even to the point of complete silencing of their discourse, was a basic condition of any disciplinary regime. In fact, the push to regulate prisoners' association formed the guiding principle of prison reform decades before the institutional struggles between the 'separate' and the 'silent' systems became the central feature of the reform movement. As early as 1823, the Gaol Act attempted to put an end to the evils of contamination by dividing convicts into groups characterized by a similar degree of criminality. Assessing the measure of badness in an individual criminal was no easy matter, however. To counter an intuition of radical idiosyncrasy of every case to be classified, reformers concentrated on what was in those cases repeatable and objective: the nature of the offence, and the age and gender of the offender. But in classifying individual cases, the reformers were also classifying personal stories, those 'gross and guilty stories of [prisoners'] lives' whose trading constituted the favourite, and in reformers' view the most corroding, pastime in pre-reform prisons.[5]

These attempts, however, led nowhere. Under the System of Classification British prisons remained the same proverbial 'schools of vice' as they had always been, thus exposing the failure of the new system to fulfil its main objective of improving inmates' morals. The main problem was that a workable principle of classification turned out to be unattainable. As the Surveyor General of Prisons Colonel Jebb wrote bitterly, 'There does not exist any moral standard by which [the System of Classification] can be regulated so as to avoid the mischievous effects of bringing together criminals of different degrees of criminality and of every shade of character.'[6] When it was finally abandoned in the early 1830s, the reformers acknowledged more than just the fact that the observable commonalities in criminals' personal histories (age, gender, the nature of the offence) failed to yield a meaningful basis for an accurate determination of their 'moral perversity.' They also recognized each prisoner's personal history as a class in itself and acknowledged that the infinite variety of 'gross and guilty stories' that the law enjoined them to order subverted their attempts at systematization. The stories that they could not classify needed to be rendered innocuous by other, more radical means.

Far from disclaiming the importance that the System of Classification implicitly attributed to the prisoner's personal narrative, the new prison reform movement foregrounded it even further. Indeed, as they tried to silence the prisoner completely, both the 'silent' and the 'separate' systems revealed that despite all other disagreements, they shared one important goal – to disrupt the circulation of pernicious narratives and to enforce what Henry Mayhew once called a 'criminal quarantine.' 'Of late years,' Mayhew wrote in 1862 in reference to the recent developments in prison regulations, 'we have made rapid advances towards the establishment of a kind of criminal quarantine, in order to stay the spread of that vicious infection which is found to accompany the association of the morally disordered with the comparatively uncontaminated; for assuredly there is a criminal epidemic – a very plague, as it were, of profligacy – that diffuses itself among the people with as much fatality to society as even the putrid fever or black vomit.'[7] To the extent that the orbits of infection were prisoners' 'gross and guilty stories,' one can also see Mayhew's 'criminal quarantine' as a sort of 'narrative quarantine.'

Prison Sentence and the 'Transfusion' of Language

This quarantine, however, was not absolute. In the 'separate' system in particular, the inmate's solitude was to be broken by frequent visits from prison officials and chaplains, who were to spend substantial amounts of time daily in morally improving conversation with their charges. (For a number of practical reasons, such as overcrowding and lack of personnel, these visits were neither as long nor as frequent as the more conscientious chaplains desired.) Prisoners were also given books to read. Most of the books and periodicals were supplied by the Society for the Promotion of Christian Knowledge, and although lists of approved titles varied from prison to prison, the main criterion for selecting a text was its morally edifying character.[8] Besides the Bible, a prison library could include a variety of religious tracts, some philosophical treatises, and, occasionally, some historical narratives, usually with a moral lesson. In some places, most notably at Reading Gaol, prisoners were assigned to memorize substantial portions of the Bible. In others, the literate were encouraged to write their autobiographies, an exercise that people like the Reverend John Clay, the chaplain at Preston, believed to have important therapeutic value.

All of these activities were designed to help to rid the convict of his criminal 'germ.' In the silence of 'criminal quarantine,' the convict was to be drained of his pernicious vernacular in which he was used to boasting of his life of vice and depravity, and to become infused with a new language and a new set of representational conventions in which to tell his new story, a story of the reformed self. The reformers' nervousness about the corrupting effects of criminals' speech in general and criminal argot in particular underscores the importance they attached to a peculiar transfusion of language that was to take place in prison. The juxtaposition of the corrupt language of the inmate population with the language of the Bible and prayer books that we find in the following lines from John Field is entirely typical. Criticizing prison association, Field, an ardent separatist and the chaplain at Reading, writes: 'Oaths, cursing, swearing, blasphemies, obscenity, and the cant phrases of criminals, were the current language of the ward. Bibles, prayer books, and other books were provided, but generally despised, and frequently destroyed, and if any attempted to read or seek instruction he became the object of ridicule and scorn, and almost every effort was defeated.'[9] He goes on to quote extracts from the testimony given by prisoners themselves to the Inspectors of Prisons in 1837:

> The conversation of prisoners is generally bad; it relates to their exploits out of prison; how they performed them, &c., and they boast of these things. No doubt a man might learn every mode of committing crime; they learn of each other the cant language, and are proud of shewing their knowledge of it. There are words for highway robberies, for picking pockets, for house-breaking, &c. Most of the prisoners are anxious to learn this kind of language: there are names for almost everything. I suppose the prisoners must get worse by this kind of conversation, which takes place I know throughout the prison.[10]

'They used to learn the cant words,' adds another prisoner, 'and repeated them to each other as boys used a spelling-book.'[11]

The persistent appearance of such testimonies in numerous official reports bespeaks the reformers' anxiety about criminal slang and reflects their belief that it was not compatible with the reformative process. The stakes of inculcating the criminal with a new language were particularly high, one would think, because reformation, just like criminality, could not be measured by any objective test, or, to use Jebb's words again, by any 'moral standard.' It could only be known in its effects, that is, in the absence of recidivism. But since even this outcome, when and if achieved, was highly problematic (because not easily distinguishable from the effects of deterrence), one important evidence of moral reform seems to have lain in the story the criminal would tell upon his release. It is largely from the way the prisoner narrated both his pre-prison life and prison experience that one could gauge the success of his reformation. In this sense, one of the most important goals of a reformative regime was to train one to fit one's personal narrative into the appropriate mould. That this is indeed how many officials 'measured' reformation's success is evident from the fact that appeals to convicts' own stories figure in the reformers' writings, including official reports, nearly as often as appeals to statistics and other hard data. *Memoirs of Convicted Prisoners* (1853), a collection of convicts' letters published by H.S. Joseph, the chaplain of Chester Castle, for example, is representative of how, in the eyes of many, personal stories could in fact constitute proof of moral reformation.[12] They needed, however, to be narrated properly. What emerges from the pages of

Joseph's *Memoirs* is a whole narrative genre with its own laws and conventions that govern both their structure and rhetoric.

Structured around the set of questions that the inmate writers learnt from their encounters with prison officials – what is your family, when did you commit your first crime, when did you last attend church, do you know how to pray, did you ever see your mother pray – the stories these letters told were designed to confirm Joseph's, and by extension the middle-class super-addressee's, understanding of the origins of crime and channels of reformation (the collection's full title is *Memoirs of Convicted Prisoners; Accompanied by the Remarks on the Causes and Prevention of Crime*).

In a curious illustration to the post-structuralist view of discursively constituted subjectivity, the inmates' letters disclose the process whereby in constructing themselves as objects of bureaucratic knowledge, prisoners were also expected to learn to interpret their (criminal and prison) experience according to the generic conventions prescribed by the institution of the penitentiary. Lack or absence of religious instruction, idleness, bad company, fickleness of desires, and restlessness of temperament – all the familiar elements of Victorian discourse on crime – figure prominently in these accounts of individual moral demises. Their narratives abound in expressions of contrition and proclamations of the newly found faith and are cluttered with biblical allusions, references to religious practices, and Christian rhetoric. Many authors talk with gratitude about their prison experience. 'Since I have been here,' writes one convict, 'I have thought very differently of religion. I feel that I am a very great sinner in the sight of God. I hope to spend the rest of my days in a very different way.'[13] Others express appreciation of the chaplain himself: '[It] is to you that I am indebted for the benefits which I receive from our Lord Jesus Christ … When I first came to Chester, I did not care whether I heard the Word of God or not; but now, thanks to the Almighty Providence, I could sit the whole day to hear it.'[14] Still others refer to the most memorable sermons, 'I shall often think of that sermon you preached to us from Luke, 15th chapter, 7th verse. Oh that the Lord may convert my soul. I tremble when I think how much I have resisted the workings of God's holy spirit in my soul.'[15] Many wish that their former companions shared with them their blessed state and found their way to repentance, 'I only wish many of my partners could hear from you. They are a wicked set, and never go to church. "The Lord have mercy upon us all."'[16]

It is on the basis of these and similar statements that H.S. Joseph judged with unperturbed confidence of their authors' successful reformation. 'From the foregoing letters, which have been received from convicted felons,' Joseph writes in the conclusion of the *Memoirs*, 'we may trust that the good seed which has been sown among them, has not been in vain. Indeed we have great reason to believe that many of *them*, as well as many discharged prisoners, have been brought from "darkness to light, and from the power of Satan unto God." For these mercies we would give all the praise and all the glory to Him, who hath given the Gospel treasure unto earthly vessels, "that the excellency of the power might be of God and not of man."'[17] This sample of Joseph's own style explains why he felt the need to preface *Memoirs* with the assurance that he was giving the reader 'the statements of the different prisoners as they were narrated by them without any alteration.'[18] This disclosure was indeed in order, for what followed resembled Joseph's own arguments not only stylistically but also thematically. One convict's letter in which he blames his love of novels and romances for his moral failings illustrates the striking resemblance between the assessments of the inmates and the opinions of their chaplain. Joseph's own conclusion to *Memoirs* features an extended argument for suppressing publication and circulation of 'thrilling narratives,' which in his opinion constituted 'one great cause of crime.'[19]

It is of course tempting to dismiss the letters of Joseph's correspondents as the phony drivel of crafty 'Joeys,' who, trading criminal slang for the language of religious hypocrisy, simply substituted one kind of canting for another, just as it is tempting to dismiss Joseph's optimistic confidence in the reformation of his flock as the mere prattle of a gullible man who mistook assumed contrition for the real thing.[20] But since Joseph and his congregation represent a definitive strain in the history of Victorian prison reform, it is a credit to Victorian sceptics like Dickens that they did not simply dismiss 'Joeyism' but attempted to analyse its cultural significance.

'Pattern Penitence' in 'Pet Prisoners'

Before dramatizing his objections to the separatists' misplaced credulity and misguided optimism in the final instalment of *David Copperfield*, Dickens aired his arguments in 'Pet Prisoners,' a leading article that appeared in *Household Words* on 27 April 1850.[21] In it, Dickens condemned the mixture of narcissism and hypocrisy that, he believed, 'the system' promoted in the convict when it made him the centre of universal attention, often at the expense of the forgotten victim. Even murder victims and their families, Dickens bitterly complains, have but a weak claim on anybody's memory or consideration, least of all on the murderer's. His persona and his salvation become the pre-eminent concern:

The state of mind into which a man is brought who is the lonely inhabitant of his own small world, and who is only visited by certain regular visitors, all addressing themselves to him individually and personally, as the object of their particular solicitude – we believe in most cases to have very little promise in it, and very little of solid foundation. A strange absorbing selfishness – a spiritual egotism and vanity, real or assumed – is the first result. It is most remarkable to observe, in the cases of murderers who become this kind of object of interest, when they are at last consigned to the condemned cell, how the rule is ... that the murdered person disappears from the stage of their thoughts, except as a part of their own important story; and how they occupy the whole scene. *I* did this, *I feel* that, *I* confide in the mercy of Heaven being extended to *me*; this is the autograph of *me*, the unfortunate and the unhappy; in my childhood I was so and so; in my youth I did such a thing, to which I attribute my downfall – not this thing of basely and barbarously defacing my Creator, and sending an immortal soul into eternity without a moment's warning, but something else of a venial kind that many unpunished people do. I don't want the forgiveness of this foully murdered person's bereaved wife, husband, brother, sister, child, friend; I don't ask for it, I don't care for it. I make no enquiry of the clergyman concerning the salvation of that murdered person's soul; *mine* is the matter; and I am most happy that I came here, as to the gate of Paradise.[22]

'Now, God forbid,' Dickens continues, 'that we, unworthily believing in the Redeemer, should shut out hope, or even humble trustfulness, from any criminal at that dread pass; but it is not in us to call this state of mind repentance.'[23]

If such is the case with convicted murderers awaiting execution, the picture Dickens paints of less serious offenders is gloomier still. 'The dread of death not being present,' their 'tendency to hypocrisy' is even stronger.[24] 'If I, John Styles, the prisoner,' Dickens dramatizes the thoughts of a fictional convict,

don't do my work, and outwardly conform to the rules of prison, I am a mere fool. There is nothing here to tempt me to do anything else, and everything to tempt me to do that ... I should be weary of myself without occupation. I should be much more dull if I don't hold these dialogues with the gentlemen who are so anxious about me. I shouldn't be half the object of interest I am, if I don't make the professions I do. Therefore, I John Styles go in for what is popular here, and I may mean it, or I may not.[25]

Further in the piece, Dickens introduces the narrative of a 'reformed' offender, which he goes on to analyse to show the same 'spiritual egotism and presumptions of which we have already spoken.'[26] He makes a point of borrowing this letter from *Prison Discipline; and the Advantages of the Separate System of Imprisonment* (1848), a treatise by John Field, the chaplain at Reading Gaol and Dickens's adversary, whose criticisms of the chapter on the Philadelphia penitentiary in *American Notes* (1842) had cut Dickens to the quick.[27]

The letter Dickens considers could have easily made it into Joseph's *Memoirs* or other such collection. It follows the same conventions and has the same tone and feel. Anticipating Uriah Heep's sermonizing in *David Copperfield*, the letter's author expresses his enthusiasm about his 'present state' and prays day and night for God's forgiveness; he frets about his parents and sends his respects to his companions, hoping that they will see their folly, as he has seen his. Seizing on the letter's language, Dickens invites the reader to observe a characteristic preaching on the part of its felonious author about 'the wickedness of the unfelonious world.'[28] Then he goes on to contrast this piece of writing to a different kind of reformation narrative, written, as Dickens puts it, of his own (i.e., convict's) mind. In this alternative narrative (composed of course by Dickens himself), an imaginary author faces his degradation instead of pointing at the sinfulness of others, names his crime frankly and clearly instead of glossing over it, admits his evil influence on those 'littler' than he instead of casting himself as a victim of bad associates, and promises 'to work [his] fingers to the bone to make restitution' instead of avoiding as much as a mention of the wronged party. [29]

What would happen if a letter like this would fall, say, into Joseph's hands? 'Would that be better? Would it be more like solid truth?' Dickens asks. The answer, he believes, is no. A narrative such as this would not strike anybody as more truthful because it 'is not the pattern penitence.' 'There would seem to be,' Dickens goes on to explain the term, 'a pattern penitence, of a particular form, shape, limits, and dimensions, like the cells.' While he goes on to make another quick foray against Field, suggesting insidiously that in their 'overweening readiness to lecture other people,' pattern penitents in fact imitate chaplains like him, the point that Dickens makes rises above personal attacks.[30]

What this brief comment reflects is Dickens's understanding of the process by which the system appears to have coped with the same absence of 'moral standard' that we saw Colonel Jebb lament earlier in the paper. It is as if to deflect the challenge that this void posed to the practicality of the institution's goals that the separatists welcomed a rigid set of parameters for the genre of 'pattern penitence.' Having failed to classify convicts' stories on the way in, the system attempted to synchronize them on the way out. If reformed subjectivity could indeed be recognized only through the story one told about one's reformation, this genre, just like the process of reformation itself, called for strict routinization. It was formalized in the same way as diet, uniforms, hours of work, exercise, and worship, and allowed no infractions to its narrative discipline. Just as any violation of prison regime entailed a penalty, violation of this genre's conventions threatened a rhetorical failure. Once its protocol was spurned, the system, personified by people like Field and Joseph, could not, according to Dickens, recognize the message.

Curiously, however, Dickens does not seem to suggest that the penitent's reliance on a pattern always and necessarily discredits the authenticity of his protestations. In theory, he allows for the possibility that an account of the authentic moral conversion can assume the form of a patterned tale. The off-hand remark 'I may mean it' that Dickens assigns to his 'pet prisoner' John Styles suggests precisely this possibility. It reveals that Dickens does not dismiss all and any professions of reform as disingenuous solely because they are articulated with reference to the institutionalized script. To be sure, he is sceptical of the uncanny resemblance that he detects in 'doubtful converts,' and yet the lack of variation in the language of patterned protestations is only one cause for concern. As 'Pet Prisoners' demonstrates, Dickens's repudiation of 'pattern penitence' has at least as much to do with its content as it does with its form.[31]

Indeed, one could say that in dramatizing the alternative reformation narrative, a narrative of the genuinely reformed inmate, Dickens simply offers a different pattern by which to organize penitence. As we have noted above, this narrative is characterized by the penitent's heightened emphasis on personal responsibility, a frank acknowledgment of his blame, and a willingness to repay, as far as possible, the damage inflicted upon his victims. But while the purpose of this narrative may seem as largely rhetorical – to highlight, by means of a contrast, the 'strange absorbing selfishness' that was typical of the officially endorsed 'pattern penitence' – it nevertheless provides an important insight into Dickens's understanding of a genuine reformation, should it indeed occur.[32]

It appears that, according to Dickens, to be authentic, reformation would need to involve a shift in one's understanding of one's social embeddedness and of the power of one's situatedness.[33] As he recognizes his evil influence on those 'littler' than he instead of presenting himself as a victim of bad companions, Dickens's fictional penitent makes an important step towards asserting himself as a self-determining subject that nevertheless generously acknowledges the social embeddedness and malleability of others. In a striking contrast to the 'pet prisoner,' he recognizes the power of circumstances in the lives of other people but refuses to take advantage of this defence to account for his own moral failings. If we translate the sentiments of Dickens's penitent into the language of today's social sciences, he might be thinking along these lines: 'Although I recognize that others may be products of outside influences, and that in fact my own involvement in their lives must have affected their moral character and actions in adverse and destructive ways, for my own part, I refuse to appeal to the power of circumstances to rationalize my criminal conduct, for the power of situatedness ends with me.' It is this renunciation of the idea of social determinism and the embracing of one's moral freedom and responsibility that appear to be as necessary to the subject's spiritual reformation as his sincere and heartfelt remorse. Defying the culture of 'Nobody's Fault,' the genuinely reformed penitent remembers both his crime and his victim,[34] resisting the typical gestures of, at best, effacing 'the murdered person,' or, at worst, of monstrously presenting the victim's demise as a necessary element in the story of his own spiritual awakening.[35]

As he starts on the path of self-mastery and self-creation, the penitent thus takes an important step towards reshaping himself in the mould of the autonomous, rational, and responsible subject valorized by the Victorian discourse of character. This embracing of one's autonomy and responsibility is particularly important because therein lies the only assurance that the positive change the penitent claims to have undergone in prison will not be reversed as soon as he steps outside. Indeed, one important aspect of Dickens's critique emerges from his distrust of the power of patterned reformation to withstand the test of the 'working world.'[36] Repeatedly, Dickens alludes to the fleeting nature of patterned transformations, suggesting that the converts' enthusiastic readiness to fight temptations is best accounted for by their virtual absence within prison walls.[37] The fortitude necessary to withstand the power of one's circumstances, the conviction needed to resist the corrupting influence of wicked associates, the firmness requisite to follow one's resolutions can only originate in the penitent who has embraced his autonomy and responsibility, and has recognized himself as a self-determining and self-creating subject. As the content of 'pattern penitence' reveals, this is emphatically not the kind of penitent that one encounters in Dickens's John Styles and 'pet prisoners' like him.

What Dickens's discussions foreground then is the paramount importance that the reformers attributed to language both in enacting and in gauging moral reform in the individual criminal. Dickens himself, however, remains deeply suspicious of patterned professions of reform, repudiating them as much on account of their form as their content. Equally mistrustful of the pattern and of the penitence, he rejects both the language that is already inscribed with the categories that legitimate the institution that promotes it and the categories themselves. While one can argue that the alternative narrative of reform Dickens offers is just another institutional script, it nevertheless reveals an important difference between his and the officially endorsed conceptions of reformed subjectivity. Whereas the reform of the 'pattern penitent' consists, according to Dickens, in merely mastering the language of penitence, the spiritual revival of Dickens's genuinely reformed subject consists in mastering the self.

'Pattern Penitence' in *David Copperfield*

The polemic against the 'separate' system that Dickens began in *American Notes* and particularly in 'Pet Prisoners' continued in *David Copperfield*. But whereas 'Pet Prisoners' points to the system's failure to distinguish between discourse and lived experience, *David Copperfield* suggests its inability to distinguish between different kinds of discourses.

In chapter 61 of the novel, which relates David's visit to the model prison, Dickens satirizes the gullibility of the separatists, eager to believe the professions of penitence that both David and the reader know to be fraudulent. Coming as they are from Uriah Heep and Littimer, the novel's villains and confirmed hypocrites, they can be nothing else. But 'the system,' represented here by Mr Creakle, David's old schoolmaster-turned-magistrate, and his colleagues is blind to the fact. The officials appear to be fully taken by the professions of the two hypocrites, as do the majority of the visitors who tour the prison along with David.[38] Adapting the conventions of 'patterned penitence' to oral discourse, the duo take turns preaching at David and calling on him and others 'to see [their] wickedness, and amend.' They bless their 'present state' and declare that prison has made them 'sensible of [their] follies.'[39] They only wish that their visitors could all be 'took up and brought here.'[40] 'When I think of my past follies, and my present state,' Uriah concludes his sermon, 'I am sure it would be best for you. I pity all who ain't brought here!'[41]

Dickens's representation is, of course, a caricature of the conventions of 'pattern penitence' and an attack on the institution's readiness to credit the obviously fake displays of contrition and professions of moral reformation. Like any caricature, it exaggerates the features that it targets, hyperbolizing the obvious duplicity of Uriah and Littimer and overstating the gullibility of the officials. But regardless of how dullwitted (or self-serving) the officials are made out to be, one may argue that it is in principle unfair to expect of them the same insight into the penitents' subjectivity as David and the reader possess. The perceptiveness that we share with David (and that is denied to the officials and the visitors) is an effect of our privileged position. It originates in the surplus of knowledge that we have and that they don't. After all, what constitutes chief evidence of Heep's and Littimer's insincerity is precisely their 'moral character.' But what is literally an open book to us, Heep's and Littimer's past being delineated in David's autobiographical novel where both figure as characters, is not at all an open book to Mr Creakle and others. They are invited to assess these characters' morality without the benefit of the information that David and the reader are privy to, and get ridiculed when they misjudge. And although Mr Creakle's own moral failings authorize our laughter on other grounds, it is still worth remembering that what he, and 'the system' in his person, has at his disposal is, for the most part, representations made by these characters themselves. The question then arises as to how Mr Creakle (and the system he represents) interprets them.

In the remaining section of the paper I consider this issue through the lens of Mikhail Bakhtin's discourse analysis developed in his study of Dostoevsky. Reading the novel's chapter 61, as well as the historical professions of 'pattern penitence,' with reference to Bakhtin's instrumentality suggests that separatists viewed the penitential language as 'direct,' 'unmediated,' 'object oriented' discourse (all terms come from Bakhtin's analytical arsenal), that is, a discourse that is used for 'naming, informing, expressing, representing,' and that is intended for 'unmediated, object-oriented understanding.'[42] Oblivious to the (inevitably) stratified nature and multivalent meanings of the words it uses, a direct unmediated discourse, Bakhtin explains, 'recognizes only itself and its object, to which it strives to be maximally adequate.'[43] It is a discourse that knows no irony and is well fitted for speaking in earnest. And this is apparently how both Joseph and his fictive counterparts in *David Copperfield* see the penitents use the language of 'pattern penitence.'

As we have seen already, the fact that Joseph's charges probably learnt this language from Joseph himself does not trouble the solemn reformer. And, according to Bakhtin, there may indeed be no cause for concern. As Bakhtin explains, the fact that a direct unmediated discourse may imitate someone or learn from someone 'does not change things in the slightest.'[44] As long as the project of an utterance does not include the task of giving the stage to the imitated voice next to the imitating one (becoming double-voiced in the process), it remains single-voiced, direct, and unmediated.[45] Confident about its semantic authority, it has no doubt that this authority is located within its borders. And if the language of penitence accurately reflects – or so the penitents feel – the process they claim to have undergone, its uniformity and resemblance to the language of their spiritual mentors does not in itself constitute evidence that it is used spuriously. It is apparently this possibility that Dickens has in mind when in 'Pet Prisoners' he suggests in reference to the professions of the fictitious convict John Styles that he 'may mean it.'[46]

Most likely, however, he does not. At least, Styles's novelistic counterparts do not. And yet following real-life models like Joseph and Field, the officials in *David Copperfield* fail to see the deception. They fail to see, in other words, that Littimer's and Heep's speech is not a direct unmediated discourse but represented and objectified one. In fact, it is objectified on two levels, by Dickens and by the characters themselves. To sort out this point, I need to turn briefly to Bakhtin's discussion of objectified discourse.

Objectified discourse, Bakhtin explains in *Problems of Dostoevsky's Poetics*, is different from direct unmediated discourse in that it itself becomes an object of representation. The most typical form of represented discourse is the direct speech of characters.[47] It is treated, Bakhtin continues, 'as someone else's discourse, as discourse belonging to some specific characterological profile or type,' that is to say 'as an object of authorial understanding and not from the point of view of its referential orientation.'[48] While a character's speech does, of course, have a referential meaning, it is also 'at the same time the object of someone else's intention, the author's.'[49] Its task to carry out referential intention is subordinated to an overriding task posited by the author. Objectified discourse itself, however, knows nothing of this superseding task. Nor is it aware of serving any functions other than those that are consistent with what is expected of direct unmediated discourse that it knows itself to be and that it is, if viewed from within the character's field of vision.

For example, in Heep's professions of repentance Dickens represents the discourse of 'pattern penitence.' While Heep himself uses this discourse to make representations about his alleged moral conversion, Dickens surrounds it with the text (of the entire novel), which clearly exposes Heep's speeches as lies, making thus a critical statement not only about Heep but also about the discourse itself. Dickens's intention, however, does not penetrate inside the objectified speech of Heep, who remains unaware that he participates in the debunking of his own discourse, but is realized through the contrast between Dickens's and Heep's semantic goals. It is this opposition between the author's and the character's semantic intentions that constitutes this representation as parody.

But while it is easy to see how Dickens objectifies the discourse of 'pattern penitence,' it is more important for my argument to see how Heep and Littimer do the same. Just as Dickens's intention to discredit Heep's and Littimer's objectified discourse lies outside its parameters, so do these characters' real intentions lie outside the scope of 'pattern penitence' and have little to do with its referential powers. Their intention, after all, is not to use the pattern to represent the penitence but rather to use this discourse to construct the kind of selves that are consistent with the system's conception of reformed subjectivity. It is in this sense that their use of 'pattern penitence' is analogous to a novelist's use of objectified discourse of another.

Indeed, in chapter 61 Littimer and Heep no longer function as just characters in Dickens's novel; they also function as authors of selves that match the institutional definition of a reformed criminal. It is in authoring these new selves, these new characters in their own novels, so to speak, that they make use of a newly learnt discourse that is, after all, a discourse of another. A murderous look that David detects on Heep's face, a look that is so radically at odds with the spirit of Heep's preaching, communicates exactly that otherness.[50] Not only does it indicate to David and to the reader that Heep's declarations of contrition are opportunistic and untrustworthy, but it also frames his words as a quote, as discourse of another that Heep the author puts in the mouth of Heep the character that he forges for the consumption of the system.[51]

That David can see through Heep's and Littimer's dissembling while 'the system' remains blind to it can be attributed then just as much to David's familiarity with their inglorious past as to his occupation as a professional writer. It is only natural that as someone who himself is in the business of making characters he has a better eye for detecting similar activities of others. Adept in creating subtle double-voiced utterances, as his own discourse amply demonstrates, he is understandably more conscious of other people's discursive manipulations.[52]

It is David's sensitivity to language that accounts for his mistrust of the uniform letter of protestations of penitence, a mistrust which, by his own admission, is even stronger than his mistrust of their spirit (on his prison tour, we remember, he finds 'a great amount of profession, varying very little in character: varying very little (which I thought exceedingly suspicious), even in words'). This mistrust signals David's belief that such an intensely personal process as spiritual rebirth can only be articulated in ways that are non-repeatable and unique. The standardized, institutionalized format into which such protestations are channelled strikes David as a sign of their inauthenticity.

Furthermore, what David hears in Heep's and Littimer's professions of penitence is a dialogized, double-voiced discourse, a discourse which has at least two centres and two worldviews, one consistent with the ideology that has given birth to 'pattern penitence,' and the other that disputes and challenges it. He discerns, in other words, a profound separation between the author and the character in the authoring activities of the 'two interesting penitents,' who activate the discourse of 'pattern penitence' not to refer to any change that has occurred in their self-understanding but to plagiarize the kinds of selves that comply with the institutional definition of reformed subjectivity.

In contrast to David, the separatists, both in the novel and in real life, welcomed and cultivated precisely the standardization of penitents' self-expressions. To them such uniformity was crucial to the very project of 'pattern penitence': to transmute a stubbornly elusive content into an easily assessable bureaucratic text and to serve, in the absence of referential verifiability, as the only obtainable evidence of reform's success. And yet the separatists' willingness to view self in terms of a discursive program does not signal a forward-looking proto-post-structuralist conception of subjectivity, for they saw this program as a means of subverting any further possibility of fluctuation, contradiction, stratification, or tension in the self-describing subject. As *David Copperfield* reveals, the separatists approached patterned professions of reform as a plainly referential discourse that describes a unitary and now permanently fixed self. Insensitive to the deployment of language that departs from univocal and transparent expression, the system ignored the possibility of separation between authors and characters in patterned tales of reform. Choosing to view the self-describing self as indivisible and its description as plainly referential, it overlooked its plagiarized nature.

Conclusion

Dickens's formulation 'pattern penitence' reveals his insight into one of the central conflicts of the institution of the penitentiary. What the wording recognizes in the system's encouragement of patterned self-delineation is the institution's effort to cope with the challenges ingrained in the very nature of the penitentiary as it attempted to deal uniformly with the infinite variety of individual experience and yet to accomplish change that was the same. In relating the empirically unverifiable process (moral reform) with reference to the rigid discursive paradigm of reformation narrative, 'pattern penitence' externalized the imperatives of the two major epistemologies underlying the penitentiary project. While the 'pattern' in 'pattern penitence,' with its emphasis on the formulaic and repeatable, exemplified the institutional recognition of the demands of empiricist rationalism, with its prizing of the objective, verifiable, and reproducible, 'the penitence' in the same formulation belonged to the province of evangelical idealism, where it was conceived as a transforming experience of a profoundly personal and therefore unrepeatable kind. By recounting experiences that were characterized by radical specificity with reference to conventions that were characterized by strict uniformity, 'pattern penitence' helped to neutralize and homogenize what was diverse and unverifiable on the level of content by making it appear homogeneous and repeatable on the level of form. And it was precisely the form, the patterned penitence itself that, according to Dickens, the separatists naively mistook for evidence of moral reform in the individual criminal, and thus for a measure of the institution's success. In the end, however, whether we look for the origins of 'pattern penitence' in the ideological foundations of the penitentiary or in the institutional need for self-legitimation, whether we account for its popularity with the officials by reference to their gullibility or ambition, what Dickens exposes behind the separatists' readiness to credit uniform accounts of moral reform is the institutional tendency to see all discourse as direct, object oriented, and monologic, a tendency that ultimately results in the institution's failure to distinguish between discourse and lived experience.

NOTES

1 Philip Collins, *Dickens and Crime* (London: Macmillan, 1962). I would like to acknowledge a great debt to Philip Collins's invaluable study, which has informed many of my discussions.

2 Harry Stone, ed., *Charles Dickens' Uncollected Writings from Household Words, 1850–1859*, 2 vols. (Bloomington: Indiana University Press, 1968), 2:484.

3 For a history of the 'separate' system in Britain, see U.R.Q. Henriques, 'The Rise and Decline of the Separate System of Prison Discipline,' *Past and Present* 54 (1972): 61–93.

4 For a detailed discussion of Dickens's views on various prison regimes, see Collins, *Dickens and Crime*, and David Paroissien's contribution to this collection. For a critique of the 'silent' system in Dickens, see Adam Hansen's essay in this volume.

5 William Hepworth Dixon, *The London Prisons, with an Account of the More Distinguished Persons Who Have Been Confined in Them: to Which Is Added, a Description of the Chief Provincial Prisons* (London: Jackson and Walford, 1850), 9.

6 *British Parliamentary Papers*, vol. 11 of *Crime and Punishment: Prisons* (Shannon: Irish University Press, 1970), 439.

7 Henry Mayhew, *The Criminal Prisons of London, and Scenes of Prison Life, by Henry Mayhew and John Binny* (1862; New York: A.M. Kelley, 1968), 80. For a detailed analysis of this text, see W.B. Carnochan's contribution to this volume.

8 Janet Fyfe, *Books Behind Bars: The Role of Books, Reading, and Libraries in British Prison Reform, 1701–1911* (Westport, CT: Greenwood Press, 1992), 3.

9 John Field, *Prison Discipline; and the Advantages of the Separate System of Imprisonment with a Detailed Account of the Discipline Now Pursued in the New County Gaol, at Reading* (London: Longman, 1848), 40.

10 Field, *Prison Discipline*, 42.

11 Ibid., 43.

12 Henry Samuel Joseph, *Memoirs of Convicted Prisoners: Accompanied by the Remarks on the Causes and Prevention of Crime* (London: Wertheim, 1853).

13 Joseph, *Memoirs of Convicted Prisoners*, 63.

14 Ibid., 85.
15 Ibid., 69.
16 Ibid., 78.
17 Ibid., 142.
18 Ibid., 18.
19 Ibid., 142.
20 This is Victorian prison slang for a convict who fakes reformation by displays of religious feelings. Mayhew explains this slang term in *The Criminal Prisons of London*, 169. See also Sean C. Grass's essay in this collection.
21 The piece appeared about four weeks following the publication of 'Model Prisons,' a violently critical pamphlet by Carlyle written upon his visit to Coldbath Fields, a prison organized on the 'silent' system. While Dickens never mentions Carlyle's pamphlet and, in contrast to Carlyle, focuses on Pentonville – a model prison on the 'separate' system – many of the attitudes that he expresses in 'Pet Prisoners' are similar to Carlyle's.
22 Michael Slater, ed., *Dickens' Journalism*, vol. 2, *The Amusements of the People and Other Papers: Reports, Essays, and Reviews, 1834–51* (Columbus: Ohio State University Press, 1995), 220.
23 Ibid.
24 Ibid.
25 Ibid., 220–1.
26 Ibid., 223.
27 On the exchange between Dickens and Field, see Collins, *Dickens and Crime*, 119–21.
28 Slater, *Dickens' Journalism*, 2:222.
29 Ibid., 223.
30 Ibid.
31 Ibid., 225.
32 Ibid., 220.
33 I am borrowing the term 'situatedness' from David Simpson, *Situatedness, or Why We Keep Saying Where We're Coming From* (Durham, NC: Duke University Press, 2002).
34 While in the case of a (male) criminal, Dickens emphasizes the importance of remembering the crime as pivotal to the penitent's moral reclamation, in the case of a prostitute, he seems to suggest the necessity of a balance between remembering and forgetting. In his letters to Miss Coutts concerning Urania Cottage, Dickens both insists that the staff never refer to the women's past lives and emphasizes the need for the women themselves to remember the 'lessons' about the consequences of poor choices. See David Paroissien, ed., *Selected Letters of Charles Dickens* (Boston: Twayne Publishers, 1985), 193–210.

35 In 'The Murdered Person,' a *Household Words* article from 11 October 1856, Dickens uses the phrase 'the murdered person' as a shorthand for the kind of instrumental thinking that remembers the victim (be it a murdered human being or the cheated nation) only as part of the perpetrator's own story of success (be it the murderer's spiritual reformation or the illusory triumphs of certain military administrators). See Michael Slater, ed., *Dickens' Journalism*, vol. 3, *'Gone Astray' and Other Papers from Household Words*, 1851–59 (Columbus: Ohio State University Press, 1999), 396–402.

36 Slater, *Dickens' Journalism*, 2:223. Dickens expresses similar sentiments in a 1846 letter to Miss Coutts: 'A kind of penitence is bred in our prisons and purgatories just now, which is a very pretty penitence inside the walls, but fades into nothing when it comes into contact with worldly realities.' See Paroissien, *Selected Letters of Charles Dickens*, 199.

37 See, for instance, 'Perfect Felicity in a Bird's-Eye View,' a *Household Words* article from 6 April 1850. In Slater, *Dickens' Journalism*, 2:192.

38 Charles Dickens, *David Copperfield* (London: Penguin Classics, 1985), 917.

39 Dickens, *David Copperfield*, 927, 928.

40 Ibid., 929.

41 Ibid., 928.

42 Mikhail Bakhtin, *Problems of Dostoevsky's Poetics*, trans. Caryl Emerson. (Minneapolis: University of Minnesota Press, 1993), 186.

43 Bakhtin, *Problems of Dostoevsky's Poetics*, 187.

44 Ibid.

45 Ibid.

46 Slater, *Dickens' Journalism*, 2:221.

47 Bakhtin, *Problems of Dostoevsky's Poetics*, 186.

48 Ibid., 187.

49 Ibid., 189.

50 Ibid., 928.

51 A similar effect can be detected in Mr Littimer's admonition to David to 'repent of all the wickedness and sin to which he has been a party.' See Dickens, *David Copperfield*, 927. While obviously amusing in its impudence, coming as it does from a convicted thief and one of the novel's worst villains, the remark is also comical in its clashing of dissonant discourses. As he has the language of evangelical preaching break into the register of bureaucratic communications, Littimer not only solicits the reader's smile at his discursive fumble but also invites a suspicion that he, too, is only 'quoting.' The interpolation of discourses we find in Littimer's language points to the existence of a second speech centre, and consequently, at the presence of what Bakhtin calls an axiological orientation that is alien to the language of evangelicalism.

52 Consider, for instance, the following sentence from the same chapter. In reference
to the invitation he has received from Mr Creakle to visit the model prison under his
supervision, David says to his friend Traddles: 'And he writes to me here, that he
will be glad to show me, in operation, the only true system of prison discipline; the
only unchallengeable way of making sincere and lasting converts and penitents –
which, you know, is by solitary confinement. What do you say?' (Dickens, *David
Copperfield*, 921). This is a classic example of Bakhtin's 'hybrid construction,' that
is, an utterance that appears to belong to a single speaker but that contains within its
formal boundaries two different voices. Juxtaposed with the voice of Mr Creakle,
who diligently reproduces in his letter the language of treatises advocating the 'separate' system of prison discipline, the reader can 'hear' David's voice, which says
'You know' and 'What do you say?' The interjection and the question cast a thick
ironic shade on Mr Creakle's stilted official language. The chapter features several
more examples of the same use of official prison reform discourse. On hybrid constructions, see the chapter on heteroglossia in Bakhtin's 'Discourse in the Novel.'
See *The Dialogic Imagination: Four Essays by M.M. Bakhtin*, trans. Caryl Emerson
and Michael Holquist. (Austin: University of Texas Press, 1996), 303–24.

7 Prisoners and Prisons in Reform Tracts of the Mid-Century

W.B. CARNOCHAN

Visiting a prison brings with it a troubled blend of emotions: sympathy mixed with understanding that sympathy can be too easy; the conditioned reflex of those who are fortunate in the presence of those who are unfortunate; the knowledge that some of those who are imprisoned would or could be danger-ous company in a different setting; awareness that one has at least imagined doing things that could have meant living behind the bars and walls topped with razor wire that are the grim insignia of incarceration; a sense that, what-ever the deprivations of prison, the regimen imposes an order and simplicity on prisoners' lives that may be missing from one's own; discomfort to the point of embarrassment in the role of spectator, walking down the brightly lit corridor of a cell block and wondering how to look at occupants of the cells without appearing to stare (should you smile? try to say something encourag-ing?); anger, perhaps, at the very nature of the human situation; admiration for the strength of will that enables some inmates to lead productive lives under conditions of confinement; awareness that one simple difference separates you, the visitor, from 'them,' namely, that you will walk through the gate to the world outside when you want to while they can't; and, finally, awareness, too, that this may be an illusory or at least a trivial difference: for those within and for those without the prison walls, there is only one way out in the long run, and those without, as much as those within, may feel like inmates – of their bodies and of the world.

Of course it is the modern prison – as it was created in the West towards the end of the eighteenth century – that generates this mixture of feelings; or, we might want to say with John Bender, it is this mixture of feelings, a product of the modern world as it forced and fumbled its way into existence, that brought about the very possibility and structure of the modern prison.[1] It is a fair pre-sumption that prison reformers, often visitors themselves within the walls, will experience these same feelings. They also have an explicit agenda: tolerable prison conditions, concern for the humanity of inmates, and measured assessment of the penal system are their goals. But along with this agenda comes the need to gain the attention and commitment of an audience with interests that may not be limited to the hopes of reform. Victorian reform tracts are typically balancing acts, poised between claims of reason and the secret allure of the unknown. We read on, persuaded (probably) by the claims of reason but drawn in more firmly still by the promise of hidden knowledge. The prisoner, always a cog in the immense penal system by which the modern world deals with those who deviate from its behavioural codes, also figures as a human example, sometimes for good, sometimes for ill. Prisoners have stories, and reformers tell them when they can – because we like to hear stories. If the penal system will not allow the stories to be told, that creates a story of its own.

The mid-nineteenth century was a heyday of prison reform, and the public had an insatiable appetite for reform tracts, as indeed for anything relating to prison life. The reforming craze and the literature it generated helped fill the gap left when the straightforward genre of criminal biography, with its calendar of sensational crimes and punishments, was in a measure eclipsed by the changing conventions of the Victorian world that yielded the reform agenda itself and by evolving penal customs. A recent series of reprints, edited by Martin J. Wiener, with the umbrella title *Crime and Punishment in England, 1850–1922* offers thirty titles spanning the years from 1849 to 1922. Of these titles, eight were published between 1850 and 1863. Not included, for reasons no doubt both of size and greater availability, is Henry Mayhew and John Binny's monumental *The Criminal Prisons of London and Scenes of Prison Life*, a sequel to Mayhew's *London Labour and the London Poor. The Criminal Prisons of London* was published in 1862, though much of it had been completed in the 1850s. In little more than a decade, the reading public was offered its fill, and then some, of 'scenes of prison life.'

Among the texts from these middle years of the century – both included in the series *Crime and Punishment in England* and both known to Mayhew – were William Hepworth Dixon's *The London Prisons: With an Account of the More Distinguished Persons Who Have Been Confined in Them; To Which is Added a Description of the Chief Provincial Prisons* (1850) and George Laval Chesterton's *Revelations of Prison Life; With an Enquiry into Prison Discipline and Secondary Punishments* (2nd edition, 1856). Between them, Dixon and Chesterton offer a sample of reform narratives during the period. This essay will consider both texts before going on to Mayhew and Binny, whose survey, like *London Labour and the London Poor*, achieves something like the grandeur of epic, and similar to many a Dickensian fiction is panoramic in range, all the while anticipating considerations of prison life and its inmates, now a staple of the literature, that view the prisoner as a demographic counter within a controlled sociological setting. The monumental narrative structure of *The Criminal Prisons of London* sets Mayhew and Binny apart, but these texts all display stresses and strains intrinsic to the genre, as well as the normal stylistic mannerisms of Victorian prose, so well fitted to express the psychological shocks of prison experience that it is as if the subject required the style; or as if, in the subject of the prison, the style found its most appropriate vehicle of expression. If one were to reduce the ambiguities of these texts to a single, simple formula, it would be, on the one hand, the analytical (including any amount of data concerning the demographic characteristics of inmates, their daily lives, their offences, and the setting, architecture, and costs of prisons); on the other, the emotional and evocative (such as we associate with criminal biography, with tales of the powerful and the famous who, falling afoul of authority, find themselves in some inhospitable dungeon, or with tales of human wretchedness and misfortune). I propose, as a thesis that could be further tested, that such a combination of modes is a defining – or at least a common – feature of the genre; and even, in a more attenuated form, that it underlies much of the vast fictional literature relating to the experience of prisoners and prisons. Reform tracts of the 1850s, in their ambiguities of feeling, anticipate attitudes and strategies that are with us to the present.[2]

I

William Hepworth Dixon (1821–79) was one of those substantial, if not quite eminent, Victorians who can still dazzle us by their sheer output and the breadth of their work and life. He was not Charles Dickens, but he was a near contemporary who, like Dickens and others, ranged far and wide over the literary and journalistic landscape, including the landscape of the prison. He was first of all a journalist, serving as editor of *The Athenæum* from 1853 to 1869. He was a writer of fiction, a traveller whose voyages yielded a double-decker called *New America* (1867), a historian, and a reformer, though perhaps a reformer who knew above all that reform suited the public taste. His first major publication, in 1849, was *John Howard and the Prison-World of Europe*. *The London Prisons*, based on but much expanded from an earlier series of papers in the *Daily News*, followed the next year. As a journalist Dixon understood what his readers liked and wanted; and, to the papers in the *Daily News*, written 'to paint the actual condition' of the London prisons and to enable readers 'to form a judgment on the comparative merits of the various schemes of criminal treatment,' he added sections in *The London Prisons* 'to take in the Past as well as the Present' – including chapters on the Tower of London, with its galaxy of famous occupants, and on the Queen's Bench, with still another roster of illustrious names.[3] Only after he has milked these celebrity tales does he move on to survey contemporary prisons, not only in London but also in the provinces, beginning with the infamous hulks, good fodder always for a hearty Victorian shudder. Reform is a fine thing, especially when a touch of spice is added to the brew.

Dixon's style, at its most purple moments, blends rhetorical questions, exclamatory exhalations, and anaphoric repetition. The Tower of London section, for all its sensational material, is a relatively restrained historical chronicle; the material itself, with all its turns of fortune's wheel, is largely allowed to carry the burden of feeling. But when Dixon comes to the fate of (mostly) debtors, past and present, in the Queen's Bench, he hits his full organ-throated stride, at least in the chapter's opening lines:

> Who has not heard of Queen's Bench prison? Who, that has come to years of discretion, and inherited that "right of man," the privilege of going to gaol for his own debts, has not more than heard of it? Is there a lounger in Pall-mall, a saunterer in Regent-street, who has not had a friend there at one time of his life or another? Has not every one known men prefer it to Rome, Baden-Baden, or Vienna? In fact, where is the statesman, poet, artist, noble, wit, politician, or philosopher, who has not paid a visit to its secluded courts – taken momentary shelter from the storms of life within its peaceful haven – and gathered there new strength to contend against a wasteful world? Queen's Bench! Why, the very words sound like an oracle, and stir the depths of memory as a dream. There are history and romance in its sound. Before the mind's eye moves a procession of glorious and spectral forms – authors, heroes, artists, who for a time have hallowed with their life, and thought, and fancies, the precincts which it names. Queen's Bench![4]

Nor is this the entire passage, which ambles on in the same vein for another 150 words or so. For any connoisseur of prison journalism and prison writing generally, this is a considerable find. Seldom can the sensational trope of the prison as sanctuary, even as monastery – a trope familiarized once again in the prison meditations of Jean Genet – have been more grandly deployed, while at the same time exhibiting an almost sly mock-heroic awareness of its own excess.

It is worth pondering Dixon's baroque ornamentation, so *Victorian* in kind, in this apostrophe to the Queen's Bench. Of course there are occasional loungers in Pall Mall who haven't had a friend there; and it would not be hard to discover statesmen, poets, artists, nobles, wits, politicians, and philosophers who had never paid a visit. But Dixon knows that. He is invoking the prison mystique. In one sense everybody is a debtor, thus a visitor, metaphorically, to the Queen's Bench. It is the language of the sacred and of the visionary that gives the passage its special cast. The prison is a cloister with 'secluded courts,' a peaceful haven against the fierce storms of life, a counterforce to that of the 'wasteful' world where debtors are made. Its very name is an oracle, proclaiming the visionary landscape of dream. Authors, heroes, and artists, in 'glorious and spectral forms,' pass before the mind's eye in a dreamlike procession – authors, heroes, and artists who have 'hallowed' the ground.

It is a long way from this lavish apostrophe to the prison as sanctuary to the ultimate close of the chapter, where Dixon warns his readers against those idle inhabitants of the actual prison who constitute 'a whole colony of low beggars and letter-writing impostors.' One man, he reports, 'has been in the prison seven-and-twenty years. He won't go out,' even though 'liberty has been all the while in his own hands.' Therefore, readers beware: 'We would strongly counsel every one to make proper inquiries before sending money to persons confined in the Queen's Prison, however plausible the tale of their distress may seem. The officers can usually give the information that is desired.'[5] The ground that has been hallowed by authors and heroes and artists is, here, more like a den of low-life thieves.

II

Chesterton's *Revelations of Prison Life*, though gossipy and rambling, is a more managerial and matter-of-fact affair than *The London Prisons*. That is not surprising, for Chesterton was no mere visiting reformer; he had been governor of Coldbath Fields, the Middlesex County house of correction for men, for twenty-five years from 1829 to 1854. During his final year in office, Coldbath Fields housed 'the extraordinary daily average of 1400 souls' and, at one point during the year, no less than 1596 inmates. Governing the prison must have been no easy job, and Chesterton, a former artillery officer who was studying for holy orders, his military career behind him, had been appointed when a previous incumbent was dismissed on charges of 'neglect, mal-administration, and incompetence.' Chesterton's tenure was not only long but successful, and he was eager to take credit: 'My emphatic claim is to have been one of the humble instruments in the hands of Providence (and my conscience tells me I was no sluggish or lukewarm participator) in that onward and eventful movement, by whose civilizing influence the chief prison of the metropolitan county (perhaps the most extensive in the world), was transformed from one of the worst specimens of corruption and misrule into an establishment distinguished for industry, order, and impressive discipline.' In *Revelations of Prison Life* he sets out to tell how he made the prison a model institution of industry, order, and discipline by instituting and rigorously enforcing the 'silent' system, in which prisoners worked together but with no communication allowed between them: 'During the extended period of twenty years, did I maintain, with unyielding strictness, the silent system in the prison of Cold Bath Fields.'[6] With his military training and his earlier hopes of a vocation in holy orders, Chesterton was well suited to the task of taming an unruly institution.

Yet, like Dixon, he knew the public wanted something more than a bare treatise on prison discipline – a treatise that he did in fact put forth, arguing the claims of the 'silent' system against those of its chief rival, the 'separate' system, embodied in Bentham's famed proposal for the Panopticon and in use at prisons other than Coldbath Fields, both in Britain and America. Chesterton thought the 'silent' system more humane than the isolation of the cell block and more likely to induce reform. But 'revelations of prison life' were better designed to sell books than theories of penology. As the title makes apparent, *Revelations of Prison Life; With an Enquiry into Prison Discipline and Secondary Punishments* sought to reap the related yet independent benefits that came with, on the one hand, an enquiry into prison regimen and, on the other, revelations – with their hint of what might turn out to be strange or shocking – of prison life.

Chesterton was fascinated as much as he was repelled by those in his charge. This becomes clear very early in his first volume when he teases the reader with an account of the 'ordinary' – and shocking – 'language of public reprobates.' This language 'is not only to the last degree foul and revolting, but it is, moreover, intensely curious. Some studious miscreant appears to have closely analysed, and industriously sifted the elements of language, in order to select and embody its most refined abominations. The ordinary conversation, therefore, of such outcasts is a compound of whatever is gross, brutal, and disgusting; but still so wickedly ingenious as to constitute a startling science.' This description matches the familiar response by guardians of public decency who cry out against, say, the grossness and brutality of pornography but study its startling science with attention. Chesterton has studied the language of his reprobates, a language so shocking that, though it bears description, it does not bear repetition, and 'propriety forbids one solitary example'; a language that is 'dreadful, indeed, but yet singularly curious; and exhibiting a depth and subtlety of research which betokens a laborious diligence in the construction of sentences devoid of decency.'[7] Even the nineteenth-century reader, no doubt dazzled by the surpassing genius, or at least the wit, that has created such unspeakable speech, would have been happy (if only under cover of night) to have seen a few examples. Now, 150 years later, we would welcome examples as eagerly as we read Dickens. Chesterton has grabbed the attention of his audience from the outset.

While contemplating the wickedness of hardened reprobates and their speech habits, both foul and unforgettable, he also turns to the theatrics of innocence, in the person of a naive prisoner confronted with a language unknown to him before. This young man – convicted, with others, of a gold-dust robbery 'some years ago' – is even more shocked than Chesterton: 'oh, sir, I had heard of the language and conversation of the lowest criminals, but I had not the remotest idea of its reality! It is too dreadful to contemplate!!'[8] It is when he is confronted with this surpassing innocence that Chesterton responds, sagely but also strangely, that, yes, the language is dreadful but also 'singularly curious; and exhibiting a depth and subtlety of research.' Would the naive young man have been impressed by the 'research' that Chesterton believes to have created prisoners' cant? The shocking (the speech of reprobates) and the sentimental (the innocent young robber's reaction) thrive in each other's company. The narrator, wise, experienced, and impartially above it all, quite revels in his mixed bag of revelations.

This coexistence of the shocking and the sentimental confirms, in its way, reforming aspirations: inmates may be wicked reprobates when they arrive at Coldbath Fields, but they are susceptible to enlightened treatment. Maybe they are even innately good: 'the manifestation of innate, but long-concealed virtue, is a fact too largely observable by the philanthropic supervisor, to admit of any doubt whatever.' Chesterton's prison world is peopled with the unfortunate victims of social circumstance. Show them 'kindly deportment,' 'gentle words,' and a patient attention to their small requests and there will follow 'a grateful expression in the eye' and 'an unmistakable gleam of satisfaction.' This is the prelude to reform: 'After a short period of submission to the discipline and instruction of a well-ordered prison' – such as Coldbath Fields – 'a softening influence seems imperceptibly to improve the expression of the features of many an hitherto neglected child of misery, and gleams of growing intelligence begin to irradiate the countenance' in a 'silent march of amelioration.'[9]

And yet it would be wrong to think that 'these remarks are of universal application.' Quite the contrary, and now Chesterton does a 180-degree turn back to the unredeemably wicked: 'There are vast numbers of criminals who appear to be dispossessed of every hopeful quality. Their sole instinct seems to be that of blind selfishness.'[10] And so on, at some length and in the same lurid accents. In the official imagination of the 'philanthropic supervisor' there is little room for nuance. It is either/or: essential goodness or immutable evil.

Yet Chesterton also shares Dixon's appetite for 'distinguished persons' who have been confined – not the unlucky denizens of the Tower of London in this case nor poet-debtors, but those who have come into his charge at Coldbath Fields.[11] These distinguished persons, on the human scale, occupy another category from ordinary prisoners: that of the rich or well-born who fall from grace – the Martha Stewarts, one might say, of their time.[12] One of Chesterton's high-born examples was in fact a woman. Presumably she was held at Tothill Fields, the Middlesex House of Correction for women and boys. She was 'the wife of Sir W-------l B-----e, Bart, then separated from her husband,' and she would probably not have been hard to identify for many of Chesterton's readers. She 'possessed, from various sources, about £800 a year, and lived near the Regent's park.' But, being 'extravagant, and indifferent to her credit,' she allowed her furniture to be seized, then printed and circulated hand-bills charging her creditor with theft. Her creditor in turn had her indicted for libel, a jury found against her, 'and a full bench of magistrates resolved to teach her a useful lesson'– two months in a house of Correction, where she proved to be 'pert, supercilious, and disobedient.'[13] Unlike the turns of fortune's wheel that bring great ones down, eliciting melancholy reflections on the transitoriness of worldly things, prison for the merely rich or merely famous is more likely to elicit a clandestine – or maybe not so clandestine – *Schadenfreude*. Who, if seriously pressed, would not admit to a certain satisfaction in Lady B----e's discomfiture – or, so far as that goes, in Martha Stewart's? Chesterton's revelations of prison life are attuned to our sometimes all-too-human feelings. Lady B----e's two months of incarceration are a crowd pleaser as well as a useful lesson. They have nothing to do, one way or another, with the merits or demerits of any prison regimen or indeed of any reform agenda at all.

III

The Criminal Prisons of London also displays its share of feeling responses to prison life but quite otherwise than in Dixon or Chesterton, and in ways more firmly tied to a reform agenda. What had defined the Mayhew brothers' *London Labour and the London Poor* was its extraordinary combination of statistical data, in the form of endless, massive tables containing mountains of information about almost everything, and human portraits in the form both of Dickensian monologues by London's street people and portraits from photographs. Images of an Irish crossing-sweeper; of Jack Black, ratcatcher to the

Queen; of 'Old Sarah,' a hurdy-gurdy player; and of many others; all look out at us from the pages of *London Labour and the London Poor* – sometimes peering across facing pages of the text itself, a text in which we find, for example, such matters as the amount of 'food consumed by and excretions of a horse in twenty-four hours' or a calculation 'that, including the horses of the cavalry regiments in London, which of course are not comprised in the Stamp-Office returns, as well as the animals taken to Smithfield, we may, perhaps, assert that the annual ordure let fall in the London streets amounts, at the outside, to somewhere about 1000 tons weekly, or 52,000 tons per annum.'[14] Thus set side by side, the oddly quantitative and the cheerfully human reflect a world in which sociology and statistics have not yet been surgically detached from the imperatives of individual lives, as they would be in due course.

In *The Criminal Prisons of London*, on the contrary, real, live prisoners are almost entirely absent because Mayhew was unable to interview them. We do see prisons close up and receive, much as in *London Labour and the London Poor*, quantities of data, in this case about prison life. We do not see prisoners, except in quick, occasional glances or in illustrations, again taken from photographs, that show communal and regimented activity: inmates as the indistinguishable cogs in the daily machinery of institutional life. If *London Labour and the London Poor* brought us close to life as it was lived in the streets, *The Criminal Prisons of London* gives us quite a different experience: a sense of psychological and spatial separation between 'us,' outside observers who come and go, and 'them,' figures in the shadows, anonymous inmates beyond our reach, no matter how much we discover about the daily conditions of their lives. What is most evocative in the volume is our awareness of so many missing persons – the prisoners themselves.

The Criminal Prisons of London begins curiously – Mayhew had in mind a grand (but never-to-be-realized) vision of a work that would take in much more than the city's prisons – with a panoramic view of London from the high vantage of an air balloon: 'it was a most wonderful sight to behold that vast bricken mass of churches and hospitals, banks and prisons, palaces and workhouses, docks and refuges for the destitute, parks and squares, and courts and alleys, which make up London – all blent into one immense black spot – to look down upon the whole as the birds of the air look down upon it, and see it dwindled into a mere rubbish heap.'[15] And so on, in an immense tumbling sentence, itself a whole paragraph, that adds up to over three hundred words. The common denominator of the bird's-eye views that Montgolfier's invention made real was their capacity for effacing difference and diminishing persons into remote ant-like figures in the landscape. Mayhew's balloon view of the great metropolis, as it turned out, was aesthetically congruous with his eventual subject: the remoteness of life in the prisons from our own and the utter, methodical sameness of life in what Erving Goffman, a century later, was to call 'total institutions.'[16]

To underscore the difference that divides 'us' and 'them,' Mayhew often adopts a simple-seeming yet unusually effective narrative strategy: he brings us with him from the moment he sets out in the morning, then along the route that brings him to his destination and, only then, through the gates of the prison and into its carceral heart. Going to visit a prison is like boarding a conveyance to some other world.

Let us imagine first, by way of comparison and illustration, that our destination is not one of London's nineteenth-century prisons but, instead, the Louisiana State Penitentiary in Angola, Louisiana, a maximum security facility famous until recently as brutally harsh and violent, now much changed for the better but still forbidding in its aspect, eighteen thousand acres of former plantation land, isolated on much of its perimeter by the Mississippi River and by dense wilderness. It is the setting for the film *Dead Man Walking*, with Sean Penn and Susan Sarandon.[17] Anyone who has seen the film will probably recall the quick but defining shot of the prison gateway as Sarandon, in the role of Sister Helen Prejean, drives in to begin her ministry.

But what the shot of the gateway does not by itself convey is the experience of getting there. The site, originally, of a slave plantation – hence its African name – Angola is at the end of a road, perhaps fifteen or twenty miles long, leading off a main north-south highway. On the highway you pass old plantation houses and lands that bespeak the *Gone with the Wind* gentility of their slave-owning society. But after the turn-off to Angola, the antebellum aura fades into a landscape of small and uninspired homes scattered here and there along the edge of the road. The prison awaits at the end of what amounts to a long cul-de-sac – a different world that seems also to be at the very margin of the world itself. If it is summer, the atmosphere is hot and stifling; there seems to be no turning back. Going to Angola is a liminal experience, a time of being in between and a time, also, of equal threat and promise, of apprehension and anticipation.[18]

With the approaches to Angola in mind, we can rejoin Mayhew on his way to Coldbath Fields, the house of correction that George Laval Chesterton had governed for twenty-five years. Mayhew begins at the beginning of his day: 'On a dull summer's morning, when the sky was lead-coloured with an impending storm, and the air was hot as though the thick roof of clouds impeded the ventilation of the City, we left our home to make our visit to this prison.'[19] From the standpoint of the sociologist or the statistician, of course, none of this is important or necessary. Nor are the pages that follow with their evocation of the London scene – cocks crowing, a caged lark singing in a seedman's shop, a newspaper express cart on its way to Euston Station, a milkmaid waiting on a doorstep in Gower Street for the maidservant to take in milk for the day, butchers' carts, the Foundling Hospital, posters advertising an undertaker's shop that offers 'Genteel Funerals' for a guinea[20] – until the traveller arrives at last at his destination. But if the weather and the sights and the sounds along the way to Coldbath Fields are extraneous, sociologically, they are humanly important. Like the road to Angola, the road to Coldbath Fields is a long journey from home.

The gloomy day and the lead-coloured sky set the mood at the outset, in the liminal moment between darkness and dawn: 'The dull morning appeared to have made the inhabitants stop in their beds longer than usual; for, as we gazed down the now clear perspective of the different streets, we could see but few persons about. The only chimneys that were sending out their smoke were those at the bakers, but even here the curling streams of soot were gradually diminishing in blackness, as though the night's work was over and the fires dying out.'[21] Then, quickly, the light changes, black clouds turn to white, trees and gardens and flowers and windowpanes sparkle again, all in a kind of chiaroscuro: the gods of light and darkness are fighting it out. In the in-between time, threat and promise, apprehension and anticipation, equally divide the mind.

But when the voyager approaches Coldbath Fields, everything turns again to grey. The fortress-like brick wall encircling the prison is 'dull,' the buildings nearby are 'dingy and distressed,' and 'the surrounding locality wears a degraded look, as if it also had put on the prison uniform of dirty gray.' Only then, at last, do we arrive at the massive and forbidding gateway with its 'curious George the Third air.'[22] Everything contributes to remoteness of time and place and feeling as we make our way past the guard and through the entrance to Coldbath Fields; the message is: abandon hope, if you should ever have the bad luck to be incarcerated here (see figure 1).

What follows are some seventy-five pages covering 'the history and construction of the prison,'[23] its 'system of management,'[24] both past and present, and, once inside the gateway, the daily routines of the prison and prisoners laid out in the usual relentless detail. Most vivid to the imagination are the modes of hard labour imposed for dozens of offences ranging from abduction to bestiality to dog stealing to indecent exposure.[25] What distinguishes the most onerous forms of hard labour is their intentional and absolute uselessness – the mark of a retributive brutality, under the guise of a constructive work ethic, unmatched even by the later (American) institution of the 'chain gang.' The labours of the 'tread-wheel,' of 'crank work' (rotating a large drum ten thousand times), and of 'shot drill' (passing cannon shot from hand to hand) are all

GATEWAY OF THE HOUSE OF CORRECTION, COLDBATH FIELDS.

Fig. 1. Reprinted from Henry Mayhew and John Binny, *The Criminal Prisons of London and Scenes of Prison Life* (London: Griffin, Bohn, and Company, 1862), 277.

labours of Sisyphus. Picking oakum (small fibres used for caulking) from old rope is scarcely less futile. The prison regimen turns men into robots, machine-like, less than human. That is how they appear in illustrations of the oakum pickers or of prisoners at exercise, walking in single file about one of the prison yards while others, above them, work twenty-four numbered treadwheels, twelve at a time resting for fifteen minutes between turns at the wheel, twelve others arduously marching up the steps of the wheel to nowhere (see figures 2 and 3).[26]

LARGE OAKUM-ROOM (UNDER THE SILENT SYSTEM) AT THE MIDDLESEX HOUSE OF CORRECTION, COLDBATH FIELDS.

Fig. 2. Reprinted from Henry Mayhew and John Binny, *The Criminal Prisons of London and Scenes of Prison Life* (London: Griffin, Bohn, and Company, 1862), 300.

Prison life and its visual representations efface the traces of individuality and selfhood.

Some rare, though partial and revealing, exceptions to the rule that prisoners are, as persons, largely missing comes in a brief section entitled 'Prisoners' Letters.' First we learn the rules governing the sending and receiving of letters – no more than one, either sent or received, in the space of three months, though '*events of importance to prisoners may be committed by letter (prepaid) to the* **Governor**.' Then we listen in, at a distance, on a conversation Mayhew has overheard between a prisoner – 'he had a fawning manner of obsequious respect' – and 'the chief authority.' The conversation as reported includes no dialogue, but Mayhew makes up for the omission as best he can by with an extract from a letter written by the same prisoner: 'This is a finishing school for me for i hope this will be a good warning to me for the future please God spare me to come home again i shall be a altard man please God i can get some employment and have my Sunday to myself, please God i hope i shall never neglect my going to church for i am sorry to say that as been a great folly on my part.'[27] The prisoner, a hansom cab driver before his incarceration who has learned his fawning demeanour in his profession, is unlikely, Mayhew thinks, to be sincere in his avowals.[28] But the real voice and the real orthography of a real prisoner – if we assume the accuracy of

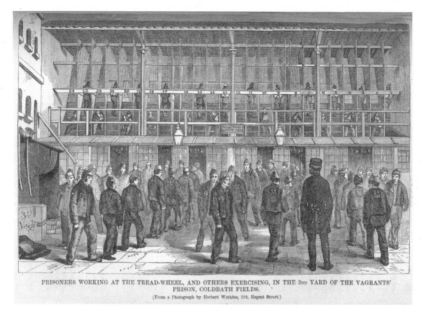

PRISONERS WORKING AT THE TREAD-WHEEL, AND OTHERS EXERCISING, IN THE 3rd YARD OF THE VAGRANTS'
PRISON, COLDBATH FIELDS.
(From a Photograph by Herbert Watkins, 179, Regent Street.)

Fig. 3. Reprinted from Henry Mayhew and John Binny, *The Criminal Prisons of London and Scenes of Prison Life* (London: Griffin, Bohn, and Company, 1862), 306.

Mayhew's transcription – offer some human comfort in the sterile terrain of Coldbath Fields.

Then there follows an even rarer, perhaps unique moment: a poem, transcribed from a prisoner's letter. The poem is in the same vernacular as the letter from the one-time cab driver or the many interviews Mayhew recorded in *London Labour and the London Poor*:

Aunt cousins and friends for a short time adieu
Once more I bid adieu to all of you
I will own liberty is a jewl
While I myself *have* been a fool
My tale myself I will unfold
I think you will say in sin I am old
* * * * * *

O that I ad the wings of a dove
I would begone with liberty and the birds above.[29]

It scarcely matters whether this effusion is entirely authentic, though I suspect it is. What does matter is the incursion of a poetic voice in the pages of

Mayhew's epic tract, thus mitigating the sense of distance created by the long roads the narrator travels to reach his destination and by the immense collection of information that he gathers when he finally arrives. This lone voice, uttering familiar words from the 55th Psalm, stands out bravely among the tables, the lists, the varieties of discipline, the daily schedules, the menus, the data of every sort that fill the volume. Suddenly a lone speaker asserts his presence in a grim setting that is otherwise defined largely by a pervasive and foreboding sense of human absence.

IV

Underlying the large differences between Dixon, Chesterton, and Mayhew is a broad and symptomatic sameness: the claims of prison reform, in their hands, are fortified – or qualified – by claims of the theatrical, the sentimental, or the existential. Whether it is Dixon's celebrated occupants of the Tower or his not much less famous authors, heroes, and artists who have hallowed the grounds of the Queen's Bench; whether it is Chesterton's inmates speaking their deep and subtle, but indecent and troubling, language, or his innocent young prisoner shocked by that language, or his haughty and spendthrift Lady B----e; whether it is Mayhew's Sisyphean world where we see prisoners at a distance labouring at useless tasks but seldom as persons, or the rare occasion when feeling breaks through in the form of an inmate's vernacular poetry – in every case the demands of a reform agenda take their place beside, or even subordinate to, the spectacle of prison experience and the feelings born of that experience. In this context the enigma of Gladstone comes to mind, Britain's prime minister walking the streets of London at night and picking up prostitutes, not for sexual purposes but hoping to rescue them from their wicked ways. The drama of innocence and alluring wickedness is a staple plot of human nature. For the Victorians, it was especially powerful, a dominating text of the age.[30]

NOTES

1 'I shall argue that attitudes toward prison which were formulated between 1719 and 1779 in narrative literature and art – especially in prose fiction – sustained and ... enabled the conception and construction of actual penitentiary prisons later in the eighteenth century.' John Bender, *Imagining the Penitentiary: Fiction and the Architecture of Mind in Eighteenth-Century England* (Chicago: University of Chicago Press, 1987), 1.
2 On themes of prison literature, both from within and without the prison, see W.B. Carnochan, 'The Literature of Confinement,' in *The Oxford History of the Prison:*

The Practice of Punishment in Western Society, ed. Norval Morris and David J. Rothman (New York: Oxford University Press, 1995), 424–55.

3 William Hepworth Dixon, *The London Prisons: With an Account of the More Distinguished Persons Who Have Been Confined in Them; To Which Is Added a Description of the Chief Provincial Prisons* (1850), ed. Martin J. Wiener, *Crime and Punishment in England, 1850–1922* (New York and London: Garland, 1985), vii, viii.

4 Ibid., 102.

5 Ibid., 120f.

6 George Laval Chesterton, *Revelations of Prison Life; with an Enquiry into Prison Discipline and Secondary Punishments* (1856), 2nd and rev. ed., 2 vols., ed. Martin J. Wiener, *Crime and Punishment in England, 1850–1922* (New York and London: Garland, 1984), 1:4, 1:34, 1:3–4, 2:1.

7 Ibid., 1:8, 1:8–9, 1:9.

8 Ibid., 1:9.

9 Ibid., 1:10, 1:10–11, 1:11.

10 Ibid., 1:11, 1:11–12.

11 For further ways in which nineteenth-century narratives may stage the prison as a site of social demarcation, see Greta Olson's contribution in this volume.

12 Perhaps Martha Stewart's name is not so well known elsewhere as it has become in the United States. Chief executive of her own company, Martha Stewart Living, she was convicted and served five months for perjury in connection with sale of stock in another company, on the basis of insider information.

13 Chesterton, *Revelations of Prison Life*, 1:283, 1:284.

14 Henry Mayhew, *London Labour and the London Poor*, 4 vols, intro. John D. Rosenberg (1861–2; New York: Dover, 1968), 2:134, 2:196.

15 Henry Mayhew and John Binny, *The Criminal Prisons of London and Scenes of Prison Life* (London: Griffin, Bohn, and Company, 1862), 9.

16 For Goffman on total institutions, see Erving Goffman, *Asylums: Essays on the Social Situation of Mental Patients and Other Inmates* (New York: Anchor, 1961), especially xiii – 124.

17 *Dead Man Walking*. Dir. Tim Robbins. Gramercy Pictures, 1995.

18 The concept of 'liminal' experience is associated with the late anthropologist Victor Turner. Cf. Bender, *Imagining the Penitentiary*, 26–7.

19 Mayhew and Binny, *The Criminal Prisons of London*, 277.

20 Ibid., 278.

21 Ibid., 277.

22 Ibid., 278, 279.

23 Ibid., 280.

24 Ibid., 284.

25 Cf. ibid., 280, 284, 300.

26 Ibid., 301ff.

27 Ibid., 298, 299.

28 On this question, see also Anne Schur's contribution to this collection.

29 Ibid., 299.

30 Stephen Marcus on pornography, especially on Henry Spencer Ashbee, collector
    and bibliographer extraordinaire, is essential to this story. Cf. Steven Marcus, *The
    Other Victorians: A Study of Sexuality and Pornography in Mid-Nineteenth-
    Century England* (New York: Basics, 1964), 34–76.

8 *Great Expectations*, Self-Narration, and the Power of the Prison

SEAN C. GRASS

Of all Charles Dickens's fictional returns to the prison, none is at once as seductive and enigmatic as *Great Expectations*. No other Dickens novel is so dominated by prisons, though he wrote of them obsessively during thirty-four years as a novelist. From the opening scene on the marshes to Pip's final return to Satis House, literal and figurative prisons brood over the novel, shaping its action, scarring Pip's narrative, and making *Great Expectations* into a protracted account of the guilt engendered by the cell. Yet *Great Expectations* is also the novel in which Dickens's interest in the prison is least literal – least concerned with its concrete realities and ideological failures. The prison may pervade the novel, but there is no wide-eyed Samuel Pickwick here to learn about its horrors; no William Dorrit to show the permanence of its taint; no Alexandre Manette, buried alive and driven mad by solitude, to remind us that the prison depends upon the cruel and capricious operation of power. Instead, *Great Expectations* gives us Abel Magwitch, whom we see in prison only just before his death, and who appears so fleetingly during the first two volumes that he seems more bogeyish than Miss Havisham, that surreal figure of 'wax-work and skeleton' come suddenly to life.[1] In *Little Dorrit* and *A Tale of Two Cities*, which just preceded *Great Expectations*, Dickens had relied at least partly upon his usual practice of narrating the prison through its concrete realities: first in writing of the Marshalsea that had blighted his youth, then in drawing Manette from his memories of prisoners at Philadelphia's Eastern Penitentiary.[2] But *Great Expectations* contains almost nothing of this approach to the cell. The novel is haunted by the prison but scarcely portrays it – is 'about' the prison in tenuous ways. The prison is seductive and enigmatic in the novel because it is stubbornly present, but less as a quantity to be reckoned than as a quality of the narrative itself.

Perhaps because of the prison's equivocal status in the novel, critics have often focused on its obvious symbolic functions. Fifty years ago, in the first sustained study of Pip's guilt, Julian Moynahan observed that 'Pip has certainly one of the guiltiest consciences in literature,' and that his encounters with prisons serve to heighten his sense of the 'deep affinity between him and a world of criminal violence.'[3] Though many critics have assessed the prisons of *Great Expectations* since, they have tended to reach similar conclusions about their role. For J. Hillis Miller, the prisons belong to the novel's drama of guilt and redemption, their relentless recurrence forcing Pip to 'accept the guilt that has always haunted him,'[4] and Michael Peled Ginsburg calls Pip's first encounter with Magwitch 'a primal event ... [that] does not simply *create*, or *originate* the feeling of guilt; rather, it *confirms* a feeling of guilt which predates it.'[5] Such readings make the prison the cause and sign of Pip's psychic unease, a chronic reminder that the boy who once fed a convict on the marshes cannot ever after erase the prison's taint. And they persuade precisely because they reinforce Pip's narrative, which insists throughout that his life has been maimed by prisons: not just by the hulks, but by Mrs Joe and the forge; not just by Newgate, but by Magwitch's designs and Miss Havisham's ruined and ruinous sexual desire. Indeed, Pip emphasizes so strongly the prison's power to shape him that even new essays tend to reach old conclusions about the cell. As David Trotter writes in his recent introduction to the novel – and in language that echoes Moynahan's – Pip's guilt '[is] less a gradually intensifying recognition of moral failure than a deep mysterious affinity with criminal conduct.'[6]

The novel's prisons certainly belong to the poetics of guilt that shape Pip's narrative, but critics who discuss the prison *only* in these terms underestimate its broader significance to the novel. From *The Pickwick Papers* to *The Mystery of Edwin Drood*, Dickens evolved from a comic novelist and social critic into an author concerned deeply with narrating private identity and desire – not an identity *created* by language but an interior identity that language must come to express, a complex psychological self that we might call the Freudian subject. Perhaps because Dickens's work returns so often to the prison, his accounts of it show this artistic transformation. Early works like 'A Visit to Newgate,' *Pickwick*, and *Barnaby Rudge* treat the prison realistically and even historically, only hinting at the intangible psychological consequences of confinement. But during the 1850s, as *David Copperfield* and *Bleak House* show, Dickens became increasingly interested in techniques for narrating the private self. For Dickens the prison was embedded in this narrative project, and not only because of his miserable past. During the 1840s England had adopted a new prison system based upon solitary confinement, self-reflection, and the demand that prisoners produce autobiographies to attest to their moral and psychological reform – a system that turned prisons into sites for the narrative production of the private self and resulted in prison authorities rather than prisoners assuming final control over the self-narratives that emerged. In this dynamic of imprisonment, psychological transformation, and the narration of the private self, Dickens found a model that allowed him to explore the distinctly narrative implications of the cell. Together, in their increasingly complex portraits of prisoners like Wilkins Micawber, William Dorrit, and Manette, Dickens's mature novels show more than a hovering obsession with the prison; they show, in their formal complexities, his growing artistic concern with the relation between the prison, the novel, and the private self.[7]

Great Expectations is Dickens's fullest expression of this relation, for it shows the prison's power not only to shape Pip's identity but also to control and impel his construction of that identity through language. As Jeremy Tambling writes, *Great Expectations* is generally about the operation of power and 'the creation of identities, imposed from higher to lower, from oppressor to oppressed,'[8] but the novel also traces more particular relations between Pip's self-accounting and the prison's narrative power. Pip is not literally a prisoner in the novel, nor is he forced by wardens or chaplains to produce his autobiography. But in this novel, so much about Pip's attempt to construct a coherent identity in language, he shows repeatedly that his long subjection to real and metaphorical prisons is the origin of his psychological and narrative disarray – the cause of a gap between the guilty self-account he writes and the fairy story of his life that he wants so desperately to tell. Pip's prisons produce guilt, then, but also, as John Jordan writes, self-division, a sense that his private identity is 'a concatenation, a linking together of heterogeneous, often contradictory parts.'[9] In the process, they force him to recognize that self-narration is never a discovery or disclosure of 'truth' about identity so much as it is an act of power that imposes order upon the disorder and discontinuities of the private self. The novel *is* and *is about* Pip's attempt to claim this power – to use self-narrative to bring coherence to the guilty, divided identity the prison has made. More to the point, it is a process of narrative self-ordering that takes place in solitude, when he is forced to look upon the disorder of his identity and desire. In this portrayal of imprisonment, guilt, solitude, and self-narration, *Great Expectations* recreates the narrative mechanism of the Victorian prison. The novel suggests that Dickens understood the new prison and the way in which it exposed the subject to narrative power. It also suggests that *Great Expectations* is finally 'about' the prison because – imaginatively – Dickens required the prison's narrative power to invent his most complex account of the private self.

II

Though Pip is never really a prisoner in *Great Expectations*, he takes pains to show us from the opening chapter the psychological and narrative damage inflicted upon him by his prisons. The novel's famous beginning records his 'first most vivid and broad impression of the identity of things,' an impression that unfolds as an Edenic act of naming by which Pip calls himself into linguistic being: 'At such a time I found out for certain, that this bleak place overgrown with nettles was the churchyard; and that Philip Pirrip, late of this parish, and also Georgiana wife of the above, were dead and buried ... and that the dark flat wilderness beyond the churchyard ... was the marshes; and that the low leaden line beyond, was the river; and that the distant savage lair from which the wind was rushing, was the sea; and that the small bundle of shivers growing afraid of it all and beginning to cry, was Pip.'[10] The syntax suggests that Pip's sudden self-apprehension involves a sense of his 'thing-ness' – his split existence as a thing that names and must be named. But at this very instant, so 'richly suggestive of the problem of identity, self-consciousness, naming, and language,'[11] Pip is arrested and overwritten by the prison. Rising from 'among the graves,' Magwitch creates a mirror scene in which Pip sees himself not as in a glass darkly but in the competing signs of his symbolic fathers: the tombstone, which bears his name and promises him a place 'above'; and the convict, an abject figure who calls him a 'little devil' and threatens to cut his throat.[12] In the questions that follow – what is your name, where are your parents, where do you live – Magwitch forces Pip to an infant act of self-narration, a miserably insufficient account of origins that is really a first draft of the novel. Magwitch is not a prison but an embodiment of its power, for he arrests Pip, demands self-narration, and threatens the self with mutilation. Small wonder that when Pip returns home and asks, 'What's a convict?' the only part of Joe's answer he can understand is 'Pip.'[13] From his earliest recollections, he has always been subject to the narrative power that names him a prisoner.

Like the opening chapter, the rest of Pip's story unfolds as an elaborate display of the prison's psychological and narrative power. His waking hours are haunted by real reminders of the prison, like Magwitch, the mysterious man at the Three Jolly Bargemen, the convicts on the coach, and the fears that he will be taken by 'officers of the County Jail' for having pummelled the pale young gentleman.[14] His dreams are troubled, meanwhile, by awful visions of 'the file coming at [him] out of a door' and of himself trapped as 'a brick in the house-wall ... entreating to be released.'[15] On the day he is bound apprentice, too, he is dogged by the prison, for he is given a tract called 'TO BE READ IN MY

CELL' and 'ornamented with a woodcut of a malevolent young man fitted up with a perfect sausage-shop of fetters.'[16] The metaphor recalls Magwitch's savage hunger in the churchyard and ties Pip's new apprenticeship to the misery of the cell. It also shows that the language of his self-narration, like the action, is marked indelibly by the recurrence of the prison. His old Sunday clothes, he writes, were 'a kind of Reformatory ... [designed] on no account to let [him] have the free use of [his] limbs,' and in an especially suggestive scene, Pip peeks into Pumblechook's seed-drawers and wonders 'whether the flower-seeds and bulbs ever wanted of a fine day to break out of those jails, and bloom.'[17] Pip, too, is a 'seed' shadowed by the prison, an association that tells more strongly when he visits Newgate with Wemmick, who 'walk[s] among the prisoners ... as a gardener might walk among his plants' – and as he walks along so often with Pip, tending him from the day he arrives in London.[18] Such moments reveal that for Pip the prison is an inescapable linguistic mode, a perpetual return to the trauma inscribed by the cell.

As Pip describes the various prisons that blight his childhood, it becomes clear that they *are* prisons less because of their literal realities than because they claim the broad power to narrate, from the outside, the hidden story of the private self. At home, in the shadow of the hulks and under the discipline of Tickler, Pip's imprisonment is largely verbal, the result of adult jailors who name him a convict, a Bolter, a questioner, '[n]aterally wicious,' a Swine, and a Squeaker.[19] As his life expands beyond the margins of the forge, his story reads less like a liberation from prison than an oscillation between literal and figurative cells. He escapes Christmas dinner only to end up at the hulks, all '[c]ribbed and barred and moored by massive rusty chains,' and he escapes the forge only to arrive at Satis House, with its upper windows walled up and lower ones 'rustily barred.'[20] Mostly, though, Satis House is imprisoning in its narrative implications, because it recreates Pip's narrative impotence from the beginning of the novel. Though Miss Havisham, like Magwitch, demands that Pip name himself, he does so only to have Estella narrate another identity for him: as the 'boy,' coarse and common, another abject figure from the marshes.[21] In the process, she renews Pip's sense of self-division, humiliates him, and provokes him to invent outrageous fictions about Satis House when he returns to the forge. His lies seem to be an act of narrative defiance, but Pip blames them on his powerlessness as a narrator: his childish 'dread of not being understood,' and his tormentors' ability to make him 'a reckless witness under the torture ... [who] would have told them anything.'[22] As Pip explains to Joe, the lies have 'come ... somehow' of his encounter with Estella, who has created this narrative disarray by declaring him an ignorant and backward boy from the marshes.[23] After visiting Satis House, even Joe proves adept at lying, inventing fictions that he hopes will mollify Mrs Joe. Like Pip's lies, Joe's affirm the prison's narrative power, reminding us that self-narration in a carceral world is a matter of *inventing*, not *disclosing*, the self – a matter of creating an orderly self-account that mends the private disorder engendered by the prison.

This private disorder is Pip's characteristic problem, not in the sense of insanity or imbalance but in the sense of his deep apprehension that his identity is multivalent – that he is at once a young gentleman and the guilty boy from the marshes. It is a sense of self-division that originates in Pip's earliest recollections of the churchyard, and that he records by insisting upon his chronic association with the prison. Though Pip wants to tell the story of his place 'above,' in which Miss Havisham will ask him to 'restore the desolate house ... [and] do all the shining deeds of the young Knight of romance,'[24] his story shows repeatedly that 'every encounter with the world of Miss Havisham, Estella, and great expectations [is] preceded by a return of the world of the convict.'[25] On the day that Estella comes to London, Pip visits Newgate with Wemmick but ends in contemplating 'how strange it was that [he] should be encompassed by all this taint of prison and crime ... starting out like a stain that was faded but not gone.'[26] Indeed, he thinks 'with absolute abhorrence' of the contrast between Estella and the prison, considering them irreconcilable parts of his identity and story.[27] As Hilary Schor writes, though, '[f]or all that [Pip] fears ... the "Newgate cobwebs" on him when he meets Estella, she *is* the Newgate novel at this romance novel's center.'[28] Pip's detective work regarding Estella shows that his self-narration depends upon making these stories converge and creating narrative coherence from the discontinuities of his possible selves. In the meantime, his self-division remains a considerable narrative problem, reinscribed each time the prison recurs and leaving him in an always-already state of alienation from his own story. Thus he reads himself constantly as the object of another's narration: as George Barnwell for Wopsle, or 'Hamlet to Miss Havisham's Ghost,' or Victor Frankenstein, or the sultan's enemy annihilated at a stroke.[29] As Pip writes, significantly, after his quarrel with Bentley Drummle, he is so profoundly uncertain what story of himself he can tell, he must 'repudiate, as untenable, the idea that [he is] to be found anywhere.'[30]

By writing this way, Pip offers himself as one example of a larger concern with aberrant and guilty selves who become the objects of others' narration: the Aged P., whose nods and non sequiturs must be interpreted by Wemmick; Mrs Joe, whose indecipherable drawings are given meaning by Biddy; and Miss Havisham, self-imprisoned and emotionally diseased, whose sad history is related by Herbert Pocket. Such characters underscore the way that the novel's world wrenches narrative power away from those who seem unable to narrate for themselves. No one shows this more clearly than Jaggers, whose dealings with criminals and outcasts reveal their vulnerability to narrative invention undertaken from a position *outside* the self. At the Three Jolly Bargemen, Jaggers scolds Wopsle for 'pronounc[ing] a fellow-creature guilty, unheard,' and Pip's first visit to Jaggers ends in his seeing the feckless Mike, whose witness is prepared to swear 'in a general way, [to] anythink' at trial.[31] Both scenes imply that the story of the guilty self can be multiple, a set of narratives the relative validity of which will be determined by the law – the same authority that supports the carceral and narrative power of the prison. Thus Jaggers can rewrite Molly as a childless housekeeper, imprisoning her through the story he might tell, and he can defy London's criminals by leaving his house unlocked since they are subject to his narrative power. Though Magwitch narrates his story in a separate chapter of the novel, that story is mediated by Pip's role as amanuensis, and his ability to place the story within his own text and thus control the meaning it might convey. More important, Magwitch's story testifies explicitly to his perpetual narrative subjugation. From childhood, he has been in and out of jail, with the result that he has been narrated constantly by others: jailors, who tell visitors that he is 'a terrible hardened one'; Compeyson and his attorney, who make him 'much the worst one' at their trial; the judge, who singles him out among the thirty-two prisoners as an especial 'scourge to society.'[32] The aim of the law in *Great Expectations* – and the broader aim of power – is to tell the story of the guilty self, whether or not that story is verifiably 'true.' Even Pip's efforts to discover Estella's origins end in allowing him to narrate especially the identities of those others – Estella, Molly, and Magwitch – whose psychological and narrative vanishing point is the prison.

Perhaps this explains why *Great Expectations* is preoccupied with doubled selves, which serve collectively to show the narrative implications of a world pervaded by prisons. Wemmick leads his double life at Walworth and Little Britain, and Orlick not only echoes other brutes like Drummle and Magwitch but also serves as 'Pip's "bad double," a hateful and sadistic version of the hero.'[33] Likewise, Estella resembles Molly but remakes Miss Havisham, and Compeyson, that accomplished fraud, appears ghost-like behind Pip at the theatre and 'writes fifty hands,' creating an explicitly textual profusion of selves.[34] Narrated repeatedly by the prison and its agents, Magwitch becomes a proliferation of symbolic and textual identities, a composite of the narrative harm inflicted by the cell. When Pip returns to the churchyard bearing the stolen food, Magwitch seems already to have become a second convict, and later he becomes Pip's benefactor, Uncle Provis, and Mr Campbell. He is, Martine Dutheil writes, 'paradigmatic of the nature of signification … a key to Pip's initiation to ... the duplicity of the sign.'[35] At the end of chapter 1, Pip even observes that Magwitch leaves 'clasping himself, as if to hold himself together' – a fitting gesture for a man so fragmented by the prison.[36] Pip, too, is the narrating Pip and the narrated one, not to mention Philip Pirrip, the boy, silly boy, dear boy, and Handel. The proliferation of identities mirrors the pro-liferation of his prisons, each one inscribed differently upon the text as a warn-ing that Pip must constantly reify the value of the sign – the prison, of course, and its place in his story, but also the name he can give himself through his self-narration. Christopher Morris argues that Pip believes 'that by naming or narrating he is imparting some truth,'[37] but the novel's prisons show Pip unambiguously that naming is always and only an act of power, the inscription of one identity that the self might contain. It is fitting in this respect that Pip responds to his childhood prisons by learning to read and write, for the prison's narrative power means that these 'are not just skills but semiotic codes constitutive of personality and social order.'[38] The prisons teach Pip that forging an identity is nearer to Compeyson's work than to Joe's: not a matter of rendering the subject's 'true' shape but a contest over representation that ends in rendering one of the self's many possible shapes, each one an expres-sion of the author's power.

Remarking Pip's inability to shape the events of his life, Eiichi Hara argues that 'the author of the story is not Pip but Magwitch,' who figures symboli-cally as 'the writer and the father.'[39] But this is not true even at the level of story, or *fabula*, since Pip's life is shaped also by Miss Havisham, Estella, and especially Compeyson, who weaves the novel's plot from the threads of his guilty desire.[40] Taking *Great Expectations* on its own terms, Pip is its author, and the novel reflects mostly his need to author himself and to use narration to bring coherence to an identity divided by the prison. Though Brooks argues famously that Pip has 'outlived plot,'[41] his argument depends upon what one takes the plot to be. In *Great Expectations*, the plot is not in the plot of this life that hovers between fairy tale and guilty confession; rather, the plot is the plot-ting of that life, the process by which Pip comes to construct his identity through language. For Pip, surrounded by and subject to innumerable real and symbolic prisons, this narration means imposing order and coherence upon his self-divisions and telling the guilty story that the prison has inscribed upon him. He undertakes this process of narrative self-ordering in solitude, when he must look full upon the disorder of his identity and desire, and when he most resembles the solitary Victorian prisoner. Dickens makes the prison central to the novel, a thing that disfigures and controls Pip's self-narration but also enables and even forces him to it. In this vision, which liberates the intense compressions of the opening scene, *Great Expectations* expresses Dickens's most radical insight into the relation between the prison, the novel, and the narration of the private self.

In a broad sense, Dickens's decision to write of the prison in this way belongs to a broader mid-century impulse to expose the private self to the prison's narrative power. Michel Foucault's analysis of the Panopticon in *Discipline and Punish* has been influential for so long in scholarly circles that it has been hard to see other links between the prison and the novel. It is true, of course, that Jeremy Bentham wrote his proposal for the Panopticon in 1786 in response to a crisis of prison overcrowding that had begun more than a decade before. But by the time he gave the proposal to Sir William Pitt five years later, Pitt's cabinet had already decided that convicts could be kept in Australia more easily than they could be kept in prisons at home. Though Bentham lobbied for his penitentiary for the next twenty years, government officials ultimately favoured other forms of confinement.[42] In 1810 Parliament endorsed a new national penitentiary system premised upon solitary, or 'separate,' confinement that would be mitigated by the moral influence of a prison chaplain, their decision based partly upon solitude's power 'to create a sense of guilt and awareness of folly' and also upon fears that an 'industrial' prison like Bentham's would emphasize utility and profit rather than spiritual salvation and moral reform.[43] When Millbank Penitentiary opened in 1816 as England's first real attempt to implement reformative discipline, it adopted a mostly 'solitary' scheme and, in the years that followed, moved steadily toward a program of nearly unbroken solitary confinement. Though certain writers on penal matters always opposed 'separate' discipline, two decades later Parliament passed a new Prisons Bill that established separation as the standard for all of England's prisons and paved the way for a new 'Model Prison' at Pentonville that would serve as the institutional fulfilment of that design.

Advocates of 'separate' discipline based their arguments upon the power of solitude to effect lasting moral and psychological transformations. In the Inspectors Report for 1837–8, the Reverend Whitworth Russell – an inspector for the Home District and former chaplain at Millbank – praised the way that, for prisoners in solitude, 'the moral machinery of the system is brought to bear … as if the prison contained no other but the culprit himself.'[44] The other Home District inspector, William Crawford, became a supporter of separation after visiting the same Eastern Penitentiary that had appalled Dickens in Philadelphia. Though the penitentiary had been plagued by rumours that its solitary discipline caused insanity, Russell, Crawford, and their allies assured Parliament that such a program could be milder in England, and that it would produce more satisfactory results. Periods of separation would not exceed eighteen months, and the chaplain would guide prisoners through solitude and self-reflection to an awareness of their wickedness and a desire to reform. The key was helping the inmate to review his past life and recognize and interpret his old failings – to make correct moral 'sense' of the guilty self-account. In his remarks on the Prisons Bill, the Marquis of Normanby lauded separation for being 'calculated to promote ... repentance' and therefore 'consonant with the spirit of our religion.'[45] The Reverend John Field, chaplain at Reading Gaol and another proponent of separation, put it more strongly: 'Deprived of most of the resources of educated men; constantly reminded of the cause which brought him to this situation; undisturbed by any distracting objects; enveloped in silence – he needs must *think.*'[46] As Field implies, the solitary prisoner was to 'think' in a confessional, autobiographical way. The aim was complete narrative coherence, a program of self-reflection that would include the causes of criminality, the commission of crime, an awareness of guilt, and – as a final chapter – the moral and psychological transformation engendered by the prison.

With literate inmates, chaplains turned 'separate' confinement into an auto-biographical exercise by requiring prisoners to write their lives during their hours of solitude; more often, chaplains became amanuenses, recording illiter-ate prisoners' stories either verbatim or in notes meant to reflect the substance of oral accounts. In both cases, the tacit requirement was that the story must end with a return to moral thinking inspired by the cell. While prison chap-lains like Russell and Field argued publicly that prisoner autobiographies were proofs in favour of separate discipline, England's penal experiment had really become a struggle for narrative power. Since prison chaplains had the most contact with solitary inmates, they naturally had, too, the most credibility in describing their reform. As a result, authorities from local magistrates to national prison inspectors based many of their 'official' findings on the chap-lains' reports. Predictably, many chaplains planned these reports as defences of separation, complete with testimonials in the prisoners' own words. In 1853 the Reverend H.S. Joseph published *Memoirs of Convicted Prisoners*, a vol-ume of autobiographies and letters from reformed convicts, the reading of which, he wrote in the preface, would inevitably 'have a tendency to diminish the number of inmates in our gaols.'[47] Two years later, Walter Clay published *The Prison Chaplain: A Memoir of the Reverend John Clay*, excerpting hun-dreds of pages of his father's notes from conversations with solitary prisoners at Preston Gaol. The picture that emerges from these notes is of John Clay the amanuensis, adopting the self-narrative 'I' on behalf of prisoners who wish to narrate but cannot write for themselves.[48]

Such examples only begin to suggest the extent to which prison officials controlled the discursive framework by which prisoners' stories could be known. For chaplains like Joseph, Field, and the Clays, prisoner narratives were not so much records of imprisonment as stories-within-the-story of the prison's power to reform. Joseph's preface ensures that we cannot misunderstand the narratives that follow, and Field claimed to have 'thousands of letters' from convicts praising the morally salutary effects of solitary confinement. In the case of the Clays, prisoner narratives are twice-distilled, filtered through the dual lens of the father's notes and the son's purposeful biography. More telling, when prisoners' pens and voices failed, their bodies were made to speak. A prisoner's tears, John Clay writes, stem from 'softening of the heart' or 'relief' or 'the springs of good feeling' – not from creeping insanity – and the 'countenance' reveals not only whether a prisoner is serene or disturbed but also whether serenity is real or feigned.[49] Because our records of inmates come primarily from such sources, we must conjecture that prisoner narratives were shaped partly by official demands, and that narrative control and autobiographical truth are always in question, even when prisoners seem to speak for themselves. Indeed, since criminality was thought to stem from a kind of self-narrative failure to review and make moral sense of the past, one wonders how often chaplains pressed inmates to 'complete' their stories by narrating more guilt than they owned. To curry favour with prison authorities, many convicts would gladly have bent their stories, though more often probably they exaggerated the heights of their religious fervour, like Dickens's humbugging 'Model Prisoner,' Uriah Heep. The Victorian prison's deliberate aim was to transform inmates by driving them to solitude, self-reflection, and self-narration that would impose order upon the narrative disorder that had brought them to the cell. Its effect was to create a socially authorized mechanism for wrenching self-narrative power away from the self and exposing that self to narrative invention by the prison.

This is the prison that we find in *Great Expectations*: a prison that at once subjects Pip to narrative power and drives him, in solitude, to self-ordering and self-narration. Tambling writes that panoptical power is what fixes Pip's guilt and makes his narrative 'carceral ... an automatic, unstopping confession, which pauses not at all in its recounting.'[50] But if social power fixes Pip's guilt, solitude enables him finally to narrate it, since Pip's moments of solitude are what allow him to look full upon his private disorder and find a place for guilt in his identity and self-narration. At the Hummums, where Pip goes to escape Orlick's spying only to fall prey to the 'foolish Argus' of his rushlight and the 'staringly wideawake pattern' it makes on the walls, Pip does not record being watched so much as he records his own staring at the nightmare apparitions conjured by his thwarted desire.[51] Believing that he and Estella have 'parted that day forever,' Pip and the rushlight 'stare[d] at one another'

while he imagines the crawling things that infest the ceiling and the recent suicide found there 'weltering in blood.'[52] He also sees the ominous message
'DON'T GO HOME' written in every unblinking eye the rushlight casts upon
the wall, and his obsessive conjugations of this command show him working
linguistically through the complexities of his relation to home: to his apartments, the forge, the marshes, the churchyard, the tombstone, and the innumerable regressions that belong to his tracing of origins.[53] The scene is, in
other words, a narrative wrestling with recurrence, a puzzle of temporal order-
ing that performs the same-but-different iterations of the private trauma he
must bring to order if he wishes to account for himself. Pip's guilt may begin,
then, with the panoptical inscription of power, but his movement from disorder to self-narration requires solitude and remakes the narrative dynamic of
the Victorian prison.

Even the first chapter shows that Pip requires solitude to narrate his guilt,
for he begins to understand the implications of his encounter with Magwitch
only after he returns to the forge and 'the dreadful pledge [he is] under to commit larceny ... [rises] before [him] in the avenging coals.'[54] Partly, his trepida-
tion is bound to surveillance and detection, his dread of Tickler, and his
uncomfortable likeness to the other 'Bolter.' But Pip takes the full measure of
his guilt only after he has retired to the solitude of his bedroom. There he
writes: 'I was in mortal terror of the young man who wanted my heart and
liver; I was in mortal terror of my interlocutor with the ironed leg; I was in
mortal terror of myself, from whom an awful promise had been extracted ...
[and] I am afraid to think of what I might have done, on requirement, in the
secrecy of my terror.'[55] The tumbled phrases are, using Jordan's word, a 'concatenation': of prisons, jailors, violent rending, self-division, and guilty self-
apprehension. Reduced to this terror, Pip recounts his theft and flight back to
the churchyard in language that reveals for the first time his lurking sense that
he has become the guilty object of another's narration. The floorboards and
the cattle on the marshes seem to call him a 'thief,' and a black ox with 'something of a clerical air' elicits from him a blubbering confession.[56] Just as terrible, Pip writes, 'instead of my running at everything, everything seemed to run
at me,' so that he becomes the passive observer of his own story rather than the
agent performing its action.[57] He also lapses into confusion over which convict is which when he stumbles across Compeyson on the marshes. Pip's first
descent into solitude thus forces him to acknowledge his guilt and reduces him
to narrative disarray.

Such solitary scenes punctuate the novel, and they are crucial because they
allow Pip to escape his various prisons and their narratives of his identity, and
to reflect instead upon his psychological and narrative ruptures. When Estella

humiliates Pip during his first visit to Satis House, he retreats to the ruined courtyard where he considers in solitude whether his abjection has always given his sister the 'right to bring [him] up by jerks.'[58] When Pip returns to the forge filled with lies and confesses them to Joe, he goes to bed considering Joe's advice to pray for forgiveness but finds that his 'young mind' remains 'disturbed' – preoccupied with the gap between his life at the forge and what he 'used to do' at Satis House, 'as though,' he writes, 'I had been there weeks or months, instead of hours; and as though it were quite an old subject of remembrance.'[59] Looking back on his childish confusion, Pip closes the chapter by reflecting upon 'the long chain of iron or gold, of thorns or flowers, that would never have bound you, but for the formation of the first link on one memorable day.'[60] Disorder made orderly, temporal confusion made logical sequence: it is the invariable pattern of Pip's solitary reflections. In solitude, after he has been bound apprentice, Pip is first struck by the 'conviction ... that [he] should never like Joe's trade';[61] in solitude, he has dreams of displacement that force him to look upon the frightful fragmentation of his identity.[62] In solitude, before he goes to London, he strolls onto the marshes only to return to the trauma and language of his infant naming and the problematic relation between his childhood, 'the wretch ... with his felon iron and badge,' and his new expectations.[63] He writes, 'No more low wet grounds, no more dykes and sluices, no more of these grazing cattle ... farewell, monotonous acquaintances of my childhood, henceforth I was for London and greatness.'[64] Like Pip's other solitary moments, his reflections on the marshes are a perpetual consideration of the gap between the multiple stories that constitute his self-narration.

This is especially clear on the night of Magwitch's return, the first of three scenes in the last volume that show Pip working in solitude towards self-narration. Magwitch arrives on a night when Pip is isolated profoundly: Herbert is in Marseilles, and the storm has blown out even the winking eyes of the lamps in the courtyard. Pip writes, 'I was alone, and had a dull sense of being alone,' and the next moment hears a tread on the stairs that he 'connect[s] ... with the footstep of [his] dead sister.'[65] From the moment Magwitch arrives the scene is a return to childhood, and his conversation with Pip records the psychological and narrative collapse of Pip's new life into his old, a shift from the certain 'I did not know him' to the feverish 'I knew him!'[66] This awakening – and Magwitch's warning that Pip would be 'sorry arterwards' to catch hold of him – reduces Pip to the terrified child on the marshes and forces him to the despairing awareness of the revelation's meaning for his relationship with Estella.[67] In this movement from origins to desire, and only after Magwitch has gone to bed, Pip considers the entire wreckage of the fairy story he has cherished: 'Miss Havisham's intentions toward me, all a mere dream; Estella not designed for me; I only suffered in Satis House as a convenience, a sting for the greedy relations ... those were the first smarts I had. But, sharpest and deepest pain of all – it was for the convict, guilty of I knew not what crimes, and liable to be taken ... and hanged at the Old Bailey door, that I had deserted Joe.'[68] 'To find his identity,' as Henri Talon writes, '[Pip] must embrace his whole career, totalize and interpret all that is significant.'[69] In other words, to narrate a life disfigured and disordered by the prison, he must learn to tell the guilty story inscribed upon him by the cell.

This need is what makes Pip's final confrontation with Orlick so crucial, and what makes the sluice-house an essential site for Pip's eventual self-narration. Throughout the novel Orlick has been Pip's double and shadow; he has reflected and enacted Pip's guiltiest desires. And though Orlick has often been a spy as well, the scene at the sluice-house is less panoptical than an attempt to isolate Pip, inscribe power upon his body, and – by renewing the trauma of the opening scene – do violence to the story that Pip can tell. Instructing Pip to come alone to the desolate marshes, Orlick becomes a corruption of the Victorian prison chaplain, forcing upon Pip an account of identity that is based upon narrative power and that cannot ever suffice in its attestations of guilt. Pip writes that he 'could have summed up years and years and years' while listening to Orlick's accusations, suggesting that his life passes before his eyes even as Orlick narrates it, as Orlick makes Pip guilty for costing him his place at Satis House, for ruining his prospects with Biddy, and for providing the weapon and the cause for his brutal attack on Mrs Joe. While Orlick speaks, what flashes across Pip's mind is not a dread of death but rather of 'being misremembered after death.'[70] It is the closest that Pip comes to admitting the reason for his self-account, and he rejects Orlick's charges only to acknowledge the reality of his other sins – especially his injustice to Joe and Biddy, who 'would never know how sorry [he] had been.'[71] In other words, Pip's struggle for self-narrative power does not end in innocent self-narration; rather, it culminates in his ability to assimilate his guilt and narrate himself a guilty self in the cell. It is Orlick's 'vision of Pip that prevails,'[72] for his accusations appear not only in Pip's retelling but also in the guilty reflections that pervade his self-account. For Pip, progress towards self-narration is measured by his ability to reify permanently the status of guilt in his story – to narrate himself as a Victorian prisoner, scarred ineradicably by the cell.

Perhaps this explains why Pip slips so easily into a place at Newgate during Magwitch's final days, and why Pip's illness rather than Magwitch's reads like the novel's last return to the prison. In fact, Pip comes under the literal threat of imprisonment while he is ill, not for aiding the returned transportee but for debt, a transgression of his own making. As Stanley Friedman observes, the denouement subjects Pip to a symbolic punishment that starts with solitary confinement in his apartments and ends in a kind of self-imposed exile to the East.[73] In solitude – and in a scene that recalls Esther Summerson's delirium, Jane Eyre in the red room, and Lucy Snowe during the long vacation – Pip's illness drives him one last time to the private disorder he must resolve if he is to reach the possibility of self-narration. After the first night of his illness, Pip tries 'to settle with [himself] and get into some order' the murky events of the evening before.[74] In the hours that follow, he has terrifying dreams in which he 'confound[s] impossible existences with [his] own identity,' but which have 'an extraordinary tendency ... to settle down into the likeness of Joe.'[75] So profound is the effect of his illness and recovery that he fancies he is 'little Pip again.'[76] He emerges from the greatest solitude and mental disorder of his life into a return to origins that again makes Joe his benefactor and restores Biddy rather than Estella as the object of his desire. Even so, and though Magwitch's death and the confiscation of his property have dissolved any concrete ties between Pip and the prison, this last descent into solitude is what finally enables Pip to tell the guilty story the prison has inscribed.

As he mends, Pip offers to tell Joe the old secret of his first encounter with Magwitch – to give him, in effect, a preliminary draft of the novel that will incorporate Pip's guilt into a self-account that links the prison to his birth into perceptual and linguistic awareness. But Joe refuses to hear Pip's confession, telling him instead: 'Supposing ever you kep any little matter to yourself, when you was a little child, you kep it mostly because you know'd as J. Gargery's power to part you and Tickler in sunders, were not fully equal to his inclinations. Theerfore, think no more of it as betwixt two sech, and do not let us pass remarks upon onnecessary subjects.'[77] Instead of recording Pip's guilt, the novel reinscribes Joe's, as if to suggest the archetypal nature of Pip's experience – the superfluity of confessing guilt in a world where the prison maims every subject and every act of self-narration. Pip emerges from solitude and self-reflection to find that he can tell no story of his identity that does not include the prison. This is true of Pip's narration, and of Magwitch's, Joe's, and Miss Havisham's, and it is even hyperbolically true of Mrs Joe's, which is doomed after the attack to inscribe perpetually the symbol of her punishment. At the end of the novel, Iain Crawford writes, Pip's 'sense of alienation ... from himself, remains,'[78] but of course it cannot do otherwise in this carceral world. *Great Expectations* is finally the story of this alienation, the story of the prison's power to shape Pip's identity and self-account. In the end, it makes very little difference, either, which ending one prefers, for both endings and all possible endings will leave Pip's self-narration to linger where it has always been: in the shadow cast by the Victorian prison.

III

Because *Great Expectations* rehearses the autobiographical concerns that shaped *David Copperfield* and pervaded so much of Dickens's mental life, it is tempting and perhaps even right to conclude that the novel reflects mostly Dickens's sense of the prison's inescapable power over his own life. As Anny Sadrin writes, Dickens's fiction is 'the work of a man … who remained to the end a prisoner … and who, novel after novel, like Dorrit in dotage, welcomed his readers to the Marshalsea.'[79] Though Dickens was for three decades the most celebrated writer in the world, even late in life he always found 'at extreme points … the explanation of himself in those early trials.'[80] But *Great Expectations* is not autobiographical in the same way as *Copperfield*; it is at once more symbolic and more intensely real, more impressionistic yet more immediate in the life that it unfolds. Its story belongs to the psychic and linguistic rhythms of desire and accounts for the subject even as, in Dutheil's words, it casts 'doubt on the possibility of making definite and definitive sense' of the self.[81] This is so because *Great Expectations* has more to do with the prison than *Copperfield*, because instead of making a sinister caricature like Uriah Heep a 'Model Prisoner' it reconstitutes in the complex storytelling of its protagonist and narrator, Pip, the prison's model for imprisoning and narrating the self. For Dickens, as we see throughout the fiction of his mature period, the privacy of the subject was a considerable narrative problem, one that he tried to work through by returning again and again to first-person narration by characters as various as David Copperfield, Esther Summerson, Miss Wade, and Alexandre Manette. In the end, it was a problem that the Victorian prison solved by showing, in its transparent application of narrative power, that the self declared guilty could become entirely a matter of narrative invention.

The prison is what showed Dickens, in other words, the possibility that subjectivity – or at least the story of it – could always be a linguistic construct, so long as the self to be narrated belonged imaginatively to the prison. Partly, perhaps, because this is so, the novels engaged most deeply with the prison are the ones in which Dickens gestures most certainly towards literary modernity: towards Freud, and interior narration, and linguistic representations of the divided subject. We find such gestures in the prison narrative of Alexandre Manette, and in the unfinished portrait of John Jasper's divided psyche – which, according to Forster, Dickens intended to have culminate in a moment of self-narration from the condemned cell. We also find such gestures in Pip's self-narrative, so pregnant with irruptions, recurrences, and repressions that critics have regarded it for more than a century as Dickens's most complete and ambitious attempt to narrate the complexities of the private self. During the last fifteen years of his life, Dickens wrote only one novel, *Our Mutual Friend*, that did not centre upon some version of the prison, and that did not reconsider artistically the prison's relation to subjectivity and private narration. In his study of the repressions and recurrences that shape *Great Expectations*, Ginsberg contends that the novel shows us above all that 'pure repetition, cannot generate a story,' that it is rather the recurrence that is *not* pure repetition that 'opens up a space where a story can be told.'[82] In Dickens's mature fiction and in *Great Expectations*, nothing recurs more often or more strongly than the prison, and it is in these recurrences that Dickens found the imaginative space he required to undertake his most compelling account of the Victorian subject.

NOTES

1 Charles Dickens, *Great Expectations*, ed. Charlotte Mitchell (London: Penguin, 1996), 58.

2 Trey Philpotts points out in 'The Real Marshalsea' that William Kent cited *Little Dorrit* in 1927 as the most detailed extant description of the prison, which had closed in 1849 and was subsequently demolished. Trey Philpotts, 'The Real Marshalsea,' *Dickensian* 87 (1991): 133. For studies of Dickens's careful realism regarding the prison in these novels, see Philpotts and Harry De Puy, 'American Prisons and *A Tale of Two Cities*,' *Cahiers Victoriens et Édouardiens* 25 (April 1987): 39–48.

3 Julian Moynahan, 'The Hero's Guilt: The Case of *Great Expectations*,' *Essays in Criticism* 10, no. 1 (1960): 60. Though Moynahan was the first critic to focus on guilt in the novel, he cites Robert G. Stange, 'Expectations Well Lost: Dickens' Fable for His Time,' *College English* 16, no. 1 (1954): 9–17 and Dorothy Van Ghent, *The English Novel: Form and Function* (New York: Harper and Row, 1953) as important precursors to his work.

4 J. Hillis Miller, *Charles Dickens: The World of His Novels* (Cambridge, MA: Harvard University Press, 1958), 274.

5 Michael Peled Ginsburg, 'Dickens and the Uncanny: Repression and Displacement in *Great Expectations*,' *Dickens Studies Annual* 13 (1984): 117; emphasis in original. So many critics have discussed guilt in *Great Expectations* that one cannot list them all. Among early studies, Joseph Hynes's and John P. McWilliams's are the most careful discussions of guilt in relation to the novel's prison imagery. See Joseph A. Hynes, 'Image and Symbol in *Great Expectations*,' *ELH* 30, no. 3 (1963): 258–92, and John P. McWilliams, '*Great Expectations*: The Beacon, the Gibbet, and the Ship,' *Dickens Studies Annual* 2 (1972): 255–66. More recently,

Peter Brooks (*Reading for the Plot* [Cambridge, MA: Harvard University Press, 1984]), Michael Peled Ginsburg ('Dickens and the Uncanny'), Monique Morgan ('Conviction in Writing: Crime, Confession, and the Written Word in *Great Expectations*,' *Dickens Studies Annual* 33 [2003]: 87–108), and Jeremy Tambling ('Prison-Bound: Dickens and Foucault,' *Essays in Criticism* 36, no. 1 [1986]: 11–31) have written of Pip's guilt, and Kathleen Sell has observed that guilt's close corollary 'shame ... is central to the narration and thematics of identity in the novel.' Kathleen Sell, 'The Narrator's Shame: Masculine Identity in *Great Expectations*,' *Dickens Studies Annual* 26 (1998): 203.

6 David Trotter, introduction to *Great Expectations*, ed. Charlotte Mitchell (London: Penguin, 1996), viii.

7 I argue this point more fully in Sean C. Grass, *The Self in the Cell: Narrating the Victorian Prisoner* (New York/London: Routledge, 2003), 103–50.

8 Tambling, 'Prison-Bound,' 18.

9 John O. Jordan, 'Partings Welded Together: Self-fashioning in *Great Expectations* and *Jane Eyre*,' *Dickens Quarterly* 13, no. 1 (1996): 23.

10 Dickens, *Great Expectations*, 3–4.

11 Brooks, *Reading for the Plot*, 116–17.

12 Dickens, *Great Expectations*, 3–4.

13 Ibid., 13–14.

14 Ibid., 94.

15 Ibid., 79, 462.

16 Ibid., 105.

17 Ibid., 23, 53.

18 Ibid., 260.

19 Ibid., 26.

20 Ibid., 40, 55.

21 Ibid., 56.

22 Ibid., 65, 68.

23 Ibid., 70.

24 Ibid., 231.

25 Ginsburg, 'Dickens and the Uncanny,' 120.

26 Dickens, *Great Expectations*, 264.

27 Ibid.

28 Hilary Schor, *Dickens and the Daughter of the House* (Cambridge: Cambridge University Press, 1999), 171.

29 Dickens, *Great Expectations*, 258.

30 Ibid., 309.

31 Ibid., 135, 169.

32 Ibid., 346, 351, 457.

33 Brooks, *Reading for the Plot*, 127.

34 Dickens, *Great Expectations*, 427.

35 Martine Hennard Dutheil, '*Great Expectations* as Reading Lesson,' *Dickens Quarterly* 13, no. 3 (1996): 171.

36 Dickens, *Great Expectations*, 6.

37 Christopher Morris, 'The Bad Faith of Pip's Bad Faith: Deconstructing *Great Expectations*,' *ELH* 54, no. 4 (1987): 944.

38 Murray Baumgarten, 'Calligraphy and Code: Writing in *Great Expectations*,' *Dickens Studies Annual* 11 (1983): 64.

39 Eiichi Hara, 'Stories Present and Absent in *Great Expectations*,' *ELH* 53, no. 3 (1986): 593. Baumgarten also argues that 'Magwitch is [Pip's] author, as Miss Havisham creates Estella' ('Calligraphy,' 66).

40 Hilary Schor argues that Estella has been much underemphasized in discussions of the characters that shape Pip's life. See Schor, *Dickens and the Daughter of the House*, 154–5 and 164.

41 Brooks, *Reading for the Plot*, 138.

42 For more on Bentham's plan for the Panopticon and wrangles with Parliament, see Grass, *The Self in the Cell*, 3–5, and Jeremy Bentham, *The Correspondence of Jeremy Bentham*, 11 vols, ed. Ian R. Christie (London: Athlone Press, 1971), 3:509 and 4:xxiv-xxvii.

43 William Forsythe, *The Reform of Prisoners, 1830–1900* (London: Croom Helm, 1987), 20.

44 Qtd. in ibid., 27.

45 *Times*, London, 14 April 1840, 6b.

46 John Field, *Prison Discipline: And the Advantages of the Separate System of Imprisonment, with a Detailed Account of the Discipline Now Pursued in the New County Gaol at Reading*, 2 vols. (London: Longman, Brown, Green, and Longmans, 1848), 1:347.

47 H.S. Joseph, *Memoirs of Convicted Prisoners: Accompanied by Remarks on the Causes and Prevention of Crime* (London: Wertheim and Co., 1853), viii.

48 Walter Lowe Clay, *The Prison Chaplain: A Memoir of the Reverend John Clay, B.D., Late Chaplain of the Preston Gaol* (Montclair, NJ: Patterson Smith, 1969).

49 Ibid., 287.

50 Tambling, 'Prison-Bound,' 25.

51 Dickens, *Great Expectations*, 366.

52 Ibid., 366–7.

53 Ibid., 367.

54 Ibid., 10.

55 Ibid., 15.

56 Ibid., 15, 17.

57 Ibid., 17.

58 Ibid., 63.

59 Ibid., 72.

60 Ibid.

61 Ibid., 106.

62 For an intriguing analysis of Pip's dreams, see Clare Pettitt's 'Monstrous Displace-ments: Anxieties of Exchange in *Great Expectations*,' *Dickens Studies Annual* 30 (2001): 248.

63 Dickens, *Great Expectations*, 147.

64 Ibid., 147.

65 Ibid., 313, 314.

66 Ibid., 315.

67 Ibid.

68 Ibid., 323.

69 Henri Talon, 'Space, Time, and Memory in *Great Expectations*,' *Dickens Studies Annual* 3 (1973): 123.

70 Dickens, *Great Expectations*, 425.

71 Ibid.

72 Helen von Schmidt, 'The Dark Abyss, the Broad Expanse: Versions of the Self in *Jane Eyre* and *Great Expectations*,' *Dickens Quarterly* 2, no. 3 (1985): 89.

73 Stanley Friedman, 'Estella's Parentage and Pip's Persistence: The Outcome of *Great Expectations*,' *Studies in the Novel* 19, no. 4 (1987): 415.

74 Dickens, *Great Expectations*, 461.

75 Ibid., 462–3.

76 Ibid., 466.

77 Ibid., 469.

78 Iain Crawford, 'Pip and the Monster: The Joys of Bondage,' *Studies in English Literature* 28, no. 4 (1988): 629.

79 Anny Sadrin, *Great Expectations* (London: Unwin Hyman, 1988), 70.

80 John Forster, *The Life of Charles Dickens* (London: Chapman and Hall; New York: Oxford University Press, 1903), 1:34.

81 Dutheil, '*Great Expectations* as Reading Lesson,' 165.

82 Ginsburg, 'Dickens and the Uncanny,' 123.

9 From 'Dry Volumes of Facts and Figures' to Stories of 'Flesh and Blood': The Prison Narratives of Frederick William Robinson

ANNE SCHWAN

At the heart of this essay lies a methodological question: how do we write a history of non-elite people, and, more specifically, nineteenth-century female convicts? The embodied knowledge of women (and men for that matter) in nineteenth-century prisons remains largely unrecorded, due to a number of factors – illiteracy and the generally low cultural capital among prison inmates, who mainly came from disadvantaged socio-economic backgrounds; but also the cultural sanctioning of certain forms of (institutionalized) knowledge over others. Michel Foucault's *Discipline and Punish* famously explores how institutional discourses produce criminal subjectivities, rather than how criminal subjects experience disciplinary mechanisms or how alternative formulations resist such discursive constructions.[1] Yet, Foucault was equally interested in considerations of agency, subjective and collective experience, and the production of alternative knowledges – issues outlined in his genealogical method in a series of lectures delivered at the Collège de France in 1975–6, just at the moment when *Discipline and Punish* was first published.[2] Inspired by Foucault's concern with the recovery of 'subjugated knowledges' – a critical (and indeed *political*) agenda neglected in the predominant reception of Foucault that usually reduces him to his 'disciplinary thesis' – this article will analyse efforts to record the experiences of female convicts by the little-known Victorian popular fiction writer Frederick William Robinson in his commercially successful prison narratives, written under the pseudonym of 'A Prison Matron': *Female Life in Prison* (1862), *Memoirs of Jane Cameron: Female Convict* (1863), and *Prison Characters Drawn from Life with Suggestions for Prison Government* (1866). I will argue that *Memoirs of Jane Cameron* in particular constitutes a deliberate and self-reflexive attempt to reinstate not only the voices of female convicts, but also those of other non-elite women – especially those of prison matrons. As I will demonstrate, Robinson explicitly constructs his tales of female prisoners in opposition to other, institutionally legitimized modes of representing these women, such as parliamentary reports. Although Robinson's narratives also employ and reinscribe conventional notions of gender and class familiar from other writings on women's criminality and punishment – both official and reformist – his work differs from such accounts in crucial ways, providing an early social history approach that validates the marginalized experience of non-elite females.

I am not arguing for the recovery of a supposedly 'authentic' or homogeneous voice of women convicts and prison matrons here; yet Robinson's writings do provide an insight into the lives of these women, and into the ways in which the experiences of female criminals and matrons were imagined and represented. Although various critics have drawn on the 'Prison Matron's' narratives, mainly as a source of empirical evidence regarding women's imprisonment, they do not usually consider the textuality of these sources.[3] By contrast, questions of narrative construction and authorship concerning the three prison narratives are one of my key interests here. It is the techniques through which Robinson's tales attempt to ventriloquize the life-narratives of non-elite women that this article aims to problematize. In particular, I will consider Robinson's use of and meta-reflexive comments on competing genres of penal enquiry and voices from prison, including that of the 'Prison Matron' herself, and their implications for the representation of female prisoners, and non-elite women more broadly speaking. In this context, the relationship between Robinson and the 'Prison Matron' and the impact of that relationship on the representation of female life in prison need close critical attention. As I will suggest, Robinson constructs the Matron as a female narrative persona whose first-person narrative voice occasionally coincides with, and occasionally diverges from, the voice of the implied male author.

A successful writer and journalist, Frederick William Robinson (1830–1901) published prolifically from the mid-1850s until well into the 1890s.[4] Highly formulaic, Robinson's fiction led its readers into the world of romance, often with strong religious overtones. But as Gerald Le Grys Norgate in his entry in the *Dictionary of National Biography* formulates it, 'Robinson was also a pioneer in novels of low life,'[5] writing about society's outcasts, such as abandoned children, if in hardly less formulaic fashion, and rarely without a love interest. Robinson's prison narratives belong to this part of his opus. In his review of Robinson's life in the *Athenaeum* in 1901, Theodore Watts-Dunton, by his own account a friend of the writer for over thirty years, comments on the tremendous success of the first book in the prison series, *Female Life in Prison*, and its reception:

No one dreamed for a moment but that it was the work of a prison matron who had recorded her real experiences. The book was indeed extraordinarily vivid and vital. The *Times* had a long article upon it, accepting it as a true record, and used it as the basis of a discussion on prisons and prison discipline. Not unfrequently donations were sent to the author from benevolent people for him to make use of for the welfare of the prisoners. These donations were embarrassing, but they were all scrupulously devoted to that purpose.[6]

Watts-Dunton also claims that Robinson's prison tales were indeed 'based in part upon the personal record of a real prison matron.'[7] Although this is not impossible, it is hard to verify the accuracy of Watts-Dunton's statements – his primary purpose here may well have been to protect the moral integrity of his friend. But Robinson's decision to write the three books as 'A Prison Matron' is certainly more than the choice of a pseudonym (or anonym); it is part of his narrative strategy. As Watts-Dunton's article suggests, it was clearly the illusion of authenticity that made the tales so powerful and successful. The use of 'A Prison Matron' as alleged author of the tales surely helped to fuel the curiosity of potential readers interested in 'racy,' entertaining accounts of crime and imprisonment, promising an all-female prison context and the possibility of same-sex romance – a romance that indeed develops in *Memoirs of Jane Cameron* most explicitly.

In his prison narratives, Robinson draws on various other writings on criminality and the penal system, thus situating his own work within the context of a number of discourses on crime. Robinson's background as a reporter is significant, since the prison tales combine a fictional, novelistic style with that of documentary journalism. This specific construction of the tales facilitates a Bakhtinian heteroglossia or polyphony, since they contain a 'multiplicity of social voices' with regard to crime and punishment.[8] The texts mentioned in Robinson's three narratives include official reports of prison authorities, governors, physicians, surgeons, and chaplains of Brixton and Millbank to the Secretary of State between 1855 and 1860.[9] Robinson also explicitly draws on Henry Mayhew's *Great World of London*,[10] newspapers,[11] and George Laval Chesterton's *Revelations of Prison Life*,[12] as well as Mary Carpenter's *Our Convicts*.[13] *Memoirs of Jane Cameron* furthermore acknowledges the assistance of 'the principle public functionaries of Edinburgh and Glasgow,'[14] as well as members of prison boards, governors, chief constables, superintendents, detective officers, the secretary of the Prisoner's Aid Society, and 'those good Christians and kind friends who have helped to throw a light upon the after and better life of Cameron.'[15] Again, whether Robinson actually met with all of these alleged informants, or whether he simply uses them as another authenticating device, apart from the 'Prison Matron,' is difficult to determine. Regardless, Robinson explicitly criticizes and departs from some of these named sources, while siding with others. His own ideological position is an ambiguous one, oscillating between pro-working-class statements, Christian paternalism, and the use of familiar stereotypes and colonial tropes with relation to female convicts. But as I will argue, the paternalism of Robinson's narratives is counteracted by the fact that they also record and affirm aspects of the lives of non-elite women not usually given a space in reformist writings. In this respect, Robinson's tales share some of their contradictions and ambiguities – if not the writerly skill – with the publications on female criminality and imprisonment by another contemporaneous writer, Charles Dickens. Dickens's work, too, is characterized by a mixture of compassionate commitment to draw attention to the lot of these women, and an apparent aversion to some of their behaviour.[16]

In his obituary, Watts-Dunton records how the 'genius of Charles Dickens' had captured the interest of the young Robinson and possibly inspired him to become a writer himself.[17] Le Grys Norgate in the *Dictionary of National Biography* also calls Robinson a 'disciple of Defoe and Dickens.'[18] Apart from Dickens, there are striking parallels between Robinson's writing and Mayhew's representations of London's East End – a contemporaneous source acknowledged by Robinson – when it comes to his treatment of abject poverty and women's criminality. Indeed, Robinson's use of the local thieves' dialect and the description of Croiley's Land in the New Vennel, the poorest, most densely populated section of Glasgow where 'Jane Cameron' grows up,[19] reminds one of Dickens's *Oliver Twist*. Robinson's Prison Matron, speaking with the voice of the implied male author, aligns herself with Dickens and his representations of criminal women at various points. In *Female Life in Prison*, the Matron draws on Dickens's conviction that even fallen women retain a better self and need sympathy.[20] Yet the Matron carefully qualifies this view, continuing: 'But to see some of these women hour by hour, and listen to them in their mad defiance, rage and blasphemy, is almost to believe they are creatures of another mould and race, born with no idea of God's truth, and destined to die in their own benighted ignorance.'[21] *Prison Characters*, however, referring back to *Memoirs of Jane Cameron*, sides with Dickens, clearly and explicitly, against a letter in the *Times* attributing the schools of crime described in *Oliver Twist* to the novelist's imagination rather than factual existence.[22] Arguably, Robinson's tales share Dickens's impulse to both write for commercial reasons and educate readers about social conditions. The charge of false representation against another male author must have rung particularly true for Robinson, who packaged his prison tales as the authentic account of an insider.

While I have no evidence that Robinson actually visited women's prisons himself, the chapter entitled 'Visitors' in *Female Life in Prison* is suggestive in this regard. The narrative alludes to the 'steady and incessant stream of visitors [to Millbank and Brixton prisons], furnished with orders from Parliament-street or the Secretary of State,' maintaining that '[s]carcely a week in the year occurs without some one from the outer world passing by order through the gates and being conducted from pentagon to pentagon, and ward to ward, by a matron of the establishment.'[23] In what sounds like a self-reflexive statement, the writer – hidden behind the identity of 'A Prison Matron' – refers to 'the poet or novelist, in search of a new idea, which the wild lives of prisoners may suggest' as one type of visitor to women's prisons.[24] The acknowledgments in the first volume of *Memoirs of Jane Cameron* may also imply that Robinson did actually research prisons and criminal life on a first-hand basis. Here his Prison Matron thanks the Scottish functionaries, 'gentlemen who, partly ignorant of the object which took me and a valuable co-operator to Scotland, were yet most anxious, by every means in their power, to show me the interior of their prisons, the working of their criminal law, the darkest secrets of their streets.'[25] Dickens and Mayhew, of course, visited prisons, so it seems reasonable to assume that this path was open to Robinson as well.

In a metafictional comment at the end of the first volume of *Female Life in Prison*, the writer foreshadows more comprehensively the task he would complete two years later, with the writing of *Memoirs of Jane Cameron*. Relating some incidents of '[p]risoners' freemasonry' at Millbank that, the narrator promises, 'take[s] us to the world of romance,'[26] Robinson's tale suggests that female prisons harbour a plethora of ideas for the fiction author: 'If the hearts of these prison women could be laid bare, there would be found a story in each which has hitherto escaped the poet and the novelist; the matter for a thousand books is floating amidst the desolate wards that echo to these women's sighs, or ring with their defiance. Theirs have not been quiet lives, and from the elements of life's discord spring the incidents to interest mankind.'[27] This passage illustrates the problematic status of Robinson and his prison fiction. Although the author's call to record the lives of female convicts validates the experiences of such women and gives them a voice to a certain extent, Robinson also exploits the stories of female prisoners for his own economic benefit – the sale of his books. In this regard, his fiction shares the commercial impetus central to other popular narratives of crime and punishment, such as execution broadsides, which ventriloquized, and profited from, the experiences of non-elite women in similar ways.

The fact that Robinson writes disguised as 'A Prison Matron' – 'one retired from Government service'[28] – deploying gender strategically to feign authenticity, further complicates his position. The writer's agenda to 'convey to the reader some idea of what prisoners are, and what prison life really is' is two-sided.[29] If it presents itself as an explicit attempt to rectify misrepresentations of women convicts, it is likewise not free from (nevertheless unacknowledged) biases and misconceptions regarding the biographies, behaviour, and treatment of incarcerated criminals, not least because the author is not the insider he pretends to be but a commercial writer.

Robinson's claims to authentic representation, however, are embedded in interesting broader reflections on which discursive forms can adequately render a truthful account of prison life. In the introductory chapter of *Female Life in Prison* – which can also be regarded as a mission statement for the two later prison narratives – Robinson's Prison Matron expresses her belief that she offers 'for the first time, a true and impartial chronicle of female prison life.'[30] The Matron legitimizes her project by pointing to her inside view, contrasting her woman's perspective, and her more immediate access to the prisoners' feelings, with that of male officials: 'Directors may issue their annual reports, the governors of prisons may write their ponderous tomes upon the question, the chaplains may preach, and pray, and visit, but their opportunities of judging fairly and honestly are few and far between, and they are misled and deceived every week in the year. In men's prisons I believe it is the warder, and in female prisons I am convinced it is the matron, who alone has the power to offer a true picture of prison life.'[31] Promising to provide a more balanced account, the matron suggests she has a better insight into more positive aspects of the prisoners' character: 'And of that better side to prison character which a Matron has the greatest chance of observing, of that evidence of affection for some kind officer who has screened offenders from a trivial punishment, or has listened to some little story in impulsive moments, about a mother, sister, brother, child, they loved once, the great report books utter not a word.'[32] When Robinson's Matron promises to give an insight into prison life beyond official reports and statistics, 'the life within the outward life that Blue Books speak of, and Parliament agitates concerning,' the life of which 'there are no records kept,'[33] she offers a social history that aims to note down formerly unknown aspects of the lives of female convicts (and prison matrons). Indeed, Robinson's agenda here converges with Foucault's concern to insurrect 'subjugated knowledges ... buried or masked in functional coherences or formal systematizations.'[34] Robinson's tale makes the struggle between different social voices explicit, decentres the linguistic and social authority of official documentation, and reinstates the authority of formerly peripheral agents.[35] In this context, the narrative works in support of women's professional roles and validates the matrons' labour and their perspective within the penal system, attributing to it a special status and power. Robinson's project does not only argue for the improvement of matrons' working conditions,[36] but it also aims to recover the delegitimized knowledge of minor female employees in the penal system, contrasted with the institutionally sanctioned knowledge of male directors, governors, and chaplains.[37] The fact that this female 'subjugated knowledge' is – at least in part – fictionally mediated through Robinson's narratives detracts from the more radical potential of this act of recovery, of course.

The Matron's motto to turn 'dry volumes of facts and figures, – skeletons of prison life' into accounts of 'flesh and blood to make them living, breathing truths'[38] is not only an affront to the professed truthfulness of official documents; it is also the mantra of a commercial novelist. Interestingly, the status of the male fiction writer – who has relinquished authority into the hands of the 'Prison Matron' – is affirmed later on in *Female Life in Prison*, at the expense of the Matron's status. Struggling to represent the particularly violent character of the prisoner 'Towers,' Robinson's Matron expresses her reluctance and conviction that 'it is impossible for a woman's pen to fill the shadings in all that depth and intensity necessary for a truthful portraiture.'[39] By contrast, the Matron suggests that '[t]wo men, whose minds loved to grope in dark places, might have been glad of such an eccentric character for a story or romance – Edgar Allen Poe and Eugene Sue.'[40] Subtly, the narrative thus reinstates the male ghostwriter's power and implicitly suggests that it is ultimately in fiction authored by male novelists that the stories and personalities of female convicts can best unfold. Ironically, Robinson here simultaneously undermines his own narrative by calling into question the adequacy and reliability of his narrator.

Although Robinson's prison narratives clearly argue in favour of a new and different perspective on women's criminality, the accounts are complicated by the fact that in writing this social history – however authentic or inauthentic it may be – he appropriates women's voices in multiple ways, both those of female criminals and that of 'A Prison Matron.' The fact that Robinson's Matron explicitly insists that no other matron knows she is speaking on their behalf indicates some awareness of the implications of this rhetorical move on Robinson's part,[41] although it does not mitigate entirely the appropriation of 'A Prison Matron's' perspective. Female prisoners and matrons themselves have no unmediated voice in his writings, even if his recording of their allegedly authentic experiences in itself ascribes a different, more positive cultural value to them.

Robinson's prison narratives follow a highly formulaic pattern, with regard to both form and subject matter. *Female Life in Prison* and *Prison Characters* have a comparable structure, alternating between chapters containing general information on women's prisons and brief case studies of specific female convicts, mainly organized around little anecdotes, thus offering a mixture of education and entertainment. *Memoirs of Jane Cameron* fuses all of these elements into one life-narrative – a form of conversion tale – starting with Jane's childhood of neglect, her fall into criminality, her repeated incarceration, and her eventual death after a successful reformation. The lack of unmediated speech power for convicts manifests itself most obviously in *Memoirs of Jane Cameron*, which is not the autobiographical account the title suggests. The narrative is, however, occasionally intersected with passages that record Jane's train of thought, such as her feelings over her first theft, instigated by her jealousy and desire to join her unfaithful lover at a dance (for which she needs some money). Reporting the young girl's nervousness in the process of stealing some items from a haberdasher's shop, the Matron cites her: "'I thought my heart would burst,' was her comment upon this incident, "I was sae afeard o' bein' foond oot – naethin' else. I didna think o' anythin' but my Johnnie dancing with the Frazers, and if I could ony get at the ribbons or the gloves and mak' awa' wi' them!"'[42] Although the narrative gives Jane Cameron a voice and cites her at various points in her local Glaswegian dialect, authorial control ultimately rests with the Prison Matron, that is, Robinson.

The Matron begins *Memoirs of Jane Cameron* by asserting that she is rendering 'an authentic record of a female criminal's career,'[43] based on nothing but 'this woman's word.'[44] Robinson here creates the illusion that it is the character of Cameron herself who stands behind this 'faithful chronicle of a woman's fall and rescue.'[45] Quotations from Jane are inserted into the chapters again and again, but often to back up the 'moral' of the narrative, thus resembling the use of convicts' testimonies in conversion tales and other writings authored by prison chaplains in support of their own ideological argument. John Field's *Prison Discipline* (1846), for instance, contains the 'evidence of prisoners' extracted from testimonies given to the Inspectors of Prisons in 1837.[46] Generally, these statements are deployed in order to back up the message intended by the Reverend, confirming the disadvantages of association in prison.[47] Similarly, the Prison Matron records Jane Cameron's admiration of her prison cell during imprisonment in Scotland, which, according to the narrator, 'tells its own moral': "'If we all had a room to our ainsel' like this, we should na get into half the trooble, and many o' us would ne'er gae bad at a.'"[48] While this statement draws attention to the material conditions at the root of women's criminality, it can also be deployed in the service of an agenda of social control, aiming at the sanitizing and reformation of the lives of the poor.

Even if the narrative does not provide an unmediated prisoner's perspective, Robinson's Matron draws attention to this very act of mediation and the problematic task of giving an insight into and a 'truthful' transcript of Jane Cameron's thoughts and feelings, thus going beyond a mere appropriation of the prisoner's voice in support of a particular ideology – a method characteristic of Field's account, for example. Towards the end of *Memoirs of Jane Cameron* – Jane in the meantime has left prison to take up a position as a servant, but is seduced into leaving through a chance encounter with a former prison 'pal' – the Matron gives a record of Jane's decision-making process in the form of free indirect speech, subsequently commenting on her own writing:

> No; she could not write her warning, or give warning in any fashion. She could not remain another month in that house with her mistress wearying her with well-meant advice … She could not wait a month, she could not endure service a week longer, she must go away at once!
>
> I do not attempt to say that this was exactly the train of thoughts or their sequence in the mind of Jane Cameron that night, but I believe that she had all these thoughts, and that they beset her and kept her restless till the morning. In that confession of her conduct, made at a later period of her life, she explained forcibly and simply the motives which led her to go, and the reasons which urged her to adopt this course, and they approximate to that analysis which, in the preceding pages, I have attempted to set before the reader.[49]

Through free indirect style, Robinson's Matron here explicitly tries to gain an insight into Jane Cameron's world of thoughts and emotions in order to paint a more sympathetic and complex picture of the servant's escape. As John Bender notes in his study of eighteenth-century narratives, including prison tales, '[t]he device of free indirect discourse creates the illusion that the unvoiced mental life of fictional personages exists as unmediated presence.'[50] Importantly, though, while Robinson's tale employs such a device to create a sense of immediacy, the narrative draws attention to the limits of representation, a self-reflexive gesture uncommon in other writings on female convicts. Although *Memoirs of Jane Cameron* draws on the conventions of confessional tales and conversion narratives, it moves beyond the ideological constraints of these genres by including a meta-perspective.

The attempt to access the personal motivations of a criminal in itself constitutes a departure from other, positivist representations of female prisoners as objects of enquiry, or mere repositories of the failures and advantages of a particular 'system,' rather than subjects with an emotional, intellectual, and social agenda. At the beginning of the second volume of *Memoirs of Jane Cameron*, the Matron renders an account of Jane's reflections after being arrested for her involvement in a robbery:

> In the cell at Glasgow Prison, awaiting her sentence, she was left to reflect upon the fate that lay before her in the future. Would it be four years, seven years, ten years – how many years taken from her life? How many years set aside from the streets which had been life to her, and confinement apart from all that had consti-tuted '*happiness*,' would be fixed upon her? The thought and the suspense were horrible, and, as her trial did not come on at once, she begged for work to relieve her from the monotony which preyed upon her, and seemed to drive her mad.
>
> She felt bewildered by the importance and gravity of her trial, by the judge on the bench, and the state and solemnity surrounding her. In the midst of her sus-pense, her incertitude of the sentence which would be passed upon her, there came at times a little spasm of pride to think that all the pomp and parade of jus-tice were for her, that all those people before her were interested more or less in her case, and that the crowd representing the public had come to hear about her, and would go home talking about her.[51]

In passages like this, Robinson's narrative provides the reader with a history of emotion from below – a history of the experiences (imagined, but not neces-sarily that far from actual, lived experience) of an incarcerated individual not recorded elsewhere. Although some of the ideas put forward here overlap with arguments made by prison authorities and reformers – such as the need for prison labour to counter the effects of solitary confinement – the passage also gives room to Jane's transgressive sensations during the trial. The description humanizes the figure of Jane Cameron during the process of imprisonment, implicitly inviting a better understanding on the reader's part of the challenges faced by the prisoner. At various other points, the narrative makes an attempt to depict and account for the emotional life of the convict. For instance, the Matron reports Jane Cameron's different moods during imprisonment, her desperation in her cell with 'the old monotony of labour' and 'nothing to look at but the four walls,' as well as her desire for change, resulting in the refusal of food and the carrying out of 'all the evil arts which are in vogue at pris-ons.'[52] Again, the Matron quotes Jane, reflecting on the anxiety-ridden period in Glasgow Prison before her transfer to Millbank Prison in London: "'I ken that I was hardenin' fast eno' at that time," were her remarks; "that I ne'er felt a warse woman in a' my leef. The fourteen years made me care for naethin'; I had the fancy that I should die lang afore my time was up, and that I was na gude warking hard for a character."'[53] Thus the narrative describes the psychological aspects of incarceration in a more nuanced way than other sources, like official reports, which merely record the prisoners' moods but do not attempt to understand them. Robinson's analysis, then, is a qualitative rather than a quantitative approach, more attuned to the representation of individual prison lives and convict experience.

Although Robinson's narratives encourage readers to pity rather than condemn people like Jane Cameron, they do not consider convicts as equals. The narratives' paternalism manifests itself in the language employed by the Prison Matron to describe her prisoners. Robinson's Matron repeatedly draws analogies between the prison inmates and children or describes them as irrational, diseased, or physically abnormal, hence identifiable by the observer. In *Female Life in Prison*, the Matron expresses paternalistic pride, contradicting 'the satirist' who critiques the management of prisoners and their release as 'a paternal government.'[54] She insists instead that the government '*has* a fatherly interest in its misguided children – and the satirist is not always in the right.'[55] Reflecting on violent behaviour by female inmates, the Matron concludes that '[h]urried as by a will beyond their own – impelled by a force that seems bestowed upon them to work evil in the hour of their desperation – we can but wonder, pity, pray for these wild natures.'[56] If individualized treatment, characterized by special attention from the prison matron, and reformation succeed, however, the Matron maintains that convicts – like 'Macklin' in *Female Life in Prison* – develop an attachment to their matron that is 'almost the fond, faithful attachment of a dog to its mistress.'[57] The narrative alternates between such patronizing images of ultimate docility and total lack of restraint, suggesting the need to supervise these women at all times.

Yet, there is another side to Robinson's representations of female prisoners, which complicates his accounts and distinguishes him from other commentators such as Mary Carpenter, who deployed similar, often colonial, tropes to describe them.[58] Although Robinson's Matron uses a whole catalogue of jungle creatures to refer to female convicts – lionesses, tigresses, hyenas, panthers, and elephants, among others[59] – the depictions occasionally seem to bear the traces of gleeful admiration (and simultaneously provoke such in the reader) for the strength, agility, and grace of these powerful women. The same is true for Robinson's desire to tell about the secret alliances, communication, and romantic attachments between female prisoners. Although, arguably, this keenness could be interpreted as a strategy to render his prison narratives 'racier' and hence more commercially profitable – *Memoirs of Jane Cameron* offers a popular mixture of crime and romance,

detailing Jane's early involvement with men alongside her criminal career –
the stories also acknowledge aspects of convicts' lives not usually given that
much attention in official publications or most reformers' writings.

The same holds true for the depiction of 'palling-in,' the formation of
romantic bonds between women convicts.[60] Robinson's Matron draws attention to the value of these attachments, despite the problems and quarrels they
cause in penal institutions, because they 'indicate[s] in most cases that craving
for affection, that wish to be loved, and to find some one to love, which is the
natural instinct of woman, however low in the scale of humanity.'[61] A sense of
voyeuristic sensationalism certainly plays a role in these instances of desire
between women, occurrences which the Matron occasionally describes in
medicalized terms as 'strange, morbid fancies'[62] and 'spasmodic liking[s].'[63]
Telling the story of Jane Cameron's prison romance with another woman, the
Matron's words acknowledge the nature of same-sex desire more forcefully
and positively, though, suggesting the existence of a hidden lesbian history
rarely hinted at so explicitly in other contemporaneous documents dealing
with women in penal institutions:

> But she *fell in love* with this woman; I know no phrase that can more truly convey
> my meaning. And women do fall in love with each other in prisons; exhibit for
> each other at times strange passionate and unselfish attachments, lasting, as a rule,
> nine or twelve months, and then ending in a whirl of rage and jealousy, a desperate
> quarrel, and a new 'pal.' I have known one woman leave her baby to a stranger's
> care, and fight her way to the dark, where she knew her 'pal' was confined.[64]

Robinson's Matron also alludes to the possibility of strong ties between convicts and matrons, noting Jane Cameron's 'strange attachment, almost devo-
tion' for Miss Weston, the Brixton prison matron who begins to take a special
interest in her. Jane Cameron's 'love' for Weston is described as 'intense,'
and the Prison Matron's narrative is highly suggestive of secret moments of
intimacy between officer and inmate: 'She [Jane Cameron] had a strange
habit of crouching on the floor of her cell, and watching the dress of Miss
Weston pass her ... Cameron would lie extended along the floor of her cell,
watching for the matron, occasionally reaching forth her hand, and touching
her foot gently, if she approached too near.'[65] When Jane Cameron's release
from prison is imminent, their relationship is sealed with another breach of
rules and secret encounter:

> The preceding night, let it be confessed, to the amazement of disciplinarians,
> Miss Weston had found her way to the ward – adjacent to her own at that time –

and whispered her 'good-bye,' and heard the woman call God's blessing on her head for all the interest she had taken in her.

Matron and prisoner touched each other's hands beneath the door, and then the interview had ended – a fugitive interview, that the rules would have punished by a fine for Miss Weston, and for the matron who had allowed her to pass in, and Cameron flung herself on the bed and covered her head with the clothes to stifle her sobs.[66]

It seems quite obvious that here, Robinson, prolific writer of romance fiction, could not resist his impulse to embellish the 'couple's' separation with dramatic and sentimental detail. According to the Prison Matron, the eventual parting between Jane and Weston in the outside world – after Weston, sought out by Jane Cameron, successfully assists in restoring the former prisoner's servant-position with the employers she had abandoned, now about to move their household to America – constitutes 'a trial' for both of them.[67]

The regime promoted by Robinson's narratives thus relies on occasional subversions of official institutional rules, manifesting themselves particularly in close alliances between individual matrons and prisoners, and their conversations that are 'not in the books.'[68] This advocacy of female-female coalitions is sometimes combined with an explicit critique of governmental policies. With reference to Miss Weston, Robinson's Matron notes that '[i]n my time, she was even a critic of the Government under which she held office, and had Colonel Sir Joshua Jebb or Captain O'Brien condescended to have solicited her opinion upon many requirements of the prison service, it is just possible that her practical opinions would have shaken their faith in the wisdom of a few of the "Rules."'[69] Robinson's narrative skilfully packages the critique of government 'Rules' by reporting it as another's opinion (interestingly, the earlier prison tale, *Female Life in Prison*, was dedicated to O'Brien, the director of convict prisons, who here does not receive more than a snide comment). The narrative presents the occasional alliances of non-elite women – the matron Weston is characterized as a woman 'who had known trouble and seen better days' herself so that 'the trouble of others always drew her towards them'[70] – as a possible, sometimes more effective, alternative to the strict disciplinary regime instituted by influential men. In contrast to official publications of the period, Robinson's tales explicitly support the subversion of discipline in some cases and present secret bonds and attachments as potentially helpful elements in the process of convict reformation.

Robinson's Prison Matron also joins in the debate around cheap female prison labour and its dire consequences for needlewomen in the outside world, who, she suggests, are forced into crime because of 'this obnoxious policy.'[71]

Aligning herself with a popular song of protest, the Matron predicts that '[t]here will be living illustrations to Hood's "Song of the Shirt" to the end of time, if some better and more just system be not presently adopted.'[72] In strong language, the Matron blames both the City firms that are seeking out prisons as an alternative market – 'shame on the City firms who seek so cheap a market as our Government prisons!'[73] – and the government for selling to them: 'it is an unnatural expedient to reduce prison expenditure, that in moral and enlightened England, with a thoughtful, feeling Lady on its throne, should be cried down by every honest soul with power to raise a voice against its glaring inconsistency.'[74] Surely, in these passages, Robinson's passionate voice fuses with that of his persona, the Prison Matron, in an evident way.

Robinson's Matron repeatedly points to the economic causes at the root of crime and female criminality more particularly. In a chapter on circumstances encouraging criminal activities, the Matron criticizes the regulation of street trade and insists that 'to throw difficulties in the way of the huckster is to add to his difficulties of living honestly.'[75] Similarly, the narrative traces Jane Cameron's misfortunes back to economic problems. After her alcoholic mother has kicked her out of the apartment to have more space for paying lodgers, Jane is befriended by a couple in the building who take her in at night. They are matmakers but disappear after prices for mats fall so that they cannot sell them anymore and are forced to move out.[76]

In spite of these instances, Robinson's narratives shy away from a more substantial, consistently materialist critique of the distribution of wealth. It is the character of Elizabeth Harber, a cell mate of Jane Cameron's – portrayed in a rather unsympathetic light as a 'crafty, hypocritical prisoner'[77] – who formulates this critique most clearly: '"If people will see us starve rather than give us money, why, we must help ourselves. If anybody would give you and me a hundred a-year and a house to live in, why, we should be honest people, and go to church every Sunday."'[78] Although Robinson's call for Christian philanthropy supports this statement to a certain extent – the Matron formulates the desire to awaken the interest of philanthropists as one of her original aims in the writing of these stories[79] – the portrayal of Harber as Jane's temptress who gives her advice and 'whispers' to her throughout the night, against Jane's will,[80] suggests that Harber's response, legitimizing crime as a response to social inequality, goes too far. Nevertheless, the fact that the narrative provides a space for this voice in itself suggests that it is willing to allow for different perspectives, beyond a coherent, socially conservative message.

The transformation of Jane Cameron's criminal career is exemplary of the kind of reformation promoted by Robinson's narratives. The former convict leaves Britain, sailing towards 'the new world and the new life' with her employers.[81] Her mistress, Mrs Evans, an 'energetic' and 'Christian woman, with a great and undying interest in the progress of the weak and the erring to repentance,'[82] sees 'evidence of a new religious feeling, without which, perhaps, no reformed prisoner ever kept strong to the last.'[83] Jane Cameron's health declines only a few months after she starts service with her family in America, and she dies. The narrative concludes with a letter from Mrs Evans to Jane's old prison matron, Miss Weston, and a comment by Robinson's Matron: '"To the last she was a good servant and a faithful friend – she died truly penitent for all past sins, and truly thankful for the mercies which had been vouchsafed to her." This was the last news of Jane Cameron – the last and the best!'[84]

In this account, the 'good' news of Jane Cameron's complete reformation and penitent death obviously outweighs the bad news of the loss of her life. Implicit in this eventually successful conversion of the former convict, so close to a relapse, is the wider rationale behind Robinson's prison tales – a call to other 'Christian men and women,' like the Evanses, 'who may read this book,' to support organizations like the 'Discharged Prisoners' Aid Society,'[85] and to discreetly take on former prisoners like Jane 'at a fair salary.'[86] Although Robinson's Matron criticizes patrons who take women into service and do not pay 'fair' wages,[87] the general class structure of society remains intact in these narratives. As in earlier criminal reform concepts, initiated by Elizabeth Fry and other prison visitors, reformed female prisoners are advertised as a valuable resource for wealthy households, because, as the Prison Matron insists, 'there are no servants so thoroughly industrious as a discharged prisoner.'[88] It is only for a brief moment that we get a glimpse of the secret discontent some of these women might have been experiencing simultaneously. Describing the servant-existence of Jane Cameron shortly before her decision to escape, the Prison Matron reports that her life 'was very still and quiet and *prison-like* – not much resembling freedom, or what she had once believed freedom to consist of.'[89] It is her 'wild desire to have less restraint upon her actions, to be her own mistress in any way,'[90] which ultimately leads to her decision to break out. Although Jane Cameron returns and the servant's discontent is dissolved into penitence at the end, the fact that Robinson acknowledges the servant's dissatisfaction and prison-like living conditions in a wealthy household at all demonstrates that the narrative's ideological agenda is ambivalent.

The vision of Frederick William Robinson's prison narratives may ultimately not be a radical one. Rather, it calls for an organic relationship between the different classes of society, vowing to root out crime through the help of Christian benevolence. At the end of *Prison Characters*, Robinson's Matron insists that it must be possible in 'the richest country in the world'[91] to halt the increase in crime. Rather than demanding social justice, the Matron asks for '[c]leanliness, education, religion, incessant watchfulness of the children of the poor.'[92] Here, the narrative presents a strategy of surveillance and social control familiar from other social commentators during the 1860s, like Mary Carpenter, as appropriate response.

Female Life in Prison, Memoirs of Jane Cameron, and *Prison Characters* offer some sympathetic, humanizing portrayals, and an insight into some of the challenging living conditions of female prisoners – as well as non-elite people more generally – even if more positive representations are counteracted by descriptions typifying criminals as animalistic, irrational, child-like, and physically deviant creatures. Some of the stereotypes and narrative conventions used by Robinson might have been employed to satisfy audience expectations. We may even speculate whether, in the case of *Memoirs of Jane Cameron*, the conventions of confessional or conversion tales might have served a strategic function, to detract attention from the more radical aspects of the narrative.[93] But the ideological contradictions in Robinson's narratives may also be a result both of his own ambivalence – and that of his readers – with regard to social issues like women's criminality and of the constraints of the marketplace.

Although the voices of female prisoners themselves are mediated in multiple ways in Robinson's stories, they do exist. Akin to representations of criminals in gallows literature, these narratives – *Memoirs of Jane Cameron* especially – open up a space for readers to take notice of the convict's story. It is here that an analysis of Robinson's work can contribute to the 'insurrection of subjugated knowledges ... buried or masked in functional coherences or formal systematizations' that Foucault had in mind.[94] As I have argued, it is not only the prisoner's 'subjugated knowledge' that Robinson's narratives reinstate – if in a limited way – but also the delegitimized knowledge of prison matrons. Robinson's narratives thus constitute a polyphonic pastiche of different voices. Their 'social multiaccentuality' lends itself particularly to an excavation of these alternative forms of knowledge.[95] Written during a period when the broadside trade was already in decline, Robinson's tales can be seen as one of the channels in which popular interrogations into female criminality and imprisonment continued. Published in two volumes, rather than cheaper instalments, though, they cannot be assumed to have had nearly as wide a distribution as street literature.

As I have indicated, Robinson's work rarely attacks society's structural inequalities explicitly. In *Female Life in Prison*, Robinson's Prison Matron tells the story of the prisoner Sarah Featherstone, a story, she says, 'not unlike

Hetty's in "Adam Bede," from which, perhaps, Hetty's character was conceived – for novelists are quick at piecing the fragments of stern truth into a story that may touch all hearts.'[96] This ability to 'touch all hearts' may ultimately also have been the power and – simultaneously – the limitation of Robinson's narratives. The constraints of these tales consist precisely of Robinson's decision to limit his analysis of female life in prison to convict psychology, and to the humanization of individual convicts, such as 'Jane Cameron.' While these modes of representation, including his metacritical comments, depart in important ways from other, institutionally sanctioned ways of representing female prisoners, Robinson's discursive strategy cannot ultimately replace a more thorough, structural critique of the material conditions at the root of women's criminality.

To recover and reinstate the 'subjugated knowledges' of nineteenth-century convicts and minor prison employees, such as matrons, remains a crucial project for cultural and literary historians, in order to complicate traditional histories of women's (and men's) criminality and imprisonment that have largely relied on official documentation, and reformist or scientific writings. Popular narratives of crime and punishment, like execution broadsides or Robinson's tales, suggest that alternative forms of representation *were* available. These popular modes interrogated, or even explicitly resisted, the homogenizing tendencies of more institutionally sanctioned accounts of criminality and prison life. The recognition of these alternative voices suggests that nineteenth-century penal debate was not *purely* configured in terms of seemingly homogeneous disciplinary narratives, as has occasionally been suggested.

The tradition of reacting against institutional narratives of women's delinquency and imprisonment that Robinson's prison stories form a part of continues until today, even if the critical parameters of contemporary counter-narratives are very different, and certainly more radical.[97] The recovery of 'subjugated knowledges' in the context of the penal system is important on an individual, communal, and public level, but it must come in conjunction with a systemic critique that addresses both the causes, and the exact workings, of the very processes of 'subjection' that it responds to, in order to fully develop its force. As I have argued, Robinson's narratives yet stop short of a radical, materialist critique of women's criminality and imprisonment; although these stories constitute an attempt to both represent and validate convict experience, they also ultimately remain caught in the dominant concepts of social inequality characteristic of the culture they emerge from, and they even participate in the discursive disciplinary mechanisms of this culture to a certain extent. A contemporary critical agenda that wishes to address convict experience and agency – in the past or today – and to recover prisoners' voices, then, must not

come at the expense of a continued attentiveness to the strategies of disciplinary power, as well as its discursive and material effects on society's disadvantaged groups.

NOTES

1 Michel Foucault, *Discipline and Punish: The Birth of the Prison* (1975), trans. Alan
   Sheridan (New York: Vintage, 1995).
2 Michel Foucault, *'Society Must Be Defended': Lectures at the Collège de France,
   1975–76*, ed. Mauro Bertani and Alessandro Fontana, trans. David Macey (London:
   Lane, 2003).
3 The 'facts' of prison life presented in these tales may not be entirely reliable; the
   use of them as a source of empirical data is hence not unproblematic. For some
   examples of how Robinson has been employed by contemporary critics, see Russell
   P. Dobash, R. Emerson Dobash, and Sue Gutteridge, *The Imprisonment of Women*
   (Oxford: Blackwell, 1986), who attribute *Female Life in Prison* to a 'Francis'
   Robinson; Seán McConville, *A History of English Prison Administration*, vol. 1:
   1750–1877 (London: Routledge, 1981); Ann D. Smith, *Women in Prison: A Study
   in Penal Methods* (London: Stevens, 1962); Martin J. Wiener, *Reconstructing the
   Criminal: Culture, Law, and Policy in England, 1830–1914* (Cambridge:
   Cambridge University Press, 1990); Lucia Zedner, *Women, Crime, and Custody in
   Victorian England* (Oxford: Clarendon, 1991). Leon Radzinowicz and Roger Hood
   acknowledge the fictionality of *Female Life in Prison* (although they, quite rightly,
   insist that it is also a rare 'realistic' account of women's imprisonment), but they do
   not go into further detail. See *A History of English Criminal Law and its Administration from 1750*, vol. 5: *The Emergence of Penal Policy* (London: Stevens, 1986),
   5:524, n. 28.
4 I have not been able to locate any recent, detailed studies of Robinson and his work.
   Some biographical information is available in Gerald Le Grys Norgate's article
   'Robinson, Frederick William,' *Dictionary of National Biography* (Oxford: Oxford
   University Press, 1912). R.R. Bowker briefly discusses Robinson in 'London as a
   Literary Centre: Second Paper: The Novelists,' *Harper's New Monthly Magazine*
   77 (1888), 17, which also prints a portrait of the writer on page 13. A short obituary
   reference with a portrait was also published in *Black and White*: 'The Passing Hour:
   The March of the World in Picture and Pen,' *Black and White* 22 (1901), 831. One
   of the few references to Robinson that I have been able to trace in recent criticism
   is in Graham Law's study *Serializing Fiction in the Victorian Press* (Basingstoke,
   UK: Palgrave, 2000), where the writer is referred to as part of a group of 'established metropolitan authors' (77) and as a 'newspaper novelist' with 'early

metropolitan newspaper experience' (264), although his work is not discussed in further detail.

5 Norgate, 'Robinson, Frederick William,' 216.

6 Theodore Watts-Dunton, 'A Great Builder of the Old Three-Decker: F.W. Robinson,' *Athenaeum* 14 (1901): 813.

7 Ibid.

8 Mikhail M. Bakhtin, *The Dialogic Imagination: Four Essays*, ed. Michael Holquist, trans. Caryl Emerson and Michael Holquist (Austin: University of Texas Press, 1981), 263.

9 Frederick William Robinson [A Prison Matron], *Female Life in Prison*, 2 vols. (London: Hurst and Blackett, 1862), 1:39.

10 Ibid., 1:87.

11 Ibid., 2:82.

12 Ibid., 1:282. For a detailed analysis of this reform tract, see W.B. Carnochan's contribution to this volume.

13 Frederick William Robinson [A Prison Matron], *Prison Characters Drawn from Life with Suggestions for Prison Government*, 2 vols. (London: Hurst and Blackett, 1861), 1:7.

14 Frederick William Robinson [A Prison Matron], *Memoirs of Jane Cameron: Female Convict*, 2 vols. (London: Hurst and Blackett, 1864), 1:5.

15 Ibid., 1:6.

16 Dickens explicitly comments on female prisoners and conditions in women's prisons in a number of his journalistic writings. See, for instance, 'Philadelphia, and its Solitary Prison,' in *American Notes for General Circulation*, ed. F.S. Schwarzbach (London: Everyman, 1997), 113; 'The Prisoners' Van' (1835), in *Sketches by Boz* (1839), ed. and introd. Dennis Walder (London: Penguin, 1995), 314–17; and 'A Visit to Newgate' (1836), in *Sketches by Boz*, 234–48. See also Henry Mayhew and John Binny, *The Criminal Prisons of London and Scenes of Prison Life* (London: Griffin, 1862), e.g. 466–7. For a discussion of contradictions in Dickens's penal philosophy in general, see David Paroissien's contribution to this volume.

17 Watts-Dunton, 'F.W. Robinson,' 813.

18 Norgate, 'Robinson, Frederick William,' 216.

19 Robinson, *Memoirs*, 1:10–12.

20 Robinson, *Female Life*, 1:45.

21 Ibid.

22 Robinson, *Prison Characters*, 2:233.

23 Robinson, *Female Life*, 2:159.

24 Ibid., 2:160.

25 Robinson, *Memoirs*, 1:5–6.

26 Robinson, *Female Life*, 1:291, 1:300.

27 Ibid., 1:301.
28 Ibid., 1:1.
29 Ibid., 2:34.
30 Ibid., 1:3.
31 Ibid., 1:6.
32 Ibid., 1:7.
33 Ibid.
34 Foucault, 'Society,' 7.
35 On decentralizing tendencies and heteroglossia in popular fictional genres more generally, see Bakhtin, *The Dialogic Imagination*, 273.
36 Robinson, *Female Life*, 1:36–7.
37 McConville discusses the financial situation of prison employees in the nineteenth century. According to his figures, the matron's annual income was significantly smaller than that of all other staff, including that of lower-rank turnkeys and the nightwatchman. See McConville, *History of English Prison Administration*, vol. 1, 291.
38 Robinson, *Female Life*, 1:40.
39 Ibid., 1:283.
40 Ibid.
41 Ibid., 1:41.
42 Robinson, *Memoirs*, 1:56.
43 Ibid., 1:7.
44 Ibid., 1:4.
45 Ibid., 1:5.
46 Reverend J. Field, *Prison Discipline: The Advantages of the Separate System of Imprisonment, as Established in the New County Gaol of Reading, With a Description of the Former Prisons, and a Detailed Account of the Discipline Now Pursued* (London: Longman, 1846), 32–9.
47 Most of the speakers in Field's account are male by implication. Only one explicitly refers to evidence given by a female convict. Regardless of whether these testimonies are 'authentic,' their value is compromised by the environment in which they were given; the position of the questioners (in this case of Prison Inspectors) may well have influenced the prisoners' answers. See Sean C. Grass's discussion of the use of prisoners' statements by the prison chaplains John Field, H.S. Joseph, and John Clay (*The Self in the Cell: Narrating the Victorian Prisoner* [New York: Routledge, 2003], 15–36). See also Anna Schur's and Sean C. Grass's contributions to this volume.
48 Robinson, *Memoirs*, 1:233–4.
49 Ibid., 2:205–7.
50 John Bender, *Imagining the Penitentiary: Fiction and the Architecture of Mind in Eighteenth-Century England* (Chicago: University of Chicago Press, 1987), 211.

51 Robinson, *Memoirs*, 2:24–5.

52 Ibid., 2:33.

53 Ibid., 2:34.

54 Robinson, *Female Life*, 1:64.

55 Ibid., 1:64–5.

56 Ibid., 1:145.

57 Ibid., 1:235–6.

58 See Mary Carpenter's *Our Convicts* where she associates criminal women with that which is non-British, non-Christian, non-civilized (Mary Carpenter, *Our Convicts*, 2 vols [London: Longman, 1864], e.g., 2: 208). See also M.E. Owen, 'Criminal Women,' *Cornhill Magazine* 14 (1866): 153.

59 Robinson, *Female Life*, 1:108, 213, 2:58, 60, 63.

60 Zedner discusses cases of so-called 'tampering' with prisoners by female attendants (Zedner, *Women, Crime, and Custody*, 161–2). For a contemporary attempt to recover a hidden lesbian history in the penal sphere, see Sarah Waters's historical novel *Affinity* (London: Virago, 1999), which explores the theme of desire between a lady visitor and a female prisoner at Millbank in the 1870s and is discussed by Rosario Arias in the epilogue of this volume.

61 Robinson, *Prison Characters*, 1:31.

62 Robinson, *Memoirs*, 2:46.

63 Ibid., 2:176.

64 Ibid., 2:93–4; emphasis in original.

65 Ibid., 2:125–6. Although one might be inclined to doubt the practical feasibility of this gesture, the Matron maintains that physical touch was possible through the aperture at the bottom of the door.

66 Ibid., 2:147–8.

67 Ibid., 2:297.

68 Ibid., 2:113.

69 Ibid., 2:115.

70 Ibid., 2:282.

71 Ibid., 1:120.

72 Robinson, *Female Life*, 1:185, see also Robinson, *Prison Characters*, 1:94.

73 Robinson, *Female Life*, 2:275.

74 Ibid., 2: 292. On the debate, see also William Ellis, 'The Distressed Needlewomen, and Cheap Prison Labour,' *Westminster Review* 50 (1848–9): 371–94. The article discusses the objects of the Distressed Needlewomen's Society.

75 Robinson, *Prison Characters*, 2:239.

76 Robinson, *Memoirs*, 1:26–30.

77 Ibid., 1:131.

78 Ibid., 1:140.

79 Robinson, *Prison Characters*, 1:1–2

80 Robinson, *Memoirs*, 1:138–9.

81 Ibid., 2:299.

82 Ibid., 2:291.

83 Ibid., 2:299–300.

84 Ibid., 2:301.

85 Ibid., 2:155.

86 Ibid., 2:159.

87 Ibid.

88 Ibid., 2:167.

89 Ibid., 2:169; emphasis in original.

90 Robinson, *Prison Characters*, 2:195.

91 Ibid., 2:248.

92 Ibid., 2:249.

93 A similar argument has been made with regard to the moralistic frames of execution broadsides. See, for instance, Richard D. Altick, *Victorian Studies in Scarlet* (London: Dent, 1972), 49.

94 Foucault, *'Society,'* 7.

95 The phrase is the Soviet theorist Valentin Voloshinov's. See Michael Denning, *Mechanic Accents: Dime Novels and Working-Class Culture in America* (London: Verso, 1987), which draws on Voloshinov/Bakhtin, for an application of the concepts of multiaccentuality (and the dialogic) to a reading of nineteenth-century American dime novels (especially 82–4).

96 Robinson, *Female Life*, 2:272–3.

97 For an early feminist attempt to recover contemporary female prisoners' voices in order to counter the ramifications of 'monocausal and global' (9) models of female criminality, see Pat Carlen, ed., *Criminal Women: Autobiographical Accounts. Diana Christina, Jenny Hicks, Josie O'Dwyer, Chris Tchaikovsky and Pat Carlen* (Cambridge: Polity Press, 1985).

10 The Sensational Prison and the (Un)Hidden Hand of Punishment

JASON HASLAM

The terms on which much recent work about prisons and prison writing is structured are, implicitly or explicitly, confined by Foucault's analysis of the transformation from public to private punishments at the end of the eighteenth century, and his argument that this change is symptomatic of a transformation in dominant notions of subjectivity from the embodied to the docile subject. More specifically, this is a change from a notion of identity defined – and regulated or controlled – by its exterior relations to a heightened sense of a self-regulated interiority that is nonetheless created within a diffuse ideological matrix characterized by surveillance or, more properly, by the assumption of surveillance. Of course, several penologists and literary and cultural critics have critiqued Foucault's overall map of panopticism, focusing on extending his historical framework or denying what seems to them to be his overly constraining notion of this social panopticism.[1] I mention these general arguments in order to situate the reading I want to give of E.D.E.N. Southworth's immensely popular sensation novel *The Hidden Hand, or, Capitola the Madcap*, originally serialized in 1859, reserialized twice afterwards, and published in book form in 1888.[2] Written after the dramatic shift in penological practice – it started just before the turn of the nineteenth century – had taken a firm hold in U.S. prisons, Southworth's novel critiques some of the cultural practices that lie at the heart and origin of this new penology by returning, time and again, to the central sites of socially sanctioned punishment.

In order to analyse this critique, I need to begin by situating the 'culture of punishment' with which the novel engages. Certainly, no one questions that, at the turn of the nineteenth century, theories of punishment at the very least underwent a shift in emphasis, as Foucault details. These practices were defined, as the by now traditional narrative goes, by the competing, but in many ways similar, Auburn and Philadelphia systems. By the mid-nineteenth century, as Orlando Lewis states, the practices of and theories behind these systems had become ingrained in American penology: 'principles had become fairly well established; methods were fairly well fixed; traditions had already formed.'[3] In other words, the cultural discourses informing the practice of imprisonment were becoming entrenched in the U.S. imagination. Such punishment, moreover, was understood as a means of deterring further criminal activity (by both the inmate and the general population), and the prisons were, at least theoretically, supposed to be institutions designed to reform the criminal into a civil, socially productive individual, among other effects.[4] At the root of these new methods of prison reformation was the use of silence, based on the assumption that personal reflection could lead to a spiritual redemption that would bring with it concomitant behavioural changes. Tied to this, prison punishments were to be made private, rather than the previously public spectacle of corporal punishment.

These alterations in the aims and methods of punishment represent a radical departure in Western penology, a departure that, as Thomas L. Dumm argues, both echoes and enables the U.S. democratic experiment:

> Inside the walls of the penitentiary, the absence of freedom had the ironic effect of establishing the conditions necessary for the reconciliation of liberal and democratic assumptions about the behaviour of men. The penitentiary was already liberal and was to become democratic. It was liberal because the entire force of its operations was designed to reconstruct the psychology of individual persons. It was to be democratic because the same operations applied to each individual.[5]

In this utopian figuration of punishment, the criminal is reconstituted as an individualized, Enlightenment self through the new methods of isolation and discipline, thus correcting what were perceived as the external and non-essential contaminants that had brought about his criminal behaviour.[6] As a direct result of this reindividuation, as Dumm outlines, the reformed solitary individual was, somewhat paradoxically, seen to become part of the collective citizenry.

These aims and methods of the U.S. penitentiary experiment, as I note in *Fitting Sentences*, rapidly became the centre of penological discussion throughout the Western world. This dissemination of penological theory and practice is most prominently highlighted by Gustave de Beaumont and Alexis de Tocqueville's oft-discussed study of the U.S. prison system and its potential application to France. Indeed, Frank Lauterbach has noted that both the Auburn and Philadelphia prisons 'were visited extensively by foreign penologists in the 1830s (and were written about by many more who had never even visited them at all), an exchange that culminated in the first international prison congress at Frankfurt (Main) in 1846. Among those visitors were Gustave de Beaumont and Alexis de Tocqueville for France in 1831, William Crawford for the United Kingdom from 1832 to 1833, Dominique Mondelet and John Neilson for Canada in 1834, and Nicolaus Heinrich Julius for Prussia in 1835.'[7] Given the centrality of the early American experiments to the future of penology in the Western world, U.S. reactions to these systems (be they specifically legal or, as in the focus of this paper, cultural) can help to highlight the pitfalls embedded in the modern penitentiary system.

Against the theoretical motivations of penitentiary reform, additionally and as I have argued elsewhere, the actual practice of the prisons belies not only the effectiveness of the rule of silence, but also the general notions of human subjectivity that enable it. While the spectacle and practices of corporal punishment do indeed diminish in the nineteenth century, violent physical punishment did not disappear, but was reorganized in relation to the institution. Indeed, early in the history of prison reform – at the origin of the Philadelphia system, in fact – U.S. founding father Benjamin Rush included both pain and silence as means for reformation: 'The punishments should consist of bodily pain, labour, watchfulness, solitude and silence,' he wrote.[8]

Perhaps in part due to the grotesqueries of such punishments, the prison has a long history of representation in gothic fiction and its adventurous sibling, sensationalist fiction. What is significant for the current argument, though, is not the physical grotesquery of these punishments and their representations, but instead that such literary endeavours were themselves explicitly lauded as part of the prison project at its very inception. The brief meditations on prison reform by Rush (who was a driving force behind the new Philadelphia penitentiary) largely support Foucault's conclusions about the transformation of subjectivity – a transformation that is embodied, so to speak, by the penitentiary system. Rush, however, approaches the issue from a different angle. Rush may also use the idea of the sympathetic subject, the person defined by interiority, in his argument against public punishments, but he argues that public punishments can give rise to sympathy *for* the criminal, which can cause the unravelling of civil society: 'While we pity, we secretly condemn the law which inflicts the punishment: hence, arises a want of respect for [laws] in general, and a more feeble union of the great ties of government.'[9] Rush's desire for private, hidden punishments thus has more to do with silencing social dissent than lessening other forms of criminal behaviour.

In keeping with this perspective, Rush envisioned the penitentiary and its private punishment as not only effecting prisoners' reformations, but also as 'diffus[ing] terror through a community' (in what could be called an eighteenth-century liberal humanist version of the present-day 'Scared Straight' program).[10] Rush stated that if his prison reforms were made, then 'Children will press upon the evening fire in listening to tales that will spread from this abode of misery. Superstition will add to its horrors: and romance will find in it ample materials for fiction, which cannot fail of increasing the terror of its punishments.'[11] Rush argues that the true social benefits of private punishments are in their cultural effects, in the creation of cultural forms that will remove sympathy from the realm of punishment, and subsequently create a 'terror' perpetrated primarily through literary fictions. The gothic and sensationalist depiction of prison, then, was seen by Rush as a desired terrorist action against the citizenry, one that was aimed at maintaining law and order. In Rush's vision of the culture of punishment, literature becomes a primary form of creating Foucault's 'docile' subject.[12] The internalized self-surveillance of Foucauldian discipline becomes instead an internalized terror of external, though hidden, social violence. It is an interiority that is nonetheless culturally (re)produced. And this fear, as Dumm argues, is conceived precisely as a reduction of a subject's freedom of action in the service of the industrial machinery of the state: 'This uniform legal punishment underscored and supported a uniform model of behaviour, so that there was less and less psychic space available for the growth of individuals, for the development and nurturance of difference. U.S. citizens would have one dimension in which they could develop ... namely, the desire for wealth ... in terms not of alienation but of mechanization.' One could think here of Edgar Allan Poe's 'The Pit and the Pendulum' as a thematic exploration of the horrors of the hidden punishment and its reduction of the subject's 'space.'[13]

Southworth, however, in keeping with other sensationalist and gothic authors sympathetic to abolition, subverts this literary terror. She depicts the prison and its punishments as horrible and terrifying, to be sure, and does combine this to a certain degree with the removal of the notion of the sentimentalized punished subject.[14] But, beyond Lynette Carpenter's observation that 'the novel pits ... house against prison or asylum,'[15] *The Hidden Hand* highlights these horrors precisely in order to force the reader to actively question the methods and aims of the penitentiary (exactly what Rush wanted to avoid by creating this terrorist, non-sympathetic situation). In other words, Southworth exploits the implicit desire of Rush's reading subject – if readers 'press upon the evening fire' for stories of prison horror, then their readerly desire opens up possibilities for public discussion, the hidden gothic object of their private desire transforming into the subject of public dialogue, while their lack of sympathy and sentiment opens up, for Southworth, the possibility of rational debate. Southworth even goes beyond the tropes of sympathy, demonstrating how tales of horror, and horror itself, become objects of desire per se. The imaginative horrors of hidden punishment do terrify some of the citizenry into proper behaviour, but they also spark curiosity and drive people towards the criminal, deterrence becoming incentive. In turn, this form of criminal desire leads characters to expose some of the hidden biases of the law and society in general. In Southworth's tale, private horrors are corrected through the public sphere, making cultural dialogue the curative to the prison's horrors, rather than the other way around (as Rush would have it).

Fear and Sentimentalizing

Attempting to summarize all of the intricately intertwined plots of Southworth's novel is a fearsome task in itself. A classic sensation novel, it follows several plots, intertwined by characters who are related and married to, or cheated or abandoned or murdered by, various other characters. The two main storylines follow, first, the adventures of the title character, Capitola Le Noir, aka Capitola Black, who was raised as an orphan in the streets of New York, and who dressed as a boy both to get work and to avoid abuse by men. Capitola is taken in as a ward by a Virginia gentleman, Major Ira Warfield (who is often referred to by the moniker Old Hurricane). His adoption of Capitola becomes part of Warfield's ongoing feud with the villain of the piece, Capitola's evil, murderous uncle, Colonel Gabriel Le Noir. Second, we are introduced to Marah Rocke, a destitute working woman, and her prodigy son, Traverse, who is likewise taken in as a ward and apprentice by the kind and sentimental Dr Day. Day trains Traverse to be a medical doctor, hires Marah Rocke as a governess figure for his daughter, Clara, and eventually betroths his daughter to Traverse. All of Day's efforts, which seem to be leading to an Edenic household, are, of course, also nearly thwarted by the evil Colonel Le Noir.

Each of these main plots also details several different dealings with the justice and prison systems, both literally and figuratively. Indeed, Southworth's novel runs the gamut of nineteenth-century punishments, from juvenile workhouses, to full-scale prisons, to asylums, to slave punishments, to a military tribunal. Tied to this, several characters are at various points kidnapped and, in the words of the novel, 'imprisoned' by private individuals. Capitola's narrative is, in fact, largely framed by imprisonment or the threat thereof. Capitola is arrested off the streets as a vagrant, and tried, seemingly, for vagrancy and/or cross-dressing. What is telling about this early section in terms of my argument is that Capitola is more versed in the law and its systems of punishment than most of the adults around her. Major Warfield is horrified to learn that she may be sent to the workhouse:

> 'To the *work*-house – *her*, that *child*? – the wretches! Um-m-m-me! Oh-h-h-h!' groaned Old Hurricane, stooping and burying his shaggy, gray head in his great hands. He felt his shoulder touched, and looking up saw that the little prisoner had turned around, and was about to speak to him. 'Governor,' said the same clear voice that he had even at first supposed to belong to a girl – 'Governor, don't you keep on letting out that way! You don't know nothing! You're in the Recorder's Court! If you don't mind your eye, they'll commit you for contempt!' 'Will they? Then they'll do *well*, lad! *lass*, I mean, I plead guilty to contempt. Send a child like *you* to the – – ! They *shan't do it!*' ... 'But, you innocent old lion, instead of freeing *me*, you'll find *yourself* shut up between four walls, and very narrow ones at that, *I* tell you! You'll think yourself in a coffin! Governor, they call it – *The Tombs!*' whispered the child.[16]

The feelings of sympathy that are elicited by the sight of the girl in the dock could illustrate the cultural legitimacy of Rush's worry that public displays of punishment – what Foucault termed the 'spectacle' of punishment – could cause sympathy for the punished and lead to a questioning of civil authority.

Warfield's sympathetic reaction in fact mimics that which readers were supposed to feel upon perusing the works of such prison-reform writers as Southworth's contemporary Charles Dickens. Indeed, a passage from *Sketches by Boz* that describes a young girl seen visiting her mother in prison – written some two decades before *The Hidden Hand* – closely mirrors Warfield's vision of Capitola:

> The girl belonged to a class – unhappily but too extensive – the very existence of which should make men's hearts bleed. Barely past her childhood, it required but a glance to discover that she was one of those children, born and bred in neglect and vice, who have never known what childhood is: who have never been taught to love and court a parent's smile, or to dread a parent's frown ... Talk to *them* of parental solicitude, the happy days of childhood, and the merry games of infancy! Tell them of hunger and the streets, beggary and stripes, the gin shop, the station house, and the pawnbroker's, and they will understand you. [17]

Writing of this passage in relation to Dickens's portrayal of prisoners, Monika Fludernik states that 'the sentimental parameters are put in place by the phrase "make men's hearts bleed,"' which Dickens uses with 'the clear intention to create a tear-jerking scene.'[18] While Fludernik argues that this is not a scene of the 'spectacle' of punishment as in some of Dickens's other prison passages, Dickens does, through his writing, focalize the image of the girl as a spectacle in and of herself. The reader is meant to 'see' this girl in such a way as to respond emotionally and to want to act against the 'injustices' of the social system that placed her there. Like Warfield, who sees Capitola precisely as this girl 'barely past her childhood,' our hearts should bleed at the sight (and site) of Capitola's civically ordained punishment. Rush's fear of the social effects of the spectacle of punishment is thus made manifest.

The passage from *The Hidden Hand* is not, however, as simplistically sentimentalized as that of Dickens's text. The scene of Cap's trial seems to walk the line between sympathy for the punished (and concomitant feelings of insurgency) and fear of punishment itself (with its quelling of anti-social behaviour). At the end of the passage, we seem to have the horror of the hidden, private punishment that Rush recommends, the terrifying tale of what prison *really* is, told specifically in order to teach the overly sentimental Warfield, and presumably the reader in need of such an education, why he should want to stay out of prison. Capitola herself becomes part of Rush's new penology, frightening Warfield with the explicitly gothic threat of the hidden '*Tombs*' (the name used for the prison on Centre Street in New York).[19] From the sentimental figure, Capitola becomes Rush's cautionary example, espousing the horror of punishment by equating it (as everyone else did through the common name of the prison) with death. Warfield's sentimental reaction (and presumably that of the reader of such sentimental narratives as Dickens's) is seemingly portrayed as one that is ignorant of the material horror of prison, and therefore ignorant of the necessity of keeping quiet when one disagrees with the magistrate (or the government he represents).

The Hidden Control of Law

Or is it that simple? Rather than Rush's domestic, pedagogical setting of children being educated about the horrors of prison, here we have a young, cross-dressing street urchin educating a grown, socially responsible, and respected member of high society, and not just teaching him the horrors of prison through setting a sympathetic example, but explaining to him the specific legal code (contempt) by which he might be convicted. Capitola shows *no* fear for herself or of her situation. In fact, throughout the novel, Cap is portrayed as largely fearless, and this lack of 'proper' sentiment is specifically tied to her early position as a member of the underclasses, those groups of people characterized by Henry Mayhew as the criminal class. However, rather than being predestined to commit crimes, Capitola is instead educated in the inner workings of the law and of imprisonment, and is rendered what we would now call 'desensitized' to the educational horror of Rush's fireside prison tales. 'Of a naturally strong constitution and adventurous disposition, *and inured from infancy to danger*,' we are told later, 'Capitola possessed a high degree of courage, self-control, and presence of mind.'[20] As she says at one point when threatening legal action of her own, 'I wasn't brought up in New York for nothing!'[21] – a statement she later reiterates and clarifies by saying, 'I wasn't brought up among the detective policemen for nothing.'[22] Like Dickens's urchin, Capitola was not 'taught ... to dread a parent's frown.'[23] The fear that Rush would inspire in the citizenry in order to prevent them from committing crimes is precisely the emotion that is lacking in Dickens's girl and in Capitola, in the latter's case because of her possession of particular knowledge about the prison system itself.

Several critics have discussed the gendered nature of Capitola's character-ization, pointing out that, unlike the traditional self-sacrificing 'angel in the house,' Cap continually expresses supposedly masculine traits, especially related to her roles in the public sphere (and often associated with her cross-dressing childhood).[24] But the classed descriptions of Cap's upbringing go beyond subverting traditional gender types, and beyond inuring her to the ter-rors of the law. Her life on the street also makes her better equipped to subvert and counter anyone who tries to harm her, be it through legal or illegal means. Her cross-dressing, as many critics point out, is an early attempt at such a defence, since, in her words, 'being always exposed, sleeping out-doors, I was often in danger from bad boys and bad men,' which is what 'finally drove me to putting on boy's clothes.' In her words again, she 'took care' of herself.[25] Moving on from this early self-defence from sexual abuse, the novel shows that Cap can always 'take care' of herself, precisely because she does not fear 'the *unknown*.'[26] The material threats that exist for Cap render Rush's more literary and ethereal horror of private punishments completely ineffective.

This lack of fear distinguishes Cap from the more traditional sentimental heroine of the novel, Clara Day, as Joanne Dobson argues.[27] Identified throughout by her relationship to men – in the classic domestic roles of daugh-ter, then bride – Clara continually adopts the passive role of suffering saint, whose faith alone, and not action, will save the day. This passivity, moreover, is figured not only as a general, cultural form of gender submission, but is also represented as a 'proper' submission to the particularities of law. When Clara's father dies, he leaves an oral testimony with his friends that she should be allowed to stay in the family home until she is of age, when his student, Traverse, can marry her. Unfortunately, his earlier written will leaves her as a ward of Le Noir. Because Le Noir is a member of the upper classes, the courts of the town will not recognize Clara's rights (as a woman) or Traverse's rights (as a member of the working class) over Le Noir's fully sanctioned rights. Clara becomes Le Noir's ward, and he subsequently 'imprisons' her in his 'Hidden House.' Speaking to her fiancé, Clara says 'gravely and sweetly: The law, you see, has decided against us, dear Traverse! let us bend gracefully to a decree that we cannot annul; it cannot at least, alter our sacred relations ... It would be strange if one did not learn *something* by suffering. *I* have been trying all night and day to school my heart to submission.'[28] Unfortunately for Clara, proper feminine submission is quite explicitly rendered here as ideological and legal domination, and Le Noir comes very close to altering Clara and Traverse's 'sacred relations' by *legally* trying to force her to marry his son, the equally villainous Craven Le Noir.

Luckily for Clara and Traverse, Capitola comes to the rescue, something she is able to do precisely because she 'show[s] very little sympathy, for there was not a bit of sentimentality about our Cap.'[29] As Dobson and others have argued, Capitola and Clara are figured as diametrically opposed, with Clara serving as the traditional domestic angel, and Capitola as its subversive reflection. More specifically, however, the scene in which Cap rescues Clara (which I discuss at greater length below) demonstrates that Clara's sentimentality renders her a victim to the ideologically and practically class- and gender-biased operations of the law, whereas Capitola can see through and counteract them.

Once this hegemonic operation of the law is noted, we can go beyond the traditional gendered readings of the critique offered by Capitola. Indeed, masculine sentimentality is also portrayed as rendering people subject to the ideological, class-reinforcing aspects of law and punishment. Part of the background to *The Hidden Hand* is the war with Mexico.[30] Traverse, Clara's fiancé, joins the army as a private after his attempt to gain fame and fortune in the West as a medical doctor fails – a failure that results from the fact that he is young and part of the working class, and so does not have the social connections he needs. The army and the war itself, however, turn out to be hyperbolic replications of Traverse's subjugated position. In keeping with the abolitionist politics of her earlier novels – but here disguising such politics in the voice of an emotionally fraught character for the more conservative politics of *Ledger* readers[31] – Southworth damns the war (in terms that may ring relevant to contemporary ears). When Traverse tells his friend Herbert, an officer (and also friend to Warfield and Capitola), about his less than stellar performance as a soldier, Herbert says, 'Well, well, it is honorable at least to serve your country,' to which Traverse replies, 'If a foreign foe invaded her shores, yes; but what had I to do with invading another's country? – enlisting for a war of the rights and wrongs of which I know no more than anybody else does! Growing impatient because fortune did not at once empty her cornucopia upon my head! Oh, fool!'[32] Joining the army solely because he 'grow[s] impatient' with his economic and social status, Traverse finds only an extended and more violent form of that same status, both in terms of how he himself is treated and in the overall invasion (which many contemporaries saw as a land grab to increase slave territories). Southworth could be read here as prefiguring Jürgen Habermas's critique of the ways in which the public sphere of a Lockean democracy can become the ideological apparatuses that control, rather than the tools exercised by, the public itself (one should again recall here Rush's program of cultural terror). 'According to the liberal model of the public sphere,' Habermas writes, 'the institutions of the public engaged in rational-critical debate were protected from interference by public authority by virtue of their being in the hands of private people. To the extent that they were commercialized and underwent economic, technological, and organizational concentration, however, they have turned during the last hundred years into complexes of societal power.'[33] In Traverse's role in the army, once again, control over the supposedly public systems of 'punishment' (be it the punishment of an individual or a nation) is shown by Southworth to be a silent – even hidden – control by private individuals, one that does not respond directly to its material or public surroundings, but instead bends those surroundings to the will of those who are shown to be in control of 'societal power.'

Moreover, Traverse, in keeping with the logic of sensational novels, finds himself under to direct control of Colonel Le Noir, who proceeds to torture Traverse by not allowing him to sleep. Traverse at first wants to lash out and resist this treatment, exclaiming 'And this man, … This demon – this beast – is now commanding officer! the colonel of our regiment!' But his friend Herbert reminds him of his proper place:

> 'Yes,' replied Herbert, 'but as such you must not call him names; military rules are despotic; and this man … will leave no power, with which his command invests him, untried, to ruin and destroy you! Traverse, I say these things to you, that being "forewarned" you may be "forearmed." I trust that you will remember your mother and your betrothed, and for *their* dear sakes practice every sort of self-control, patience and forbearance under the provocations you may receive from our colonel.'[34]

Calling on both Traverse's sense of masculine 'self-control,' as well as the proper forbearance that a private should show his commanding officer, Herbert commands, and Traverse performs, the same kind of passivity in the face of punishment that Clara does.

Indeed, this submission results in Traverse being brought up before a court martial, because Le Noir's efforts to keep Traverse awake and perform dangerous duties cause Traverse to fall asleep at his post, a misstep punishable by death under martial law during wartime. And, once again, the law is shown not to function in an unbiased and public manner, but to be largely under the direct control of the ruling classes. No matter the extenuating circumstances, Traverse's position does not allow him a voice in the proceedings with which to change his fate: 'The FACT of the offence, and the LAW affixing the penalty of death to that offence was established, and as the Judge Advocate truly said, nothing remained but for the court to find their verdict in accordance to both.'[35] On its own, Traverse's passivity merely mimics the passivity that is socially, militarily, and legally forced onto one of his rank, rendering him a mere object of, rather than a subject within, the legal systems of punishment (which are reified through the capitalization of 'LAW' in the text and its typographic connection to 'FACT'). In direct opposition both to contemporary theories of prisoner reform (as evidenced in the 'silent' system) and Rush's theories of social control, here the horror of punishment results not in the cessation or deterrence of crime; instead, the true criminals control the courts through power – and it is a power ensconced in the legal tradition itself, in which punishment is shown to be only embodied, and justice not universal and objective, but particular and subject to the desires of the powerful.

Of course, Traverse lives, but only because Herbert is in a position to insert his voice into the system, not by finding any legal reason to free Traverse, but instead by challenging the court to create a precedent that stands outside of the law. After Herbert suggests that Traverse be freed even though he is guilty of the charge, the tribunal's president 'sternly' replies, 'Gentleman ... this thing is without *precedent!* In all the annals of courts martial, without *precedent!*' Herbert then responds, 'Then, if there *is* no such precedent, it is quite time that such a one were *established*! so that the iron car of literal law should not always roll over and crush justice!'[36] Herbert, as an officer and a gentleman, is able to add lines to and alter the course of the 'iron car of literal law,' saving Traverse's life, whereas Traverse must remain fully and completely passive on the tracks; he can traverse social structures in Herbert's name only. Indeed, Traverse's straight and narrow – and passive – path puts him in harm's way to begin with. The very privacy of his and Clara's suffering (private for him in that it is 'self-controlled,' and private for her in that it is literally locked away inside the hidden domestic sphere) is what renders it powerful, paralleling Rush's motivation for hidden punishments. However, the hidden nature of the law and its punishments is once again shown to succeed only in hiding the biased functioning of the law, and the only way to assert what the novel situates as 'justice' is to publicly declaim the rectitude and justness of state law. From the everyday functions of ideological gender paradigms to the extreme end of the state's repressive apparatus in its military, the law's hidden motivations lead to a questioning of state power. Both the ideological and repressive functions of legalized punishment, rather than reinforce the state's control as Rush argued, instead call the very mechanisms of that control into question.

Publicizing the House of Horror and Other Entertainments

Capitola, however, quite actively and consistently traverses gender, class, and legal boundaries, consistently frustrating the disciplinary regimes that surround her, working through the sensational terror that all others in her position(s) feel. Beyond being unafraid of legal and other horrors, Cap begins to seek them out, since traditional housebound roles make her feel as if she is 'decomposing above ground for want of having my blood stirred,' because the feeling of 'safety makes [her] low!'[37] Cap's desire for sensation leads her to Le Noir's home, which is called 'Hidden House.' In the midst of all of the actual prisons, workhouses, asylums, and courts in the novel, Hidden House comes to embody the cultural image of the gothic prison for which Rush calls. Indeed, the chapter titled 'Hidden House' is followed by the chapters 'The Inmate of Hidden House' and then a little later 'Cap Frees the Captive' and 'Cap in Captivity.' Furthermore, Capitola describes the road to the house as having 'as many doubles and twists … as there are in a lawyer's discourse,'[38] thus allegorically figuring the same confused, and therefore 'hidden,' nature of legal language that nearly condemns Traverse.

Hidden House, at the end of this twisted legal road, can thus be read as the epitome of the problems with hidden punishments and the legal framework that supports them. When combined with Le Noir's various controls of (or attempts to control) law courts and punishment, Hidden House therefore becomes the symbolic centre of the novel's various portrayals and analyses of the prison. The fact that the house is a physically hidden one has, as per Rush's theory, increased the terror it holds over the local population. But not for Cap: 'The Old Hidden House, with its mysterious traditions, its gloomy surroundings and its haunted reputation, had always possessed a powerful attraction for one of Cap's adventurous spirit. To seek and gaze upon the sombre house, of which, and of whose inmates, such terrible stories had been told or hinted, had always been a secret desire and purpose of Capitola.'[39] Moving from the novel's argument that a life on the streets has inured her to fear, we come to Cap being portrayed as actively *seeking* the fearful, desiring the private carceral horrors of Hidden House. This active desire on her part to seek out these hidden punishments is tied to her absolute refusal to accept dictums of either 'natural' law (as in traditional figurations of gender) and human law (again in terms of cross-dressing, but also fighting duels and freeing a convicted felon, to name a few). Seemingly paradoxically, it is because of these conjoined transgressions that Capitola becomes both the hero/heroine and title of the novel; her transgressions of the law and her evasions of punishment are precisely what enable her to become the central figure for stopping the 'iron car of literal law' in the name of justice.

In every instance she finds or creates justice by removing privacy, by publicizing those punishments that were hidden. The primary example of this publicizing occurs immediately after Cap finds Hidden House and helps Clara escape from Le Noir's clutches. While forced to stay in Hidden House, Clara has suffered from Warfield's treatment in proper, stereotypically sentimental ways. By switching clothes with Clara and acting the role of the sentimental heroine (in what could constitute another combined class and gender cross-dressing), Capitola is able to allow Clara to leave before her forced marriage, to shake off the constraining submissiveness her sympathetic figure necessitates. Meanwhile, Capitola simultaneously permits the Le Noirs to take her to the church for the ceremony, thus placing them firmly within the public sphere, in an institution that is tied to, but still separate from, the state. She tells an audience at the church the entire sordid tale of Le Noir's abuse of Clara, which makes the public 'prevent the escape of those men,'[40] while ensuring her own freedom. Indeed, when she is thereafter 'subpoenaed to give testimony' against Le Noir, she laughingly says, 'Oh, *won't* I tell all I know! Yes, and more too! ... I will, for I'll tell all I suspect.'[41] And this frustrates any attempt within the law to contain her: 'Stringfellow, the attorney for Colonel Le Noir, evidently thought that in this rash, reckless, spirited witness, he had a fine subject for sarcastic cross-examination! But he reckoned "without his host." He did not know Cap! ... And before the cross-examination was concluded, Capitola's apt and cutting replies had overwhelmed him with ridicule and confusion, and done more for the cause of her friend than all her partisans put together!'[42] Cap's avowal to 'tell all' and publicize these private horrors, an ability arising out her fascination with hidden terrors, effectively undermines the legal footing of class and gender dominations. Capitola thus exercises a role in the public sphere in ways that not only challenge contemporary gender (and class) mores, but also legitimize the public sphere in a Lockean sense. In a sense, Capitola fulfills Habermas's claim that 'The subject of this publicity is the public as carrier of public opinion; its function as a critical judge is precisely what makes the public character of proceedings – in court, for instance – meaningful.'[43] Capitola's avowal to 'tell all' renders, in this framework, the hidden and twisted nature of law and punishment impotent, and simultaneously gives rational meaning to the court proceedings.

Later in the novel, through Traverse, Southworth also shows this need for what Habermas calls a 'critical publicity.'[44] Traverse finally gains his true station in life only by publicizing the fate of a woman whom Le Noir imprisoned in a private asylum, and whose identity had been purposefully hidden from public knowledge (this woman turns out to be Capitola's mother). But, lest we suspect that this need for public awareness is limited to those unjustly condemned, Capitola also frees the criminal highwayman Black Donald from prison. Although he is likely innocent of the murder with which he is charged, he is certainly not innocent of several other criminal misdeeds. But it is only through his *escape* from the prison – effected by Capitola – that he becomes, in the words of the text, a '*Reformed Robber.*'[45]

The novel thus forms a complex response to Rush's theory that the populace must be terrorized by the gothic fear of the hidden and the unknown in order to ensure a proper respect for what is commonly referred to as 'law and order.' The very horror that is created through the 'Hidden House' of punishment *is* shown at first to terrorize people into passive behaviour, but this reading is then roundly critiqued, as 'proper' passivity and sentimental feeling leave Clara and Traverse to be victimized by a class- and gender-based legal system. Carpenter states that 'the world [in *The Hidden Hand*] cannot be neatly divided into family homes and prisons,'[46] but I would argue that Southworth goes beyond even this argument, showing how Rush's private punishments and the horror they create contain the seeds of their own undoing in terms of this ideological control they are supposed to disseminate. The gothic horror of tales of punishment becomes an object of public desire, until, as the novel says of Hidden House, the site (and sight) of punishment becomes 'a scene fascinating from its very excess of gloom and terror.'[47] This fascination leads Cap to want to publicize the atrocities taking place within it. For Southworth, then, the public sphere becomes the cure for the unjust legal system that attempts to hide both its punishments and its class and gender biases; conversely, the 'public' of Rush's call for a 'public' terror falls closer to Habermas's definition of the contemporary use of the term: 'In the realm of the mass media, of course, publicity has changed its meaning. Originally a function of public opinion, it has become an attribute of whatever attracts public opinion.'[48] As Michael Meranze argues in his study of the punishment debate in Philadelphia at the turn of the nineteenth century (a debate that included, of course, Rush's own contributions), 'The disciplinary realm offered an inverted extension of the public sphere. Within disciplinary institutions, the power of the better argument was supplanted by the argument of power, and the reason of the

public materialized on the bodies of those without 'sufficient' reason ...
Social discipline worked to individualize and contain those citizens who
remained outside the bourgeois public sphere – and who thereby embodied its
limits.'[49] Capitola, and Southworth it seems, want to shatter these limits.
Slightly altering Meranze's conclusions, I would argue that Southworth's and
Rush's prisons occupy a space where the public and private spheres meet in
the attempt to (re)form the citizenry itself, and what constitutes proper behav-
iours within both spheres. This space must necessarily be hidden from public
for Rush because, since it is this space where private and public spheres and
their relations are formed, it must remain separate from both. Otherwise, the
repressive nature of the (supposedly positive and preferably unconscious)
dominant ideology is rendered visible – which is precisely what happens in
The Hidden Hand. The novel as a whole constitutes a call for public debate
about issues of law and punishment as a means to counter Rush's hegemonic
publicizing, through hiding, of horror.

Southworth also realizes that this public space of ethical discussion, rather
than the ideological and disciplinary control of prison publicity, is messy,
leading the narrator to state (in what constitutes in part an obviously gendered
revisioning of society):

> I wish I could say 'they all lived happy ever after.' But the truth is, I have reason
> to suppose that even Clara had sometimes occasion to administer to Doctor
> Rocke dignified curtain lectures; which no doubt did him good. And I know for
> a positive fact, that our Cap sometimes gives her 'dear, darling, sweet Herbert,'
> the benefit of the sharp edge of her tongue, which of course he deserves. But,
> notwithstanding all this, I am happy to say that they all enjoy a fair amount of
> human felicity.[50]

Passive, hidden, and silent no more, the private sphere is no longer controlled by public tales of horror; instead, a continually public sphere of ethical discussion and critique is fully accessible by all. Rush's utopia (perhaps
more of a dystopia) of ideological control is here replaced by a '*fair* amount'
of dialogue.

NOTES

1 See, for example, David Garland, *Punishment and Modern Society: A Study in
  Social Theory* (Chicago: University of Chicago Press, 1990), 165; C. Fred Alford,
  'What Would It Matter if Everything Foucault Said about Prison Were Wrong?

Discipline and Punish after Twenty Years,' *Theory and Society* 29 (2000): 125–46; Sean C. Grass, *The Self in the Cell: Narrating the Victorian Prisoner* (New York and London: Routledge, 2003); Jan Alber, *Narrating the Prison: Role and Representation in Charles Dickens' Novels, Twentieth-Century Fiction and Film* (Youngstown, NY: Cambria Press, 2007). For an outline of some of these arguments, and a case for the usefulness of Foucault's model in the face of recent critiques, see my introduction to *Fitting Sentences*. Jason Haslam, *Fitting Sentences: Identity in Nineteenth- and Twentieth-Century Prison Narratives* (Toronto: University of Toronto Press, 2005).

2 E.D.E.N. Southworth, *The Hidden Hand or, Capitola the Madcap*, ed. Joanne Dobson (1888; New Brunswick, NJ: Rutgers University Press, 1988). See Joanne Dobson, 'The Hidden Hand: Subversion of Cultural Ideology in Three Mid-Nineteenth-Century American Women's Novels,' *American Quarterly* 38, no. 2 (1986): 223–42 for a summary of the novel's publication history.

3 Orlando F. Lewis, *The Development of American Prisons and Prison Customs, 1776–1845* (1922; repr. Montclair, NJ: Patterson Smith, 1967), 324.

4 For discussions of North American and European perceptions at this time of prisons, penitentiaries, and the related issues of crime and criminality, see Lewis, *The Development*, esp. 323–45; Peter Oliver, *'Terror to Evil Doers': Prisons and Punishments in Nineteenth-Century Ontario* (Toronto: University of Toronto Press, 1998), esp. 105–29; David J. Rothman, 'Perfecting the Prison: United States, 1789–1865,' in *The Oxford History of the Prison: The Practice of Punishment in Western Society*, ed. Norval Morris and David J. Rothman (Oxford: Oxford University Press, 1995), 111–29; Seán McConville, 'The Victorian Prison: England, 1865–1965,' in *The Oxford History of the Prison*, 131–67; Randall McGowen, 'The Well-Ordered Prison: England, 1780–1865,' in *The Oxford History of the Prison*, 79–109; and Martin J. Wiener, *Reconstructing the Criminal: Culture, Law, and Policy in England, 1830–1914* (Cambridge: Cambridge University Press, 1990), 1–45.

5 Thomas L. Dumm, *Democracy and Punishment: Disciplinary Origins of the United States* (Madison: University of Wisconsin Press, 1987), 95.

6 Dumm elaborates on the ways in which the external forces were seen to corrupt and possess a person's being in a manner that mimicked the way in which outside stimuli affected one's physical or mental health; Dumm pertinently connects this, through the figure of Benjamin Rush, to new asylum strategies. See Dumm, *Democracy*, esp. 91–6.

7 Frank Lauterbach, '"From the Slums *to* the Slums": The Delimitation of Social Identity in Late Victorian Prison Narratives,' *Captivating Subjects: Writing Confinement, Citizenship and Nationhood in the Nineteenth Century*, ed. Julia M. Wright and Jason Haslam (Toronto: University of Toronto Press, 2005), 140n.54.

8 Benjamin Rush, 'An Enquiry into the Effects of Public Punishments upon Criminals, and Upon Society. Read in the Society for Promoting Political Enquiries,

Convened at the House of Benjamin Franklin, Esq. in Philadelphia, March 9th, 1787,' in *Essays Literary, Moral, and Philosophical* (1806), ed. Michael Meranze (Schenectady, NY: Union College Press, 1988), 89. For my extended reading of the rule of silence, its relation to subjectivity, and theoretical discussions thereof, see the introduction and first chapter of Haslam, *Fitting Sentences*. For a discussion of Rush in relation to a particular branch of captive literature, see Douglas Taylor's discussion of Rush and Harriet Jacobs's *Incidents in the Life of a Slave Girl*. Douglas Taylor, 'From Slavery to Prison: Benjamin Rush, Harriet Jacobs, and the Ideology of Reformative Incarnation,' *Genre: Forms of Discourse and Culture* 35, nos. 3/4 (2002): 429–47.

9 Rush, 'An Enquiry,' 83.

10 'Youth Violence: A Report by the Surgeon General' in the United States briefly outlines the Scared Straight program as one of several 'Ineffective Tertiary Programs And Strategies' for deterring youth violence. The Scared Straight program, as this report states, 'is an example of a shock probation or parole program in which brief encounters with inmates describing the brutality of prison life or short-term incarceration in prisons or jails is expected to shock, or deter, youths from committing crimes.' The report concludes that such programs do not work: 'In some studies, rearrest rates were similar between controls and youths who participated in Scared Straight. In others, youths exposed to Scared Straight actually had higher rates of rearrest than youths not involved in this intervention' (see chapter 5 of the report). While the comparison between this program and Rush's tales of 'terror' is, of course, limited, that both rely explicitly and solely on fear could provide a sociological parallel to my literary argument concerning the problems of Rush's project. See 'Youth Violence: A Report by the Surgeon General,' January 2001, available at http://www.surgeongeneral.gov/library/youthviolence/default.htm.

11 Rush, 'An Enquiry,' 88.

12 Taylor similarly points out that Rush advocated the removal of the punishment of criminals from the public gaze in order to make such punishment *more* frightening to the populace: 'Secrecy surrounding the site of the prison, Rush argued, would generate speculation in the form of rumor, superstition, and popular fiction. Such speculation, Rush believed, would be worse than the actual realities of punishment, and would continue the work previously done by the spectacle of public punishment in spreading a crime-inhibiting terror among the multitude.' Taylor, 'From Slavery to Prison,' 438–9.

13 Dumm, *Democracy*, 137. For a similar discussion, but in a British context, of the ways in which prison discipline figures in the creation of a paradoxically individual but uniform citizenry, see Wiener, *Reconstructing the Criminal*. For an extended discussion of Rush, in relation to Poe, see Jason Haslam, 'Pits, Pendulums, and Penitentiaries: Reframing the Detained Subject,' *Texas Studies in Literature and Language* 50, no. 3 (2008): 268–84.

14 The relationship between sentimental literature and abolition has been widely
    analysed, especially in relation to slave narratives. See Bruce Burgett, *Sentimental
    Bodies: Sex, Gender, and Citizenship in the Early Republic* (Princeton, NJ:
    Princeton University Press, 1998); Beth Maclay Doriani, 'Black Womanhood in
    Nineteenth-Century America: Subversion and Self-Construction in Two Women's
    Autobiographies,' *American Quarterly* 43, no. 2 (1991): 199–222; Franny Nudelman,
    'Harriet Jacobs and the Sentimental Politics of Female Suffering,' *ELH* 59, no. 4
    (1992): 939–64; and Mauri Skinfill, 'Nation and Miscegenation: *Incidents in the
    Life of a Slave Girl*,' *Arizona Quarterly* 51, no. 2 (1995): 63–79. Russ Castronovo
    also analyses sentimentality in relation to pro-slavery plantation novels ('Incidents
    in the Life of a White Woman: Economies of Race and Gender in the Antebellum
    Nation,' *American Literary History* 10, no. 2 [1998]: 239–65). For an analysis of
    the gothic and its relation to abolition, see, for example, Teresa A. Goddu, *Gothic
    America: Narrative, History, and Nation* (New York: Columbia University Press,
    1997). For a discussion of the rather complex relationship between Southworth's
    works, abolition, and the plantation novel tradition, see Paul Christian Jones, '"This
    Dainty Woman's Hand ... Red with Blood": E.D.E.N. Southworth's *The Hidden
    Hand* as Abolitionist Narrative,' *American Transcendental Quarterly* 15, no. 1
    (2001): 59–80. Jones also makes an interesting argument for reading *The Hidden
    Hand* as a coded abolitionist novel, but the blatantly racist portrayal of blacks in the
    novel does perhaps undercut Jones's reading more than he admits. Katharine
    Nicholson Ings provides a complementary argument concerning Capitola's meta-
    phorical 'blackness,' in which this category is used 'to express rebellion against the
    more passive and static' figurations of whiteness, and white femininity in particu-
    lar. Katharine Nicholson Ings, 'Blackness and the Literary Imagination: Uncover-
    ing *The Hidden Hand*,' in *Passing and the Fictions of Identity*, ed. Elaine K.
    Ginsberg (Durham, NC: Duke University Press, 1996), 133.
15 Lynette Carpenter, 'Double Talk: The Power and Glory of Paradox in E.D.E.N.
    Southworth's *The Hidden Hand*,' *Legacy* 10, no. 1 (1993): 17.
16 Southworth, *The Hidden Hand*, 40.
17 Charles Dickens, *Sketches by Boz and Other Early Papers 1833–39*, ed. Michael
    Slater, Dent Uniform Edition of Dickens' Journalism (London: Dent, 1994), 202–3.
18 Monika Fludernik, '"Stone Walls Do (Not) a Prison Make": Rhetorical Strategies
    and Sentimentalism in the Representation of the Victorian Prison Experience,' in
    *Captivating Subjects: Writing Confinement, Citizenship, and Nationhood in the
    Nineteenth Century*, ed. Jason Haslam and Julia M. Wright (Toronto: University
    of Toronto Press, 2005), 160.
19 For a brief history of the Tombs, see 'A Tale of the Tombs' on the New York Cor-
    rection History Society's website. Available at http://www.correctionhistory.org/
    html/chronicl/nycdoc/html/histry3a.html.

20 Southworth, *The Hidden Hand*, 114; my emphasis.

21 Ibid., 124.

22 Ibid., 307.

23 Dickens, *Sketches by Boz*, 202.

24 See, for example, the articles by Joanne Dobson ('The Hidden Hand') as well as Patricia Okker and Jeffrey R. Williams, '"Reassuring Sounds": Minstrelsy and *The Hidden Hand*,' *American Transcendental Quarterly* 12, no. 2 (1998): 133–44. Ings also deals at length with Capitola's rejection of sentiment ('Blackness and the Literary Imagination').

25 Southworth, *The Hidden Hand*, 45.

26 Ibid., 112; emphasis in original.

27 Dobson, 'The Hidden Hand,' 232–6.

28 Southworth, *The Hidden Hand*, 255; emphasis in original.

29 Ibid., 305.

30 This war began on 11 May 1846 as a result of Texas's entrance into the Union. The addition of Texas as a slaveholding state was felt to 'increase substantially the influence of the South in national politics' (Len Gougeon, 'Thoreau and Reform,' in *The Cambridge Companion to Henry David Thoreau*, ed. Joel Myerson [Cambridge: Cambridge University Press, 1995], 200), so many abolitionists opposed both that and the war which was seen to inevitably arise from it. Southworth's engagement with the war also places *The Hidden Hand* firmly within Shelley Streeby's summary of mid-nineteenth-century sensation literature, which, she writes, 'responds ... to a double vision of Northeastern cities divided by battles over class, race, national origin, and religion, on the one hand, and, on the other to scenes of U.S. nation- and empire-building in Mexico, Cuba, and throughout the Americas.' Shelley Streeby, *American Sensations: Class, Empire, and the Production of Popular Culture* (Berkeley and Los Angeles: University of California Press, 2002), 5. Southworth's use of prison and prison-like punishments could also inform this 'double vision,' since the nineteenth-century prison was not only an internal national concern, but was, as Julia M. Wright and I argue, inherently connected to the formation and maintenance of empire (see introduction to *Captivating Subjects*, esp. 8–9).

31 Quoting an unpublished paper by Christopher Looby, Jones details the politics of the *New York Ledger*, writing that this 'very popular story magazine ... had "an editorial policy of studied neutrality on the question of slavery" ... because the editor "Bonner ... wanted it to circulate and sell both North and South, among anti-slavery and pro-slavery readers."' Jones, 'This Dainty Woman's Hand,' 70.

32 Southworth, *The Hidden Hand*, 345.

33 Jürgen Habermas, *The Structural Transformation of the Public Sphere: An Inquiry into a Category of Bourgeois Society*, trans. Thomas Burger with the assistance of Frederick Lawrence (Cambridge, MA: MIT Press, 1991), 188.

34 Southworth, *The Hidden Hand*, 346.
35 Ibid., 417.
36 Ibid., 423.
37 Ibid., 173.
38 Ibid., 270.
39 Ibid., 269.
40 Ibid., 317.
41 Ibid., 330; emphasis in original.
42 Ibid., 333.
43 Habermas, *The Structural Transformation*, 2.
44 Southworth, *The Hidden Hand*, 235.
45 Ibid., 485; emphasis in original.
46 Ibid., 24.
47 Ibid., 270.
48 Habermas, *The Structural Transformation*, 2.
49 Michael Meranze, *Laboratories of Virtue: Punishment, Revolution, and Authority in Philadelphia, 1760–1835* (Chapel Hill: University of North Carolina Press, 1996), 11–12.
50 Southworth, *The Hidden Hand*, 485.

11 Prisons of Stone and Mind: Henry James's *The Princess Casamassima* and *In the Cage*

GRETA OLSON

Aptly described in Joseph Conrad's phrase as the 'historian of fine consciences,'[1] Henry James has heretofore been little associated with Victorian prisons and penitentiaries.[2] Therefore, James's explicit exploration of carceral
spaces and tropes in *The Princess Casamassima* (1886) and *In the Cage* (1898)
represents an area of critical oversight that deserves investigation. Explicating
imprisonment in these two works reveals larger preoccupations in James's oeuvre, including an awareness of how mental sequestration can be caused by class
divisions and social prejudices as well as by perceptual limitations.

    The Princess Casamassima and *In the Cage* instance James's political fic-
tion. More explicitly than in any of his other works, the author explores class
tensions, money pressures, and the lack of social mobility in late Victorian
society. Whereas the prison scene in *The Princess Casamassima* seems to be
a throwback to Dickensian prison scenarios or even gothic prison tropes, the
rest of the novel suggests that social reality imprisons its modern urban subjects. It also evidences a modernist awareness of the subjectivity and partiality of experience. The prison in *In the Cage* is literally a barred-in workplace
and figuratively a symbol for the inflexible limits of the protagonist's future.
It serves as a metaphor for the mental confinement women enter into when
they buy into the conventions of romance fiction, and it also works as a model
for the limits of tellability in reflector-mode narrative. On the one hand,
incarceration is figured in both texts as an emblem of social immobility and
prejudice. However, another form of confinement is experienced by the
reader of these texts, in that the narrators' lack of omniscient knowledge and
the reflector figures' fallible perceptions force readers to be continuously
aware of the gaps in their knowledge about storyworld events.[3] I argue that
both *The Princess Casamassima* and *In the Cage* demonstrate the transition
between Victorian and modernist consciousness and modes of representation

with recourse to prison motifs. Millbank Prison and the telegraph box give way to the protagonists' realizations of their lack of agency and sense of alienation. These realizations also occasion readers' recognition of the epistemological uncertainty that is inherent in narratives that are related with limited omniscience and focalization.

I

The prison scene that inalterably changes Hyacinth Robinson's image of himself and marks him as stained – he is the illegitimate son of a French murderess – has much the same atmosphere of shame as the debtor's prison in *Little Dorrit* and the dark terrifying quality of the prison cell where the reader finds Fagin just before his execution in *Oliver Twist*. Like the Marshalsea, this prison has a stench about it that infiltrates visitor's clothes and leaves a stain on their person. Children of these prisons like Hyacinth and Amy Dorrit remain part of the institutions that imprisoned their parents, even if they themselves are sympathetic characters who have committed no crimes. In this respect the prison scene has a distinctly Dickensian feel to it, and as has been pointed out, James may have been making a conscious reference to his predecessor's work.[4]

Within the course of the novel, however, the 'old' dungeon-like prison is replaced by a 'new' prison type in which the mind is incarcerated.[5] In the middle of the novel Hyacinth commits himself to a form of absolute and unquestioning servitude to the revolutionary Diedrich Hoffendahl. With this step he gives his life away, knowing that he is on a self-imposed death row where the call to commit a revolutionary act entails certain demise. Significantly, both the prison scene and the passage in which Hyacinth swears his obedience are followed by narrative breaks. A period of nearly ten years follows Hyacinth's embrace of Florentine Vivier on her prison deathbed before the narrative resumes with the loud note of Millicent Hennings forcing her way into Pinnie's shop. Hyacinth's actual meeting with Hoffendahl is also elided. Perhaps the most significant event of the novel, this meeting is, like Hyacinth's actual suicide, shrouded in narrative silence.[6]

Similar to Conrad's modernist *Lord Jim*, significant details of seminal scenes are left out or are related non-linearly, and then only incompletely. Readers enter into a form of indebtedness to the narrator, as we impatiently wait to learn how Hyacinth reacted to meeting his mother and what happened on the evening when he was introduced to Hoffendahl. The readers' being forced into a state of epistemic limbo in which we lack essential knowledge about events in the novel mimics the sensory deprivation typical of many types of physical imprisonment. We then, like Hyacinth, are forced to do time, to await what the narration will allow us to know about the fate of the protagonist. These lapses in the narrative demonstrate the heterodiegetic narrator's lack of omniscient knowledge about characters and their actions. Such gaps are part of James's nascent critique of the realist novel's attempt to represent reality as a teleological sequence of completely detailed scenes. By examining different types of imprisonment, including narrative encagement, James's texts demonstrate that the project of transparent realism is an impossible one.

Ultimately, the first prison scene foreshadows the later sense of imprisonment that colours Hyacinth's life. Yet the transition from an actual scene of imprisonment to a felt one also demonstrates the movement in novelistic writing towards more modernist forms. Physical incarceration within Millbank's formidable walls makes way for self-induced sequestration of alienation and self-scrutiny. Before analysing the prison scene, it is important to delineate the motivations of the three individuals who cause it to occur. These are Mrs Bowerbank, a 'female turnkey,' who plays an unannounced call upon Miss Pynsent in order to ask her to bring Hyacinth to visit his dying mother; Anastasius Vetch, a musician and a sort of surrogate father; and, finally, Miss Amanda Pysent (Pinnie), a struggling seamstress and the boy's foster mother. The formidable Mrs Bowerbank appears to Pinnie, as Hyacinth and the narrator refer to her, to be by metonymic association part of the prison itself. Representing the 'possibility of grating bolts and clanking chains,' she visits Pinnie as an 'emissary of the law,' bringing with her 'the cold light of the penal system.' Millbank is in turn a prominent feature in the whole edifice of the law.[7]

With her capacity for violence and narrow prejudices, Mrs Bowerbank personifies aspects of the contemporary penal system as well as attitudes towards prisoners that the novel appears to criticize. Mrs Bowerbank proudly reports that she knows how to 'hush up' raving prisoners during the night as well as how to distinguish those who feign illness from the genuinely ill. We are led to suspect that she and her fellow wardens beat inmates. Moreover, Mrs Bowerbank voices conventional prejudices about convicts that mirror the press coverage of crime. In Mrs Bowerbank's view Florentine Vivier is 'a wicked low foreigner that carries a knife.'[8] Typifying those whose attitudes turn a prison into a site of social demarcations, she assigns a lower-class and, in this case, also an ethnicized identity to the incarcerated individual.[9] For her, as for the reader of *The Times*, where Florentine's trial and conviction were reported as a '*cause célèbre*,'[10] the foreign woman is automatically a whore and a vicious murderess. No mention is made of the slain Lord Frederick Purvis being the probable father of the woman's child or of his unwillingness to fulfil his parental duties.

Although a part of 'one of the dreadful institutions' of London's prisons,[11] Mrs Bowerbank has a weakness for maudlin narratives. What she aims to achieve by bringing about a meeting between the dying convict and her son is the melodrama of a deathbed reunion of long-lost family members. That her wishes are informed by the mores of Victorian sentimental fiction is shown in her confidence that mother and son will recognize one another, even though they have been separated since his infancy.[12] She reasons that Florentine will resist death until she receives '[t]he kiss her lips have been famished for, for years.'[13]

Combining sinister elements with sentimentalist longings, Mrs Bowerbank shuts prisoners up at night but also wishes them to perform heart-rending reunions with their children. Exemplifying public attitudes, she believes that prisoners should be severely punished. Yet she also wishes to have the rightness of her punitive attitudes proven: she orchestrates a death scene in which the convict is meant to silently acknowledge her repentance and the efficacy of her punishment.

Down-on-his-luck Anastasius Vetch, by turn, wants Hyacinth to visit Millbank so as to make an early acquaintance with the miserable facts of quotidian existence.[14] Visiting his inmate mother, Vetch believes, will show the boy that his aristocratic affectations will be to no effect. Another motivation works on Vetch. As a sympathizer with revolutionary causes, he desires to wake up the boy politically: 'I haven't the least objection to his feeling badly; that's not the worst thing in the world! If a few more people felt badly, in this sodden, stolid, stupid race of ours, the world would wake up to an idea or two, and we should see the beginning of the dance.'[15]

Knowing that she dislikes his political inclinations, Vetch also works to convince Pinnie by referring to conventional wisdom about deterring criminality in the young. He belabours her with the view that it will be a good dose of preventative medicine for him to see how frightening prison is: 'there are people that would tell you it would do him good. If he didn't like the place as a child, he would take more care to keep out of it later.'[16] Here, he echoes views of individuals like Mrs Bowerbank who believe in intimidating individuals into abstaining from crime.[17]

Pinnie remains reluctant to visit Millbank despite Mrs Bowerbank's and Vetch's arguments. Only her conviction that she will not be able to sleep at night if she denies Florentine's dying wish moves her. Yet she anticipates that this visit will inalterably change her adopted son's sensibilities; it may in fact 'subject[ ] ... him to a mortification that might rankle for ever and perhaps even crush him to the earth.'[18] This premonition proves true. As she later muses: 'She had sown in her boy's mind the seeds of shame and rancour; she had made him conscious of his stigma, of his exquisitely vulnerable spot, and condemned him to know that for him the sun would never shine as it shone for most others.'[19]

The imagery in this passage is certainly carceral, corresponding to the darkness that is a feature of the dungeon scenario outlined by Monika Fludernik.[20] It also corresponds to Miss Pynsent's former observations about Millbank. From the outside it appears to throw 'a blight' over the Thames and its banks;[21] on the inside it erases the colour of the day (see the passage quoted below). The image of a lack of sunlight bespeaks both the dark interior of the labyrinthine prison, which contributes to the death of Hyacinth's mother, and the shadow the prison casts over Hyacinth's future, cutting out the light of respectability. Millbank's blight is then one of social condemnation based on prejudices about class, foreignness, illegitimacy, and inherited criminality. The visit to the prison marks the moment in which social barriers appear to Hyacinth to grow up between him and happier participants in London life.

Pinnie takes Hyacinth to the prison without having told him who they are visiting. Her omissions contribute to her feelings of guilt when she enters Millbank:

> She only had a confused impression of being surrounded with high black walls whose inner face was more dreadful than the other, the one that overlooked the river; of passing through grey, stony courts, in some of which dreadful figures, scarcely female, in hideous brown, misfitting uniforms and perfect frights of hoods, were marching round in a circle; of squeezing up steep, unlighted staircases at the heels of a woman who had taken possession of her at the first stage, and who made incomprehensible remarks to other women, of lumpish aspect, as she saw them erect themselves, suddenly and spectrally, with dowdy untied bonnets, in uncanny corners and recesses of the draughty labyrinth. If the place had seemed cruel to the poor little dressmaker outside, it may be believed that it did not strike her as an abode of mercy while she pursued her tortuous way into the circular shafts of cells, where she had an opportunity of looking at captives through grated peepholes and of edging past others who had temporarily been turned into the corridors – silent women, with fixed eyes, who flattened themselves against the stone walls at the brush of the visitor's dress and whom Miss Pynsent was afraid to glance at. She never had felt so immured, so made sure of; there were walls within walls and galleries on top of galleries; even the daylight lost its colour, and you couldn't imagine what o'clock it was.[22]

Through the narrator's reporting of the dressmaker's vivid thoughts – her 'perfect frights of hoods' and 'dowdy untied bonnets' – we experience the prison as maze-like and deindividuating. We read here repetitions of the word that this reflector figure most often uses to describe anything she fears or disapproves of. The inner face of the prison is 'dreadful,' as are the figures within it. Her comparison of the hideous faces of Millbank prison suggests entombment and the supernatural. This description of Millbank may also remind readers of another example of gothic urban architecture, the comparison of the entrance to Dr Jekyll's laboratory with a sinister face, a face that reveals the owner's hidden self in Mr Hyde:

> It was two storeys high; showed no window, nothing but a door on the lower storey and a blind forehead of discoloured wall on the upper; and bore in every feature, the marks of prolonged and sordid negligence. The door, which was equipped with neither bell nor knocker, was blistered and distained. Tramps slouched into the recess and struck matches on the panels; children kept shop upon the steps; the schoolboy had tried his knife on the mouldings; and for close on a generation, no one had appeared to drive away these random visitors or to repair their ravages.[23]

Both *Dr Jekyll and Mr Hyde* and *The Princess Casamassima* feature architecture that resembles a two-headed Janus figure. The two faces reveal the nature of the persons within the structures as well as the negative effects these buildings have on those who come near them.

Having never felt herself to be 'so immured' as while moving within its walls, Pinnie is 'surrounded' by Millbank.[24] Entering the prison produces an effect on the visitor of being criminalized herself. In this vein of imagery, she is taken control of by the warden, who silently leads her towards Hyacinth's mother. Correspondingly, she will later experience herself as having indeed committed a crime by entering Millbank, as this event poisons Hyacinth's sense of his own identity.

On another note, the prison is figured in this passage as diminishing personal differences. The prisoners there are 'scarcely female,' 'lumpish' and 'silent,' having lost the attributes of gender. Even their ability to articulate themselves has been taken from them, as they speak unintelligibly. This literal labyrinth of a prison resembles a dungeon or an imprisoning gothic castle; it is vast, dark, cold, stony, and threatening. Just as its spaces seem imponderable and like a puzzle, Millbank erases one's sense of time: 'you couldn't imagine what o'clock it was.'

Nine years of imprisonment has had a defacing effect on Hyacinth's mother. She has been robbed of the markings of womanhood, her beauty, and her proper age: 'Above all she seemed disfigured and ugly, cruelly misrepresented by her coarse cap and short, rough hair.'[25] Moreover, as Mrs Bowerbank's bigoted remark reveals, she has also lost her fluency in English: 'since she has been so bad – you can't get a natural word out of her.'[26] The prison has the effect of levelling its inhabitants into a state of general ugliness and deprivation.[27] Florentine has become as deindividuated as the spectral 'silent women' who withdraw from Pinnie when she enters the prison.

In a sense all three of the individuals who contribute to Hyacinth's visit to Millbank are correct about its effect on him. For the formidable warden Mrs Bowerbank, the melodramatic Victorian family reunion scene is successfully staged, and the murderess's child is shamed. In keeping with her conventional prejudices about foreigners and criminals, the prison, moreover, proves to be a site of social delimitation. There the protagonist internalizes the attitudes that inform the public's treatment of prisoners, as revealed in the following exchange: '"There's a many that begin like that!" laughed Mrs Bowerbank, who was irritated by the boy's contempt for one of Her Majesty's finest establishments.'[28] Her response implies that if a boy's mother is a murdering prostitute, he can hardly scoff at the place he will most likely end up.

Vetch also achieves his desired end of forcing Hyacinth to recognize that his world is to be a prison. As a young adult, Hyacinth is acutely aware of his limited possibilities. He cannot speak of his parentage without shame, and he lacks funds for a formal education or the entrance into a gentleman's profession. Finally, Pinnie's fears are confirmed. She never forgives herself for informing Hyacinth of his awkward social standing in the world. Even on her deathbed, she relives Mrs Bowerbank and Florentine's request in 'a passion of repentance, of still further expiation.'[29] She knows that for Hyacinth the immensity of the knowledge of his social imprisonment has replaced the image of Millbank. She, too, has been stained by her proximity to the prison.

Being caught between a rock and a hard place marks the limits of Hyacinth's mental experience during the remainder of the novel. This corresponds to James's comment in the preface to the novel that he wrote for the New York Edition of his works: his walks through London streets had suggested a story to him about 'some small obscure intelligent creature whose education should have been almost wholly derived from them [the streets], capable of profiting by all the civilisation, all the accumulations to which they testify, yet condemned to see these things only from outside – in mere quickened consideration, mere wistfulness and envy and despair.'[30] Due to his birth, spotty education, and lack of connections or money, Hyacinth believes that he can only be a distanced spectator. The image of being perpetually on the outside is repeated in the Princess's reaction to learning about his background: 'Fancy the strange, the bitter fate: to be constituted as you are constituted, to feel the capacity that you must feel, and yet to look at the good things of life only through the glass of the pastry-cook's window!'[31] This speech adopts a common vehicle for describing confinement – the container. In this case, however, the usual perspective is reversed, with the confined individual's being figured as looking into a desirable space rather than looking out from inside an undesirable one. By virtue of his constitution – presumably his gentleman's blood – and his capacity to appreciate 'the good things,' Hyacinth knows about his inability to engage in a desirable type of life, figured here as expensive consumables.

The Princess's metaphor describes the confinement of being a spectator to the desirable rather than a participant in it. This image is dramatized in two scenes that mark important stages in Hyacinth's gradual renunciation of his claim on life. In the first of these he finds himself during a foggy night observing the Princess from outside her house in the company of her estranged, jealous husband, and watching her enter that house with her lover, his best friend Paul Muniment. Typically, the reader does not learn about the effect of this scene on Hyacinth until another chapter has gone by. Then recalling the scene, he muses: 'The movement repeated itself innumerable times, to his moral perception, suggesting to him things that he couldn't bear to learn.'[32] This sentence in psycho-narration condenses many themes in Hyacinth's experience: his pain in perpetually observing as an outsider, his frustration – in a Freudian reading – of not being able to enter the Princess, and of not knowing what he fears to know. The novel's readers mimic Hyacinth's lack of comprehension in having to accept the inchoate quality of the narrative. We are forced to renounce transparent representation by a narrative agent that delays the recitation of important events and admits narrative gaps, and by our own reliance on the reflector figure Hyacinth's limited perception. Such narratives force the reader to actively construct an alternative perspective to compensate for the novel's opacity.

During the last scene of the novel that relates Hyacinth's experience, he visits Millicent at the department store where she works as a saleswoman. There he finds her in the process of exhibiting a dress for that one-time admirer of the Princess – and now probably Millicent's lover – Captain Sholto. Pretending to be a customer in order to see Millicent just as Hyacinth was planning to do, Sholto lets his rival know that he should leave without alerting Millicent to his presence. Here Millicent acts as a substitute for 'the good things in life' that the Princess once referred to. Her job also comments on the general frustrations to be encountered in a wealthy urban society in which goods are constantly being presented in ways to maximize their desirability but are only available to those who possess currency to buy them. Entrapped in a position of specular confinement, Hyacinth sees what he desires but cannot touch it. This will be the reader's final experience of the narrative as well.

The reversal of the container metaphor marks a larger movement within the text away from depicting imprisonment as literal constraint to exploring forms of mental incarceration. In the first part of the novel Hyacinth's metonymical imprisonment takes place through his association with his convict mother. His status as the foster son of a lower-middle-class struggling seamstress further limits him. These constraints appear to briefly give way after Hyacinth is introduced to the seeming social and aesthetic freedom of the Princess's universe. Yet his pecuniary state limits him to being only a temporarily tolerated visitor to this glamorous world. The tenuousness of Hyacinth's association with all he finds beautiful is driven home to him when the Princess tires of him. He is then just as permanently shut out of the life he has found so desirable as he and Pinnie once felt themselves to be perpetually immured within Millbank.

The narrative suggests that Hyacinth's physical constitution as well as social circumstances cause him to suffer. His being the child of a proud daughter of a Parisian revolutionary, who in the most heroic version of her life dies because of her efforts to attain justice for her child, and an English lord makes him susceptible to conflicting impulses. Forced to be one of 'the people' through the attributions of baseness that were made to him in Millbank, he initially wants to fight the 'hideous social inequality' he sees. Later, he comes to find the people's cause 'beastly' and to believe that it is motivated by 'invidious jealousy.'[33] Here, he mimics essentialist attitudes about the inherent inferiority of the poor. More than in other texts, James seems to flirt with ideas of biological determinism in this novel, suggesting that the protagonist's genetic inheritance directs him. Aristocratic blood spoils Hyacinth for the working-class success he might have achieved in his artisan's profession. À la William Hogarth's good apprentice in *Industry and Idleness*, he might have married his master's daughter and taken over the bookbinding business. His father's blood, however, renders Hyacinth a lousy revolutionary:[34]

> There was no peace for him between the two currents that flowed in his nature, the blood of his passionate, plebeian mother and that of his long-descended, super-civilised sire. They continued to toss him from one side to the other; they arrayed him in intolerable defiances and revenges against himself ... The thought of his mother had filled him, originally, with the vague, clumsy fermentation of his first impulses toward social criticism; but since the problem had become more complex by the fact that many things in the world as it was constituted grew intensely dear to him, he had tried more and more to construct some conceivable and human countenance for his father – some expression of honour, of tenderness and recognition, of unmerited suffering, or at least of adequate expiation. To desert one of these presences for the other – that idea had a kind of shame in it, as an act of treachery would have had; for he could almost hear the voice of his father ask him if it were the conduct of a gentleman to take up the opinions and emulate the crudities of fanatics and cads.[35]

Figured in this passage as a boat caught between mighty currents, Hyacinth ultimately cannot move forward or backwards. His binational status contributes as much to his inanition as does his dual-class parentage. Foreigners like the Poupins, Schinkel, and Hoffendahl act as movers and shakers in the underground world of the London revolutionaries. British reformers such as Anastasius Vetch, Lady Aurora, and Paul Muniment are, by contrast, ineffectual. The Princess comments on this as follows: 'the English can go half-way to a thing, and then stick in the middle!'[36]

That the physical prison of Millbank with its gothic horrors and Dickensian warden gives way to the prison of the mind – to the indecision and inanition of Hyacinth as a modern subject – is a mark of the transitional nature of the novel and James's experimentation with narrative form. The change in prison typologies is mirrored in the narration. The omniscient narrator of the realist novel is replaced by a reliance on focalization – chiefly through Pinnie and Hyacinth – and the comments of a disembodied, limitedly knowledgeable first-person narrator. This narrator does not wish to or cannot relate important information such as the contents of the letter Hyacinth receives from Hoffendahl. Like Hyacinth, the reader must wait and wait and wait while Schinkel belabours the details of how he received the missive.[37] This waiting mimics the novel's central image of being forced to view what one desires from outside a window without being able to touch it. Similarly, the incapacity for taking action echoes the experience of being in prison.

Acknowledging the gaps in the telling, the narrator comments on a conversation between the Princess and Lady Aurora that has been given a one-sided presentation: 'These remarks, which I have strung together, did not, of course, fall from the Princess' lips in an uninterrupted stream; they were arrested and interspersed by frequent inarticulate responses and embarrassed protests.'[38] Just as we can only imagine what transpires when Lady Aurora replies to the Princess, we are constrained by our incomplete knowledge of characters' experience. Similarly, we, like Hyacinth, never conclusively learn the facts about his parentage. We witness his oscillations between the conviction that he is a nobleman's son and the conventional view that he is a French whore's bastard. The betrayal by those he most loves, including Paul, the Princess, and, finally, Millicent, only adds to his sense of profound alienation.

Readings of *The Princess* disagree on whether it should be classified as a realist, naturalist, romantic, or urban gothic novel.[39] My interpretation of its carceral imagery suggests that the novel has to be read as a transitional work, lying somewhere between realist Victorian social criticism, narratorial omniscience, and occasional naturalist detail, and the partiality of telling and atmosphere of alienation that characterize more modernist fictions. *The Princess Casamassima* cycles through sentimental, gothic, and naturalistic tropes to arrive finally at a proto-modernist sensibility. In this line Mike Fisher describes the novel as marking the point at which James turns away from realist forms of representation in order to undermine 'the author(itarianism)' inherent in all writing processes.[40]

In terms of its imagery, the Millbank scene works to condemn contemporary penal practices. We recall the narrator's assessment of Pinnie's experience of Millbank quoted from above: 'If the place had seemed cruel to the poor little dressmaker outside, it may be believed that it did not strike her as an abode of mercy while she pursued her tortuous way into the circular shafts of cells.' Even the conservative Pinnie's critique of the institution can be heard in her idiom: 'cruel' and 'abode of mercy.' However, the effect of this scene on Hyacinth's, and in turn the reader's, consciousness is more modernist. It effects a turn from the preoccupation with external appearances and plot events to the drama and non-communicability of internal experience.

Departing from Millbank, we enter into the rest of the novel with a sense of the profound limitations that mark Hyacinth's life. We come to see his larger sense of imprisonment; this may alternately be experienced as a being locked out of life (as in the metaphor of the pastry cook's window) or of a being contained (as in the image of the boat) in a vessel that one cannot control. Hyacinth's lack of agency arises from his conviction that he may neither partake in the aesthetic pleasures of life nor sufficiently believe in the levelling process of revolution. The carceral motif and materialist critique of prison institutions is transformed then into a portrait of mental alienation. Hyacinth becomes an unhappily self-conscious modern subject who is profoundly aware of both his material and perceptual limitations and his radical aloneness in a crowded city.

As readers, we share Hyacinth's awareness that our knowledge of the novel's universe is incomplete. The narrative will not allow us to forget that we only visit the novel's projected world. We must content ourselves with our limited ability to comprehend those sights we are invited to see there. Along these lines, James wrote that the novel's representation of revolutionary politics was intended to create 'the effect … of our not knowing, of society's not knowing, but only guessing and suspecting and trying to ignore, what "goes on" irreconcilably, subversively, beneath the vast smug surface.'[41]

Contrary to the promise of storyworld transparency that is the hallmark of Victorian realist fiction, *The Princess Casamassima* demonstrates that states of mind can be at best only impressionistically conveyed and partially understood. Demonstrably, we can merely guess at the entirety of the Princess's conversations or about Hyacinth's sensations before death; like Hyacinth, we are made cognizant of our limited process by which we know. We, interpretative prisoners, have bars in front of our eyes rather than an unencumbered view of the novel's cityscape.

II

Like *The Princess Casamassima*, James's novella *In the Cage* examines various kinds of imprisonment a sensitive young Londoner must endure when material conditions fail to correspond with her imaginative horizon. In the New York Edition preface to the novella, James makes an explicit connection between the two narratives. Both are explicitly urban tales that were suggested by the author's daily experiences of walking through the streets and by 'the commonest and most taken-for-granted of London impressions,' the postal-telegraph office. Both works concern 'the range of wonderment' of their socially and economically constrained protagonists.[42] As reflected in its title, the novella measures the actual physical confines of the protagonist's workplace, a barred-in post and telegraph office space that is situated within a grocery store in the wealthy London neighbourhood of Mayfair. The text thus portrays contemporary anxieties concerning the new visibility of white-collar women knowledge workers and the potentially danger of having women in charge of communication media.[43] Just as importantly, *In the Cage* renders visible the telegraphist's awareness of the barriers against her freedom caused by her class and gender. Nascent social critique informs this rendering. Yet, as I will argue, the novella's central concern is with the crisis of interpretation the telegraphist undergoes. *In the Cage* dramatizes this crisis and suggests that it is innate to the experience of reading modernist fiction.

Beyond its obvious mention in the novella's title, the cage motif is constantly invoked in the reflected thoughts of the unnamed telegraphist. The telegraphist's physical captivity takes place on a number of levels. It consists of her being placed behind bars when she works at the post office, or even worse, when she is confined to the smaller space of the glassed-in telegraph sounder.[44] Forced to work at the sounder by her co-worker, the telegraphist feels her sense of agency most reduced there. The sounder, as she thinks of it, 'was equally his business to mind, being the innermost cell of captivity, a cage within the cage, fenced off from the rest by a frame of ground glass.'[45] Whether or not, as John Carlos Rowe suggests, the sounder also marks the space where the telegraphist is made the object of routine sexual harassment, we do not conclusively learn.[46] Clearly, she dislikes the maximal sense of sensory deprivation she experiences there.

Variations on phrases that substitute images and metonyms of a cage for the post office highlight the reflector's awareness of her captivity. These include references to her looking 'through the bars,' her being 'in the cage' while at work, or in the 'hole,' or in 'the little hole-and-corner,' as well as the word 'confinement' to describe her situation. Working in the post office is further referred to as being 'in the stocks,'[47] an image that suggests the particular humiliations of a woman being punished publicly. However, the phrase also refers to the new and potentially disorienting effect that educated women workers had on the public. All of these images refer to punitive techniques. They imply that the telegraphist's pronounced visibility within her cage and her repetitive tasks are in themselves penalizing.

The prison is one obvious vehicle for the frequent cage metaphors and metonyms in the text; another is animals. The workplace is figured as holding its workers like livestock. Thus, the reflector remarks internally: 'But the summer "holidays" brought a marked difference; they were holidays for almost everyone but the animals in the cage.' This is also the note with which the novella begins: 'It had occurred to her early that in her position – that of a young person spending, in framed and wired confinement, the life of a guinea pig or a magpie – she should know a great many persons without their recognizing the acquaintance.'[48] Magpies, it should be noted, are not the songbirds of romanticized visions of imprisonment whose transcendent singing surmounts high walls.[49] Rather, guinea pigs and magpies are considered ugly. Due to their frequency, they are associated with the lower classes, a highly relevant distinction for this socially descended young woman. Invoking the same line of imagery, she later responds with hostility to a question from an upperclass interlocutor about whether she has already eaten with the pointed: 'Yes, we do feed once.'[50]

In keeping with common images of a guinea pig running around in circles in its cage and a magpie senselessly collecting objects, the telegraphist's work consists of fruitless repetition and meniality: 'Her function was to sit there with two young men … and dole out stamps and postal-orders, weigh letters, answer stupid questions, give difficult change and more, than anything else, count words of the telegrams thrust, from morning to night, through the gap left in the high lattice, across the encumbered shelf that her forearm ached with rubbing.'[51] Like the young woman, the guinea pig repeats actions in a setting where it is constantly subject to the depersonalizing gaze of its owner. Seen by her customers as identical with her tasks, she is reduced in their eyes to a means to an end: getting telegrams and mail off or acquiring stamps and information. Recognizing the one-sidedness of these interactions, the telegraphist knows she is being made a commodity.

This process of reification in which relations between people become analogous to those with objects is mirrored in the protagonist's recorded words and thoughts.[52] She has her customers' 'silly, guilty secrets in her pocket,' and she compares her efforts to help Everard to 'a little hoard of gold in her lap.' Similarly, her decision to marry Mudge is informed by her conviction 'that he

would build up a business to his chin.' These tropes suggest that her being
seen as a thing by her customers and her strained material circumstances have
made the telegraphist conceive of all relationships in terms of whether they go
'beyond the sixpence.'[53] The cage-like circumstances of her working life are
then mirrored in the telegraphist's confining calculations of her relations to
others in terms of money.

Such thinking extends to the disgust she feels about the money her wealthy
customers squander in telegraphing 'their expensive feelings' to one another.
To do so, they employ the services of those for whom their casual sums would
mean the end of poverty. In a moment of acute class consciousness, the reflector angrily reflects on her customers' 'vague gestures that cost the price of a
new pair of boots.' The money that flows from their hands through her own
into the post office's treasury represents completely different things for them:
a few words expressing 'compliments and wonderments,'[54] or nourishment
and needed clothes.

Yet another form of encagement concerns the young woman's prospects in
terms of her gender. Her position as a telegraphist represents a 'rebound' for
her distressed family. It pays for her mother's and her rent and groceries and
saves the young woman from performing more disreputable work. Yet, her
intercourse with the public represents a kind of publicity that overwrites her
education as a gentlewoman and also marks a social reality, the 'turn-of-the-
century world in which inventions such as the first commercially successful
typewriter (1873) and the telephone (1876) would help give rise to a new
class of female information-workers: secretaries, stenographers, and switch-
board operators.'[55]

While she tries not to acknowledge the presence of the clerks in the grocery
store, so as to underline the distinction between her white-collar work and
their handling of hams and cheeses, she has agreed to marry one of them, the
commercially successful Mr Mudge. A telling mixture of 'mud' and 'drudge,'
his name reminds the reader of the foodstuffs he works with and the material
nature of trade in general. That Mudge inspires no passion is made clear by
her feelings about reading his 'daily, deadly, flourishy letter' and her attempts
to use a minimum of words 'to keep him imperturbably continuously going,'[56]
while she pursues her own thoughts.

Contrary to the modes of imprisonment described above, the post office
cage is also experienced by the telegraphist as the site of reading pleasure and
interpretative fantasy. Indulging in the 'amusements of captives,' she uses her
unoccupied moments to read 'borrowed novels, very greasy, in fine print and
all about fine folks, at a ha'penny a day.'[57] Such novels fuel her constructions
of her customers' affairs, the details of which she gleans from their telegrams.

She takes a particular pleasure in the fact that telegrams are not returned to her post office due to its small size, for this forces her to employ her critical abilities more vigorously in order to flesh out the plots she parses out from reading the senders' correspondence. This rush of interpretative pleasure differs entirely from her readings of Mr Mudge's daily letters. By suggesting that physical captivity may heighten reading pleasure, James explores the dialectic of the prison experience, suggesting an erotic connection between enclosure and interpretation. The prison as a site of physical limitation and simultaneous mental freedom has been explored by Victor Brombert in *The Romantic Prison* (1978), among others. For James, the telegraphist's reading pleasure represents a covert payment for drudgery and depersonalization.

As a captive – in both senses – reader, she interprets her surroundings through the medium of print and numbers and telegraph clicks. She fills in the gaps of knowledge about the illicit affair between two particularly interesting customers and their various aliases: the married and – like a figure in romantic fiction – requisitely beautiful Lady Bradeen and her lover, the requisitely debonair Captain Everard. Her involvement in this couple's telegraphed communication and imagined intercourse is so high that she puts off her marriage. In interpreting this couple's texts the telegraphist appears to break out of the physical confinement of her cage and rebel against her commodification as a service worker. Unlike Hyacinth, she appears to make her confining container permeable. Rather than waiting and suffering, she may become the author of her own future.

Due to her interpretative acuity, she is in a position to alter the lovers' correspondence. When Lady Bradeen makes a mistake about the code word for the next place of assignation, the telegraphist provides her with the missing term, thus becoming co-sender of the telegrammed text. She thus forcefully demonstrates to the Juno-like Bradeen not only that she is much more than a nameless functionary, but also that she has successfully deciphered numerous messages that were intended to be secret. This fills the telegraphist with an eroticized sense of knowing, of enjoying an 'intimacy' with the principals in the telegraphed drama, and also of having power over them.[58] It also, by contrast, sends Mrs Bradeen away in a panic.

The power to alter messages was intrinsic to the change in communication media that the telegraph brought with it. Messages could be sent and received virtually instantly, but the act of writing content was separated from the act of sending the message through code and later sound. Not only was the conduit of electricity necessary to the transmission, but also the persons who sent and received them. The telegraphist had the power not only to read private correspondence but also, potentially, to abuse her knowledge of what she was transmitting. According to Christopher Keep, 'James's point is clear: the variety of stimulus and excitation experience by women in their role as telegraphists is a potential threat not only to the security of the information network, but to the class divisions of the social order.'[59] With the opening of once-private letters to the perusal of public servants like the telegraphist, the pastry cook's window appears to have been permanently shattered.

According to the gender expectations of the day, the telegraphist might be feared to have feelings about the messages she relayed and hence prove to be untrustworthy. Alternatively, she might threaten the new economy of communications by refusing to simply be its medium. She might rebel against the class of people she despises by making them pay for her knowledge. This is an alternative plot that the telegraphist contemplates with some relish.

Yet the telegraphist chooses a role that is informed by the 'greasy' novels she reads as a form of mental escapism. In protecting Everard from scandal, she wishes 'that he should recognize her forbearance to criticise as one of the finest, most tenderest sacrifices a woman had ever made for love.' In this passage we recognize the exaggerated sentiment of romance fiction with its formulaic promise of the woman being redeemed in marital security in exchange for her selfless sacrifice for a man. '[F]inest, tenderest sacrifices' and 'forebearance' strike a completely different tone from the protagonist's otherwise unsentimental thoughts about herself as a magpie and her refreshing descriptions of callous customers as 'awful wretches.'[60] Rather than sticking by her understandable class resentments, the telegraphist prefers 'the bright improbability that her prison is synonymous with the literary heroines' mouldering gothic dungeon or cage of genteel poverty in the domestic romance – that, in effect, physical, financial, and social rescue could be imminent.'[61] Thus, the romance storyline she subscribes to proves to be another form of confinement. Here, as in *The Princess Casamassima*, an implicit critique of prevalent literary mores and their ideological underpinnings is being performed. Just as Mrs Bowerbank's desire to enact a happy family reunion on an individual inmate's deathbed helps her to justify her vicious treatment of prisoners in general, so the telegraphist's half-penny novel belief in the redemption of socially advantageous love matches serves to displace her awareness of social inequality and diffuse her appetite for political action.

Whether through interpreting the glamorous messages of her customers or imagining herself into a Cinderella plot, the telegraphist uses her position at Cocker's to escape mental desultoriness and depersonalization. These are the reading pleasures of a consciousness that is larger than the space allowed for it, and here the telegraphist again resembles Hyacinth. As long as she can delay interpretive closure and finality, she is in effect free within her cage.

She may indulge in a sense of authorial power and oneness with Everard and even, by extension with Lady Bradeen.

The novella's denouement occurs when interpretative closure is forced upon its protagonist. She learns a number of bracing realities through a butler's gossip rather than her divinations of the telegrams' hidden meanings: Everard will soon marry Lady Bradeen, even if he does not want to. Lady Bradeen 'holds him,' 'has still another pull,' 'has him tight,' and has 'just nailed him.'[62] These verb phrases strongly suggest an element of physical coercion on Lady Bradeen's part and Everard's resultant captivity in marriage. His being under her figurative thumb has to do with his debts and the socially compromising nature of their affair. Perhaps, the telegraphist's recovery of the lost telegram is also one of the instruments with which Lady Bradeen has nailed her man.

These revelations and the cognizance of the pointlessness of her own romantic speculations hurry our young woman out of her incarcerating workplace and into the confinement of a marriage. The once-dashing Everard has proven to be a saleable item, a consumable piece of goods on the marriage market. He, like the telegraphist's friend and rival Mrs Jordan, has been bought by his spouse and saved from economic ruin.

The physical cage of the woman's workplace is replaced by the realization of her inevitability inhabiting a narrow social and sexual role. She cannot be the heroine of a greasy novel. Nor can she continue to pen amorous fiction by altering telegrams or, potentially, blackmail the rich. No prince can discover her, for the prince himself has a price. Far too low to be anything but a public servant and perhaps partner in an illicit affair with Captain Everard, she is too high to remain friends with Mrs Jordan, a butler's wife. She can only then become Mr Mudge's wife, and, in effect, invisible, since relegated to the feminized private sphere.

Significantly, the telegraphist remains unnamed within the text, suggesting that she is interchangeable with any number of young women doing her kind of white-collar work. Her namelessness, like the narrative's lack of specificity about what actually happened between the Bradeens and Everard, concur to make the reader only partially cognizant of events. The reader gleans knowledge through the potentially fallible perceptions and interior comments of the reflector. Experiencing the telegraphist's thoughts in the modes of psycho-narration and narrated monologue, we are faced with the imbrication of her impressions with the narrator's sometimes ironic and sometimes empathetic comments on them. Figuratively speaking, we too only read half of the telegraphed correspondence. A complete relation is refused. For instance, the telegraphist is quite biased by her conviction of her cleverness and by her hunger for challenging mental activity. This leads her to read volumes into Everard's every signal, from his glances to his handwriting:

> They would never perhaps have grown half so intimate if he had not, by the bless-ing of heaven, formed some of his letters with a queerness –! It was positive that the queerness could scarce have been greater if he had practiced it for the very purpose of bringing their heads together over it as far as was possible to heads on different sides of a cage. It had taken her in reality but once or twice to master these tricks, but, at the cost of striking him perhaps as stupid, she could still chal-lenge them when circumstances favoured.[63]

'[T]he blessing of heaven,' 'queerness,' and the emotionally hyperbolic exclamation mark signal the lexis and syntax of the telegraphist. We are placed squarely within her perceptions here. Yet other textual evidence sug-gests that Everard is a dolt. One notes that his verbal utterances do not extend much beyond 'See here – see here!'[64] Given the discrepancy between the telegraphist's views and the reader's inferences, one may suppose that Everard's oddly formed letters are products of poor penmanship rather than a strategy to engage personal interest. This passage forces the reader to first doubt the veracity of its literal content and then to develop alternative reading strategies that require more activity in the sense-making process. Thus inter-pretative and perceptual processes are highlighted, rather than objective knowledge of narrated events. While the telegraphist experiences a let-down of her imaginative and material expectations, the reader realizes the impossi-bility of narrative transparency.

As Richard Mencke has written of the novella, James uses the trope of telegraphy with its promise of instantaneous communications to question and problematize the project of Victorian realism. Pointing out that authors such as Dickens and Elizabeth Glaskell had seen the telegraph as a model for their realist prose, he states that 'Henry James scrutinized the telegraphic muse with a keener sense of telegraphy as social and material practice and with a more skeptical eye for the claims of a fictional realism that had once found a coun-terpart in the telegraph's idealized image.'[65] The telegraph may conceal as well as transmit. A medium that had been thought to ensure immediate, com-plete communication is shown to be as fallible as those who employ it.

The reader's dawning awareness of the partiality and fallibility of the telling mimics the telegraphist's movement to a more critical mental standpoint in the last four chapters of the novella. In a conversation with Mrs Jordon that con-cerns more its participants' interest in presenting facts favourably and less in revealing them, knowing becomes anything but transparent. Not only must the telegraphist discard the romantic storyline offered by her half-penny novels and dishearteningly accept her materially and emotionally limited future, but the reader is confronted with the limits of reflectoral narrative and the gaps in the communicative medium.

III

This essay has traced James's exploration of prison motifs from the 'high black walls' of Millbank Prison to various forms of captivity in a young woman's mind. In both texts an awareness of mental confinement supersedes actual physical and spatial incarceration. By virtue of his parentage and his conflicting values, Hyacinth feels himself to be doomed to inanition and hence also to death. The telegraphist hates the cage-like postal office where she works and the treatment she receives there. As a result, she indulges in a fantasy of class ascension with a man who is not only uninterested, but who is also unable to further her socially, economically, or imaginatively. She also imagines herself into a position in which she exercises an authorial power over the texts that pass through her hands, which is quite in opposition to her actual material possibilities. In both cases the protagonists come to realize just how confining their material circumstances are. Moments of breaking through material barriers – of Hyacinth no longer being locked out, and the telegraphist no longer being barred in – prove illusory. Hyacinth commits suicide and the telegraphist recognizes the inevitability of an uninspired marriage. By experiencing epistemological denouements, in which they become aware of their misperceptions, these characters are also awakened to the subjectivism of experience.

Running parallel to the focalizers' realizations of material and perceptual limitations are the readers' experience of the epistemological limits involved in reading these texts. In these fictions readers rely on characters whose internal words and perceptions conflict with other textual evidence, and on narrators who eschew omniscience. This phenomenon forces us into an awareness of the gaps within our knowledge, and we enter into a state of conscious mental and interpretative encagement. Such epistemological confinement is a feature of modernist fiction. It includes the awareness of the limitations of telling and knowing and a foregrounding of the textual medium itself.

With his prison scenarios James offers images of materially as well as mentally confining states. Hyacinth's and the telegraphist's stories provide salient illustrations of the impossibility of sensitive individuals surmounting the barriers of economics and class. The narratives show social inequality to be painfully real. In Hyacinth's case, prejudices about foreigners and criminals further constrain his freedom, just as gender expectations curtail the telegraphist. In another way, *The Princess Casamassima* and *In the Cage* show that Millbank's walls and the telegraphist's cage relate to more than socioeconomic restrictions. They inspire their readers with a sense of the lack of complete intelligibility of experience. Made aware of the inherent partiality of mediated telling and the limits of realist representation, we are invited at once to read more actively and to relinquish our expectation that narration be authorial and complete. Through the confrontation with narrative subjectivity, we emerge from these fictions – just as Hyacinth once exited Millbank – inalterably changed. We have become modernist readers and selves.

NOTES

My gratitude goes to Richard Franklin for his detailed, critical reading of this essay.

1 Compare, for instance, *The Oxford Illustrated History of English Literature*, ed. Pat Rogers (Oxford: Oxford University Press, 1987), 391.

2 A notable exception to this rule is Daniel Schneider's extended analysis of the motif of encagement in the entirety of James's fiction. Daniel J. Schneider, *The Crystal Cage: Adventures of the Imagination in the Fiction of Henry James* (Lawrence: Regents Press of Kansas, 1978), 117–50.

3 In James's figural narratives readers find an overlapping of voices and perceptions: the heterodiegetic narrator offers comments in a more erudite and typically Jamesian voice. These observations are seamlessly embedded in passages of psycho-narration and quoted monologue. An example of this can be found in Pinnie's quoted words about the 'misfitting uniforms and perfect frights of hoods' worn by the inmates of Millbank, a passage quoted from at length below. To the degree that it is not immediately clear whether we are experiencing the storyworld through the focalizer's perceptions and words or through the viewpoint of the narrator, a degree of ambiguity about the reliability – one, of the narration itself and, two, of the reflector figures' perceptions – is introduced.

4 Margaret Scanlan, 'Terrorism and the Realistic Novel: Henry James and *The Princess Casamassima*,' *Texas Studies in Literature and Language* 34, no. 3 (1992): 394; Anne-Claire Le Reste, '*The Princess Casamassima*: Jamesian (Urban) Gothic and Realism,' unpublished manuscript; Derek Brewer, introduction to *The Princess Casamassima* (1886) (London: Penguin, 1987), 23.

5 Monika Fludernik, 'Carceral Topography: Spatiality and Liminality in the Literary Prison,' *Textual Practice* 13.1 (1999): 44.

6 Henry James, *The Princess Casamassima* (1886; London: Penguin, 1987), 311.

7 Ibid., 57.

8 Ibid., 56, 57.

9 See Frank Lauterbach's exploration of the prison as a site of identity demarcations: 'the prison becomes culturally significant as a marker to delimit different social realms; that is, a criminal nether world, seen to be inevitably associated with the prison by the respectable bourgeoisie, represented by political and legal authorities at the various stages of the penal process.' Frank Lauterbach, '"From the Slums *to* the Slums": The Delimitation of Social Identity in Late Victorian Prison Narratives,' in *Captivating Subjects: Writing Confinement, Citizenship and Nationhood in the Nineteenth Century*, ed. Julia M. Wright and Jason Haslam (Toronto: University of Toronto Press, 2005), 113–14.

10 James, *Princess*, 167.

11 Ibid., 65.

12 For an exploration of the sickroom as a site of marital and familial reconciliation, see Miriam Bailin, *The Sickroom in Victorian Fiction: The Art of Being Ill* (Cambridge: Cambridge University Press, 1994).

13 James, *Princess*, 59.

14 I am borrowing a phrase from Shaw's reading of the prison as an extension of everyday life. Harry E. Shaw, 'Realities of the Prison: Dickens, Scott, and the Secularization of their Eighteenth-Century Inheritance,' in *In the Grip of Law: Trials, Prisons and the Space Between*, ed. Monika Fludernik and Greta Olson, (Frankfurt: Lang, 2004), 172–3.

15 James, *Princess*, 76.

16 Ibid., 70.

17 For more on this topic, see Jason Haslam's essay in this volume.

18 James, *Princess*, 69.

19 Ibid., 98.

20 Fludernik, 'Carceral,' 44.

21 James, *Princess*, 79.

22 Ibid., 82.

23 Robert Louis Stevenson, *Dr. Jekyll and Mr. Hyde* (1886; New York: Bantam Books, 1981), 3. For an analysis of urban gothic topoi, see Robert Mighall, *A Geography of Victorian Gothic Fiction: Mapping History's Nightmares* (Oxford: Oxford University Press, 1999).

24 James, *Princess*, 82.

25 Ibid., 84.

26 Ibid., 85.

27 See also Anne Schwan's contribution to this volume.

28 James, *Princess*, 86–7.

29 Ibid., 370.

30 Henry James, *The Art of the Novel* (New York: Charles Scribner's Sons, 1953), 60.

31 James, *Princess*, 337.

32 Ibid., 535.

33 Ibid., 165, 336, 397.

34 A great deal of critical work has focused on James's lack of accurate knowledge about the revolutionaries he depicts. Arguably, this lack of specificity about who the London revolutionaries are and precisely what they believe in mirrors Hyacinth's own opaque beliefs: he wishes more to revenge his mother than overthrow existing social structures. See Millicent Bell, *Meaning in Henry James* (Cambridge, MA: Harvard University Press, 1991), 183.

35 James, *Princess*, 479.

36 Ibid., 487.

37 Christine DeVine, 'Revolution and Democracy in the London *Times* and *The Princess Casamassima*,' *Henry James Review* 23 (2002): 63.

38 James, *Princess*, 433.

39 Devine calls the novel 'revolutionary' ('Revolution and Democracy,' 70). Scanlan ('Terrorism'), Rowe, Tingle, and Seltzer suggest that it challenges the parameters of literary realism. See John Carlos Rowe, *The Other Henry James* (Durham, NC: Duke University Press, 1998); Nicholas Tingle, 'Realism, Naturalism, and Formalism: James and *The Princess Casamassima*,' *American Literary Realism* 2, no. 2 (1989): 54–66; Mark Seltzer, *Henry James and the Art of Power* (Ithaca, NY: Cornell UP, 1984). Finally, Anne-Claire Le Reste recasts it as gothic.

40 Mike Fischer, 'The Jamesian Revolution in *The Princess Casamassima*: A Lesson in Bookbinding,' *Henry James Review* 9, no. 2 (1988): 102.

41 James, *Art*, 77–8.

42 Ibid., 154, 156.

43 Christopher Keep, '"Exhibiting the Telegraph Girl": The Information Superrailway: Literature and Media in the Nineteenth Century.' MLA Convention. New Orleans, 30 December 2001. My gratitude goes to the author for his willingness to share this manuscript with me.

44 Brombert names the prison within the prison as one of the topoi of prison imagery. Victor Brombert, *The Romantic Prison: The French Tradition* (Baltimore, MD: Johns Hopkins University Press, 1978), 9. See also Jan Alber's analysis of increasing levels of imprisonment in actual and narrated prisons. Jan Alber, 'Bodies behind Bars: The Disciplining of the Prisoner's Body in British and American Prison Movies,' in *In the Grip of Law*, 241–69.

45 Henry James, *In the Cage*, *The Complete Tales of Henry James*, vol. 10, *1898–1899*, ed. Leon Edel (1889; London: Rupert Hart-Davis, 1964), 145.

46 John Carlos Rowe, *The Other Henry James*, 169.

47 James, *In the Cage*, 146 (further variations on the bar image: 173, 180, 182); cage references: 159, 167, 184, 207, 208, 210, 213; hole images: 175, 153; 'confinement': 189; 'stocks': 143.

48 Ibid., 189, 139.

49 Brombert, *The Romantic Prison*, 13.

50 James, *In the Cage*, 189.

51 Ibid., 139.

52 I use Wendy Graham's discussion of reification in *The Spoils of Poynton* as a starting point for my observations. Wendy Graham, 'A Narrative History of Class Consciousness,' *Boundary* 215, nos. 1/2 (Autumn 1986–Winter 1987): 41–68.

53 James, *In the Cage*, 154, 190, 167, 161.

54 Ibid., 150, 153

55 Richard Menke, '"Framed and Wired": Teaching *In the Cage* at the Intersection of Literature and Media,' *Henry James Review* 25 (2004): 36.

56 James, *In the Cage*, 143, 202.

57 Ibid., 144, 141.

58 Ibid., 181.

59 Keep, 'Exhibiting,' n.p.

60 James, *In the Cage*, 176, 169.

61 Nicola Nixon, 'The Reading Goal of Henry James's *In the Cage*,' *ELH* 66 (1999): 187.

62 James, *In the Cage*, 240, 241.

63 Ibid., 175.

64 Ibid., 199.

65 Richard Menke, 'Telegraphic Realism: Henry James's *In the Cage*,' *PMLA* 115, no. 5 (2000): 988.

12 Epilogue: Female Confinement in Sarah Waters's Neo-Victorian Fiction

ROSARIO ARIAS

The revival of things Victorian has become the subject of a substantial number of contemporary novels. Current practitioners of the neo-Victorian novel (also known as retro-Victorian or post-Victorian) include Matthew Kneale, Peter Ackroyd, A.S. Byatt, Graham Swift, and Sarah Waters, among many others.[1] To varying degrees, they are fascinated with the Victorian age and pay homage to Victorian ancestors in their historical narratives.[2] Whatever the reason that lies behind their interest in resurrecting the Victorian past, these contemporary fiction writers are using Victorian themes, personages, and literary texts to provide their novels with a credible Victorian texture; and in doing so, they revitalize our knowledge of the Victorian past.

In what follows, I will discuss Sarah Waters's *Affinity* (1999) as a reappraisal of Victorian gender issues in relation to imprisonment and madness. Sarah A. Smith suggests that one of the novel's plotlines leads to the conclusion that 'gender is a form of prison and a kind of madness [that are] predictable commonplaces of feminist studies of the Victorian period.'[3] Sandra M. Gilbert and Susan Gubar's *The Madwoman in the Attic: The Woman Writer and the Nineteenth-Century Literary Imagination* (1979) showcases this connection between gender, imprisonment, and madness in arguing that literary portrayals of imprisonment and escape are largely found in nineteenth-century women's writing, primarily 'using houses as primary symbols of female imprisonment.'[4] In addition, they argue that 'a supposedly "mad" woman [is] sentenced to imprisonment in the "infected" house of her own body.'[5] In this essay, I demonstrate that the two major characters in *Affinity* manage to escape the objectifying gaze of disciplinary society by blurring the boundaries between the spiritual and the material worlds. Selina achieves this by reproducing the potential subversion of her spiritualist activities in the confined limits of her prison cell, whereas Margaret escapes metaphorical enclosure by engaging in philanthropic activities and liberating her desire. Before undertaking the examination of Waters's neo-Victorian fiction, I will focus on the ways in which Michel Foucault moved away from his *Discipline and Punish* (1975), traditionally utilized in the study of prison narratives, in his later writings. I will also consider other critics like Lauren M.E. Goodlad who have transcended Foucault's original thesis.

I

Millbank, by far the largest criminal prison in Victorian London, nowadays 'palimpsestically the site of Tate Britain,'[6] is the setting of Waters's *Affinity*. This prison followed some of the features of Jeremy Bentham's plan for the Panopticon, which, as Henry Mayhew posits in his book on the prisons in London, basically 'consisted in placing the prisoners under constant surveillance.'[7] Taking Bentham's design of the Panopticon as his starting point, Foucault investigates not only the consequences of continuous observation but also the ways in which panopticism, or the creation of a disciplinary society, can be understood as 'a way of defining power relations in terms of the everyday life of men.'[8]

Foucault's description of 'panopticism' has proved extremely useful for studies on power, knowledge, and control in Victorian and neo-Victorian fiction. However, a recent article published by Lauren M.E. Goodlad moves away from Foucault's *Discipline and Punish* and shifts the focus of attention to Foucault's later work on governmentality and subjectivity. The main thrust of her argument revolves around the idea that Foucault's application of the mechanism of the Panopticon to the entire society is not in keeping with Victorian Britain's 'idiosyncratic, self-consciously liberal, relatively decentralized, and "self-governing" society.'[9] Goodlad's hypothesis is based on the idea that Victorianists have largely applied Foucault's genealogical method, a model in which panopticism is exercised in modern institutions (using the material conditions of eighteen-century France), to a Victorian society in which these institutions were beginning to flourish.[10] Goodlad then turns to Foucault's later writings, where he develops his own theories into more complex thoughts on the subject and governmentality, whereby individuals are endowed with the potential to resist societal codes and norms.

In his later writings, Foucault revises his own theories about power and poses questions about how human beings may turn into active subjects. He insists upon the necessity of focusing on a 'new economy of power relations,' which 'consists of taking the forms of resistance against different forms of power as a starting point.'[11] Techniques such as resistance, opposition, and struggle against authority offer a distinct mode of power, 'which makes individuals subjects.'[12]

Power relations are, then, understood as the way in which certain actions transform others since power is 'nevertheless always a way of acting upon an acting subject or acting subjects by virtue of their acting or being capable of action'; that is to say, '[a] set of actions upon other actions.'[13] Goodlad maintains that Foucault's revision of power (from the objectifying mode of domination upon docile bodies to the relational mode of subjects interacting with one another) has an important bearing upon the role played by the state in the constitution of citizens.[14] According to Foucault, the modern Western world has incorporated a power technique that derives from Christianity, the pastoral power, or pastorship, exercised primarily by public institutions, welfare societies, benefactors, and philanthropists, but also extended to the rest of the social body where there was an individualizing 'tactic' in powers like those of the family, education, and psychiatry, for example.[15] If '[e]very power relationship implies, at least *in potentia*, a strategy of struggle, in which the two forces are not superimposed, do not lose their specific nature, or do not finally become confused,'[16] the mid-Victorian concept of pastorship as supporting individuality without entailing conformity articulates the possibility of 'a glimmering potential for liberation,'[17] present in the works of authors like Charles Dickens[18] or Elizabeth Gaskell, and also invoked in Waters's novel *Affinity*.

However important Foucault's *Discipline and Punish* has been in the examination of Victorian and neo-Victorian literature, I will concentrate on Foucault's revision of his own theories about subjectivity and the ways in which power operates, not directly, but through the intervention of human subjects interacting with one another (the opposite of the objectifying gaze). The female protagonists of Waters's neo-Victorian fiction embody these ideas of the circulation of power through a relational mode of behaviour, following Goodlad and the later Foucault: they achieve agency and become human actors by engaging in relations with one another; in addition, by taking up the pen and telling their own stories, they evade the objectifying gaze, control, and surveillance of the state apparatuses, circumventing imprisonment. Some critics argue that there exists the possibility of escaping the controlling gaze in *Affinity*.[19] I would like to add that this is due to the power dynamics established between the diverse relationships of the novel, that is, between Selina and Margaret, specifically, but also between Margaret and her own mother, and finally between Margaret and the prison matrons.

II

Affinity is a contemporary historical novel, set in London in the 1870s, the heyday of spiritualism. It is told through discontinuous entries from the journals of the two main characters: Selina Dawes and Margaret Prior. Through them, the reader plunges herself in the narration of their lives for a period of a year and a half, from the time Margaret commences her philanthropic work as a 'Lady Visitor' at Millbank and happens to meet Selina, a convicted spiritualist medium, charged with '*Fraud & Assault*,'[20] and punished to a five-year sentence. The entries of Margaret's journal demonstrate that she is mourning both the death of her beloved father and the loss of her former lover, Helen, now married to Margaret's brother and with a child of her own. Originally devised to keep her occupied after her unspeakable suicide attempt, Margaret's philanthropic visits to Millbank are more and more frequent as she becomes increasingly spellbound by Selina. In turn, Selina's entries deal with her life as a notorious spiritualist medium in London before her imprisonment. However different Selina and Margaret may seem at first glance, they bear important resemblances in this prison novel.[21] Selina is imprisoned at Millbank, frequently under the observation of the matrons, whereas Margaret is trapped in her upper-middle-class home, under the near-constant supervision of her mother. Both prison and home carry 'associations of female entrapment.'[22] In what follows, I will elaborate on the imprisonment of Selina and Margaret, and the possibilities of transcending female confinement.

Waters strives to faithfully reconstruct the conditions of Millbank as a Panopticon where the constant gaze is crucial, as recorded by Margaret in her first impression of the building: 'it is in lifting my eyes from my sweeping hem that I first see the pentagons of Millbank – and the nearness of them, and the suddenness of that gaze.'[23] Interestingly, the description of Millbank conforms to the one provided by Henry Mayhew. For example, Mayhew affirms the existence of 'a chain-room,'[24] and a punishment cell, 'not exactly what we call a dark one, but an ordinary cell, with the windows nearly closed up.'[25] Similarly, Margaret is taken by two matrons, Miss Ridley and Miss Haxby, to the chain-room at Millbank: '[Each wall] was densely hung with iron – with rings and chains and fetters, and with other, nameless, complicated instruments whose purposes I could only, shuddering, guess at.'[26] Also, Waters has given life to a dark room to punish those who 'break out,' the expression used to refer to the violent outbursts by means of which female prisoners release the tension, anger, and frustration at being kept imprisoned. This is a form of protest that is inflicted 'on the inanimate objects that constituted confinement' rather than 'on the personal representatives of authority.'[27] Although the prison governor is a man called Mr Shillitoe, it is the matrons who exercise authority, power, and control through surveillance at Millbank. Several critics have dealt with the question of female observation in *Affinity* by the matrons and the ways in which they connive with power structures to maintain the status quo in systems of oppression like the prison.[28] Matrons like Miss Haxby and Miss Ridley embody the controlling power of the gaze as they are constantly supervising the prisoners (and Margaret in her visits to Selina) through the inspection slit in each cell: '[The matron] showed me how, at the side of each gate, there is a vertical iron flap which can be opened any time the matron pleases, and the prisoner viewed: they call this the "inspection"; the women term it *the eye*.'[29] Only one particular matron, Mrs Jelf, is described as 'really kind, and half-way gentle,'[30] especially when she softens the hardened daily existence of an old woman prisoner and puts some ointment on her chest. Towards the end of the novel, Mrs Jelf will be more than kind to Selina as she becomes an accomplice in the plot to secure the spiritualist medium's freedom by producing the set of keys, clothes, and a pair of shoes for Selina to 'assume' the matron's identity.

The female convicts at Millbank, following Mayhew's reports of his own visits to the prison, 'are pronounced "fifty times more troublesome than the men."'[31] This comment underlines the assumption that in Victorian times, female criminality was always considered to be more deviant, aberrant, and monstrous than male criminality.[32] The different cases of female criminals mentioned in Waters's novel reveal the main offences for which women were convicted in mid-Victorian Britain. One of the most interesting cases is that of a child murderer, Mary Ann Cook, sentenced to a seven-year imprisonment.[33] Waters incorporates some details about the socio-economic background of this girl convicted for child murder, and shows that hers is the hackneyed story of a working-class maid, abused by her master's son, and left abandoned with an unwanted pregnancy. Other female convicts are also kept imprisoned because they represent the opposite of the Victorian stereotype of womanhood; among them are thieves, pickpockets, suicidal women, and the like.

It has become a commonplace to suggest that in the Victorian age the female body, in particular, was subjected to manipulation, scrutiny and examination, as well as confined within the limits of domesticity and prescriptive behaviour. Cultural orthodoxy trapped women in the paradigm of feminine ideals as 'purveyors of religious values and guardians of home and hearth.'[34] This idealization of women contributed to their characterization as passive, permanently ill or invalid, inert, and prone to hysterical fits due to physiological dysfunctions, according to the traditional view of womanhood that was reinforced by 'scientific' evidence. At the same time, unconventional female behaviour was aligned with degenerative pathology, immorality, and criminal sexuality. Typically, the woman who overstepped Victorian norms and customs was immediately placed into the social category of 'the demonic outcast.'[35] And this also applies to the law. Nineteenth-century criminologists contributed to the perpetuation of stereotypes about women, who oscillated between two frequently invoked myths, namely, angels in the house or demons – myths which still had considerable weight in twentieth-century explorations of female criminality.[36]

Although it is accurate to maintain the view that very little attention has been paid to female convicts, it has to be remembered that the nineteenth century witnessed the publication of several studies by Cesare Lombroso, which had some influence on the perception of female non-conformity and its relation to crime. Especially relevant was Cesare Lombroso and William Ferrero's *The Female Offender*, first published in Italy in 1893, an oft-quoted text for its pioneering nature as well as for its long-lasting influence upon the work of later writers and theorists, although its authors 'did not ultimately help our understanding of women and crime.'[37] What Lombroso and Ferrero attempted to do was to explain female criminality by focusing on an 'innate' female pathology, reflected in the appearance of a vast number of female criminals, that is, their physical traits, measurements, and sizes of parts of their bodies. The main thrust of their argument is the need to establish distinctions between the occasional female offender and the born criminal. In the chapter entitled 'The Born Criminal,' the two authors develop their theories about the pathological nature of the 'born female criminal,' whose physiognomy reflects her deviance and degeneracy, 'more perverse than those of their male prototypes.'[38] Her psychology is: 'excessively erotic, weak in maternal feeling, inclined to dissipation, astute and audacious ... Added to these virile characteristics are often the worst qualities of woman: namely, an excessive desire for revenge, cunning, cruelty, love of dress, and untruthfulness, forming a combination of evil tendencies which often results in a type of extraordinary wickedness.'[39] It seems clear that the nineteenth-century vision of (female) criminality was governed by the notion of the pathological nature of the criminal, particularly in relation to female deviance. Foucault also shows that in the first decades of the nineteenth century there was an upsurge of interest in examining the phenomenon of criminality as a deviant human class, in terms of another species altogether: 'A zoology of sub-species ... Delinquency, a pathological gap in the human species, may be analysed as morbid syndromes or as great teratological forms.'[40] If the criminal was considered a subhuman species, the female criminal was even more monstrous and deviant than the male, as the inferiority of women was widely acclaimed from different quarters: criminal law, philosophy, literature, medicine, and early psychology. From the point of view of nineteenth-century criminology, it remains evident that the female criminal epitomized the need for regulation and control. Recent historical studies on the Victorian period have highlighted the pivotal role played by another type of woman who was also included in the category of deviant, aberrant subject, begging for correction and regulation: the female spiritualist, like Selina in *Affinity*. Peter Hutchings develops the connection between criminality and spiritualism as he contends that 'spiritualism and the ascendancy of criminal law are equally responses to the triumph of reason and a crisis in traditional Christianity … One junction between the worlds of spirit and crime is the emergent discourse of psychology which pathologized both the spiritualist and the criminal.'[41]

Spiritualist mediums (who were mostly women) broke down societal norms and rules when holding séances, successfully finding in the spiritualist circle an outlet for transgressive behaviour. This is not the place to undertake a thorough account of this complex movement. Suffice it to say that feminist historians such as Alex Owen, Diana Basham, and Janet Oppenheim have turned their eyes to this long-forgotten subject and have shed light on the life of underrepresented Victorian women and how spiritualism (and other spiritual trends like Theosophy) forged associations with the inception of women's rights. Contradictory as it might be, Victorian spiritualism fed on a craving for the spiritual in order to counterbalance materialistic scepticism, while simultaneously searching for material proof of the existence of the other world. Another contradiction lay in the heart of spiritualism as it was founded 'on the doctrine of female moral influence and a specific understanding of the feminine' to the extent that 'mediumship was a power strategy predicated on the notion of the female frailty and wielded from a position of social inferiority.'[42] This is clearly true with regard to working-class women, who obviously benefited from a thriving (and pecuniary) practice, as happened with the London spiritualist medium Florence Cook in the 1880s. In Waters's novel Selina embodies the collapse of social difference in the séance as the spiritualist medium, an orphan girl, ends up living under the protection of a well-off upper-middle-class women, Mrs Brink.

In *Affinity* a vast number of female criminals are kept in the female ward (as male and female convicts are imprisoned separately). Yet it is the convicted spiritualist medium Selina who stands out for many reasons. Her accent, manners, and disposition are highly commended by the matrons. Although from humble origins, she succeeded in climbing up the social ladder as she had become the protégée of Mrs Brink. Selina is doubly disruptive: on the one hand, she is a female convict; on the other, she earns her living by holding spiritualist séances and materializing a full-form spirit body, Peter Quick. Even though she is charged with fraud and assault, the reports of her trial point to her spiritualist activities as the main cause for her incarceration. It is Margaret who reads most of the clips and reports from Selina's trial, specifically from *The*

Spiritualist.[43] In *Affinity*, Waters methodically recreates real-life cases included in this newspaper when Margaret goes to the spiritualist association in order to investigate Selina's past life:

> Every spiritualist in England had his eyes upon the details of [Selina's] trial – and wept, too, when he heard the outcome of it; … 'The law has us as "rogues and vagabonds",' he said. 'We are meant to practise "palmistry and other subtle crafts" … He asked me, was I familiar with all the details of Miss Dawes' arrest and imprisonment? … 'See here,' he said, lifting the cover. 'This is *The Spiritualist*, one of our newspapers. Here are last year's numbers, from July until December.'[44]

Many points in the above-mentioned passage require further discussion. Firstly, Selina's case is presented as one of the many other stories of celebrated spiritualists who were accused of fraud and deception in late-Victorian London,[45] such as the renowned Daniel Dunglas Home, or F.O. Matthews, a real-life clairvoyant-medium who in 1880 was apprehended upon two charges under the Vagrancy Acts, that of '"Fortune Telling," and "Using subtle means and craft, thereby defrauding certain of her Majesty's subjects."'[46] The medium Henry Slade, who claimed to hold the power of communicating with the dead through slate-writing, was charged, tried, and found guilty 'of practising deception under the Vagrancy Acts, and sentenced to three months' hard labour,'[47] although he managed to escape from Britain to the Continent. His prosecution and trial are reproduced in full details in the October 1876 number of *The Spiritualist*. By holding communication with the spirits, women spiritualists like Martha Ann Houghton were charged under the Vagrancy Acts.[48]

Secondly, Selina seems to be the fictional counterpart of Susan Willis Fletcher, an American spiritualist who was first arrested on the charge of robbery by false pretences in the United States (although the case was dismissed). When she travelled to Britain to face the charges of fraud and robbery, she was condemned to spend twelve months in a London prison. Philip Priestley mentions her case very briefly and notes that 'Susan Willis Fletcher was convicted of fraud and served her sentence at Tothill Fields in the 1870s.'[49] After her release she wrote an account of her life in prison, entitled *Twelve Months in an English Prison* (1884). The success of her work, in combination with her own popularity as a lecturer, contributed to her growing fame in Britain and the States. In writing this autobiographical piece Fletcher's interest is twofold: on the one hand, she tries to defend her position as an innocent spiritualist, thus aligning with other spiritualists who claimed they had been wrongly accused of practising deception; on the other, Fletcher is eager to approach the subject of penal reform, particularly in the last section of her book. *Twelve Months in an English Prison*, then, follows the trend of certain spiritualists who turned to writing autobiographical pamphlets and texts in order to account for the veracity and truthfulness of the spiritualist movement. Like them, Fletcher manifestly tried to proselytize others as '[m]any tropes of such narratives can be found in the early part of [Fletcher's] book: spirit messages; visionary trances; the death of loved ones; crises of faith; "tests" of the authenticity of spiritualism followed by a conviction of important work to do serving the cause of spiritualism.'[50] Similarly, Selina's entries in her journal focus on her development as a consummate spiritualist prior to imprisonment and include details commonly found in real-life spiritualists' autobiographical accounts: trance states, the death of relatives, and spirit messages which instruct the medium in spiritual matters. For example, Selina records in her diary a set of questions to a spirit friend: '*What is the spirit-medium's proper home?*'[51] She gets the following answer: 'The spirit-medium's proper home is neither this world nor the next, but that vague & debatable land which lies between them.'[52]

As seen in *Affinity*, Fletcher's narrative is concerned with a detailed account of the tedious procedures of the trial, as well as the mocking tone she had to put up with when faced with her prosecutors. Her trial took place precisely when spiritualism was receiving ruthless attacks from the medical profession and the criminal law. By linking criminality with gender, spiritualism, and insanity, Victorian society attempted to exercise control and regulation over the transgression of norms and rules. For example, L.S. Forbes Winslow, the operator of two asylums, published an incendiary work on spiritualism and the tendency to madness among the population: *Spiritualistic Madness* (1877). Winslow claims that he is writing 'without prejudice' about the dangers brought about by this new religious practice. He finds that many victims, mostly women, victims of their own gullibility, suffer from mental delusions, then have to be kept confined in asylums, and affirms that in America there are 'nearly ten thousand [such] persons.'[53] As regards the criminal law, Fletcher includes an excerpt from the *Times* that clearly shows public concern over the growing popularity and increasing relevance of spiritualism in the Victorian age. According to the *Times*, 'the delusion of spiritualism is no new one ... It is certainly a very good thing that the machinations of mediums, magnetic doctors, and the like, should occasionally come within the reach of the criminal law.'[54] However distant criminality and spiritualism might be, then, both illustrate the fears and antagonisms motivated by male professionals.

However, there are more similarities between Waters's novel and Fletcher's autobiographical account. For example, on first visiting Selina, Margaret becomes fascinated with the spiritualist medium and with her holding a flower, a violet, in a confined place where nothing can possibly grow: '[Selina's] hands opened, she raised them to her cheek, and I caught a flash of colour against the pink of her work-roughened palms. She had a flower there, between her fingers – a violet, with a drooping stem.'[55] Selina tricks Margaret into believing that this is one of the gifts from her spirit friends, who accompany Selina in her solitude. Similarly, Fletcher maintains that she is kept in the company of her spirit friends at all times and that one particular spirit called Ernest held 'in his hand a little bouquet of *violets* and heliotrope' and gave it to her.[56]

In her first-person narrative account Fletcher contends that there exists the possibility of breaking up the boundary between the material and the spiritual worlds, thus transcending imprisonment. While confined in her cell, Fletcher steps out of her body by means of a trance state, crosses the Atlantic, and sees her husband (and other 'spirit friends'). Here are the thoughts she has when she returns to her earthly shell: 'It seemed bad enough to re-enter my cell, so small, so cold and dismal; but the idea of re-entering my body was still more repugnant. It was doubly a prison, a prison in a prison; and I refused to go.'[57] Fletcher is adamant about the restrictions imposed upon the body in opposition to a free spirit or soul, which refers to the religious topos of the body as prison. Prisons 'can either be represented realistically or charged symbolically,' and the most traditional prison metaphor is that of 'the world (and the body) as prison.'[58] More interestingly, Fletcher's comment also refers to a staple of spiritualism: the collapsing of the boundaries of the two worlds, the world of the living and the world of the dead; in other words, the blurring of the boundaries between materiality and spirituality.

At this point, it is worth mentioning George Du Maurier's *Peter Ibbetson* (1892), because it also hinges on questions of confinement, materiality, and spirituality/fantasy.[59] The protagonist, Peter Ibbetson, defined as an 'ex-private soldier, architect and surveyor, convict and criminal lunatic,'[60] or Gogo (the familiar name he receives), challenges and transcends his imprisonment (he is charged with the murder of his uncle) by building up an alternative spiritual world in opposition to the material world of his cell at Pentonville. While dreaming or in a 'trance,'[61] he and Mimsey, also known as Mary Seraskier, the Duchess of Towers (and his child companion in France), meet and live together for several years in their dreams, where their bodies are permanently young and fresh. The meeting between Ibbetson and Mary in their dreams is at first carried out inadvertently by their wishing to be together, but then they end up meeting every night for twenty-five years. It is clear that their souls are in harmony and maintain a link, as Ibbetson puts it: 'No two human souls can ever have interpenetrated each other as ours have done, or we should have heard of it.'[62] At the end of the novel, as Mary dies and Ibbetson is torn apart at the news, spirituality becomes more important since Mary's spirit comes to life again in Ibbetson's dreams to accomplish a mission – to instruct Ibbetson about the spiritual world and how he should undertake the task of putting pen to paper to narrate their experiences: 'to unravel and translate and put in order these voluminous and hastily penned reminiscences.'[63] Although confined in a cell, Ibbetson succeeds in liberating his spirit from the prison of the cell, and the prison of his body, by, firstly, engaging in a counter-world of dreams and fantasy, and secondly, by employing his time in writing down their experiences of how they were capable of injecting spirituality into the material world of the prison.

What Du Maurier's *Peter Ibbetson*, Fletcher's autobiographical account, and Waters's *Affinity* share is the relationship maintained between imprisonment/materiality and liberation/spirituality. As regards spiritualism, this movement managed to counterbalance the materiality of the Victorian world, seeped in scepticism and economic growth, with spirituality in providing communication with the dead. As Marlene Tromp argues, there is a crossing of boundaries between the spiritual and the material worlds when mediums conveyed messages from the afterlife, and in doing so spiritualism 'call[s] into question the stability of the categories spiritual and material, proprietous and indecorous – particularly as gender and sexuality were concerned.'[64] The doctrine of 'affinityship,' which gives the title to Waters's novel, proves how sexually indecorous the spiritualist movement could possibly be when there existed this sustained belief that two people could find their soulmates outside marriage.[65] In Fletcher's autobiographical account her prosecutrix, Mrs Hart-Davies, openly acknowledges her belief in this doctrine when she is being cross-examined by Fletcher's barrister.[66] In turn, Waters plays with this notion and opens up new possibilities of interpretation of the infatuation Margaret feels for Selina: 'We are the same, you and I. We have been cut, two halves, from the same piece of shining matter ... But my spirit does not love yours – it's *entwined* with it. Our flesh does not love: our flesh is the same, and longs to leap to itself.'[67] By utilizing a spiritual concept, Selina is trying to secure Margaret's affection to achieve freedom, as well as obtain material compensation. Contradictory as it may seem, Selina's spiritualism encompasses sexuality and corporality, which were clearly evaded by Victorian normativity.

Marlene Tromp persuasively argues that 'it is precisely in this place [the séance], at this site of fluid boundaries and metamorphosing identities that I would argue change becomes possible, that social worlds – and not just those imagined by the Spiritualists – began to shift.'[68] I would suggest that apart from the spiritualist séance, disruptive in the break-up of the distinctions between the spiritual and the material worlds, any space/text connected with spiritualist activities is liable to contain some potential for subversion and disruption. In this sense, Selina's prison cell provides her with the perfect setting to display her supposedly supernatural powers and attractions, which fascinate Margaret (and Mrs Jelf), and in doing so, she eventually manages to evade the material world of the prison. Hence, it is possible to contend that in *Affinity* a spiritual doctrine, the theory of 'affinityship,' allows Selina to transcend imprisonment. Intertwined with this fact is, following Macpherson, the subversion of the disciplining power of the Panopticon by feminizing the gaze in the liberation of lesbian desire, which 'allows for illusion, performance, and subversive control.'[69] Thus, spiritualism and lesbianism are likened in this neo-Victorian novel. In this sense, it has already become commonplace to note the importance of spectrality in lesbian criticism and fiction since the publication of Terry Castle's *The Apparitional Lesbian* (1993). This study traced a history of lesbianism in literature and propounded the spectral imagery to indicate how lesbian desire has been made 'spectral,' drawing from the notion of the return of the repressed.[70] Not only is spiritualism connected with lesbian desire in Waters's novel, but so too is spinsterhood, as Margaret Prior 'is portrayed as a ghostly, frustrated figure' who represses her lesbian desires.[71]

Margaret, like Selina, is imprisoned in the patriarchal establishment of the Victorian home where she has to fulfil the role of a dutiful daughter to her mother. Unmarried and with a hunger for a more self-fulfilling life, Margaret stands against the normative view of Victorian womanhood. She remembers her mother scolding her once for not complying with social customs: 'I saw the woman gazing at me, and think the matrons also had their eyes upon me. I thought suddenly of Mother, scolding me when I was two-and-twenty, saying I must talk more when we went calling.'[72] Like the female convicts at Millbank, she is constantly under surveillance by her mother, who colludes with patriarchal structures of power to exercise control upon the deviant, aberrant woman, in this particular case, the spinster (with a repressed lesbian sexuality). Margaret incarnates the nineteenth-century image of the woman who lived outside the prescribed normativity, the celibate woman or spinster and the lesbian, 'seen as a threat to civilization: both a threat to patriarchy and to themselves.'[73] The deployment of womanhood as monstrous or aberrant is made clear by the far-reaching implications of the links between Selina and Margaret. As explained before, both are kept imprisoned and there are many instances in the novel where the parallelism between home and prison is highlighted,[74] precisely when Margaret sees a correspondence between the imprisoned day-to-day existence of the female prisoners and herself, also noted by Selina: '"You are like me, then," she said. "Indeed, you are like all of us at Millbank."'[75] In fact, Margaret herself should have been confined in the prison because her attempted suicide deserved punishment, a fact she explicitly acknowledges.[76] However, social class intervenes as she is an upper-middle-class woman, and for that reason her crime is silenced and covered up, but never forgotten. Her own mother personally administers and measures the daily dose of chloral that keeps Margaret in a benumbed state of lethargy, thus collaborating with the medical establishment in the pathologization of her own daughter.

Considered inferior to men, women who did not comply with Victorian normative social rules were labelled as deviant and aberrant. Deviance is double, then: firstly, there is one type resulting from a woman's biological sex alone in a male-dominated society; secondly, there is 'a kind of attributed deviance [that] results from disapproved behaviors such as prostitution.'[77] Mental disease becomes synonymous with degeneracy, especially in women. Nineteenth-century investigators like Henry Maudsley and John Connolly seemed to agree on the 'belief that one of the dominant causes was repressed sexual, or uterine, energy.'[78] These medical professionals of the brain tried to demonstrate the necessity of coping with a newly emerging group of mentally ill people, whose malady was entirely due to somatic causes, and claimed their right to control the mad and their diseases. Hence, conventional notions of femininity trapped them in a state of total passivity, prey to the all-pervasive power and control of the medical authorities, who often dismissed them as hysterics, the common diagnosis for the multifaceted issue of female insanity. In the nineteenth century, madness was inextricably linked to femininity to the extent that 'women began to predominate in the statistics of the insane' from the 1850s onwards.[79] As Jane Ussher remarks, it was the upper-middle-class women who were subjected to control and scrutiny, whereas working-class women were already oppressed through their class (and gender) since 'exhaustion and extreme poverty provided an effective control for their "unnatural passions."'[80]

Again, if the spiritualist woman was dismissed as hysterical, the spinster (like Margaret) equally received the verdict of insanity. Being diagnosed with a nerve illness, Margaret is perfectly aware of the precarious position she holds at home, constantly observed and judged by every member of her family, as the following extract illustrates: 'I asked [Helen] if she remembered Mr Le Fanu's novel, about the heiress who is made to seem mad? I said, "I did think for a while: Suppose Mother is in league with Mr Shillitoe, and he means to keep me on the wards, bewildered?" She smiled at that – but checked to see that Mother could not hear me.'[81] Although it seems that Sheridan Le Fanu's *Uncle Silas* (1864) is invoked in Margaret's comment in a half-humorous tone, I suggest that Margaret is pointing out the mid-Victorian fear of wrongful confinement of vulnerable women in private asylums. In addition, I would like to indicate that this passage anticipates the subject of wrongful imprisonment, which plays a significant role in Waters's next novel, *Fingersmith* (2002), which is seeped in 1860s sensation fiction.[82] Although not confined to an asylum, Margaret in *Affinity* is equally regarded as aberrant, deviant, and dangerous; thus, she is kept metaphorically imprisoned. In fact, only through writing her diary in secret and through her philanthropic work as a 'Lady Visitor' does she find an outlet for her wishes for a more complete life.

In her visiting of women prisoners, Margaret is the fictional counterpart of real-life 'lady volunteers, who drew inspiration from the pioneering work of Elizabeth Fry.'[83] Fry was a philanthropist and penal reformer who began her visits to Newgate in the 1810s, and was appalled by the awful conditions she saw in the women's prisons. The relevance of Fry's work is noted in Waters's novel when Margaret goes to the reading room at the British Museum and orders 'Mayhew's book on the prisons of London, and the writings on Newgate of Elizabeth Fry.'[84] As Dorice Williams Elliott affirms, nineteenth-century women philanthropists such as Fry and Sarah Martin anticipated the crucial role played by women in volunteer philanthropic work from the 1850s onwards since '[b]esides the thousands of women who visited the poor and unfortunate on their own, in 1862 there were at least 640 charitable institutions in operation in England, most of them staffed and many of them administered by women.'[85] Victorian fiction equally echoes this widespread practice among accommodated classes, and novelists such as Elizabeth Gaskell and George Eliot featured philanthropic women visitors or charitable women in their novels, particularly in the 1860s.[86] George Eliot's *Adam Bede* (1859), for example, portrays a scene between a prison visitor, Dinah Morris (a young Methodist), and Hetty Sorrel (a young prisoner condemned to death for child murder) at Stoniton jail. The narrator takes pains to show that Dinah engages actively in philanthropic work by offering human contact and religious consolation: 'Let us pray, poor sinner: let us fall on our knees again, and pray to the God of all mercy.'[87] In Waters's novel, Margaret's activities are first embedded in this charitable work of nineteenth-century 'lady visitors,' whose moral guidance and humanitarian treatment were meant to alleviate the ills of the prison inmates, as Mr Shillitoe, the prison governor, states in *Affinity*.[88] At times regarded as a mere extension of a woman's domestic role, this philanthropic work has recently been studied as representing a potential challenge to the ideology of separate spheres and class relations.[89] In Margaret's case, her philanthropic occupation is even more subversive since it is to be read as 'an outlet for [her] lesbian desires, adding a distinctly sexual layer to an otherwise seemingly innocent occupation.'[90]

Therefore, Margaret succeeds in transcending her imprisonment through visiting Selina, whereby she becomes an active observer (as well as an object of observation) of the spiritualist medium, thus replacing the objectifying gaze of the Panopticon/female warders/Mother with the release of her own lesbian desire.[91] Several critics have already pointed out the deliberate repetition of the word 'queer' throughout the novel to indicate the repressed lesbian desire (also equated with spiritualism).[92] Another word, repeated as frequently as 'queer,' is 'gaze,' which is first associated with disciplining and punishment, and is then attached to the liberation of sexual desire. The feminization of the gaze is ultimately deployed through the dynamics established by Margaret and Selina, and finally recorded in her diary, which, again, first holds a disciplinary function and then enacts Margaret's refusal to conform as she becomes 'the author of her own destiny in some way,' and exerts 'control over her narrative.'[93] Her journal is the only place she can be honest in, as she herself puts it,[94] so her diary bears witness to the relationships between the different characters in the novel, relationships that 'transform rather than conform.'[95] Margaret's recognition of her own failure as an object of Selina's love comes straight from her heart to the journal where she records that '[t]here never was a cord of darkness, never a space in which our spirits touched. There was only my longing ... she has taken all that and left me nothing.'[96] Even though Margaret has not 'evolved' in spiritualist terms, she has somehow transformed herself in the actual process of facing the truth of the matter, thus achieving a sort of independence of action, which in the end procures her liberation from her gender-related imprisonment.

III

In this essay, I have shown how gender, imprisonment, and madness interact in the deployment of the main characters in Sarah Waters's neo-Victorian fiction in general, and in *Affinity* in particular. Physically imprisoned at Millbank, Selina collapses all boundaries between the material and the spiritual worlds, between physicality and spirituality, in recreating the potential subversion of her spiritualist activities in the confined limits of her prison cell, utilizing the concept of 'affinityship,' and replacing a punitive gaze with a feminized gaze. It is, then, through the interaction of subjects, particularly her relationship with Margaret (but also with Mrs Jelf, the matron who is instrumental in securing her freedom), and through the recording of her voice in the entries of her diary that she, the female criminal and spiritualist, dismissed as deviant and aberrant, resists the authority of the prison, and avoids punishment and control. Furthermore, Margaret, the unmarried woman, also considered deviant and aberrant by patriarchy, suffers from the metaphorical imprisonment of the home and the female body. At home she is under the constant surveillance of her mother, who perpetuates the objectifying gaze of the state apparatuses. In addition, being a spinster (and lesbian), Margaret is one of the most disdained female figures in the Victorian age, easily regarded as hysterical or mentally ill. Yet Margaret circumvents metaphorical imprisonment by carrying out philanthropic work as a 'Lady Visitor,' which permits an evolution, from observed object to active subject. Even though she has been deceived by Selina (and Selina's lover, Ruth Vigers), abandoned and robbed of her possessions at the end of the novel, Margaret finds an outlet for the materialization of her lesbian desire in her romantic entanglement with Selina, however faked her emotions turn out to be. Likewise, the writing of her journal allows for the incorporation of her disruptive voice, which helps her become a human actor, rather than a mere docile body. In other words, the matrons and Margaret's mother tried to suppress the transgression of these two women, respectively, but they have defied them in a final act of self-affirmation through writing/recording their own stories.

If Macpherson suggests that Selina liberates herself from the position of the observed prisoner, 'registering desire, betrayal, and refusal to conform,'[97] Margaret, despite her being denied Selina's powerful gaze and love,[98] transcends metaphorical imprisonment. She succeeds in liberating desire and refusing to follow normativity by taking up the pen and registering her unwillingness to conform. Following Foucault's later writings, then, the relationship between Margaret and Selina has finally allowed for the incorporation of human agency, the reinstitution of subjectivity, and has enabled the transformation of these two female characters who had previously been dehumanized by the disciplinary power of the prison and the home, the two sites of female confinement in *Affinity*.

NOTES

The research carried out for the writing of this article has been financed by the Spanish Ministerio de Ciencia y Tecnología: BFF2003-05143/FEDER. My thanks go to Gracia Navas Quintana for her invaluable comments on my work.

1 Dana Shiller ('The Redemptive Past in the Neo-Victorian Novel,' *Studies in the Novel* 29 [1997]: 538–60) was one of the first critics to use the term 'neo-Victorian.' Sally Shuttleworth ('Natural History: The Retro-Victorian Novel,' in *The Third Culture: Literature and Science*, ed. Elinor S. Shaffer, [Berlin: de Gruyter, 1998], 253–68) coined the term 'retro-Victorian' in her study on A.S. Byatt's *Possession* and Graham

Swift's *Ever After*. In turn, Georges Letissier ('Dickens and Post-Victorian Fiction,' in *Refracting the Canon in Contemporary British Literature and Film*, ed. Susana Onega and Christian Gutleben [Amsterdam: Rodopi, 2004], 111–28) has preferred to refer to this trend in contemporary fiction as 'post-Victorianism.'

2 Yet, by reverting to the Victorian age these writers also attempt 'to denounce the injustice towards some of its ill-used or forgotten representatives such as women, the lower classes or homosexuals' (Christian Gutleben, *Nostalgic Postmodernism: The Victorian Tradition and the Contemporary British Novel* [Amsterdam: Rodopi, 2001], 10). This paradoxical feature of the neo-Victorian novel has caused considerable controversy. Some critics like Agnieszka Golda maintain that contemporary historical novels go beyond nostalgia in that they look back to the past and also show a longing for the future: 'postmodern fascination with their Victorian predecessors could be seen as one way of a therapeutic and at the same time nostalgic insight into the historical background' ('Postmodern Post-Mortem on a Victorian Corpse or How Postmodern Fiction Rewrites the 19th Century,' in *We, the 'Other Victorians:' Considering the Heritage of 19th-Century Thought*, ed. Silvia Caporale-Bizzini [Alicante, Spain: Servicio de Publicaciones de la Universidad de Alicante, 2003], 153). However, others like Christian Gutleben argue that these novels 'cannot be deemed radically subversive' (Gutleben, *Nostalgic Postmodernism*, 218) and that retro-Victorianism illustrates syncretism (or eclecticism), loosely defined as an aesthetic form that 'cannot be fundamentally seditious and participate[s] to a certain extent in the propagation of the dominant mass culture.' Ibid., 223.

3 Sarah A. Smith, 'Love's Prisoner [Rev. of Sarah Waters' *Affinity*],' *TLS*, 28 May 1999, 24.

4 Sandra M. Gilbert and Susan Gubar, *The Madwoman in the Attic: The Woman Writer and the Nineteenth-Century Literary Imagination* (1979; New Haven, CT: Yale University Press, 1984), 85.

5 Ibid., 92.

6 Heidi Slettedahl Macpherson, 'Prison, Passion, and the Female Gaze: Twentieth-Century Representations of Nineteenth-Century Panopticons,' in *In the Grip of the Law: Trials, Prisons and the Space Between*, ed. Monika Fludernik and Greta Olson (Frankfurt: Lang, 2004), 216.

7 Henry Mayhew and John Binny, *The Criminal Prisons of London and Scenes of Prison Life* (London: Griffin, Bohn, and Company, 1862), 235. Peter J. Hutchings reformulates the fiction of an omnipresent authority in the Panopticon by arguing that 'the reformable subject of the Panopticon prison is the product of a ghostly surveillance that comes to haunt the subject themself [sic], internalizing the law of the unseen seer' (*The Criminal Spectre in Law, Literature and Aesthetics: Incriminating Subjects* [London: Routledge, 2001], 10). In this sense, it is worth noting that Bentham's fear of ghosts, and its connection with the illusion of

constant observation, has recently become the subject of critical studies (Miran Božovič, 'Introduction: "An Utterly Dark Spot,"' in *Jeremy Bentham: The Panopticon Writings*, ed. and intro. Miran Božovič [London:.Verso, 1995], 21–3). Interestingly enough, ghostly presences and spectral visitations turn out to be fundamental in the deployment of the relationship between the main characters of Sarah Waters's *Affinity*.

8 Michel Foucault, *Discipline and Punish: The Birth of the Prison*, trans. Alan Sheridan. (1975; Harmondsworth, UK: Penguin, 1991), 205.

9 Lauren M.E. Goodlad, 'Beyond the Panopticon: Victorian Britain and the Critical Imagination,' *PMLA* 11, no. 3 (2003): 542.

10 Ibid., 545.

11 Michel Foucault, 'Afterword: The Subject and Power,' in *Michel Foucault: Beyond Structuralism and Hermeneutics*, 2nd ed., Hubert L. Dreyfus and Paul Rabinow (Chicago: University of Chicago Press, 1983), 210–11.

12 Ibid., 212.

13 Ibid., 220.

14 Goodlad, 'Beyond the Panopticon,' 546.

15 Foucault, afterword, 215. Goodlad uses Foucault's relational dynamics of power among individuals as starting point for discussion of the self-conscious liberal society in nineteenth-century Britain as promoting 'moral and spiritual growth,' and simultaneously 'suspicious of government interference with individuals and their property' (Goodlad, 'Beyond the Panopticon,' 539), illustrating the tension between the ills of laissez-faire ideology and 'positive' freedom or empowerment of the sustained pastoral relations.

16 Foucault, afterword, 225, original emphasis.

17 Goodlad, 'Beyond the Panopticon,' 551.

18 For examples of such forms of resistance in Dickens's works, see Adam Hansen's contribution to this volume.

19 E.g., Macpherson, 'Prison, Passion,' 215–20.

20 Sarah Waters, *Affinity* (London: Virago, 1999), 27, original emphasis.

21 Jenni Millbank categorizes Sarah Waters's *Affinity*, Angela Carter's *Nights at the Circus*, and the English TV series *Bad Girls* as 'three narratives of violently transgressive lesbians in a prison setting' ('It's About *This*: Lesbians, Prison, Desire,' *Social & Legal Studies* 13, no. 2 [2004]: 155).

22 Paulina Palmer, 'Lesbian Gothic: Genre, Transformation, Transgression,' *Gothic Studies* 6, no. 1 (2004): 126.

23 Waters, *Affinity*, 8.

24 Mayhew and Binny, *Criminal Prisons of London*, 246.

25 Ibid., 248.

26 Waters, *Affinity*, 179.

27 Philip Priestley, *Victorian Prison Lives: English Prison Biography 1830–1914*
(1985; London: Pimlico, 1999), 208. In *Affinity*, Victorian terms for prison life such
as turnkeys (warders), taskmistresses (matrons), ticket-of-leave, and coir (punitive
work that consisted of 'picking apart tar-encrusted rope' [Millbank, 'It's About
This,' 185]) contribute to this feeling of authenticity.
28 Millbank, 'It's About *This*,' 175. Contemporary novels like Margaret Atwood's *The
Handmaid's Tale* (1985) and *Alias Grace* (1996), as well as Angela Carter's *Nights
at the Circus* (1984), portray, to varying degrees, women's complicity in perpetuating structures of oppression and control.
29 Waters, *Affinity*, 23, original emphasis.
30 Ibid., 37.
31 Mayhew and Binny, *Criminal Prisons of London*, 246.
32 See Mark Llewellyn, '"Queer? I Should Say It Is Criminal!": Sarah Waters' *Affinity*
(1999),' *Journal of Gender Studies* 13, no. 3 (2004): 209.
33 Waters, *Affinity*, 40.
34 Alex Owen, 'Women and Nineteenth-Century Spiritualism: Strategies in the
Subversion of Femininity,' in *Disciplines of Faith: Studies in Religion, Politics
and Patriarchy*, ed. Jim Obelkevich, Lyndal Roper, and Raphael Samuel (London:
Routledge & Kegan Paul, 1987), 133.
35 Nina Auerbach, *Woman and the Demon: The Life of a Victorian Myth* (Cambridge,
MA: Harvard University Press, 1982), 9.
36 Frances Heidensohn, *Women and Crime*, with the assistance of Marisa Silvestri,
foreword by Jo Campling, 2nd ed. (Basingstoke, UK: Macmillan, 1996), 39, 54.
37 Heidensohn, *Women and Crime*, 114. See also Llewellyn's study of *Affinity* for the
connection between criminality and women not only in Lombroso and Ferrero, but
also in the late-nineteenth-century sexologist Havelock Ellis (Lewellyn, 'Queer?'
209–10).
38 Caesar Lombroso and William Ferrero, *The Female Offender* (1893; New York:
Wisdom Library, 1958), 147.
39 Ibid., 187–8.
40 Foucault, *Discipline and Punish*, 253.
41 Hutchings, *The Criminal Spectre in Law*, 15.
42 Alex Owen, *The Darkened Room: Women, Power and Spiritualism in Late
Victorian England* (London: Virago, 1989), 233.
43 Established in 1869, *The Spiritualist Newspaper: A Record of the Progress of
the Science and Ethics of Spiritualism* was an extremely well-known newspaper
among spiritualists, particularly in the 1870s and 1880s, when the spiritualist
movement thrived.
44 Waters, *Affinity*, 132–3.
45 As Waters includes details of Selina's trial, following real-life cases of late-

Victorian spiritualists who were charged with fraud, she takes pains to reproduce expressions and asides to be found in those accounts: '[*Witness hesitates*]', '[*Laughter*]' (Waters, *Affinity*, 45), thus reinforcing an air of verisimilitude.

46 'The Prosecution of a Clairvoyante By a Conjuror,' *The Spiritualist*, 22 October 1880.

47 Brian Inglis, *Natural and Supernatural: A History of the Paranormal from Earliest Times to 1914* (London: Hodder and Stoughton, 1977), 276.

48 'The Prosecution of a Clairvoyante By a Conjuror,' *The Spiritualist*, 22 October 1880.

49 Priestley, *Victorian Prison Lives*, 266.

50 Bridget Bennett, 'Introduction: Susan Willis Fletcher, *Twelve Months in an English Prison* (1884),' in *Women, Madness and Spiritualism*, ed. Roy Porter, Helen Nicholson, and Bridget Bennett, 2 vols. (London: Routledge, 2003), 2:4.

51 Waters, *Affinity*, 73, original emphasis.

52 Ibid.

53 L.S. Forbes Winslow, *Spiritualistic Madness* (London: Baillière, Tindall, and Cox, 1877), 6.

54 Quoted in ibid., 257.

55 Waters, *Affinity*, 27.

56 Susan Willis Fletcher, 'Twelve Months in Prison' (1884), in *Women, Madness and Spiritualism*, 2:364, emphasis added.

57 Fletcher, 'Twelve Months in Prison,' 378.

58 Monika Fludernik and Greta Olson, introduction to *In the Grip of the Law*, xxviii, ixv.

59 I am indebted to Frank Lauterbach for drawing my attention to Du Maurier's *Peter Ibbetson*.

60 George Du Maurier, *Peter Ibbetson* (1892), intro. Daphne du Maurier, ed. Martin Seymour-Smith (London: Gollancz, 1969), 249.

61 Ibid., 239.

62 Ibid., 234.

63 Ibid., 314.

64 Marlene Tromp, 'Spirited Sexuality: Sex, Marriage, and Victorian Spiritualism,' *Victorian Literature and Culture* 21, no. 1 (2003): 67.

65 Ibid., 72. Owen, *Darkened Room*, 218–19.

66 Fletcher, 'Twelve Months in Prison,' 209.

67 Waters, *Affinity*, 275, original emphasis.

68 Tromp, 'Spirited Sexuality,' 69.

69 MacPherson, 'Prison, Passion,' 206.

70 Terry Castle, *The Apparitional Lesbian: Female Homosexuality and Modern Culture* (New York: Columbia University Press, 1993), 60–1.

71 Palmer, 'Lesbian Gothic,' 125.

72 Waters, *Affinity*, 21.

73 Jane M. Ussher, *Women's Madness: Misogyny or Mental Illness?* (Amherst: University of Massachusetts Press, 1991), 81.

74 Palmer, 'Lesbian Gothic,' 126.

75 Waters, *Affinity*, 208. When Selina is put in the darks for breaking out – to avoid being transferred to another prison – Margaret replicates Selina's outbreak at home (Waters, *Affinity*, 242, 255), thus reinforcing the correspondence between prison and home.

76 Ibid., 255.

77 Sherrill Cohen, *The Evolution of Women's Asylums Since 1500: From Refuges for Ex-Prostitutes to Shelters for Battered Women* (New York: Oxford University Press, 1992), 173.

78 Jenny Bourne Taylor and Sally Shuttleworth, 'The Sexual Body,' in *Embodied Selves: An Anthology of Psychological Texts 1830–1890*, ed. Jenny Bourne Taylor and Sally Shuttleworth (Oxford: Clarendon, 1998), 166.

79 Ussher, *Women's Madness*, 71. Elaine Showalter, *The Female Malady: Women, Madness and English Culture, 1830–1980* (1985; London: Virago, 1987), passim.

80 Ussher, *Women's Madness*, 90.

81 Waters, *Affinity*, 29.

82 *Fingersmith* focuses on the problem of wrongful confinement that attracted the Victorian public and so inspired a great many tales, stories, and newspaper accounts about men and, above all, upper- and middle-class women who became easy preys to rapacious relatives. In Waters's *Fingersmith* the fictitious portrayal of an asylum from within helps to illustrate how in the second half of the nineteenth century the image of '"woman" or "femininity" could be used to punish, to convict, to control – women out of control were clearly sexual and dangerous, and mad' (Ussher, *Women's Madness*, 74).

83 Priestley, *Victorian Prison Lives*, 104.

84 Waters, *Affinity*, 57.

85 Dorice Williams Elliott, *The Angel out of the House: Philanthropy and Gender in Nineteenth-Century England* (Charlottesville: University Press of Virginia, 2002), 160.

86 Ibid., 161.

87 George Eliot, *Adam Bede*, ed. Doreen Roberts (1859; Ware, UK: Wordsworth: 2003), 391.

88 Waters, *Affinity*, 12.

89 Elliott, *The Angel out of the House*, 5.

90 Llewellyn, 'Queer?' 204.

91 Waters, *Affinity*, 308–09.

92 Llewellyn, 'Queer?' 210; Macpherson, 'Prison, Passion,' 216.

93 Llewellyn, 'Queer?' 212.
94 Waters, *Affinity*, 242.
95 Millbank, 'It's About *This*', 169.
96 Waters, *Affinity*, 348.
97 Macpherson, 'Prison, Passion,' 220.
98 Ibid., 219.

Contributors

Jan Alber is Assistant Professor in the English Department of the University of Freiburg. He is the author of *Narrating the Prison: Role and Representation in Charles Dickens' Novels, Twentieth-Century Fiction, and Film* (2007) and has written articles that have been published or are forthcoming in journals such as *Dickens Studies Annual*, *The Journal of Popular Culture*, *Short Story Criticism*, *Storyworlds*, and *Style*. Alber also edited *Moderne – Postmoderne* (with Monika Fludernik, 2003), and he has contributed to numerous collections as well as to *The Routledge Encyclopedia of Narrative Theory*. Alber received a fellowship from the German Research Foundation which allowed him to spend the 2007–8 academic year at Ohio State University as a visiting scholar doing research on impossible scenarios in postmodernist narratives under the auspices of Project Narrative.

Rosario Arias is Lecturer in English at the University of Málaga (Spain). She is the author of *Madres e hijas en la teoría feminista: una perspectiva psicoanalítica* (2002), and was a visiting scholar at the Autonomous University of Madrid in 2001, and at Brunel University (London) in 2002. Arias has published a number of articles on contemporary women's fiction and psychoanalysis. Among them is an entry on mother-daughter relationships in *An Autobiography of Women's Autobiography* (2005). Her current research focuses on the occult, spectrality, and haunting in neo-Victorian fiction. Her recent publications include several articles in refereed journals such as *Estudios Ingleses de la Universidad Complutense*, *Revista Canaria de Estudios Ingleses* in 2005, and *Variations: Literaturzeitschrift der Universität Zürich* in 2006. Arias is currently co-editing a volume of essays entitled *Haunting and Spectrality in Neo-Victorian Fiction: Possessing the Past* (forthcoming in 2009).

Laura Berol received her PhD from Princeton University in 2003. Her work focuses on anxieties over Ireland in English fiction and political writings from the 1840s. She has published on this topic in *Victorian Literature and Culture* and has presented numerous conference papers on the works of Anthony Trollope and Elizabeth Gaskell.

W.B. Carnochan is Richard W. Lyman Professor of the Humanities, emeritus, at Stanford University. Formerly he was director of the Stanford Humanities Center. His publications on prison themes include *Confinement and Flight: An Essay on English Literature of the Eighteenth Century* (1977) and 'The Literature of Confinement' in *The Oxford History of the Prison* (1995).

Sean C. Grass is Associate Professor of English at Texas Tech University where he specializes in Dickens, Victorian fiction, and Victorian history and culture. He is the author of *The Self in the Cell: Narrating the Victorian Prisoner* (2003) as well as essays on Dickens's portrayals of imprisonment in *The Pickwick Papers* and *American Notes*. His work on Dickens and other Victorian writers has appeared in the *Journal of English and Germanic Philology*, *Nineteenth-Century Literature*, and *Dickens Studies Annual*. In 2001 he received the South Atlantic Review Essay Prize for his work on W.H. Auden, and in 2004 and 2005 he received grants from the National Endowment for the Humanities to support the research for his book-in-progress, *An Uneasy Trade: Autobiography, Sensation, and the Commodification of Identity in Victorian Narrative*, a study of autobiographical production, the literary market, and sensation fiction during the mid-Victorian period in England.

Adam Hansen is currently Lecturer in English at Northumbria University in Newcastle (UK), following teaching positions in Poland, York, Macedonia, Oxford, and Belfast. His publications, research, and teaching employ an interdisciplinary and interperiodic approach to examine the relations between history, ideology, and culture, modern and early modern. Recent pieces include 'Exhibiting Vagrancy in Victorian London,' in *A Mighty Mass of Brick and Smoke: Victorian and Edwardian Representations of London* (2007). At present, he is completing a book investigating representations of rogues and vagrants from the Renaissance to the nineteenth century.

Jason Haslam is Associate Professor in the Department of English at Dalhousie University. He is the author of *Fitting Sentences: Identity in Nineteenth- and Twentieth-Century Prison Narratives* (2005), and the co-editor of *Capti-*

vating Subjects: Writing Confinement, Citizenship, and Nationhood in the Nineteenth Century (2005). Haslam has also published articles on prison writing, American literature, and film in such journals as *College Literature, Genre: Forms of Discourse and Culture, Gothic Studies,* and *Modern Language Studies.* He has recently published, with Broadview Press, a scholarly edition of Constance Lytton's suffragette autobiography, *Prisons and Prisoners: Some Personal Experiences.*

Matthew Kaiser is Assistant Professor in the Department of English at Harvard University. He specializes in nineteenth-century British literature and culture, Victorian theatre, and gender studies. Selected works include 'A History of "Ludicrous"' in *ELH*; and 'Marius at Oxford: Paterian Pedagogy and the Ethics of Seduction' in *Walter Pater: Transparencies of Desire*, edited by Laurel Brake, Lesley Higgins, and Carolyn Williams. He is currently completing a book entitled *The World in Play: A Portrait of a Victorian Concept.*

Frank Lauterbach teaches English, Spanish, and Comparative Literature at Georg-August-University, Göttingen, Germany. His research focuses on prison writing, urban literature, the British novel of the eighteenth and nineteenth centuries, nation-building and cultural identity in the United States and Spanish America, and Chicano literature. He has co-edited a collection of essays and a CD-ROM on the formation of cultural identities in Europe and the Americas, and has published articles on early U.S. and Spanish American prose and poetry, nineteenth-century British travel writing, Charles Dickens, Victorian prison autobiographies, Raymond Williams, Juan Boscán, and Andrés Bello.

Greta Olson is *Vertretungsprofessor* for Ausgar Nünning at the English Department of the University of Gießen. The author of *Reading Eating Disorders: Writings on Bulimia and Anorexia as Confessions of American Culture* (2003), she is the editor, with Monika Fludernik, of *In the Grip of the Law: Trials Prisons and the Space Between* (2004), and the co-editor with Martin Kayman of a special issue of the *European Journal of English Studies* on law, literature, and language (2007). She has also published essays on Shakespeare's trial scenes, *Richard III,* criminalized bodies in literature and criminology, and the current torture debate. She has recently completed her faculty dissertation entitled *'Criminal Animals' and the Rise of Biocriminology – From Shakespeare to Dickens.*

David Paroissien, Emeritus Professor of English (University of Massachusetts, Amherst), and professorial research fellow at the University of Buckingham, lives in Oxford, England. Since 1983 he has served as editor of *Dickens Quarterly*; he also co-edits with Susan Shatto *The Dickens Companion*, to which series he has contributed two volumes (*The Companion to Oliver Twist*, 1992, and *The Companion to Great Expectations*, 2000). His recent publications include an edition of *The Mystery of Edwin Drood* (2002), contributions to *Dickens Studies Annual* (2004 and 2005), and an essay on Dickens's epistolary art in *A Companion to Charles Dickens* (2008), a volume of thirty-six essays, which he edited.

Anna Schur teaches Russian and Comparative Literature at Keene State College, New Hampshire. Her research interests include nineteenth-century Russian and Victorian literature and culture, law and literature, and literature and science. Her recent work has appeared in *The Russian Review*, *Law and Literature*, and *Tolstoy Studies Journal*. She is currently working on a monograph on punishment in Dostoevsky and Tolstoy.

Anne Schwan teaches English Literature and Cultural Studies at Napier University in Edinburgh, Scotland. Her main research and teaching interests are nineteenth-century studies, gender studies, and cultural theory. She has published on women's imprisonment and Foucault, on representations of the gendered body, and she is co-editor of a special issue of *Critical Survey* (17, no. 2) on 'Dickens and Sex,' which includes her article on sexual performativity and gender dissidence in Dickens's *Dombey and Son*. At present, she is working on a monograph on women convicts and prison narratives.

Jeremy Tambling is Professor of Literature at the University of Manchester, and came to Manchester from a Chair of Comparative Literature at the University of Hong Kong. He is the author of various books such as *Confession: Sexuality, Sin, the Subject* (1990), *Dickens, Violence and the Modern State: Dreams of the Scaffold* (1995), and *Lost in the American City: Dickens, James and Kafka* (2001). Tambling also edited the 2004 Penguin Classics edition of Dickens's *David Copperfield* and *Bleak House: A New Casebook* (1998). He has published numerous essays on Dickens and other Victorian writers in journals such as *Cahiers Victoriens et Edouardiens*, *Dickens Quarterly*, *Dickens Studies Annual*, *English Literary History*, and *Essays in Criticism*. His most recent book is *Going Astray: Dickens and London* (2008).

Index